MIRA SCHENDEL

Edited by Tanya Barson and Taisa Palhares

Tate Publishing
in association with
Pinacoteca do Estado de São Paulo

This edition first published 2013 by order of the Tate Trustees
by Tate Publishing, a division of Tate Enterprises Ltd,
Millbank, London SW1P 4RG
www.tate.org.uk/publishing

on the occasion of the exhibition
Mira Schendel

Tate Modern, London
25 September 2013 – 19 January 2014

Fundação de Serralves – Museu de Arte Contemporânea, Porto
28 February – 24 June 2014

Pinacoteca do Estado de São Paulo, São Paulo
24 July – 19 October 2014

Exhibition organised by Tate Modern and the Pinacoteca do Estado de São Paulo in association with the Fundação de Serralves – Museu de Arte Contemporânea, Porto

Publication organised by Pinacoteca do Estado de São Paulo and published by Tate Publishing

A catalogue record for this book is available from the British Library
ISBN 978 1 84976 090 4

Distributed in the United States and Canada by ABRAMS, New York
Library of Congress Control Number applied for

Graphic design: Leticia Moura / cj 31
Designer: Douglas K. Watanabe / cj 31
Colour reproduction by Ipsis Gráfica e Editora
Printed and bound in Italy by Grafiche SIZ S.p.A.

Front cover: *Untitled* 1963 [p.81]
Back cover: Clay Perry, Portrait of Mira Schendel with *Little Nothing*, 1966. Courtesy Clay Perry, England & Co. Gallery, London

Measurements of artworks are given in centimetres, height and width before depth

FSC
www.fsc.org
MIX
Paper from responsible sources
FSC® C005613

Foreword 4
Tate Modern and Pinacoteca do Estado

Living in between: Mira Schendel's Poetics 8
Taisa Palhares

Mira Schendel, Signals London and the Language of Movement 18
Tanya Barson

Mira Schendel in Dialogue with Vilem Flusser: Language and Reality 32
Cauê Alves

The Other World Is This:
Mira Schendel's Participation in the 10th Bienal de São Paulo, 1969 40
Isobel Whitelegg

Mira Schendel's Immanence 48
John Rajchman

Works 61

Mira Schendel Statement 196

Interview with Mira Schendel
Mira Schendel, Painter: Empty Space Moves Me Deeply 198
Jorge Guinle

Interview with Haroldo de Campos 208
Sônia Salzstein

Chronology 216

Selected Bibliography 240

List of Works 242

Foreword

Tate Modern and Pinacoteca do Estado de São Paulo

This exhibition is the first and perhaps the most emblematic in a series of collaborations between Tate and the Pinacoteca do Estado de São Paulo, Brazil. The exhibition has been organised jointly by the two institutions and reflects the proximity of the two museums in their shared outlook and desire to foster an exchange of knowledge and expertise. The collaborative relationship encompasses the development of a number of exhibitions and wider projects including joint research initiatives. As the first such endeavour, and a major undertaking, the Mira Schendel exhibition is an exemplar of the ambitions of this new, close working relationship.

Mira Schendel is acknowledged as one of the most important Brazilian artists of the twentieth century. However, despite her stature and the prolific nature and complexity of her work, she is still comparatively little known outside Brazil. Moreover, the complete repertoire of her work is also not fully known within Brazil, since considerable parts of her work remain never or rarely exhibited. Embarking on this project, the curators at Tate and Pinacoteca realised that a labour of excavation would be required to locate much of her work. In the process of researching the exhibition, they have traced and viewed a huge range of work, which has underlined that a review of the total oeuvre is necessary and timely. We are extremely proud to have brought together such a large group of Schendel's work, ranging from her early paintings from the 1950s to her last complete series from 1987, and encompassing two major installation works besides.

The Swiss-born Mira Schendel, having fled from war-devastated Europe for Brazil in 1949, developed a unique body of work in that country, in the context of a burgeoning society that was experiencing an artistic renaissance. Whilst Schendel's early life is a history of displacement and emigration, in the city of São Paulo she joined a community of émigré intellectuals that provided a fertile ground for her to explore her ideas about aesthetics and philosophy. Her first solo show, when she was thirty-one, held at the Auditório do Correio do Povo in Porto Alegre in 1950 consisted of six portraits and a selection of still lifes and landscapes. Her work was first shown in London at Signals gallery in 1965, and her first solo show in the city was staged the following year; this exhibition, also at Signals, is increasingly recognised as a key event not just in Schendel's career but also in the history of experimental art in London. For this reason it seems particularly appropriate for Tate Modern and the Pinacoteca to have worked together to realise this exhibition.

Above all, we would like to express our deepest gratitude to Mira's daughter Ada Schendel and her grandson Max Schendel, and their family, for their incredible support, generosity, time and dedication towards the realisation of this exhibition. We are delighted that the exhibition will be touring to the Fundação de Serralves – Museu de Arte Contemporânea, Porto, Portugal, and would like to thank Suzanne Cotter, Director, and her colleagues for joining the project so enthusiastically. The Secretary of Culture for the State of São Paulo and former Director of the Pinacoteca, Marcelo Araujo, was an early and ongoing supporter of the project and we would like to thank him for his role in embarking on the exhibition and in establishing the collaborative relationship between Tate and Pinacoteca. Members of the Tate and Pinacoteca teams have also played instrumental roles in developing and nurturing this relationship, in particular Judith Nesbitt and Natasha Barzaghi Geenen.

We would like to express our profound gratitude to all those who have lent to this exhibition to make such an in-depth presentation possible: Ricard Akagawa; Raquel Arnaud; Igor Queiroz Barroso; BBM Collection; Jones Bergamin; Estrellita B and Daniel Brodsky Collection; Colección Patricia Phelps de Cisneros; Daros Latinamerica Collection; Collection Antonio Dias; Eduardo Duvivier Neto; Hecilda and Sergio Fadel; Collection G. and J. Fainas; Esther Faingold; Fernanda Feitosa and Heitor Martins Collection; FEMSA Collection; The Ella Fontanals-Cisneros Collection; Marcela and Israel Furmanovich; Maria Cristina and Pablo Henning Collection; Inhotim Collection; Instituto de Arte Contemporânea (IAC); Collection of Paulo Joppert (in Memoriam); Marta and Paulo Kuczynski Collection; Marta and Marcio Lobão Collection; Gerard Loeb; Augusto Livio Malzoni; Melsohn Collection; Orandi Momesso Collection; Luiz Paulo Montenegro; Museu de Arte Contemporânea da Universidade de São Paulo; Museu de Arte Moderna de São Paulo; Museum of Fine Arts, Houston; The Museum of Modern Art, New York; Rodrigo Naves Collection; Andrea and José Olympio Pereira Collection; Max Perlingeiro Collection; Ernesto and Cecilia Poma Collection; Marcos Ribeiro Simon Collection; Collection Clara Sancovsky; mira schendel estate; Rose and Alfredo Setúbal Collection; Luisa Malzoni Strina; Collection Ivo Vel Kos; and those lenders who prefer to remain anonymous.

We are particularly grateful to Thomas Dane, Fernanda Feitosa and Heitor Martins, Andrea and José Olympio Pereira, Catherine and Franck Petitgas, Frances Reynolds, Susana and Ricardo Steinbruch and Tate Americas Foundation for their support of this exhibition. In addition, we would also like to thank the Embassy of Brazil in London for their assistance. The incredibly important role in championing Tate's ongoing activities in Latin America of Tate's Latin American Acquisitions Committee, chaired since its inception by Tiqui Atencio Demirdjian, should also be acknowledged here.

The exhibition curators Tanya Barson at Tate and Taisa Palhares at the Pinacoteca have worked closely over several years in an especially fruitful collaboration to research and realise this exhibition, supported in London by Kasia Redzisz and in São Paulo by Luiza Lian Marques who have both worked tirelessly on the exhibition research and organisation. They were assisted by Stephanie Busson, Zuzana Flaskova, Katie-Marie Ford and Katy Wan. We would also like to thank Iria Candela and Hannah Dewar for their early support on the exhibition. The curators would like to thank a number of people whose help, advice and support have assisted with their research, in particular Guy Brett whose work on Mira Schendel and a number of associated artists including David Medalla and Li Yuan-Chia, and his decisive involvement with Signals, London, is of seminal importance for this exhibition. The exhibiton has also built on the previous scholarship and substantial exhibitions featuring Schendel's work by Cauê Alves, Célia Euvaldo, Maria Eduarda Marques, Rodrigo Naves, Luis Pérez-Oramas, Sônia Salzstein, Geraldo Souza Dias and Isobel Whitelegg. The curators would also like to thank Aracy Amaral, Raquel Arnaud, Michael Asbury, Peter Cohen, Ulisses Cohen, Jane England, Heloisa Espada, Briony Fer, Stephen Friedman, Marli Matsumoto, David Medalla, André Millan, Clay Perry, Paulo Portella Filho, Ricardo Rego, Jasia Reichardt, José Resende, Nancy Roth, Sérgio Sister, Irene Small, Luisa Strina, Nick Tatchell and Sophia Whately.

The ambitious catalogue has been steered by Júlia Ayerbe and Judith Severne whose editorial support and dedication has been invaluable. We would like to thank authors Cauê Alves, John Rajchman and Isobel Whitelegg for their scholarly and informative essays on Schendel's work and Ana Cândida de Avelar for the carefully researched chronology detailing Schendel's life and career. We would also like to thank Leticia Moura and Douglas K. Watanabe for the elegant design of the publication, Isabella Matheus and Tate Photography for the new photography, Regina Stocklen for the copy editing, Anthony Doyle and Oswaldo Corrêa da Costa for the translations and the Production Department at Pinacoteca for all their support.

The exhibition would not have been possible without the work of the team at Tate Modern including: Exhibitions Registrar, Carol Burnier Magno; Programme Manager, Rachel Kent and Head of Programme Realisation, Helen Sainsbury; Phil Monk, Rhona O'Brien and the installation team; Tate conservators Pia Gottschaller, Elizabeth

McDonald and Georgina Whiteley; Marko Daniel, Corinne Scurr and the Tate Learning team who have worked on interpretation and public programmes; Christopher Griffin and Jennifer Mundy in Tate Research; Cecily Carbone and Jeanette Ward in the Press team; Sarah Briggs, Elli Cartwright, Jon-Ross Le Haye and the Tate Marketing team and all in Tate Media.

This exhibition has been made possible by the provision of insurance through the Government Indemnity Scheme. Tate Modern would like to thank HM Government for providing Government Indemnity and the Department for Culture, Media and Sport and Arts Council England for arranging the indemnity.

Chris Dercon, Director, Tate Modern
Ivo Mesquita, Artistic Director, Pinacoteca do Estado

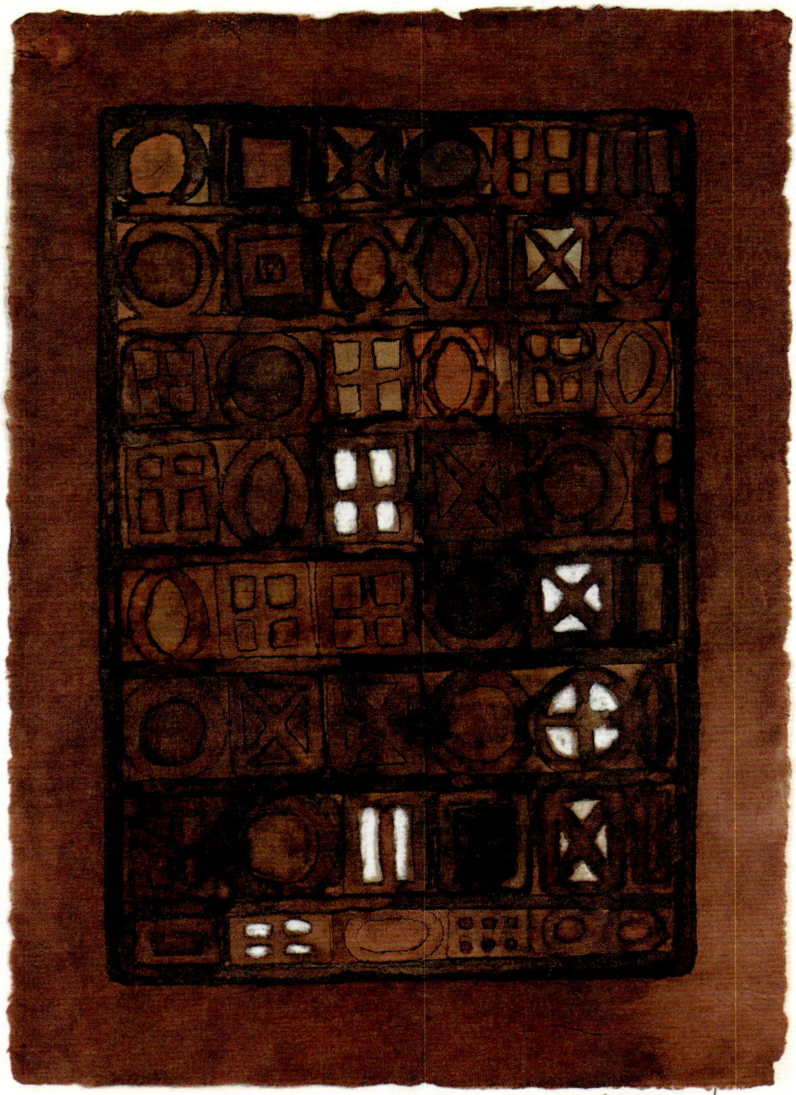

Untitled, from the series *Embroideries*
Sem título, da série *Bordados*
1963
Watercolour on rice paper
52 x 42.5 cm
mira schendel estate

Living in between: Mira Schendel's Poetics*

Taisa Palhares

Die Welt und das Leben sind Eins (The world and life are one).[1]
Ludwig Wittgenstein

To live is to wend among the living.[2]
João Cabral de Melo Neto

Active in Brazil since the early 1950s, Mira Schendel can be considered one of the most important and original artists of the second half of the twentieth century. But despite the growing visibility of her work in recent decades, particularly since the 1990s,[3] the full scope of her oeuvre remains little known to the general public, in Brazil as much as abroad. Different biographical, artistic or historical reasons could, no doubt, be listed as explanations for this: a certain isolation imposed as much by the nature of her activity and personality as by the sequence of historical events that struck Europe in the first half of the twentieth century, of which she was both victim and witness; the difficulties of artistic circulation and production as a result of the cultural and political situation in Brazil, especially during the military regime (1964–85); the lateness with which the originality of art produced in so-called peripheral countries during the postwar period was recognised; her enigmatic and cerebral presence.

However, what I see as the principal cause of this situation has to do with a particular feature of her production: the extent and variety of developments that it manifested in the course of approximately forty years of activity. Even today we are discovering works that were never exhibited during her lifetime and are aware of others that are difficult to locate. In this sense, it is evident that no overview of Mira Schendel can attempt to cover the totality of her production. Therefore, in this catalogue, in addition to her most iconic series [executed on rice paper, such as *Monotipias* (*Monotypes*), *Droguinhas* (*Little Nothings*), *Objetos gráficos* (*Graphic Objects*), and pieces that deal directly with the problematics of language], we have given special attention to her painting output from the 1950s and early 1960s, the significance of which has not previously been well evaluated.

* Translated by Oswaldo Corrêa da Costa

1 Ludwig Wittgenstein, *Tractatus Logico-Philosophicus* (CreateSpace Independent Publishing Platform, accessed 11 August 2011), pp.126–7.

2 João Cabral de Melo Neto, 'The Dog Without Feathers', in *Education by Stone: Selected Poems by João Cabral de Melo Neto*, trans. Richard Zenith (New York: Archipelago Books, 2005), p.73.

3 After her death in 1988, two major exhibitions of her work were held in Brazil: *Mira Schendel* (São Paulo, MAC USP, 1990) and *Mira Schendel: In the Void of the World* (São Paulo, Galeria de Arte do SESI, 1996–7, Rio de Janeiro, Centro de Arte Hélio Oiticica, 1997). Abroad, we can point to the exhibition *Mira Schendel* (The Drawing Center, New York, 1995). Another important moment in the history of the reception of her work in the 1990s was the Sala Especial Mira Schendel (Special Room) at the 22nd Bienal de São Paulo, in 1994.

When looking at these sets of works, it is possible to notice a subtle spiralling movement in which apparently heterogeneous groups resonate around a common nucleus, as if fundamental issues were being addressed according to different points of view. This movement is, in itself, fundamental to capturing the meaning of Mira Schendel's oeuvre and, in parallel, provides the key to understanding its relationship to art produced after 1945, in Brazil and abroad.

Attention must be drawn to a singular painting – one of the few that were not produced as part of a larger 'family' – that provides an example of what I intend to characterise as her *modus operandi*: the painting *O Retorno de Aquiles* (*The Return of Achilles*), dated 1964 [p.91]. As the title suggests, it refers to the moment in which the hero of the *Iliad* returns to battle to avenge the death of his cousin Patroclus, one of the bloodiest passages of the Homeric epic. In a white field, Mira presents a synthesis of the narrative through images and texts arranged asymmetrically. Enclosed inside a gateway, the English phrase NOW THAT I AM BACK appears diagonally ascendant in stencilled typography, slightly shifted from the centre of the picture. The word BACK is emphasised both by its location at the top of the composition and by the apparent sonority through which it appears to resonate. The reference to the poem is, in turn, crossed by a spear in a vertical position, whilst two circular figures, located inside and outside the gateway, simultaneously suggest chariot wheels and the famous shield of Achilles.

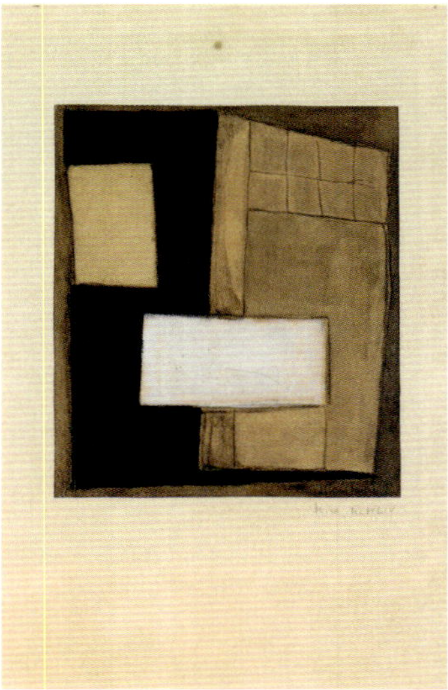

Untitled
Sem título
1954
Tempera, pencil and varnish on paper
32.3 x 21.7 cm
mira schendel estate

Beyond any symbolic value that such a narrative might have for Mira,[4] we can say that nearly all the signs contained in this painting are destined to reappear, simplified or recombined, in many of her works. This leads us to believe that the directions contained here surpass the scope of the poem itself. The drawings of arrows, spears, or even black lines crossing empty space are found in *Monotipias* from the same period, just as, ultimately, they materialise unexpectedly in the *Sarrafos* (*Battens*). For Mira, the gesture of cutting through space with this arrow-trace says something about an almost violent impulse towards individuation, the determination of the Self, the search for direction in a dense or diffuse field.[5]

The image of the gateway, in turn, suggests the issue of territory, of the boundaries and passage between two places, of threshold and entry to the home, the relationship between interior and exterior, public and private. To give some examples, this form can be found as much in the *Fachadas* (*Facades*) from the 1950s as in some pieces from the subseries of *Monotipias* known as *Arquiteturas* (*Architectures*), in which the artist humorously combines drawing with the simplicity of words like 'home', 'corner', 'window', 'door', among others.

4 The meaning of this reference to the Homeric poem in the artist's output remains an open question. For researcher Geraldo Souza Dias, the citation pushes Mira in the direction of Jean Gebser's thinking and interpretation surrounding an aperspectival world (*aperspektivischen Welt*) and the direction of writing: cf. Geraldo Souza Dias, *Mira Schendel: do espiritual à corporeidade* (São Paulo: Cosac Naify, 2009), p.184. About this, see also Isobel Whitelegg's essay in this catalogue, p.45.

5 Cf. interview given by the artist to Jorge Guinle, *Interview* magazine, São Paulo, July 1981, reproduced in this catalogue, p.198.

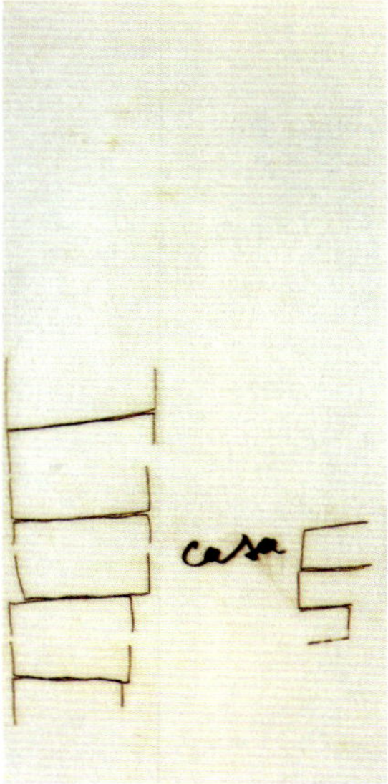

Untitled (*house*), from the series *Monotypes*
Sem título (*casa*), da série *Monotipias*
1965
Oil on rice paper
46 x 23 cm
mira schendel estate

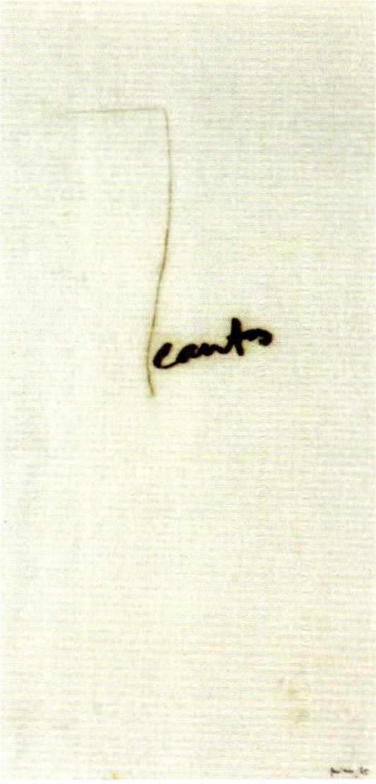

Untitled (*corner*), from the series *Monotypes*
Sem título (*canto*), da série *Monotipias*
1965
Oil on rice paper
46 x 23 cm
mira schendel estate

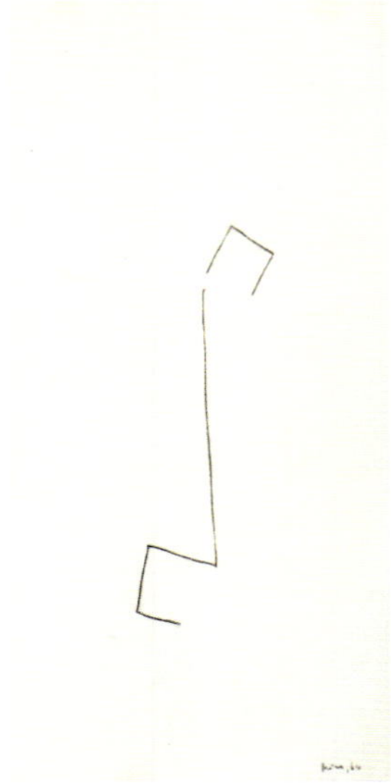

Untitled, from the series *Monotypes*
Sem título, da série *Monotipias*
1965
Oil on rice paper
46.9 x 23 cm
Pinacoteca do Estado de São Paulo, Brazil. Purchase: São Paulo State Government, 2011

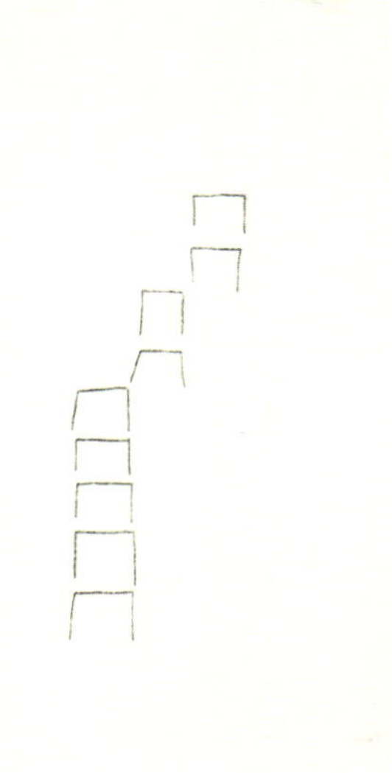

Untitled, from the series *Monotypes*
Sem título, da série *Monotipias*
1964
Oil on paper
47 X 22.8 cm
Pinacoteca do Estado de São Paulo, Brazil. Purchase: São Paulo State Government, 2011

Finally, with respect to the wheels, there is evidently an allusion here to circular movement and time: forms that could be interpreted as two clocks floating in space, symbols of the cyclic span of life [p.92]. Circular or spiral figures are so recurrent in her oeuvre that they pervade its totality, and could be identified in several places: in the 'eggs' present in still-life paintings of the 1950s [p.63]; in the fruit drawings from the first half of the 1960s; in the entire set of *Monotipias*,[6] as in *Genesis* [p.112]; in the 'matter' paintings in the 1960s [p.84], in the works using gold leaf from the 1980s [p.185]; in the circular schemes of the *Bordados* (*Embroideries*) and the *Mandalas* [p.172]; and in the spray drawings, the latter from the 1970s.

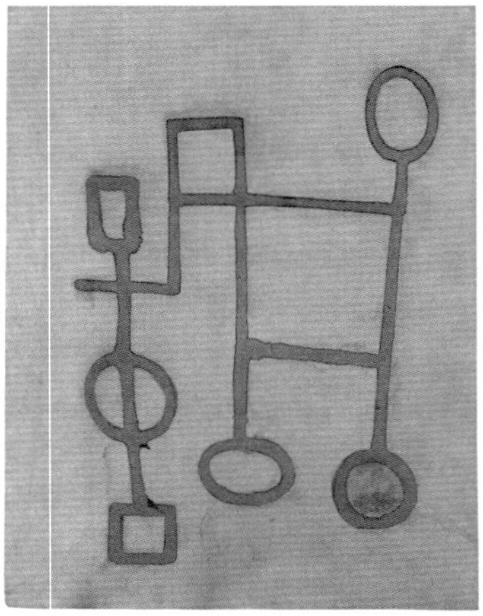

Untitled, from the series *Embroideries*
Sem título, da série *Bordados*
1963
Watercolour on rice paper
30.7 x 34.2 cm
mira schendel estate

What I would like to suggest with these brief associations is an attitude of repetition, a temporal back and forth, which is variable and, in itself, appears as a key to understanding her work. The artist herself thought of her production as a set of 'family' relationships that, despite their heterogeneous appearance, resonate based on a common driving nucleus. However, this operation of transposition or displacement makes the signs transcend the descriptive function, converting themselves into fragments of an expressive language that cannot settle on a single meaning, because they invite polyvalence and require continual reinterpretation. About a *Monotipia* drawing from the 1960s, Lorenzo Mammì says:

> a circle, drawn freehand, and next to it the phrase in Italian: 'ma che bellezza di disegno' (oh, what a beautiful drawing). Elegant self-directed irony, because that circle contains, in its simplicity, the experience of ten years (the circularity of the cups, apples, zeros and Os) and, at the same time, is a unique, immediate gesture, which refers only to the moment when it was traced – paradoxically, a geometrical figure, but not abstract. A 'bellezza di disegno' (beautiful drawing).[7]

As a matter of fact, possible meanings materialise in the moment of each work, in the here-and-now of its execution: 'the dance in time occurs within the perceptual moment', in the words of the art critic and physicist Mario Schenberg.[8]

*

A curious movement of production and reproduction of *leitmotifs* (letters, geometric figures, phrases or images), of procedures (the emphasis on making things manually[9]) and the preference for certain materials (tempera, rice paper and other artisanal papers, the use of aqueous inks, with transparent and watery results, like watercolour and China ink, acrylic, gold leaf, etc.) all provide unity to a work that had the liberty

6 According to Mario Schenberg, in a text dated 1964, 'the circle theme recurred continually in all the monotypes, even more frequently than the straight line. Closed or quasi-closed circles, flower circles, fruit circles, seed circles, tuber circles, egg circles. The qualitative variety of circular lines was surprising, as well as their combinations with other auxiliary lines.' In the same essay, the author associates this shape to the 'symbol of eternity emerging from a cyclical temporality' and concludes 'circular time is a-historical or prehistoric. In the explosion of the circle there is an image of transition from a pre-history to a history.' 'Monotipias de Mira Schendel', in *Pensando a arte* (São Paulo: Editora Nova Stella, 1988), pp.21–4 (my translation).

7 Lorenzo Mammì, *O que resta: arte e crítica de arte* (São Paulo, Companhia das Letras, 2012), p.336.

8 Schenberg 1988, p.22.

9 As the artist said, in a statement given to the Brazilian Art Research and Documentation Department, FAAP (Fundação Armando Alvares Penteado): 'Every little workshop attracts me, be it metal, glass ... any material attracts me, manual labour attracts me, let me put it this way: everything that we make with our hands', São Paulo, 19 August 1977, mimeo, p.1.

of never setting on a single path, rejecting any kind of facility that artistic dexterity might bring.

It is possible to grasp the meaning of this unity by revisiting the spiral figure. A symbol present in many cultures, it suggests the concept of permanent change issuing from a radiating centre. Its form refers to cyclical renewal and the creation of the Universe, in which opposing energies coexist: containment and expansion, centrifugal and centripetal forces, situations of internalisation and externalisation, order and randomness. It indicates a state of constant change according to a permanent order and equilibrium, without implying the exclusion of the transient. It expresses, simultaneously, the single in the multiple and vice versa [10]

Invited in 1974 by the São Paulo City Administration to present a project for an artistic intervention in a public space, Mira developed a proposal for an Archimedean aluminium spiral roughly 5 metres in diameter atop a 16-metre-tall mast at Dom Gastão Liberal Pinto square, where three bustling boulevards of São Paulo come together.[11] As justification for the project, she writes:

> Experientially and visually, the city is perceived as a set of rectangular blocks. The vertical and the horizontal predominate. The frantic movement in the streets is rectilinear, but chaotic. The rhythm is that of machines, expansive intimidation in opposition to architectural rigidity and closure. The experience, the image, is that of collision, of smashing into pieces. Of loss of form. And of time lived.

She continues:

> A large Archimedean spiral, visible against the sky, from many sides, a simple form contrasting with the rigid and excessive regularity, with architectural ecstasy and the race of the machine; a spiral evolving towards the sky (amplitude) and returning to being (narrowness) will recreate, thematically and consciously for some, but experientially for all, the sense of life in the middle of stone and machines.[12]

As an antidote to the closed orthogonality of the city's urban design, of the rigidity of the machine and of architecture, the spiral monument would revive in the artist's concept, the open and infinite circular motion of life.

It is essential to keep in mind the importance of this spiral movement, which, in a way, is mimicked by the very development of her work; because it not only helps us

10 One might remember that in Chinese philosophy, in which Mira Schendel was also interested, 'the cyclical nature (of Time) makes it a relative of the circle, in contrast with Space, whose primary characteristic is to be square'. Marcel Granet, *La Pensée chinoise* (Paris: Albin Michel, 1999).

11 They are: Rua Joaquim Floriano, and Santo Amaro and São Gabriel avenues, in the Itaim neighbourhood, near the last residence of the artist.

12 Mira Schendel, 'Projeto Conceitual', August 1974. Quoted in Souza Dias 2009, p.175.

to understand the artist's mode of operation, but also forewarns us against any type of interpretation that might seek unidirectional, linear development, which in a traditional view of art history would mean organising it according to phases that succeed and surpass one another over time. Mira's work is constructed as the realisation of an essentially qualitative temporality, since the present is not conceived as a causal link between past and future, but as instants of condensation in which diverse moments, even if contradictory, find themselves materialised in a now, like monads, in which the part, the detail, the unit reflects the whole.

There is, thus, no one-way street that would, for example, lead from figuration to abstraction, from matter to spirituality, from opacity to transparency, from immanence to transcendence, from body to soul, from subject to object, etc. On the contrary, there is an investment in the coexistence of polarities in a permanent force field that moves and nourishes the work itself,[13] and the ability to remain in this space of tension, inside this interaction of opposites, seems to be the key to the energy that feeds the poetics of her work. In this sense, it is common that, throughout her life, she would dedicate herself to heterogeneous series at the same time without seeing, in that, any sign of inconsistency.[14]

Therefore, if her artistic career began with painting, but was recognised, above all, for the *Monotipias* and the other experimental works of the 1960s such as the *Objetos gráficos* [p.125] and *Droguinhas* [p.119], this pause in her painterly output in the second half of the 1960s cannot be understood as part of the discourse concerned with superseding painting that marked movements like neoconcretism. Her approach to artistic creation would never have permitted a categorical position, given that, for Mira, formal questions were not the centre of her creation, and that, when she painted, it was not to defend the medium, but to create new possibilities for her work.

Also, only tangentially can one identify in her production any reflection the dispute between figuration and abstraction that dominated the Brazilian art scene of the 1950s. Mira was never really interested in such categorisations,[15] and there is no definitive passage from figuration to abstraction in her oeuvre. However, it would not be correct to say that she produced in a manner totally unaware of artistic trends developing around her, because there is evidently an affinity between her work and the abstract movements,[16] but she did so from a point of view that was unique, and unaffiliated to any specific group or movement.[17] Such uniqueness manifests itself in a later interview given by the artist to Jorge Guinle. Questioned about 'the dialogue between the sensual side of matter and the rigidity of construction', Mira says:

13 And in this sense, the idea of polarity as opposed to dualism in Western thought, developed by Jean Gebser (to whom Mira Schendel would grow closer as of 1965) in his book *Ursprung und Gegenwart* (The Ever-Present Origin) 1949, would help us to understand this coexistence. Cf. Souza Dias 2009, pp.141–9.

14 An example is the solo show at the Gabinete de Artes Gráficas de São Paulo in 1975 in which Mira Schendel presented *Datiloscritos* (Typed-Writings), *Mandalas* and *Paisagens (Papéis japoneses)* [*Landscapes (Japanese Sheets)*].

15 Cf. her letter to Ferdinando Tartaglia, 28 May 1952, quoted in the Chronology, p.220.

16 The attacks against 'abstraction' in Brazil took place soon after the emergence of the first groups of abstract artists in Rio de Janeiro and São Paulo between 1948 and 1949, but gained amplitude in the following decade, with the discussion already polarised between the abstraction of the concrete school (Grupo Ruptura, 1952, and Grupo Neoconcreto, 1959) and all other manifestations of informalism. Cf. Fernando Cocchiarale and Anna Bella Geiger, *Abstracionismo geométrico e informal: a vanguarda brasileira nos anos cinquenta*, vol.5, *Coleção Temas e Debates* (Rio de Janeiro: Funarte, 2004).

17 Likewise legitimate is the relationship that many scholars establish between her production, especially in painting, and the Italian modern and postwar currents, especially the names of Giorgio Morandi, Giorgio de Chirico and Lucio Fontana. About this, see: Maria Eduarda Marques, *Mira Schendel: Coleção Espaços da Arte Brasileira* (São Paulo: Cosac Naify, 2001).

in whatever kind of art, even the most abstract, or in architecture, we always have this second category of corporeality … Art that completely covers this texture, this movement of the hand, is extremely wrong. I give the utmost importance to it being manual like this, that it be handmade, that it be experienced, that it come out this way from the womb. I think this is of utmost importance.[18]

At the time of their production, this sensory character of the canvases, expressed mainly through their textures, caught the attention of such critics as Mario Pedrosa, who saw matter as a fundamental and sensitive quality of her 'abstract' paintings.[19]

On the other hand, the resonance of concrete poetry in her work should also be investigated. Schendel established, starting in 1966, through Haroldo de Campos, a rich dialogue with the German philosopher Max Bense, one of the leading theorists of the movement, and with the semiologist Elisabeth Walther-Bense, both important figures in the Brazilian artistic and intellectual milieu of the time.[20] This affinity could already be foreseen in the spatial and imagistic use of writing in the *Monotipias*, in which the artist experimented with the obverse and reverse of language, in visual texts that moved in a two-dimensional field in which letters and words were converted into events on the plane that were no longer about the line, and whose 'graphic reduction', according to Bense, 'suspends linguistic structure in favour of pictorial structure'.[21] Language receives a new extension in the *Objetos gráficos*, starting in 1967, in which the field of writing expands to three-dimensional space, and in some *Cadernos* (*Notebooks*) [p.157], dating from the early 1970s, which make use of linguistic signs, with language, here, beginning to unfold in time.

Not by chance, one of the objects present in the selection that Mira assembled for the 34th Venice Biennale (1968) [p.137] shows, at the top corner, a poem by Bense typed on rice paper, legible from both sides a true annulment of typical Western hierarchy (left to right). This work, one of Mira's most unique, is the only *Objeto gráfico* in which the vibration produced by the swarm of signs gives way to the materialisation of pause and silence, given that the field of the acrylic sheets is not completely occupied by texts and letters: there is a breathing space in the arrangement of the rice paper sheets between acrylic plates, so that the environment itself seems filtered only by the thickness of the acrylic.[22]

In this *Objeto gráfico* we find an excerpt from the poem 'O cão sem plumas' (The Dog without Feathers) by João Cabral de Melo Neto[23] and lyrics from sambas by Chico Buarque de Hollanda, like 'Madalena foi pro mar' (Madalena Went to the Sea)

18 See interview with Jorge Guinle, p.202.

19 He would also say: 'Concretism becomes denser and gains another dimension, of a subjective expressiveness with real emotional impact'. Cf. Mario Pedrosa, *Mira Schendel: pinturas*, exh. cat., Galeria São Luiz, São Paulo, 1963.

20 Starting in 1959, texts by or about the aesthetics of Bense began to circulate in Brazilian newspapers and magazines, due especially to Haroldo de Campos. In turn, the German philosopher organised shows of Brazilian art and poetry at the *Studiengalerie* of the Technical University of Stuttgart (where he taught) addressing: Brazilian concrete poetry (1959), Alfredo Volpi (1963), the creatures of Lygia Clark (1964), the design of Aloisio Magalhães (1965) and two exhibitions of Mira Schendel's work (in 1967 and 1975). Between 1961 and 1964, Bense undertook a series of trips to Brazil, and his observations were collected in the book *Brasilianische Intelligenz* (Brazilian Intelligence), from 1965.

21 Max Bense, 'Mira Schendel: reduções gráficas', in *Pequena estética* (São Paulo: Editora Perspectiva, 1975), pp.223–5.

22 Cf. artist's statement in this publication, p.196.

23 A writer and diplomat from Pernambuco, João Cabral de Melo Neto (1920–99) is a central reference for Brazilian concrete poets. 'O cão sem plumas', from 1950, written in Spain and originally published when the poet was serving at the Brazilian Consulate General in London, was also published in German, in 1964, in the journal *rot*, edited by Bense and Walther.

and 'Tem mais samba' (There's More Samba), from his debut album (1966). These songs resurface as linguistic fragments in other works from the same period. This constellation of references shows her connection to the cultural milieu of the time, in which the dichotomy *engaged art* vs. *aesthetic experimentation* was being discussed, mostly through heated debates surrounding the new popular music and avant-garde literature.

In a diary from 1969 following the occasion of her participation at the Venice Biennale, the artist noted: 'This is an attempt to show that the back of transparency lies in front of you, and that "the other world" is this one'.[24] Mira's concerns with the issue of transparency in the 1960s refer to a particular existential problematic that would accompany her throughout her life and that, in a general manner, can be glimpsed in a 1953 letter to a friend:

> Modern philosophies of spirit divide man and the world between two independent series, material and spiritual. Sometimes they accept, as brute fact, the independence of the two series (psycho-physical parallelism) abandoning matter to its determinism, whilst safeguarding the absolute right of the spirit to legislate within its own domain: the connection between the two worlds then remains unexplained. Sometimes they deny any reality to the material world, to the point of making it a mere reflection of the spirit: the importance of such an apparent world then becomes somewhat of a paradox. Such schema is rejected from the start by personalist realism.
>
> The person immersed in nature.
>
> Man is a body in the same degree that he is a spirit, wholly body and wholly spirit.[25]

Though using a theological vocabulary, this thinking echoes Mira's constant preoccupation with the non-separation between spirit and matter for the constitution of human and individual experience. What, in philosophical-metaphysical terms,[26] is characterised by the concepts of transcendence and immanence: the experience of the transcendent can only come to light on the basis of matter that makes it visible, immanent. For this reason, the other world, in truth, is contained in this one.

*

Against the universality of systematic thinking, the philosophical form of the essay claims freedom of spirit, the possibility of neither capturing the eternal nor

24 Cf. Diary image in the Chronology, p.232.

25 Letter from Mira to Vaucuccio (10 August 1953), in which the artist cites an excerpt from the book *Personalism*, by the Christian philosopher Emmanuel Mounier. I quote here from the edition published by the University of Notre Dame Press, 1970, p.3, trans. Philip Mairet.

26 It is beyond the scope of this essay to evaluate the importance that philosophical thought (Blaise Pascal, Søren Kierkegaard, Ludwig Wittgenstein, among others), and especially the German tradition of phenomenology (Edmund Husserl, Karl Jaspers, Martin Heidegger and Herman Schmitz), had in her poetics, since this would require many mediations.

distilling it in the transitory, but of 'perpetuating the transient', as the German philosopher Theodor W. Adorno[27] would say. For Bense,

> The person who writes essayistically is the one who composes as he experiments, who turns his object around, questions it, feels it, tests it, reflects on it, who attacks it from different sides and assembles what he sees in his mind's eye and puts into words what the object allows one to see under the conditions created in the course of writing.[28]

In this sense, there is something essayistic in Mira Schendel's poetics. The movement that pervades its production is also one of openness to the world, be it the situations, the materials, the environment, the places that life poses to her, all without denying their tensions. Having been forced to change places, languages, cultures, Mira Schendel knew how to say yes to the moment. As noted in her diary, in a definitive manner:

> To be faithfully of THIS world. And not be of this world.
> With love and happiness and also the inevitable suffering
> with devotion and without illusions.[29]

27 T.W. Adorno, 'The Essay as Form', in *Notes to Literature*, vol.1, trans. Shierry Weber Nicholsen (New York: Columbia University Press, 1991).

28 Quoted ibid., p.17.

29 Quoted in Souza Dias 2009, p.147.

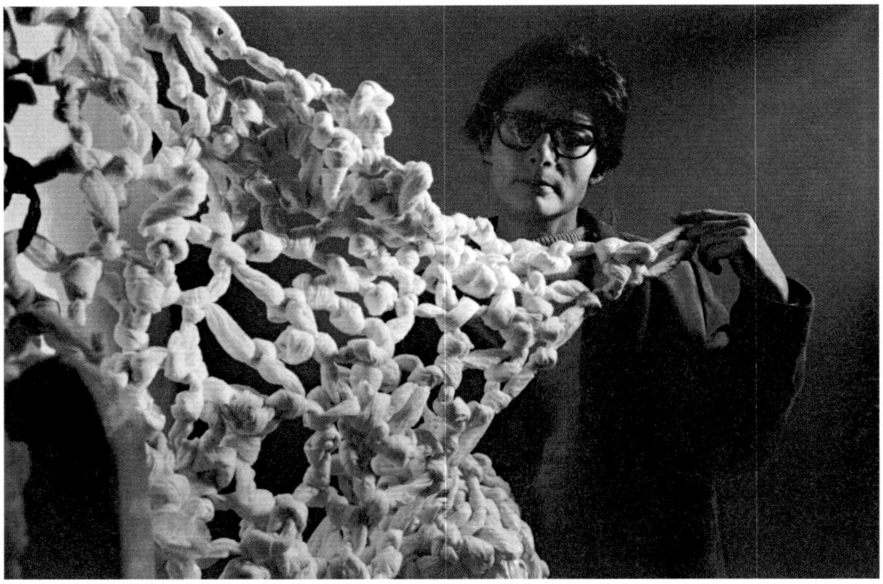

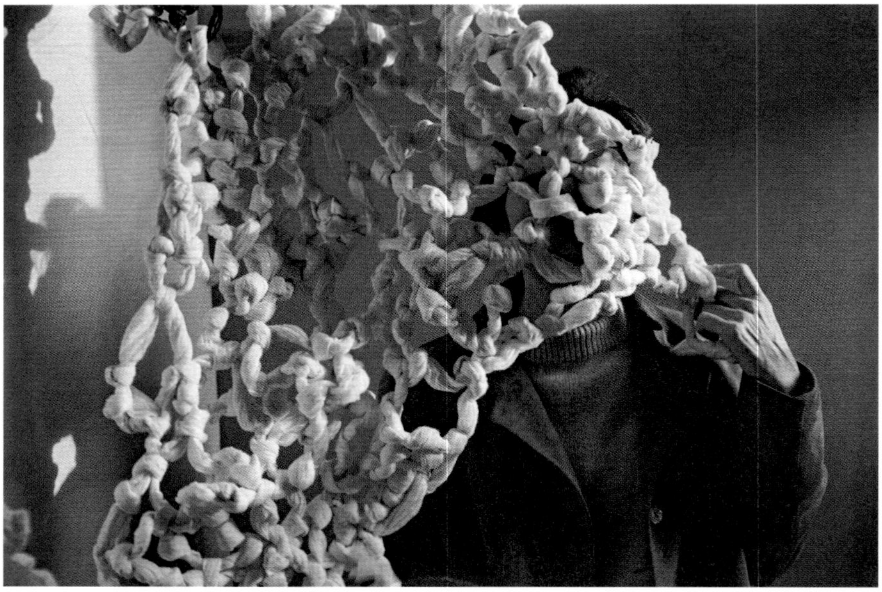

Clay Perry
Mira Schendel and *Little Nothing*, London 1966
Courtesy Clay Perry, England & Co. Gallery, London

Mira Schendel, Signals London and the Language of Movement

Tanya Barson

an art of voids
where the utmost redundancy begins to produce original information
an art of words and quasi-words
where the graphic form veils and unveils seals and unseals
sudden semantic values
... a semiotic art of icons indexes symbols ...
Haroldo de Campos (1966)[1]

I shall ... call the whole, consisting of language and
the activities into which it is woven, a 'language-game'.
Ludwig Wittgenstein, *Philosophical Investigations* (1953)[2]

The possibilities which the work's openness makes available always work within a given field of relations. As in the Einsteinian universe, in the 'work in movement' we may well deny that there is a single prescribed point of view. But this does not mean complete chaos in its internal relations. What it does imply is an organising rule which governs these relations ... the 'work in movement' is the possibility of numerous different personal interventions, but it is not an amorphous invitation to indiscriminate participation.
Umberto Eco, *The Open Work* (1962)[3]

Mira Schendel's visit to London in 1966 for her solo exhibition at Signals was her only time in Britain,[4] though it was one of a number of visits she made to Europe during the late 1960s, motivated partly by exhibitions of her work but also by her research, in which she visited philosophers and thinkers or the places associated with them.[5] She had been invited to have a show at the gallery after Guy Brett and Paul Keeler travelled to Brazil to see the São Paulo Bienal in 1965.[6] They visited her at her home and spent many hours looking through work and talking late into the night, in a characteristically intense encounter.[7] Earlier in 1965, a series of Schendel's *Monotipia* (*Monotype*) drawings had been included in the group exhibition *Soundings Two* at Signals, her work having been introduced to the gallery by the Brazilian artist Sergio Camargo.[8] Based in Paris at the time, Carmago was part of the close circle of Signals and the connecting figure between the gallery and many of the Brazilian

1 Haroldo de Campos, untitled poem, first published on the occasion of Schendel's exhibition at the Museu de Arte Moderna, Rio de Janeiro, 1966, in Sônia Salzstein (ed.), *No Vazio do Mundo: Mira Schendel*, exh. cat., Galeria de Arte do SESI, São Paulo 1996, p. 261.

2 Ludwig Wittgenstein, *Philosophical Investigations*, trans. G.E.M. Anscombe, P.M.S. Hacker and Joachim Schulte, (Oxford, Wiley-Blackwell, 2009), remark 7, p.8.

3 Umberto Eco, *The Open Work* (1962), trans. Anna Cancogni (Cambridge MA: Harvard University Press, 1989), p.19.

4 Signals was a gallery for experimental art founded in June 1964 as the Centre for Advanced Creative Study at Paul Keeler's flat at 92 Cornwall Gardens; in November 1964 it moved into a four-storey building at 39 Wigmore Street. The gallery took its name from Takis's *Signals* sculptures. The founder members were Paul Keeler, Guy Brett, David Medalla, Gustav Metzger and Marcello Salvatori. For more on Signals and its context, see Isobel Whitelegg, 'Signals Echoes Traces', in Guy Brett and Luciano Figueiredo (eds.), *Oiticica in London*, exh. cat., Tate Modern, London 2007, pp.89–92, and Carmen Julia, 'You Saw it Here First', in *Tate Etc.*, no.24, Spring 2012, also available at <http://www.tate.org.uk/content-comment/articles/you-saw-it-here-first>. For Schendel at Signals, see Geraldo Souza Dias, *Mira Schendel: do espiritual à corporeidade* (São Paulo: Cosac Naify, 2009).

5 In 1967 Schendel met Max Bense in Stuttgart, where she had an exhibition; she also travelled to Zurich, and in Milan met Umberto Eco. In 1968 she showed in the Venice Biennale but also travelled to Bern to meet Jean Gebser, visited Bense again in Stuttgart, travelled on to Hamburg and Copenhagen – the city of Kierkegaard – then to Oslo, and journeyed to the North Cape (Nordkapp) – the association of Norway with Wittgenstein was surely not incidental to her.

6 The 8th Bienal de São Paulo ran from 4 September to 28 November 1965. Brett named Schendel's drawings as among the works of great interest in his (unsigned) review 'Some Finds in São Paulo' for the *Times*, 13 September 1965, p.7.

7 Guy Brett at the 'Mira Schendel' conference, Tate Modern, 16–17 November 2012.

8 The *Soundings Two* exhibition, which included the work of forty-three artists, was shown in two parts: the first part ran from 22 July until 22 August, with the second instalment on until 22 September 1965 (see the unsigned review 'South American Paintings at Signals', the *Times*, 30 July 1965, p.13).

artists shown there. Schendel's solo show opened on 29 October 1966; writing later, Schendel herself recalled how the exhibition and its reception contrasted with another staged at the Museu de Arte Moderna, in Rio de Janeiro earlier in the year:

> That was very strange, the low attendance [at the Museu de Arte Moderna] that somehow suited the work itself. Now, it was completely different in London. I remember, in London, in 1966, it was a time of great ferment, of change; it was a very important moment. I remember the gallery. It was full. There was coming and going. There were people everywhere. A completely different atmosphere. The English must have a different mentality. They were not startled by the work. On the contrary, it was much better received. There was a more resounding effect in England than in Rio de Janeiro.[9]

A drawing Schendel made of an exhibition opening in her travel journal largely devoted to Britain, shows a gallery crowded with people in vibrant, fashionable clothing – evidently Schendel was quite taken by 'Swinging London' at its height.[10] [Fig.1]However, on 12 November 1966, quite unexpectedly the gallery closed for good, while her show was still on view. This meant that it was only up for a matter of weeks, limiting the number of people who saw it and thus also its local influence and memory of it.[11] Nevertheless, ripples of effect were registered when her work was included in two group exhibitions at the Lisson Gallery, London, in 1967 and 1968.[12] The unanticipated and abrupt end of Signals, owing to the withdrawal of financial backing, also meant that the planned edition of *Signals Bulletin* (the publication associated with the gallery, edited by David Medalla) that would have been largely devoted to her work never appeared.

Geraldo Souza Dias writes that the Signals exhibition was Schendel's most important lifetime solo show. [13] Although this is a strong claim, it has certainly become one of her landmark exhibitions and significant for the contacts it cemented in a network that now seems both prescient and remarkable in its scope and focus on radical experimentation. Although the exhibition itself was short-lived, Schendel spent several months in Britain, allowing her time to develop relationships that would remain important for her work thereafter. In a *Monotipia* produced at the time of the exhibition, in a typical act of commemoration of her personal associations, Schendel draws an arrow and an *informel* mark, and next to it writes in a column of text 'Signal for Takis and Medalla and Keeler and Guy'; lower down, the name 'Sergio' appears, referring no doubt to Sergio Camargo. [Fig.2] The list relates to the group of figures most directly involved in Signals, therefore it does not name other important figures, some of them also associated with Signals, whom Schendel came to know in Britain, such as the British-based Chinese artist Li Yuan-Chia, the Benedictine monk and concrete poet Dom Sylvester Houédard, and the scholar, art critic and Wittgenstein specialist Cyril Barrett.

9 'Mira Schendel, Painter: Empty Space Moves Me Deeply': Schendel interview with Jorge Guinle, *Interview*, São Paulo July 1981, reproduced in this publication, p.199. It also contrasted with the reception of another 1966 exhibition of Schendel's work; stopping in Lisbon both before and after going to London to visit her friend the artist Amelia Toledo, who was living in exile in Portugal, she took the opportunity to mount an exhibition in the Buchholz Bookstore in Lisbon. This was not entirely successful. Commenting dryly, Schendel said 'the exhibition in Lisbon was very well assembled. The catalogue, nothing special, and the visitors, perplexed.' Letter to Elisabeth Walther, São Paulo, 10 January 1967, quoted in Souza Dias 2009, p.193 (my translation).

10 *Time* magazine defined 'Swinging London' in its issue of 15 April 1966. In 1966, Schendel was in Europe for the first time since the end of the Second World War. Souza Dias states that she visited from August to November 1966. Souza Dias 2009, p.192. Schendel's travel journal gives us some sense of this visit to Britain and the important contacts she made. As well as the depiction of the opening mentioned, the book contains a drawing of the exterior of Signals and references to people she associated with most closely in London, such as Brett, Keeler and the artist Li-Yuan Chia. It also includes several references to Wittgenstein, the Austrian-British philosopher, including quotations from the *Tractatus Logico-philosophicus* (1921), as well as diagrams that relate to decision or game theory. The book is inscribed Paris, October 1966. While it also makes reference to Schendel being in Zurich, the majority of the book deals with her time in Britain. It does not mention Lisbon.

11 It has only been with the renewed interest in Signals and those artists associated with it that the exhibition of Schendel's work has been reassessed in the city in which it occurred. The other exhibition on at Signals alongside Schendel's exhibition was the third instalment of a series of group exhibitions called *Towards the Invisible*, which included works by Lygia Clark, Gianni Colombo, Mathias Goeritz, Gerhard von Graevenitz, Julio le Parc, Liliane Lijn, David Medalla, François Morellet, Hélio Oiticica and Takis.

12 The exhibitions were Li Yuan-Chia, David Medalla, Mira Schendel, Lygia Clark (6 July – 26 August 1967) and Ken Cox, Mira Schendel and Dom Sylvester Houédard (11 June – 29 June 1968). Documentation of these shows can be found in the Lisson Gallery Archive. I would like to thank Ossian Ward for bringing these shows to my attention. Schendel's work has been shown in a number of group exhibitions in Britain, notably *Latin America: The Modern Era, 1820–1980*, Hayward Gallery, London (1989), *Inside the Visible: An Elliptical Traverse of 20th Century Art in, of and from the Feminine*, Whitechapel Art Gallery, London (1996), *Force Fields: Phases of the Kinetic*, Hayward Gallery, London (2000) and *Experiment Experiência: Art in Brazil 1958–2000*, Modern Art Oxford (2001). There would not be another solo exhibition until that held at Stephen Friedman Gallery in 2009.

13 Sousa Dias 2009, p.193.

The last of these, Barrett, who published Wittgenstein's edited lectures and conversations in 1966, reveals another connection that provided Schendel with an ulterior motivation for being in Britain – her interest in the work of Ludwig Wittgenstein and the thought and writings of the theologian Cardinal John Henry Newman, and the ways these two interconnect on matters of faith and certainty.[14] Li, who had arrived in London from Italy also in 1966 and had links to a Europe-wide avant-garde, became Schendel's Italian-speaking interlocutor. He and Schendel had many shared interests in thought and aesthetics, and with both Houédard and Li she found a mutual interest in spirituality and in zen.[15] Whilst the influence of Houédard's *Typestracts* can be seen in Schendel's *Datiloscritos* (*Typed Writings*), Li's can be seen perhaps in her *Discos* (*Discs*), among other works. Wittgenstein was important for Schendel's work and thought, through his writings on language and logic, and later his work on certainty, particularly important is his idea that language is constituted by the actions into which it is woven – what he called language-games – and that the issue of certainty is itself at the centre of a language-game. Wittgenstein's *Tractatus Logico-philosophicus* (1921) prefigures communications theory and cybernetic thinking, influencing figures in Brazil such as Vilem Flusser as well as thinking prevalent in Britain in the late 1960s. While Schendel and Flusser had developed a close dialogic relationship by this time, in Britain, perhaps through Houédard and the concrete poetry scene, she can be linked to concerns preoccupying figures such as Jasia Reichardt who organised the exhibitions *Between Poetry and Painting* (1965) – which included Houédard's work – and *Cybernetic Serendipity* (1968) both at the ICA, London, which bracket Schendel's visit to Britain. In 1969, Flusser wrote 'the theory of communication implies the theory of decision and the theory of games.'[16]

Schendel's work embodies the preoccupations that concerned the group of individuals behind Signals and which defined both its programme and the selection of artists, writers and diverse other figures that featured in the Bulletin. Schendel's exhibition can be seen not only in the context of the other Brazilian and Latin American artists shown at Signals but within a programme that gave a platform to a wide-ranging, transnational network of experimental and kinetic art. Thus it was that through Signals, Schendel integrated into an interdisciplinary circle of radical thinkers and practitioners, much as she had done in São Paulo. The project of Signals was to foreground a poetics of a new reality that countered the dichotomy between the arts and sciences. When Signals had begun in 1964 as the Centre for Advanced Creative Study, its aim was to 'bring to the attention of the artist new developments in technology and science ...[and] to provide a forum for all those who believe *passionately* in the correlation of the arts and Art's *imaginative* integration with technology, science, architecture and our entire environment.'[17] Among many of the active and extended circle of Signals there was also a deep concern with spirituality and humankind's place in the universe or cosmos, and Schendel's work fitted particularly well within this context. In the edition of *Signals Bulletin* in which Schendel features most prominently (issued in August–October

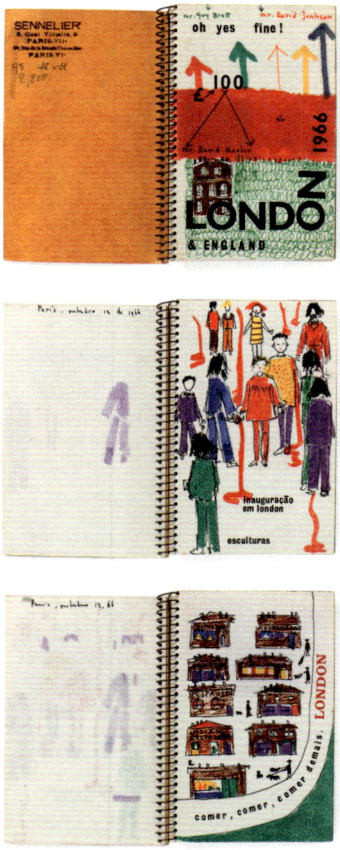

Figure 1
Untitled (London Journal)
Sem título (Diário de Londres)
1966
Mixed media on paper
40 x 22 cm
Melsohn Collection

14 Schendel was familiar with both Wittgenstein and Newman before she arrived in Britain. It is likely that the priest and theologian Ferdinando Tartalglia had first introduced her to Newman's work. Isobel Whitelegg has said: 'Cyril Barrett ... looked at connections between Wittgenstein and Newman in his writings on ethics and religious belief,' and that 'Schendel met (and argued with) [him] while in England for the first time'. Isobel Whitelegg, 'Mira Schendel: A Radical Passivity. Towards Another History of Art, Thought & Action in the Brazilian Sixties', unpublished PhD. Thesis, University of Essex 2005, p.220.

15 A full account of Schendel's engagement with zen and the correlation of her interests with those of Li and Houédard, and of the exchange of influences between them, is beyond the scope of this essay.

1965, coinciding with *Soundings Two*), a page is given over to the illustration of a *Monotipia*, accompanied by a brief yet perceptive article on her work by David Medalla. Medalla's text describes the monotypes; he was quick to the deceptive nature of their apparent simplicity and economy, and their deployment of areas of blank paper as parts of an overall composition in which a sense of spatial arrangement was critical and values of positive and negative, full or empty space were revealed not as exclusive but simultaneous – the marks and their surrounding areas forming part of a unified whole. As Medalla commented:

> Within a consciously 'restricted' working area, Mira Schendel has created a microcosmic world of great symbolic power. Her drawings on rice paper at first appear simple, but their simplicity – which is true of all great art whatever its style – is the result of an original technique quickened by a profound vision of existence.[18]

He continues:

> Here and there, among her drawings, one will find the presence of barely discernable words, half-obliterated phrases, letters removed from their usual linguistic context, letters and numbers dancing in space among simple geometric configurations, circle, triangle and square, and up and down aerial structures, the while tracing the rhythms of their dances … Thus her drawings could be regarded as the beginnings of a highly poetic Future.[19]

Crucially, in this text Medalla identifies 'a sensibility who has seen the risks and taken them' and thus creates 'visual poems … from the chaos of existence'.[20] Such a focus on language, movement, space and existence, as well as on the audacity of her compositions, served to introduce Schendel's work to London for the first time.

Schendel's show at Signals was documented, indirectly, in a series of photographs taken by Clay Perry of Mira with the works called *Droguinhas* (*Little Nothings*) – curious, seemingly 'formless' and malleable sculptures of twisted and knotted rice paper – and others of a number of *Monotipias*. These photographs give an indication of the works intended for inclusion in the exhibition, which was concentrated on these two key series of the mid-1960s – *Droguinhas* and *Monotipias*, but which also included a *Trenzinho* (*Little Train*) – one of a small series of similarly experimental sculptural works that consisted of a cotton thread onto which blank sheets of rice paper had been threaded.[21] [Fig.3] Six much more informal photographs of the show itself also exist; perhaps taken by Mira herself, these give us a rare visualisation of how she installed these works at the time.[22] These images show *Droguinhas* hanging in the windows on the street-level of the gallery (notably they are not displayed in a manner that allows for interaction), whilst a series of *Monotipias* dealing with

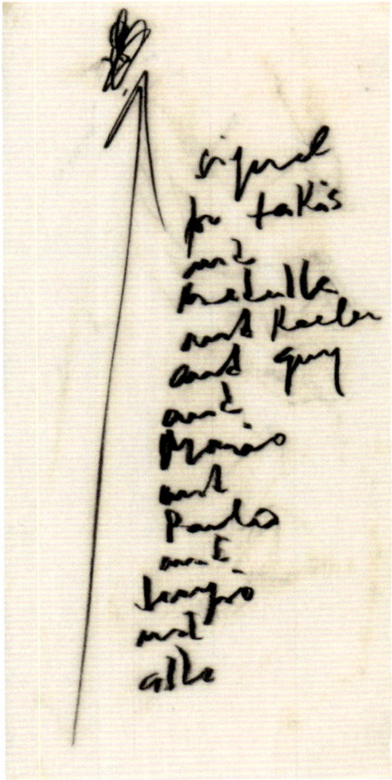

Figure 2
Untitled, from the series *Monotypes*
Sem título, da serie *Monotipias*
1966
Oil on rice paper
47 x 23 cm
Private collection, London

16 Vilem Flusser, 'In Search of Meaning', in Andreas Ströhl (ed.), *Writings*, (Minneapolis and London, University of Minnesota Press, 2002), p.205. Game theory, also called interactive decision theory, has been used to study political, economic, sociological and psychological human interactions; in philosophy, it has been applied towards understanding good, ethical or proper behaviour.

17 *Signalz: Newsbulletin of the Centre for Advanced Creative Study*, vol.1, no.1, August 1964 18 David Medalla, 'Mira Schendel', in *Signals Bulletin*, vol.1, no.9, Aug.–Sept.–Oct. 1965, p.13.

19 Ibid.

20 Ibid.

21 Whitelegg 2007, p. 92, n.6. In his book *Kinetic Art: The Language of Movement*, Brett refers to a *Trenzinho* as a *Droguinha*, suggesting how these two groups of works were closely related. Guy Brett, *Kinetic Art: The Language of Movement*, (London and New York: Studio Vista/Reinhold, 1968), p.47.

22 These 'contact' photographs were found in the archive of the mira schendel estate.

religious themes hangs on an adjacent wall. [Fig.4]. Whilst some of the monotypes Perry photographed may be connected to communication, decision and game theory[23] and to the spiral of Archimedes, which was a form that preoccupied Schendel over a number of years,[24] others are distinctly text-based and can be identified as coming from the series known as *Genesis*.[25] [p. 112] The prominent inclusion of text works telling the biblical story of Genesis indicates that in this exhibition Schendel was particularly concerned with themes of belief, faith and language which is in accordance with her interest in Newman and Wittgenstein and appropriate to the exhibition in London for that very reason.[25a]

Other photographs by Perry that were intended as portraits of Schendel show her interacting with the *Droguinhas* and thus give us a sense of these works as phenomenological-corporeal objects. [Fig.5] Schendel would later remark that 'we can never withdraw ourselves from corporeality ... artists always have had this sense of the body within space.'[26] As she attempts to hide from the camera behind or even within the works, these photographs also show the capacity of the sculptures to be a covering or veil, even if only partially. As Briony Fer has commented, 'Clay Perry's photographs of Mira Schendel ... are very compelling ... they stage a game of hide and seek that's close to the feel of the work sometimes. The play of seeing and not seeing, touching, handling, that seems important in all her work whether it's the *Droguinhas* or the other work ... in which opacity and transparency take a different form.'[27] In these images we see Schendel showing the variability of the works, the work of art *in movement*; also their playfulness, and she perhaps reveals something of her own light-hearted humour. These images suggest how the works might find some correlation in Umberto Eco's concept of the *open work* (works to be completed by the viewer, performer or reader) and raise the question of the relationship of Schendel's work to such concepts, the terms of which inflect accounts of her work in both Britain and Brazil. Eco identified 'inside the category of "open" works a further, more restricted classification of works which can be defined as "works in movement," because they characteristically consist of unplanned or physically incomplete structural units ... elementary structures which can move in the air and assume different spatial dispositions. They continuously create their own space and the shapes to fill it.'[28] The *Droguinha* forms a net-like object that embodies mathematical principles of topology, but one that might also be said to resemble a piece of loosely formed knitting – an activity Schendel herself engaged in.[29] Schendel wraps herself in the mantle-form of the *Droguinha*; the knotted-together rice paper is evidently strong enough to undergo quite vigorous manipulation.

In November 1965, some weeks after Brett and Keeler had visited her in São Paulo, Schendel wrote a letter to Guy Brett in which she announced:

> I started a new work, perhaps more important for myself than all those before. 'Sculptures' made from the same rice paper as the drawings. Something tech-

23 Whitelegg 2007, p.92, n.6. This can be seen in Perry's photographs showing monotypes with tree-like structures drawn from game theory.

24 Spiral motifs recur throughout Schendel's work – for instance, dominating the painting *Sem titulo (Todos)* [*Untitled (All)*] 1964. In 1974 Schendel designed a project for one of the Municipal Government of São Paulo's urban renovation schemes, in the form of a large aluminium spiral. This was intended to contrast the 'excessive, rigid rectangularity' of the city but was also conceived as a 'spiral of Archimedes, visible against the sky'. Schendel, quoted in Souza Dias 2009, p.175. Described by Archimedes in his treatise *On Spirals* (c.225 BC), Archimedean spirals map points corresponding with locations of a point moving away from a fixed point with a constant speed along a line which rotates with constant angular velocity. As they were also used for 'circle squaring' – constructing a square equal in area to a circle – and since several of the monotypes show circular spirals whilst others are in the form of a square spiral it seems likely that these are spirals of Archimedes.

25 Perry's contact sheets reveal that monotypes in the series *Genesis* now in Tate's collection were among those he photographed, whilst the installation photographs show them at Signals.

25a There is an important distinction to be drawn however, between the impact on Schendel of Wittgenstein's early writing and his later ideas. Flusser pointed out Schendel's contradiction of Wittgenstein's view that the limits of language necessitate silence, especially in ethics and religion, to allow for the sacred through her prayer-like 'defiance of the unutterable' (Vilem Flusser, 'Mira Schendel', São Paulo, July 1966, in *Force Fields: Phases of the Kinetic*, 2000, p.292). In contrast was the impact of Wittgenstein's later philosophy, which was more in tune with her 'experiments in linguistic structure', emphasising the multiplicity of language, its variety of relations within human activity and the rules governing its use that are established by agreement or assent.

26 Guinle 1981, p.202.

27 Briony Fer, lecture at the 'Mira Schendel' conference, Tate Modern, 16– 17 November 2012.

28 'The Poetics of the Open Work', in Eco 1989, p.12.

29 If Schendel was not making art, her restless hands and energies were focused on other kinds of production including, significantly perhaps, knitting. Her daughter, Ada Schendel, says that Schendel read philosophy mostly in German, but when she knitted, she counted in Italian – thus the *Droguinhas* – which are among other things a kind of knitting – have an oblique relationship to language and numbers. Conversation with Ada Schendel, May 2012.

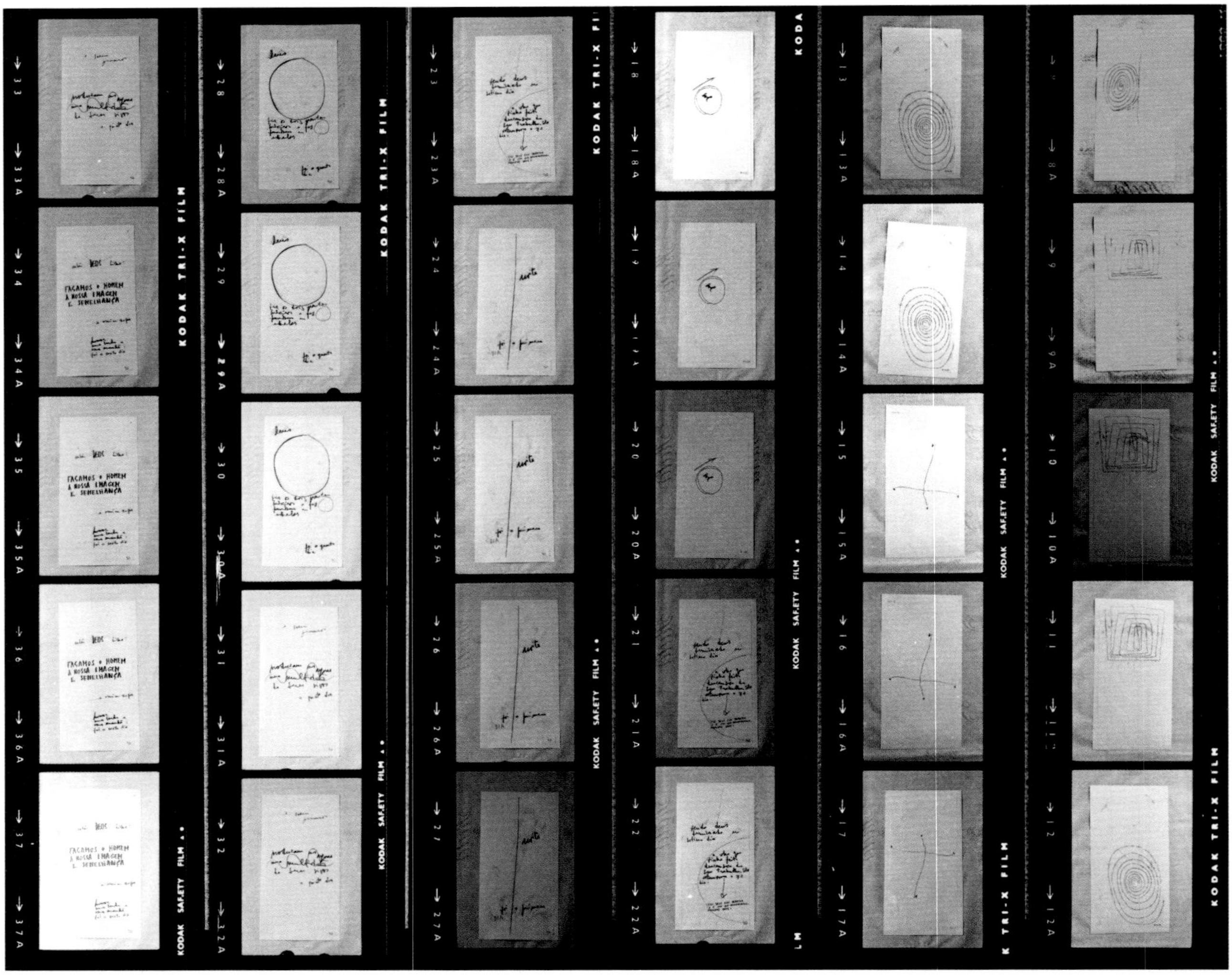

Figure 3. Clay Perry, contact sheet showing *Monotypes* by Mira Schendel, 1966. Courtesy Clay Perry, England & Co. Gallery, London

> nically primary and easy. From a western point of view these 'sculptures' (this word without sense!) could be seen from the perspective of a phenomenology of being. From the eastern point of view, well, they relate to zen.[30]

In his 1968 book *Kinetic Art: The Language of Movement*, published only shortly after Schendel's Signals show, Brett wrote, in terms similar to Eco's, of how 'Schendel's *Droguinhas* do not describe any particular movement, but they are vital contributions to the language of movement because their fragility and energy indicate space as an active thing, a *field of possibility*'; he continued that 'in open defiance of the idea of "sculpture" are Mira Schendel's *Droguinhas*. *Droguinhas* is a Portuguese word meaning literally "druglets", and also colloquially "little nothings" ... obviously they have no base, no necessary shape or position and they cannot be preserved for very long.'[31] [Fig.6] In this short passage Brett defines the particular paradox of the *Droguinhas* in that they are still objects that embody, at the

30 Letter to Guy Brett, 24 November 1965, in Souza Dias 2009, p.215 (my translation).

31 Brett 1968, p.46 (my emphasis).

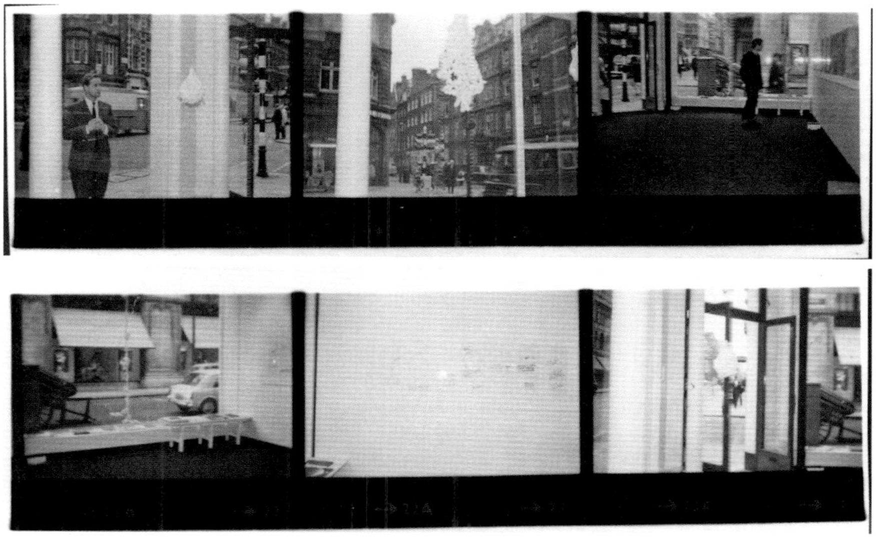

Figure 4. Anonymous (possibly Mira Schendel), Mira Schendel solo exhibition at Signals, London, 1966. mira schendel estate archive

same time, potential movement or contained energy. Thus he framed these works within a complex reading of kinetic art that, like the expansive scope of the *Signals Bulletins*, saw them connected with ideas associated with science, technology, mathematics and cosmic energies.[32] Brett would later write of the *Droguinhas* that 'with their nucleic structure they have an aura of intense energy while remaining soft, fragile, ephemeral "little nothings" in comparison to heroic monumental sculpture. These "sculptures", which can be displayed in any way one chooses, are a proposition from the 1960s which remains extremely fresh, interweaving notions of energy, matter and language by hinting at the etymology common to tissue, textile and text.'[33] Brett's allusion to language here is also critical to a reading of the *Droguinhas* in relation to other works that approach language, openness and the 'work in movement'. Likewise, the self-reflexive drawing *A trama (A fabric net)* c.1960s [p.118], one of her largest on rice paper, suggests similar weavings of drawing, textile and text.

There are also several photographs of the *Droguinhas* taken by Brett in London that emphasise their opposition to traditional or 'monumental' forms of sculpture.[34] These images show the works on the floor or spread across a shelf or step, stressing their informality, domesticity and organicism, and perhaps revealing the way that they were intended to impact on the viewer as modest rather than elevated objects. [Fig.7] They had been displayed in a similar way, located on the floor, in the exhibition at the Museu de Arte Moderna, Rio de Janeiro in 1966. In *Kinetic Art* Brett describes how, at MAM, Rio, Schendel had shown them 'merely in a heap on the floor for the spectator to discover as he wished'.[35] Schendel evidently considered these works to be eminently ephemeral objects and stated as much, commenting that to preserve them would be like preserving the foam of one of David Medalla's sculptures.[36] She was more con-

32 Brett later developed and expanded this nuanced reading of kinetic art in the major exhibition *Force Fields: Phases of the Kinetic* at the Museu d'Art Contemporani de Barcelona (MACBA), Barcelona, and the Hayward Gallery, London, in 2000. Brett argues in his catalogue essay 'The Century of Kinesthesia' that 'in particular this exhibition should sensitise the viewer to the existence of a "language of movement", which surely remains one of 20th-century art's great unknowns' and thus it aimed to reject 'the tendency to treat the historical phenomenon known as Kinetic Art as a kind of slide-show, or entertainment ... not to be treated with the same seriousness as, say, Minimal Art, Conceptual Art, or for that matter Pop Art ... the result has been that the radical implications of the best work for the evolution of art have been ignored': p.9.

33 Guy Brett, 'A Radical Leap', in Dawn Ades, *Art in Latin America: The Modern Era, 1820–1980*, exh. cat., Hayward Gallery, London, 1989, p.276.

34 Of the sculptures that Brett photographed, one has a unique addition; a small area, roughly corresponding to a circle, of black ink has been applied to the twisted paper so that it extends across several papers. This might be seen as a kind of 'cosmic point', indicating perhaps a direct influence of Li on Schendel's work.

35 Brett 1968, p.46.

36 Referring to Medella's *Cloud Canyons* sculptures, in an unpublished diary entry, quoted in Souza Dias 2009, p.215. The fact that the *Droguinhas* have survived is a testament to the interest they provoked in figures such as Brett – the person who is most responsible for their ongoing survival. Perry and Brett's photographs of them perhaps approach the manner in which the artist wanted them to be seen. Yet, these photographs are not straightforward images of the works; in different ways, Perry and Brett are both engaged in a staging of the works for the camera, in Perry's case with the complicity of the artist.

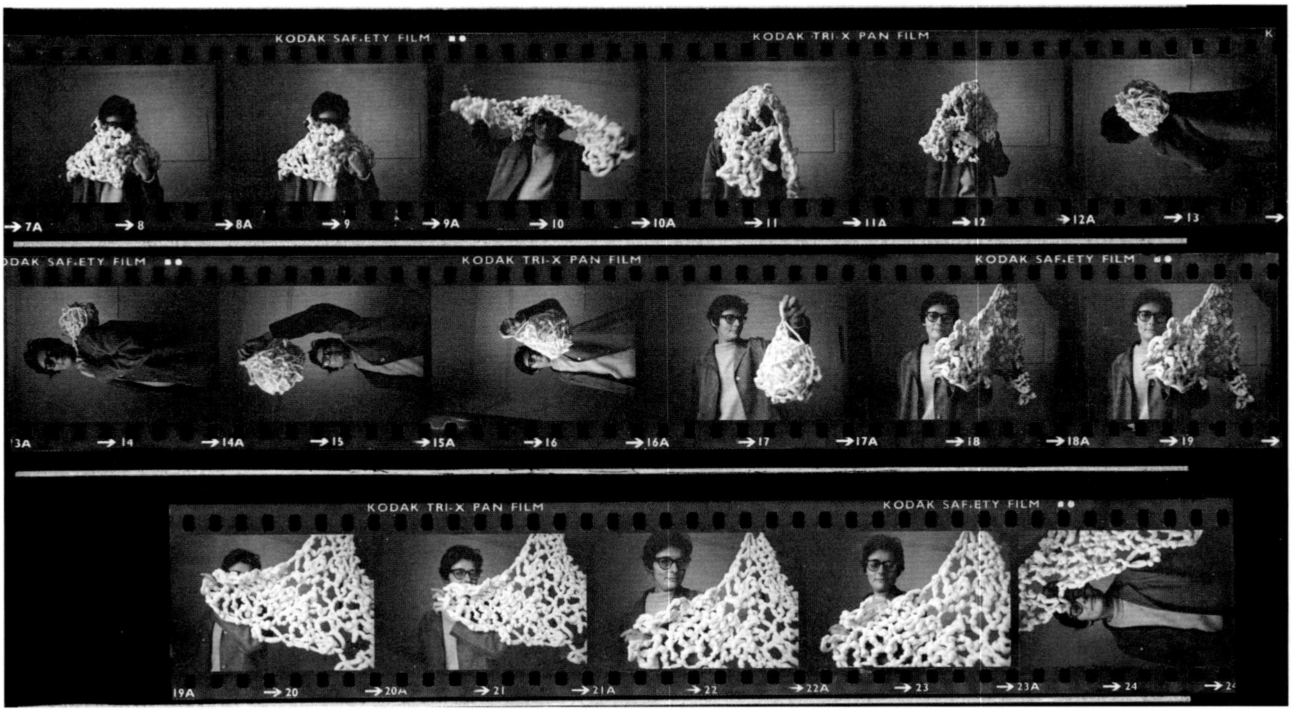

Figure 5. Clay Perry, contact sheet showing Mira Schendel and *Little Nothings*, London 1966
Courtesy Clay Perry, England & Co. Gallery, London

cerned with the meaning of the encounter than on the preservation of the material object. The emphasis, then, is on the openness of the work and its potential energy or movement, but also on their 'defiance' of the norms of aesthetics.

During the 1960s and 1970s, Schendel's work also constituted an investigation into the theme of transparency or diaphaneity, a concept she derived from the writings of the philosopher, linguist and poet Jean Gebser that corresponded to a form of the spiritual – the making transparent of all that is latent in the world.[37] Schendel developed her interest in ideas of transparency, alongside concerns with language, composition, time and the open work in the context of ongoing dialogues with the philosophers and communications theorists Vilem Flusser and Max Bense, and Bense's wife the semiotician Elizabeth Walther.[38] Formally, transparency is evident in her series of *Monotipia* drawings, the *Trenzinhos*, the *Objetos graficos* (*Graphic Objects*) and the *Cadernos* (*Notebooks*).[39] As Isobel Whitelegg has written,

> the formal motif of transparency emerges with particular coherence in Schendel's work from the late sixties to the first years of the seventies. As a physical property of her artworks Schendel attributes this to the discovery of acrylic, a support that would allow her to expose each surface of the fine rice-paper used

37 For more detailed explanations of Gebser's concept of transparency see both Cauê Alves's and Isobel Whitelegg's essays in this publication.

38 Schendel had known Flusser in São Paulo for some years, but came to know Bense and Walther in the mid-1960s. For more detail on Flusser, see Cauê Alves's essay in this publication.

39 It is not known exactly how many *Objetos graficos* there are. However, several have been numbered in the bottom right-hand corner, and examples exist numbered 117 and 121, so it seems possible that they were as numerous as other series in Schendel's oeuvre. The *Objetos graficos* were exhibited at the Venice Biennale in 1968. In his review for the *Times*, Brett wrote that 'In the first room hangs a series of transparent drawings by Mira Schendel, in which basic linguistic signs, printed letters, written letters, words and mathematical symbols form varying densities of great subtlety.' *Times Saturday Review*, 22 June 1968, p.19.

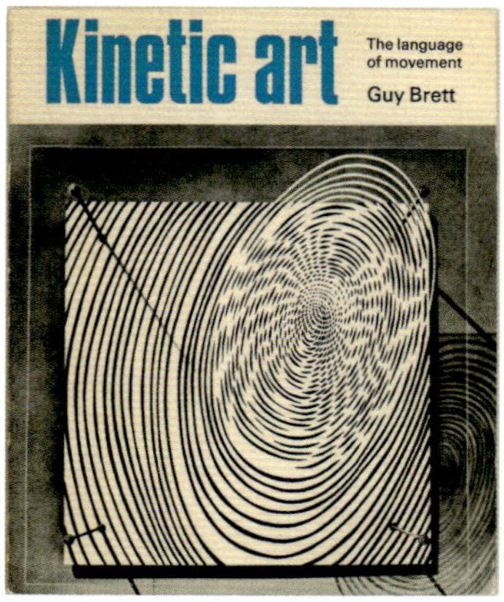

Figure 6
Guy Brett, *Kinetic Art: The Language of Movement* (London and New York: Studio Vista/Reinhold, 1968)

> to produce the multitudinous *Monotipias*. It also acted as a framing/grouping device, and as such produced different modes of seriality ... as well as a material property, 'transparency' was an expansive philosophical concept that Schendel approached in simultaneity with her use of acrylic. [40]

The spatial characteristics afforded by transparent acrylic allowed, as Schendel explained, 'a circular reading where the lettering constitutes a fixed centre around which the viewer moves. Thus time is transferred from artwork to viewer as it is bounced back from symbol to life.'[41] Pointing to the spatial and temporal significance of the deployment of transparency, emphasising simultaneity, Flusser states:

> Transparency is a temporalisation of space by which space evaporates and time disappears, resulting instead [in] an interpenetration of both structures. This means that the terms past, and future, pass into denoting aspects of the present, that is, the two terms that refer, in diachronism, to points on a progressive scale, refer in transparency, to a structured present. And the various spatial terms, that refer, in diachronism, to other such dimensions of space, refer, in transparency, only to this structured present. The linear scale of diachronism totally disappears, into an infinite cube, the emptiness called 'space'. In sum, transparency is the supersession of time and space by the presentation of both. In this sense we can say that transparency is the concrete presence of the abstract concepts 'time' and 'space.'[42]

For Flusser, the significance of transparency is that it signified a paradigm shift in human consciousness, from discursive, procedural, linear or progressive modes, to structural, dialogic or cybernetic modes, as well as an end of linear alphabetic writing and therefore the basis for historical consciousness.

Both Flusser and the Brazilian concrete poets had been aware of and in contact with European theorists such as Eco and Bense since the late 1950s. Schendel's close friendship with the concrete poet Haroldo de Campos led him to encourage her to visit Italian thinker and semiotician Eco, which she did in 1967, the year after her exhibition in London.[43] Not only might we assume that Schendel must have read Eco's published work prior to visiting him, but that she would have gained an awareness of his ideas as they had been circulating among intellectuals in Brazil. In Eco's discussion of visual art in relation to the *open work*, he places 'informal' art (*art informel*) 'in the broader sense' next to the formal experiments of moving works not because informal painting is a work in movement but because 'it is an "open work" – in an even more mature and radical way' and this is because:

40 Whitelegg 2005, p.203–4.

41 Mira Schendel Statement, undated and unsigned, reproduced in this publication, p.197.

42 Vilem Flusser, 'Diacronia e diafaneidade', *Estado de São Paulo*, 3 May 1969, quoted in Whitelegg 2005, p.207.

43 The meeting with Eco was not a success; Schendel left disappointed. Souza Dias 2009, p.218–19. Yet this in itself does not necessarily mean that Eco's ideas and writings were not useful to and employed by Schendel.

> its signs combine like constellations whose structural relationships are not determined univocally, from the start, and in which the ambiguity of the sign does not ... lead back to reconfirming the distinction between form and background. Here ... the subject of the painting is a background in continual metamorphosis. Here the viewer can (indeed, must) choose his own points of view, his own connections, his own directions, and can detect, behind each individual configuration, other possible forms that coexist while excluding one another in an ongoing relationship of mutual exclusion and implication.[44]

As Brett points out in his discussion of *informel* art in the catalogue for *Force Fields: Phases of the Kinetic*, Eco's notion of a 'field' is drawn from science, specifically from physics or field theory. Brett comments that 'translated to the artistic work it becomes "form as a field of possibilities" and provides the characteristics of the "open work"'.[45] Even though formal transparency had done away with a 'background' per se, such descriptions of the work as a 'constellation of signs' or a 'field of possibilities' might be applied to Schendel's works, particularly to the *informel* field of her *Objetos graficos* which were made in the year of her visit to Eco in Milan.

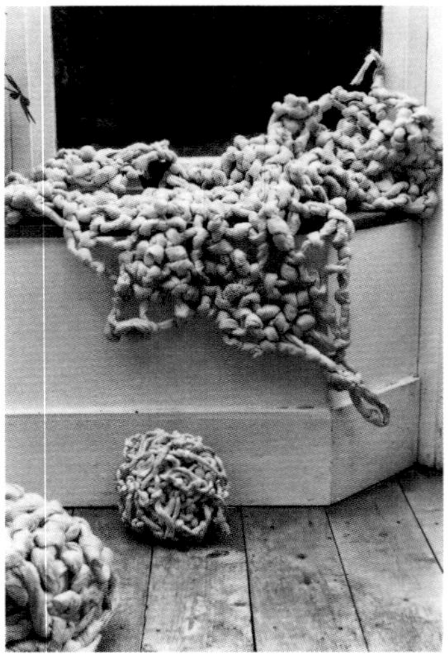

Figure 7
Guy Brett, *Little Nothings*, undated
Courtesy Guy Brett, London

In 1971, Schendel embarked on a major new series of works, the *Cadernos*.[46] Within the year she had made the vast majority of the two hundred or more books, in a characteristically prolific and concentrated period of production. These books were not sketchbooks, nor were they what we might now term artists' books, but they were a deployment of the form of the book as a work in movement. In these works, Schendel abandoned the use of acrylic in favour of making objects that could be handled more intimately.[47] The *Cadernos* vary dramatically both in size, length, format, the combination of paper and media and the subject or motifs employed. Thus in themselves they constitute a highly varied and complex sub-group within Schendel's overall oeuvre.[48] Unlike the *Monotipias* and the *Objetos graficos* , the sense of a chaotic palimpsest in the *Cadernos* is diminished. They do away with writing and include neither words nor phrases. Instead, the works are more ordered and contained, whilst language is reduced to its constituent parts – the apparent randomness of the sign expressing degrees of linguistic transparency or opacity and also informational entropy. However, in these and other works of the late 1960s and 1970s – including the *Objetos graficos*, the collages named *Toquinhos* (*Little Stubs*) and the *Datiloscritos* – these letters, numbers and symbols may not be as random as they at first appear, but might relate to the use in logic of propositional and predicate calculus to establish the truth of a statement, as in Wittgenstein's *Tractatus*, as well as to binary logic that uses only '0' and '1'. Similar, however, to the lack of any front or back in the *Monotipias* and the *Objetos graficos*, the *Cadernos* are given no narrative direction – they can be read backwards

44 Umberto Eco, 'The Open Work in the Visual Arts', in Eco 1989, p.86.

45 Guy Brett, 'The Century of Kinesthesia', in *Force Fields: Phases of the Kinetic* 2000, p.22.

46 These vary between shop-bought sketchbooks and others that were hardmade books, constructed from card, tracing paper and metal rivets, assembled and bound by the artist herself.

47 A number of books were encased in acrylic posthumously. Yet this, whilst serving to preserve the delicate books and seeming to facilitate handling, actually transforms the *Caderno* into a heavy and unwieldy object. Moreover, the addition of hinges of different types has substantially altered the kinds of subtle movement from one page to the next that Schendel carefully set in place.

48 Because of the difficulty of display and facilitating interaction they have been less often exposed and for that reason, perhaps, less frequently written about.

or forwards. If a liberation from temporal progression is integral to the importance of Gebser's transparency then this omnidirectional character of the *Cadernos* is also of fundamental significance as it challenges the traditional, diachronic structure of the book. Contrasting the time and space thematic of the *Objetos gráficos*, the *Cadernos* were specifically about temporality, countering, through transparency, the fact that the structure of books traditionally follows writing which as a 'linear organisation of signs, is what makes historical consciousness possible in the first place.'[49] Souza Dias has described Schendel's *Cadernos* as 'chains of thoughts' and identifies these books as a continuation of Schendel's investigation of transparency.[50] He argues that in these works Schendel's 'form of expression is between the traditional art object and the conceptual: they embody the unfolding of an idea in which the object, in its subtle physical aspect is present only as a point of reference for the transmission of philosophical formulations.'[51] Souza Dias also comments how the books encapsulate a gentle sense of humour and 'give rise to ludic speculations. They suggest rules according to which a visual and logical game can develop.'[52] This is further reinforced by the fact he relates that Schendel used to throw dice or coins as part of the method of making these works to determine the compositions she made on each page – referring no doubt to her use of the *I Ching* which reveals that they are manifestations of constant mutability or entropy.[53] He stresses, therefore, the balance between logic and chance in these works as well as their status as 'polisensorial' objects of inter-subjective communication and interaction between the artist and the reader.

Paulo Venancio Filho has identified an earlier moment for the inception of a radical rethinking of the book as a distinct form in Brazilian art stating that 'the role of books has probably never been reassessed and transformed in such an in depth fashion ... as in Brazil during 1959.'[54] Similarly Brett has surveyed this area of Brazilian art in his exhibition *The Enclosed Openness: Box and Book in Brazilian Art*, focusing on a history from the 1950s onwards that also encompasses Schendel's work.[55] Venancio Filho gives an overview of the magnitude of what was at stake in these new versions of the book. In his account, artists were 'attempting to renovate or recreate the very concept of the book – not just as an object, but also in terms of its writing, structure, content, and relationship with the reader' which therefore became almost unrecognisable as 'covers, title pages, and text all vanished or took different forms. Pages became three-dimensional structures. Text was slashed to a single word or none at all. There were no longer any beginnings or endings'.[56] The result was that the book became an open proposition 'altogether a different entity: alive, dynamic, ready to be discovered and reinvented, or re-experienced from scratch, far removed from traditional reading habits. A book was no longer a finished product, but was whatever was being put together or constructed in the "reading process",' thus '"reading" now meant a whole series of experiences triggered by handling this new entity. The undisputed predominance of

49 Vilem Flusser, *Die Schrift* (Writing), quoted in Ströhl 2002, p.xxix.

50 Souza Dias 2009, p.275 (all translations are my own).

51 Ibid., p.275.

52 Ibid., p.275.

53 Ibid., p.276. Ada Schendel confirms Mira's habitual use of the *I Ching* (the ancient Chinese Book of Changes) in both work and life. Conversations with Ada Schendel, May 2012.

54 Paulo Venancio Filho, 'The Recreation of the Book', in *Lygia Pape: Magnetized Space*, exh. cat., Museo Nacional Centro de Arte Reina Sofia, Madrid 2011, p.217.

55 Guy Brett, *The Enclosed Openness: Box and Book in Brazilian Art (Aberto Fechado: Caixa e Livro Na Arte Brasiliero)*, exh. cat., Pinacoteca do Estado, São Paulo, 2012.

56 Ibid., p.217.

visuality had lost its hegemony. The act of turning a page no longer evinced its mechanical aspect, or even ceased to exist.'[57] What was offered instead was 'a new open-ended reading as a multi-directional, playful, and dynamic experience ... One could no longer be passively absorbed in a book; involvement in it required that one went beyond the traditional habit of reading and bridged the steady, routine distance between subject and object.'[58] These new approaches and ideas encapsulate those first expressed by Eco to describe the poetics of the open work in his essay *L'opera in movimento e la coscienza dell'epoca* (translated as *The Poetics of the Open Work*) which was published in the critical year – 1959. Schendel's *Cadernos* can be considered as occupying a special place in this genre within Brazilian art.

Schendel's *Cadernos* were exhibited in 1971 at the Museu de Arte Contemporânea da Universidade de São Paulo, from 21 October to 7 November.[59] Aracy Amaral wrote a short text on them published in the newspaper *O Estado de S. Paulo* on 7 November 1971 in which she also described the works in terms that recall Eco's conception of the open work, saying that 'what Mira Schendel is realizing at the moment, through her "notebooks", transcends the simple artistic finished object, corresponding instead to an open visual speculation, logical and intuitive at the same time.'[60] Amaral also describes the works in relation to a 'game' in the sense of Wittgenstein's language-games as a way of building structures for communication. Moreover, the *Cadernos*, according to Amaral, revealed the 'constant presence' of mathematics and geometry in her work'.[61] More recently, Guy Brett has characterised Schendel's *Cadernos* as 'velocity books', emphasising their simultaneous deployment of time and movement in which 'the notion of velocity is reinvented in book form' and this is 'based on a fresh understanding of the simple act of turning pages'.[62] There is also in the turning page something that recaptures the 'diaphanous' character of the *Trenzinhos*. Moreover, Brett continues, 'For Mira, the use of transparent or translucent paper allowed her to create an experience of movement within the body of the book, of uncertain depth.'[63] Her use of transparency in conjunction with recession and layering that had first been seen in the *Objetos graficos* becomes more substantial in the books, where 'there is a strong sense of lines and sometimes letters arising from and sinking back into empty space as you leaf through, or flick through the pages'.[64] Thus, Brett suggests that in Mira's books energy is constantly in flux, so that her *Cadernos* are as much about contained or embodied energy as her *Droguinhas*, since 'movement in Mira's books is orbital, constantly returning to itself'.[65]

The *Cadernos* contain a variety of motifs that embody Schendel's interrelated lines of enquiry. Some relate to spirals of Archimedes that Schendel also explored in several acrylic discs called *I Ching* in 1972. Other *Cadernos* take their motifs from methods of applied mathematics and philosophy; in several, Schendel adopted the tree-like structure of nodes or vertexes suggesting points of choice used in game theory. Others are

57 Ibid., p.217.

58 Ibid., p.217–18.

59 At the time, MAC-USP was under the directorship of Walter Zanini, a key figure in the development of the Brazilian contemporary art scene, especially pioneering in his concern with conceptual art and video art. The exhibition was a presentation of three artists, Amelia Toledo, Donato Ferrari and Schendel. In the exhibition brochure, Schendel declined to make any other statement but two sentences 'Each of the notebooks displayed has as a title an element (or one of the elements) of itself. For me there isn't anything to say beyond what is said (or not said) in the works shown.'

60 Aracy Amaral, 'Mira Schendel: Os Cadernos', *O Estado de S. Paulo*, 7 November 1971. (My translation)

61 Ibid.

62 Guy Brett, 'Rough Guide to the Terrain', in *The Enclosed Openness: Box and Book in Brazilian Art*, 2012, p.44.

63 Ibid.

64 Ibid.

65 Ibid.

comprised of pages with constellations of circles or of numerous holes punched into the pages affording another formal manifestation of transparency. One of the longer of her *Cadernos* [p. 150] reveals pages of varying abstract Suprematist-like spatial motifs. In another [p. 156], the composition that develops through the book, its gradual transformation seen through the semi-transparent pages, employs large scale transfer letters. By using letters, apparently randomly, and by rotating them and thus detaching them from their usual form and syntax Schendel performed a number of potentially unending language-games. Thus Schendel's *Cadernos* can be seen as ludic-linguistic open works, designed to be completed both semantically and physically by the viewer/reader.

In 1973, Schendel collaborated with Robert Darroll, then a student at the School of Fine Art in Hamburg, to produce a film from two of her *Cadernos* which was presented at a symposium on aesthetics at the University of Stuttgart.[66] Whilst this film cannot be seen as a work of art in its own right, it does reveal much about the way in which Schendel wished the works to be activated, for them to be seen temporally and in movement.[67] However, since it is the only such experiment that exists, it seems that her access to such technology was not easy and perhaps did not satisfy her as she appears to have taken it no further. From the mid-1970s onwards a concern with communication, information and movement diminishes or took new forms in Schendel's work. Nevertheless, the notion of the work of art in movement, left open to the viewer or to chance – to the constant change of the *I Ching* – and the idea of art as a 'field of possibilities' proposed by Umberto Eco in relation to his theory of the open work; the relation between language, human actions and a defined set of rules in Wittgestein's language-games; and the interrelationship between art, science, cosmology and the language of movement advanced by Signals and by Guy Brett in *Kinetic Art*, *Force Fields* and *The Enclosed Openness*, are encapsulated no more clearly than in Schendel's *Droguinhas* and her *Cadernos*. These works reveal Schendel's exploration of decision making and the production of language, where meaning is established through dialogue and with reference to the conditions, responsibilities and freedoms afforded to the viewer by the artist within 'a given field of relations.' As Flusser would propose, 'to see the world as a set of games, and to see it as a player who knows he is playing, is to see aesthetically...and it is not enough to see, the world must be experienced.'[68]

66 Souza Dias 2009, p.245.

67 In an undated and unsigned typed statement found in Schendel's papers, the artist said 'I am still not satisfied. I do not believe acrylic is the wisdom stone, and for this reason I have begun to experiment with film.' Reproduced in this publication, p.197.

68 Vilem Flusser, in Ströhl, 2002, p.205.

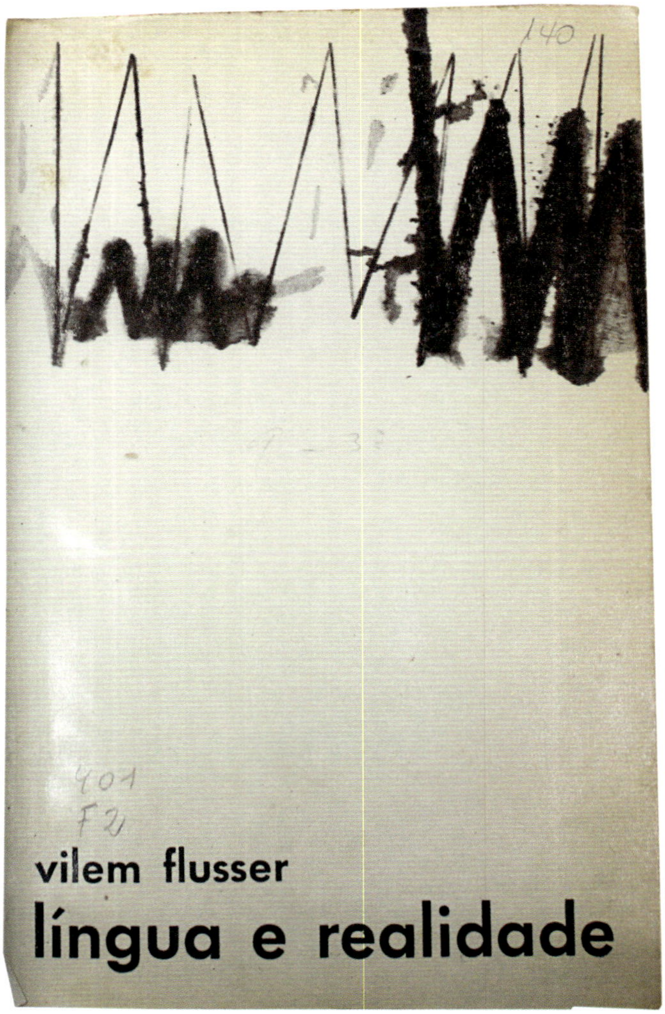

Vilem Flusser, *Língua e realidade*
(Language and Reality)
(São Paulo: Editora Herder, 1963)
Book cover designed by Mira Schendel

MIRA SCHENDEL IN DIALOGUE WITH VILEM FLUSSER: LANGUAGE AND REALITY*

Cauê Alves

The cover of *Língua e realidade* (Language and Reality),[1] by Vilem Flusser,[2] was designed by Mira Schendel. Far beyond simply illustrating the author's thought or turning out just another graphic design project, Schendel's work seemed on occasion to embody the theses Flusser defended in that book. The artist was the philosopher's friend and interlocutor, and a regular at the discussion groups he organised at his home at weekends in the early 1960s to debate major themes in the history of thought.

In his philosophical autobiography *Bodenlos* (Rootless),[3] published posthumously in 1992, Flusser recalled some of the many dialogues he maintained with Brazilian writers such as João Guimarães Rosa[4] and Haroldo de Campos,[5] as well as artists such as Samson Flexor,[6] and intellectuals, including Miguel Reale.[7] Important though these relationships were, it is Schendel to whom he devotes an entire chapter, in which he discusses her work, the most striking characteristics of her individuality and the influence they had on one another.

Calling her by her first name, which was how she signed her works, Flusser compares their friendship, which began during those philosophical get-togethers, to a roller-coaster or fever curve, such was its volatility. Despite their sometimes contrasting opinions, the sparks that inevitably came of the clash of two strong personalities, and their loss of contact after Flusser's return to Europe in around 1974, when the chapter was written, the dialogue they maintained on the notions of transparency and meaning in the early 1960s sheds much light on the philosophical dimension of Schendel's work.

The core thesis of *Língua e realidade* is that language is cosmos, the order by which the world is organised, and it is a notion that guides the author's pursuit to reveal its structure. Flusser's premise is that there is coincidence between the structures of the cosmos and of language. Heavily influenced by the German philosopher Martin Heidegger (1889–1976), for Flusser language *is* reality and, at the same time, *creates* reality; it is, basically, the raw material of thought. In other words, the world before language was chaos, as it is language which organises sensations into reality.

* Translated by Anthony Doyle.

1 Vilem Flusser, *Língua e realidade* (São Paulo: Editora Herder, 1963).

2 Vilem Flusser (1920–91) was an important Czech-born intellectual who moved to Brazil during the 1940s to escape from Nazi persecution – his entire family died in German concentration camps. During the thirty years he spent in Brazil, he studied and wrote widely on philosophy, language and communication.

3 Vilem Flusser, *Bodenlos: Uma autobiografia filosófica* (São Paulo: Annablume, 2007).

4 João Guimarães Rosa (1908–67), doctor, diplomat and widely considered to be one of Brazil's greatest authors. His work stands out for its innovative language, a mix of the erudite and oral, especially regionalisms from the Brazilian hinterlands. His best-known works are *The Devil to Pay in the Backlands* (1956) and *First Stories* (1962).

5 Haroldo de Campos (1929–2003) was a poet, translator and essayist. He was cofounder of the Brazilian concrete movement in poetry, alongside his brother Augusto de Campos and Décio Pignatari. He is best known for the poetry book *Galáxias* (Galaxies), 1984, and his Portuguese translations of works by Ezra Pound and James Joyce.

6 Samson Flexor (1907–71) was a Romanian painter who moved to Brazil in 1948, when already the author of a mature oeuvre. During the 1950s he founded Ateliê Abstração (Studio Abstraction), one of the most important spaces in the development of Brazilian abstract art. His painting went from constructive geometric abstraction to lyrical abstraction in the late 1950s, replete with organic forms. His art took a figurative turn in the late 1960s.

7 Miguel Reale (1910–2006) was a thinker who founded the Brazilian Philosophy Institute. Overtly right-wing, he welcomed Flusser on his arrival in Brazil. He was Justice Secretary for the State of São Paulo in 1963 and Chancellor of the University of São Paulo from 1969 to 1973, during the military dictatorship.

The internal rules of languages are understood as the very structure of reality. There are, therefore, as many worlds as there are languages, which are not cut off from one other, but have many roots in common. As such, translation assumes the utmost importance, as to translate is actually to move from one world to another.

The method Flusser employs in his attempt to grasp the structure of reality is to try to get as close as possible to 'naiveté in the face of language', an innocence lost over the course of the history of philosophy. On this point Flusser and Schendel would seem to have thought along very similar lines. The artist's inscriptions on paper were a way of organising her experience of the world's chaos. In her *Monotipias* (*Monotypes*), a collection of some two thousand drawings on rice paper, the sheet itself is not a space of representation, but rather an element of the world, which she activates as space by introducing modifying lines and signs.

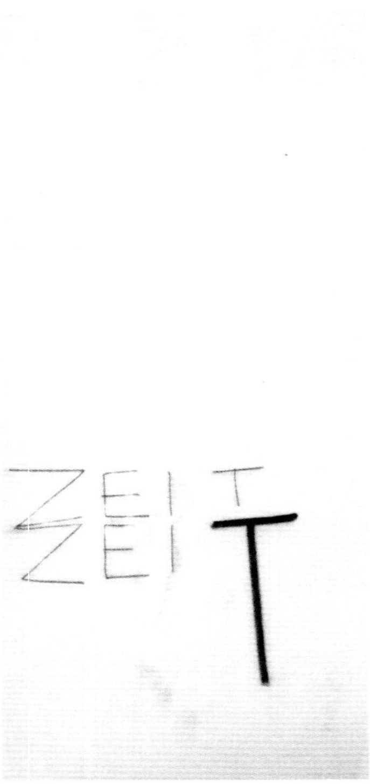

Figure 1
Untitled (Time), from the series *Monotypes*
Sem título (Zeit), da série *Monotipias*
1964–5
Oil on rice paper
47 x 23 cm
Private collection

In the monotype in which she writes the word *ZEIT* [8] ('time' in German) [Fig.1] twice in quick succession, the second *T* is thicker set and more incisive, standing out among the other graphic signs on the white page. The two *Z*s, one immediately below the other, almost meld into a single zigzag structure, while the duplicity of the *I*s suggests a dotted line, a mode of organisation in which the elements are distributed at intervals.

In a similar way, in the *Datiloscritos* (*Typed Writings*) series [p.166], begun in circa 1974, the writing serves to structure the space. The letters form homogeneous blocks, isolated units that thoroughly arrange the composition. The repetition, proximity, distance, variation – in short, the full array of relations between the blocks and the blank spaces – is what orders the universe these works create.

Another common feature of the *Monotipias* is the fluid intermingling of different languages: German, French, English, Italian, Croatian and Portuguese. There is no rivalry among them, no hierarchy, precisely because each has its own way of being and its own rules for articulating reality. Everything occurs here in an ambiguous territory in which languages can encompass each other or keep their distance.

The notion of transparency is tied in with the capacity of the gaze to bore through surfaces, burrowing abysses beyond the outer appearances of things. The eye's ability to cut through the world's crust can reveal either the fundaments that underpin things or the void that lies behind them. Flusser saw the world as becoming increas-

8 In her use of the German, Mira Schendel was probably thinking about Martin Heidegger's 1927 masterwork *Sein und Zeit* (Being and Time), which she had in her library.

ingly transparent, and with that came a corresponding and gradual loss of concreteness. If meaning is what symbols signify, and if symbols represent meanings that, ultimately, refer to the world of concrete things, then this dissolution of the world reduces everything to symbols, with each new symbol adding another meaning to the world. For Flusser, 'In the last analysis, "transparency" is the possibility of seeing the meaning behind everything. And "meaning" is the possibility of transforming everything into transparent things'.[9]

Flusser had this to say about Schendel's works on sheets of rice paper sandwiched between sheets of acrylic, known as *Objetos gráficos* (*Graphic Objects*) [pp.125–41]:

> It is as experiments that Mira's works have long concerned me. They are attempts to make concepts imaginable. Mira tries to translate the concepts of transparency and meaning into the image of transparency and the image of meaning. She strives to invert the traditional relationship between imagination and discursive reason, a relationship that can be described as follows: (a) I find something concrete in the course of my life and try to imagine it in order to move beyond it; and (b) I try to conceptualise the image I have so as to understand and succeed in manipulating the concrete. Historically, phase (a) corresponds to the mythico-magical stage of culture and phase (b) to the epistemologico-technical stage. Mira's art belongs to a phase beyond either. Her approach is the following: (a) she finds a concept in the course of her life and tries to imagine it in order to understand it; and (b) she tries to transform the image into something concrete. As such, Mira's work fulfils a violently de-alienating function. One of the aspects of our alienation is the unimaginability of our concepts, but it is an alienation that can be overcome through the new imaginative force Mira gives us.[10]

Yet language, as Schendel develops it over the course of her career, is not transparent. On the contrary, the letter and sign become opaque, intensely physical volumes. Language as it is used in her more graphic works is far removed from any denotation or explanation, but is actually an attempt to penetrate meanings, to bore into an originary world that predates language itself, a world of nascent meaning, a whorl of meanings. Hence the presence of words, of free-floating, enigmatic letters that derive their meaning from their form, from their graphic appearance and physical presence in three-dimensional space.

However, the transparency of the rice paper and acrylic sheets reveals the body in its parts, which it inserts in three-dimensional space at the same time as they allow

9 Flusser 2007, p.187. (my translation).

10 Ibid., p.190.

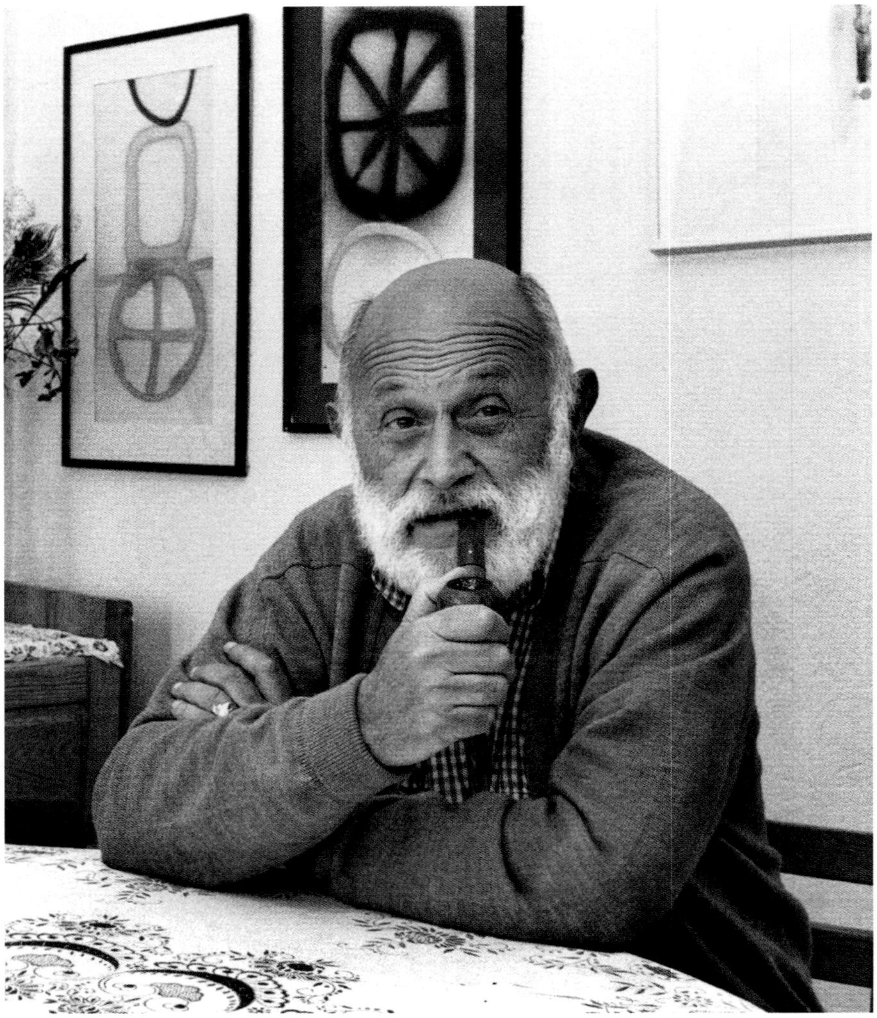

Vilem Flusser, France, 1980s

for simultaneity between inside and out. Given her dialogue with phenomenology, her work is impregnated with the notion of the body as an ambiguous field in which objective and subjective coexist. It is precisely this corporeality that will fuel the artist's drive to overcome the classical dualism.

In her *Droguinhas* (*Little Nothings*) [p.119], made of knotted braids of rice paper, the corporeal nature of the work becomes more evident. On the other hand, in the *Trenzinhos* (*Little Trains*) [p.122], sheets of paper hung from a single piece of thread evoke a frank relationship with phenomenological space that precludes any representation of it. The gesture, as movement and expression, presupposes bodily experience. Thus we can say that Mira's work emerges from the originary and primordial expression of the body. It is the corporeal gesture begotten by calligraphy and writing.

Therefore, language, such as developed by the artist during her career, is not transparent; on the contrary, signs gradually become bodies, opaque in meaning, with an accentuated physical presence. The language used in her more graphic work distances itself from denotation or explanation. Hence the presence of words and loose, enigmatic letters, that derive their meaning from form, from physical presence in three-dimensional space, from their graphic appearance.

The *Toquinhos* (*Little Stubs*) [p.144], with letters encased in acrylic stubs, are at once transparent and dense. In the *Discos* (*Discs*) [p.140], for example, there is still a discernible inside and outside, but an inside seen from the outside and an outside seen from within. The body of the object, predominantly transparent, is a mysterious, unreachable and ambiguous body that lies beyond the dichotomies of subject/object, interiority/exteriority.

There is also a clearly corporeal dimension to many of her paintings. Rather than being transparent, like the acrylic and paper works, these are thick and dense, and forsake all geometrical rigidity. In many of these, she applies thick paints, bruisingly present, and sometimes mixed with brick dust or other organic material. Her final complete series, *Sarrafos* (*Battens*) [p.192], consists of large panels of wood whitewashed with tempera and gesso onto which are attached slats of wood five centimetres thick. The result is a three-dimensional, solid object, like a black bolt of lightning, contrasting starkly against the background and destabilising the whole work.

Still on the issue of corporeality, there is also the aspect of viewer contact with the work. Mira abandoned the repertoire of modern painting in the early 1960s, or at least the idea of planarity and frontality, and embraced the notion of corporeality. However, it is important to note that her three-dimensional works do not aspire to any transformation of the human condition: they seem to reveal, in their fragility, the very impossibility of universality. They depend more on the simple, contingent gesture, and a bodily predisposition than on any univocal or utopian meaning.

As such, Mira's work resists the idea of viewer participation so much in vogue in the 1960s, which extolled the handling of the artwork, the playful aspect, and the viewer's direct action upon what the artist proposes as the liberator and trigger par excellence of creative participation. On this, the artist is ironic: 'Then came the *Toquinhos*, *Discos* and those acrylic strips [*Transformáveis* (*Transformables*)] [p.146–7], which everyone thought were DIY stuff, playthings, to be picked up, messed with and wrecked in unison'.[11] In other words, Schendel's concept of corporeality dispenses with viewer participation as a mode of political transformation. The transformation of the Other lies less in rupture with contemplation than in the individual field of experience. This does not mean that it relies upon the viewer's passivity or immobility before the work, much less the reduction of the work to merely formal problems, but rather that it reinforces the openness proper to art, that which is not foreseen in the work, but can be provided by it.

For Flusser, unlike Mira, the notion of the body does not seem to be fundamental in eliminating the above-mentioned classical dichotomies. He continued with his studies of the machine, which he understood to be the model for and condition of all technical objects and the very paradigm of rationality, and, as a result, saw that writing could be put in check by the invention of programs formulated by mathematical language.

A possible crisis of writing – and, therefore, of language – is analysed in the 1989 book *Does Writing Have a Future?*,[12] which asks whether computers might be rendering writing obsolete. Flusser's research during the 1980s led to an examination of photography and the publication of *Towards a Philosophy of Photography* in 1983,[13] followed a year later by *Into the Universe of Technical Images*,[14] which, rather than discussing photography as such, broached the proliferation of blotchy, grainy and pixelated technical images, taking him into areas with little or no connection to the issues at the heart of Mira's work.

Having never intended to assume the perspective of any one philosopher, Mira pursued her own line of research, plumbing what was effectively a metaphysics of immanence, and strove to overcome the dualisms of essence versus appearance, and subjective versus objective by taking a direction that was wholly distinct from Flusser's. Instead of delving headlong into technology, she stressed the notion of corporeality, the inseparability of interior and exterior, front and reverse.

There is little doubt that Flusser and Mira Schendel maintained a rich and fruitful dialogue throughout the early 1960s, especially on the notion of transparency and language, and this was extremely beneficial to both of them. For the artist and philosopher, it was a period of intellectual proximity and converging ideas. The discussion groups on philosophical themes that Flusser organised at weekends were important to the development of the thought behind Schendel's work and they provided the two ex-patriots with a space of dialogue in São Paulo. However, their lives and work drifted so far apart that their relationship, as

11 In an interview with the Brazilian Art Research and Documentation Department, FAAP, in 1977.

12 The book was written between 1987 and 1989, but was only published in Portuguese in 2010.

13 The German edition, *Für einen Philosophie*. The English version, *Towards a Philosophy of Photography*, was published in 1984, followed by a Portuguese edition a year later.

14 The German edition, *Ins Universum der technischen Bilder*. The Portuguese version came out in 2008 and the English translation, *Into the Universe of Technical Images*, in 2011.

Flusser would recognise in his autobiography, written after his return to Europe in 1972, came to demand of him a degree of patience that he did not normally possess. Despite their friendship and shared investigations into the possibility of overcoming philosophical problems, in the 1980s their chosen lines of response went their separate ways.

Cauê Alves holds a Master's degree and Ph.D. from the University of São Paulo (USP-FFLCH) and is a professor at the School of Philosophy, Communication, Arts and Letters of the Pontifical Catholic University of São Paulo (PUC-SP). Since 2006, he is the curator of the Print Collectors' Club of the Museum of Modern Art of São Paulo. He was one of the curators of MAM-SP's 32nd Panorama of Brazilian Art and adjunct curator of the 8th Mercosul Biennial. He is the author of *Mira Schendel: Reverse of the Reverse* (Beï Editions IAC) and curated the homonymous exhibition held in 2010. He is currently part of the *GREEN LAB: Artistic Experiments in the Amazon* project team.

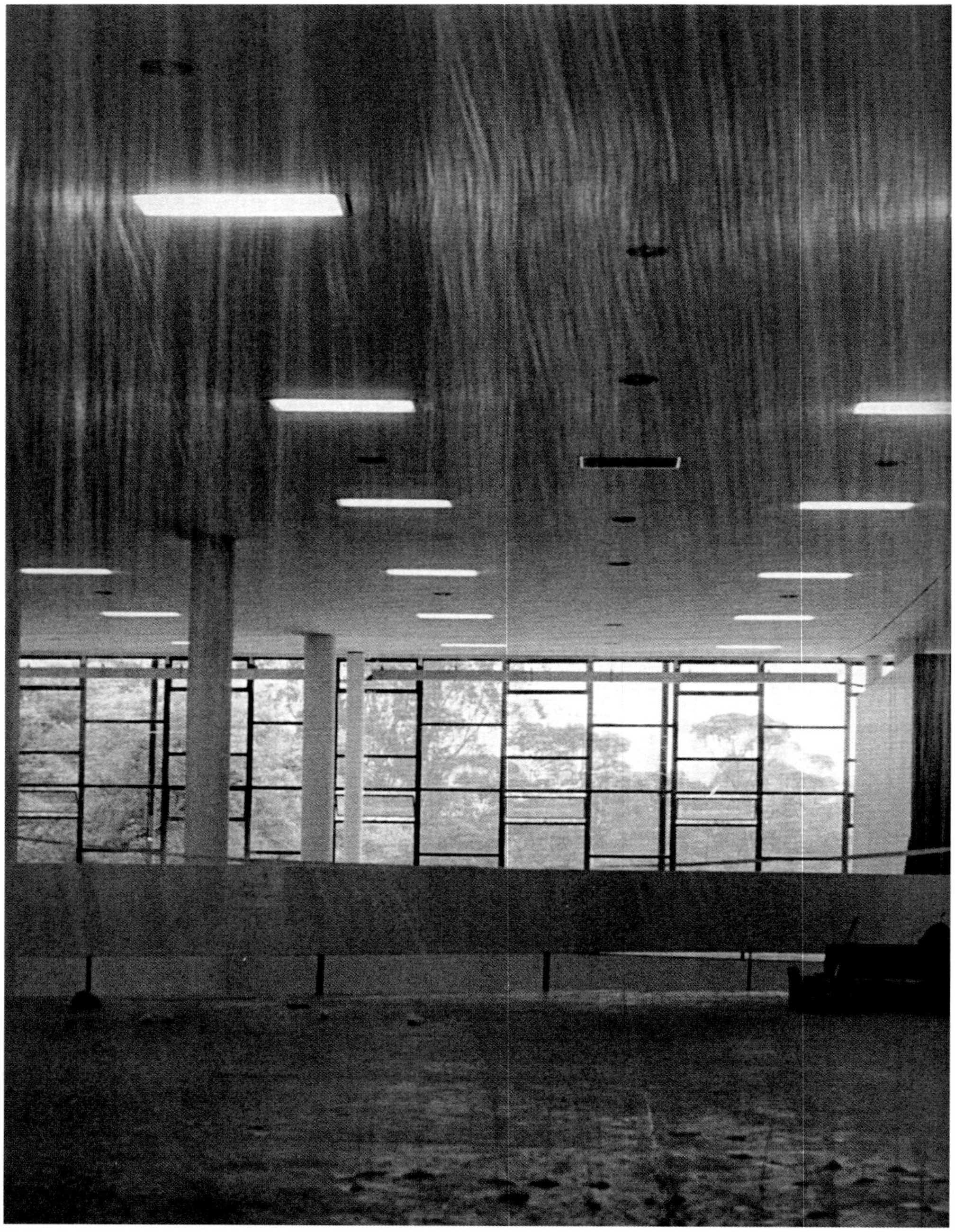

Still Waves of Probability
Ondas paradas de probabilidade
1969/1994
Nylon thread with text on acrylic
Dimensions variable
mira schendel estate
[Installation view of 22nd
Bienal de São Paulo, 1994]

THE OTHER WORLD IS THIS: MIRA SCHENDEL'S PARTICIPATION IN THE 10TH BIENAL DE SÃO PAULO, 1969

Isobel Whitelegg

> When I say that Mira was mystical what I mean is that she was a person rooted in the real looking for a justification for this real. For me the mystic is one who departs from the material in order to reach beyond it. Someone who does not accept the material is not mystical but alienated. Mira fought with the material ... She was an interrogative volcano.[1]

The question of where to locate Mira Schendel's work in relation to the reality of Brazil was frequently raised by Brazilian journalists and critics who interviewed the artist and reviewed her exhibitions during the period from the late 1970s until her death in 1988.[2] Any explicit comment from the artist on how her work related to its time (understood, that is, as its social and political context) was exceptional.[3] Such reticence perhaps contributed to her frequent characterisation as an artist who was cerebral, isolated, and 'mystical'. In a 1987 interview she defended her position in the following terms:

> It is not an escape. It is a way of saying other softer things – or saying nothing ... I have never made a work that exists outside of my time. It is always the result of the circumstances in which I live. If my works are rigorous, or if they are decorative, they are an occurrence related to a moment in my time. I might be out of fashion but I am current.[4]

The question of Schendel's relationship to reality is one that recurs now and perhaps understandably so. Schendel remained in Brazil, living, working and exhibiting in the public realm throughout the 1960s, 1970s and 1980s, a period during which the country experienced a series of devastating political and economic shifts. If she insisted that it was impossible for her work to exist outside of her time, then surely it cannot have been unaffected by this context. Therefore it is not surprising that critics or historians of art ask her work to tell us something of a past that cannot be fully comprehended in the present. The political history of Brazil, and the history of its years of military dictatorship in particular, is now a conventional device for interpreting the history of Brazilian art. But, like concretism and neo-concretism, this is a categorisation that her work refuses. Unlike that of peers who now share a similar degree of international recognition, the question of what her work can tell us of its

1 Paulo Celso de Moura Silva (São Paulo, 12 April 1997), quoted in Geraldo Souza Dias, *Mira Schendel: Do Espiritual à Corporeidade* (São Paulo: Cosac Naify, 2009), pp. 126–7.

2 Slow and successive processes of gradual democratisation within Brazil (1974–9; 1979–85; 1985–8) enabled political concerns to be addressed more explicitly within the artistic and critical milieu; Schendel was increasingly asked for an opinion on the sociopolitical role or relevance of her practice toward the end of her life.

3 The exception is her final complete series, *Sarrafos* (*Battens*), upon which she made the following comments in two separate interviews: 'If they seem more rigid, more firm, and maybe even a little aggressive, this must have something to do with the context in which they were created. I found myself in a situation of extreme disanimation in relation to the situation of the country. And for this reason my response resulted in a work that was directed.' Mira Schendel, quoted in Antonio Gonçalves Filho, 'O rigor solitário de Mira Schendel', *Folha de S.Paulo*, 5 August 1987; also Mira Schendel, interview with César Giobbi, cf. Chronology [p.238]. Schendel is here making reference to Brazil's economic crises of the late 1980s, and the implementation of 'shock' plans for fiscal reform; following the failure of the 1986 Cruzado Plan, inflation had reappeared in Brazil in December 1986 and crept upwards month by month reaching a peak in June 1987; in the same period, real wage values were not protected, and their steady decline caused widespread protest among workers.

4 Mira Schendel quoted in Doca Batista, 'As várias faces de uma artista', *Gazeta de Vitória*, 19 September 1987.

time remains unanswered. My intention here is not to find a place for Schendel's work within a genre of art under dictatorship, but rather to consider the extent to which her work might cast doubt on what can be assumed to be the obligations of art under conditions of repression, and allow for a reconsideration of how art finds its place to act, and artists their ways of acting, within such circumstances.

Thus Schendel's work consistently invites but refuses a demand to be grounded in the political real of its time, and the reason for this refusal is contained within the nature of the work itself. It contains a path of thought that continually brings the nature of the real into question, and therefore interrogates the very grounds of such a demand. But how might a speculative attitude towards what it is that we name as real contain a distinct answer to how art (and art specifically) engages in the reality of social relationships or actions grounded by political or ethical concern? In order to address this question, I here examine one moment through which Schendel's work has already been drawn into an established story of Brazilian art understood in terms of political engagement, namely her decision to participate in the 10th Bienal de São Paulo.

This 1969 edition of the Bienal holds a particular place in history because it was the object of a boycott that successfully drew international attention to the operation of censorship and arbitrary prosecution within the Brazilian cultural sphere. The boycott was initially proposed in Brazil by Mario Pedrosa, as president of the Brazilian Association of Art Critics (ABCA),[5] and gained international momentum through the production and circulation of a dossier of evidence of cultural repression.[6] It was adhered to by artists worldwide[7] including several of those invited to represent Brazil who were at that time temporarily resident in Europe.[8] International solidarity was not however matched with consensus within Brazil; a group of artists (including Claudio Tozzi, whose work had been directly targeted by censorship[9]) accepted the invitation to participate, and Mário Schenberg remained committed to his role as curator of the section of invited Brazilian artists that included Schendel.[10] To locate Schendel's perspective on the boycott, amongst a pattern of doubt or disagreement within Brazil, I here underscore the fact that her acceptance was, in a precise definition of that term, a decision, and moreover an affirmative decision. It was less a refusal to adhere to a boycott than a considered 'yes'; it was the acceptance of an invitation, an act of assent, the implications of which reached beyond the circumstances of one event.

Schendel's work for the 10th Bienal was entitled *Ondas paradas da probabilidade* (*Still Waves of Probability*) [p.149] and consisted of numerous strands of nylon thread. Extending from the ceiling to the floor, the threads marked out a diffuse space. Schendel understood the work to present a 'visual silence', the 'visibility of the

5 Written under a pseudonym, Pedrosa's text entitled 'The Duties of the Art Critic in Society' was published in the *Correio da Manhã* newspaper, Rio de Janeiro. It made reference to the removal by the military police of works from the 2nd Bienal da Bahia in 1968 and the closure of a 1969 exhibition at the Museu de Arte Moderna do Rio de Janeiro. The works at the latter exhibition were those selected to represent Brazil at the forthcoming Biennale des Jeunes in Paris. The exhibition was shut down, works were confiscated, and the director of the museum, Muniz Sodré, was arrested and detained. Pedrosa's text repudiated the government's assumed right to impose limitations upon 'the creation of artworks or the free exercise of art criticism'. It impelled the members of the ABCA (Associação Brasileira de Críticos de Arte) to refuse to judge any exhibition supported by a government that was actively imposing censorship. The fact that the Rio exhibition was linked to Paris, together with the fact that the ABCA was a branch of the International Association of Art Critics, meant that the boycott held potential to become international in scope.

6 Jacques Lessaigne, president of the Biennale de Paris, signed a letter protesting the arrest and imprisonment of Muniz Sodré, director of the Museu de Arte Moderna do Rio de Janeiro. Lessaigne was to have been the commissar for the French delegation at the 1969 Bienal, a role subsequently vetoed by the Brazilian Ministry for the Exterior. This further act of censorship added momentum. A meeting took place in June 1969 at the Musée d'Art Moderne, Paris, and 321 artists and intellectuals signed a manifesto, *Non à La Biennale*. A document entitled 'Brazil 1969: Partial Dossier of the Cultural Repression' was circulated anonymously from artist to artist within Europe and beyond, its existence eventually being cited by an article in the *New York Times*.

7 The director of the Stedelijk Museum, as well as the artists chosen to represent the Netherlands, withdrew, as did the Swedish contingent. Pol Bury and Pierre Restany withdrew a thematic cross-national exhibition for the Bienal's new Art & Technology section. The Center for Advanced Studies at MIT (Massachusetts Institute of Technology) had been chosen to represent North America, and the proposed show, organised by Georgy Kepes, was also cancelled after several of the artists withdrew. The Mexican muralist David Alfaro Siqueiros had been awarded a dedicated exhibition within the Bienal, which he refused, and two Japanese artists requested that their works, already en route to the Bienal, should be removed. The Netherlands, Sweden, Chile, Venezuela, the USSR and Mexico were among the countries to withdraw national participation entirely, with both the Netherlands and Sweden remaining absent until 1979. Other nations maintained a nominal presence. A pro-forma exhibition was swiftly prepared and dispatched to represent France, in place of the dissenting artists, and the United States was represented by only one artwork – by the sculptor Chryssa Vardea.

8 Including Sergio Camargo, Lygia Clark, Hélio Oiticica, Rubens Gerchman, Antonio Dias and Frans Krajcberg.

invisible' and an effort to show that 'the other world is this one'. Exhibited alongside the work, suspended from the ceiling on a plate of acrylic, was a text from the Old Testament Book of Kings. The text describes God's revelation to the Prophet Elijah:

> And he said go forth and stand upon the mount before the lord
> And behold the lord passed by – and a great and strong wind rent the mountains and broke into pieces the rocks before the lord
> but the lord was not in the wind
> and after the wind an earthquake – but the lord was not in the earthquake
> and after the earthquake a fire – but the lord was not in the fire
> and after the fire a still small voice

Ondas paradas da probabilidade remains a memorable part of Schendel's oeuvre; it has been recreated on several occasions posthumously. Each recreation has offered an opportunity to consider the significance of her choice of this biblical text, and its relation to the presence of this work within the context of a boycotted biennial. The still small voice of this work has, for example, been taken as a 'quietly mournful' metaphor for a 'sense of abandonment felt during the dictatorship', one that, at the same time, 'questioned the efficacy and force of artistic removal as a political strategy'.[11] Whilst it might be true that any work taking place in that context may be mobilised, now, as a means to explore the complex demands created by a call to boycott, the artist's attitude was neither as sentimental nor as plaintive as this speculative reading might suggest.

In a 1969 letter to the Norwegian gallerist Konrad Gromholt, Schendel had described the predominant concern of this work as 'the visibility of the invisible, of that which acts without us seeing it – such as, for example, the physical or spiritual'.[12] A more explicit indication that the boycott had informed and intensified her understanding of the work, however, is found in her correspondence with the German-born Swiss-resident philosopher, poet, and linguist Jean Gebser, a thinker who was influential to her work of the late 1960s and early 1970s. In a letter to Gebser, written after considering her invitation to participate in the biennial, she wrote:

> I was invited to participate in our tenth biennial. The rules have changed. Twenty-five Brazilians were invited guests this time. Another twenty-five will be admitted by jury. And what in Venice and its surroundings is already a thing of the past is new here The Netherlands, France and Switzerland apparently refused to participate. Some of the invited twenty-five Brazilian artists have also refused to participate. For reasons that (in the foreground!)

9 In 1968 Tozzi's painting *Guevara vivo ou morto* (Guevara Dead or Alive) was attacked and partially destroyed by a far-right group at the 4th Salão Nacional de Arte Contemporânea in Brasília; the source materials for the series he displayed at the 10th Bienal de São Paulo (*Multitudes*) meanwhile were photographs (both those taken by the artist and those he appropriated from press images) that depicted scenes from the political manifestations of 1968. One work for the 10th Bienal – entitled *A prisão* (*The Arrest*) – was temporarily removed (on the day of the official opening when representatives of the regime were present). See Caroline Saut Schroeder, 'X Bienal de São Paulo: sob os efeitos da contestação', unpublished MA thesis, São Paulo ECA USP 2011, available at <http://www.teses.usp.br/teses/disponiveis/27/27160/tde-26112011-133939/pt-br.php>, in Portuguese, last accessed June 2013. Schroeder's thesis offers a detailed study addressing both the artists who participated in the Bienal and the context – and contestation – of the boycott – both nationally and internationally.

10 For an examination of Schenberg's position in relation to the 10th Bienal, see Caroline Saut Schroeder (ibid.).

11 Claudia Calirman, *Brazilian Art under Dictatorship: Antonio Manuel, Artur Barrio, Cildo Meireles* (Durham, NC: Duke University Press, 2012), p.34.

12 Mira Schendel, letter to Konrad Gromholt, São Paulo, 25 August 1969; quoted in Souza Dias 2009, p.149.

> are valid. Perspectivally, I agree with them. Aperspectivally however, I have to accept the invitation. Aperspectivally it has a 'quantum value' that is also in the 'foreground'. Transparency.[13]

Schendel's letter to Gebser makes reference to the 1968 Venice Biennale, an edition in which she had participated, and one which is widely remembered now for being a site for widespread protest directed in part against bourgeois culture and that biennale's complicity in the commodification of art. Between the lines, there is an evident cynicism on her part towards cultural protest becoming a repetitively modish artistic tactic, and this might have informed her motivation not to follow the sway of a boycott. More indicative of her reasons for accepting the invitation to participate, however, is her deployment of terms relating to Gebser's philosophical work. The words 'perspectivally', 'aperspectivally', 'transparency' and 'foreground' gain particular meanings in the context of his best-known publication, *The Ever-Present Origin* (1949). As such, they are technically precise, and require some explanation in order to unpack their implications in the context of Schendel's letter.

The Ever-Present Origin describes the unfolding of different ways of experiencing and knowing reality over the long course of the history of human consciousness. Gebser's five 'structures of consciousness' are named the archaic, magical, mythical, mental and integral. In his understanding, each one of these structures has been dominant ('in the foreground') for different passages of time before falling into a 'deficient' state and being superseded by another. In his understanding, the five ways of conceiving reality were not discrete but perceptibly interconnected, with previous stages remaining operative within subsequent ones (as for example the potential for myth to infiltrate the ostensibly rational structure of Western modernity) and future structures being a 'latent' aspect of the present.

In sum, *The Ever-Present Origin* can be read as an optimistic critique of the limitations of what Gebser termed mental consciousness, a way of knowing the real associated with rational and logical thought and with an ego that locates itself in the mind, or the head. *The Ever-Present Origin* was provoked by events that he had witnessed in Europe his own lifetime, those that represented the worst conclusions of this mode of mental consciousness, including the rise of Nazism and the advent of civil war in Spain. The term 'perspectival' (as used in Mira's letter) refers to the negative aspect of the rational. For Gebser, the rational (and its Latin root *ratio*) was to be interpreted as a term that implies calculation, and division. That Schendel was able to agree with the artists that boycotted the biennial in 'perspectival' terms therefore might suggest that she understood their actions to be rational, but also

13 Mira Schendel, letter to Jean Gebser, São Paulo, 26 June 1969; quoted in Souza Dias 2009, p.149.

that she understood them to be divisive. That she understands their reasons to be valid 'in the foreground' also might indicate that she felt divisive forms of political action to be dominant within her immediate milieu. One could speculate therefore that in her view the strategy of boycott conformed to a divisive way of thinking that had proved itself ineffective in the experiences of her own lifetime.

The term that describes her act of accepting an invitation to participate points towards a different motivation: 'aperspectivally I have to accept the invitation', she states. The term 'aperspectival' in Gebser's thinking relates to a nascent structure of consciousness, named the integral. This was understood as a way of apprehending reality that was not dominant, but one that nonetheless existed. The idea of the 'aperspectival' may be grasped as a capacity to see one's own motives in the context of the motives of others, or to acknowledge other conceptions of time and history outside of the modernist logic of progress. The related concept of 'transparency' indicated an awareness of contingent relations between self and other, and a conception of time as an indivisible whole, rather than as discrete categories of past, present and future. Gebser's belief in the coming of an integral consciousness was not intended as an escape from a world evidently constrained by a divisive or rational view. It was rather as a means of insisting on the demonstrable presence of a different future within one's apprehension of present time – as was already intuited, for example, by contemporary art and by nondeterministic science. Importantly, for both Gebser and Schendel, achieving any shift in perception was not a given, but rather a process that demanded significant effort and a real conviction akin to a leap of faith, a 'primal trust' to use Gebser's term.

Here, Schendel's reading of Gebser relates to her concern with the philosophical and theological question of belief, a preoccupation that had marked her thinking since adolescence and one that relates, too, to her attraction to locating and acting upon 'gut instinct' in her mature artistic practice.[14] The question of how one knows what to do, and knows too that one is acting in good faith, when faced with decision, with the choice to say yes or to say no, finds particular resonance in the work of John Henry Newman, whose *Apologia Pro Vita Sua* (1864) was the source from which Schendel had extracted the English language phrases stencilled within her two paintings entitled *O Retorno de Aquiles* (*The Return of Achilles*) [pp.90–1]. Newman's widely revisited *An Essay in Aid of a Grammar of Assent* (1870) offers an argument for real assent (as opposed to 'notional' or abstract and rationally deduced assent) as an action based upon an intuition of multiple unproven probabilities, rather than the cool calculation of scientific proofs, or logical reason. The *Grammar* is a book referenced by one of Schendel's more consistent philosophical influences, Ludwig Wittgenstein (in his final notebooks, published posthumously as

14 In a public discussion at the Pinacoteca do Estado, São Paulo, 1976, Schendel commented: 'It is like bowling. If I do not go with my gut instinct, straight away, if instead I have an aim, make a point, I play very badly. But when I play from my belly, rather than aiming towards a point, I play a lot better. I think that in art it is more or less the same. It is also a question of gut instinct. But it is also in the head, in the mind, as I said to Lygia Clark once, in Rio, there are also guts there.' (Unpublished transcript; mira schendel estate archive.)

On Certainty, in 1969),[15] and is moreover one whose invocation of the unproven tangle of probabilities that ground 'real assent' resonates strikingly with the form of her work at the 10th Bienal: 'probabilities too fine to avail separately, too subtle and circuitous to be convertible into syllogisms, too numerous and various for such conversion'.[16] For Schendel the precision of the term probability as opposed to possibility is its significance as a measure of expectation and certainty, as not merely a blind faith divorced from the contingency and finitude of material life.[17]

Gebser understood his philosophy as a participatory form of realism, one for which verbal and visual poetics played an emancipatory role alongside new philosophical and scientific thought. For Gebser (as for another of Schendel's interlocutors, Vilem Flusser) the role and responsibility of art was to anchor what might otherwise be an abstract proposition within actual life, to make what was seemingly inconceivable conceivable by making it present.[18] In this way, the work that Schendel eventually presented within the biennale, alongside the fact that she decided to go ahead and create it, could be understood as an acceptance of this responsibility, or as a commitment to the process of making present an alternative means of conceiving of the reality of the present. In such terms, to say 'no' to this opportunity would be a refusal of a radical nature, tantamount to admitting that no alternative future could conceivably exist.

Mario Pedrosa's call for a boycott had been provoked by a betrayal of freedom or by the realisation that freedom had become impossible within his habitual sphere of action as art critic. Mira too saw the work that she placed within the biennale in terms of her own struggle to find and enact freedom. In her diary of the time she located freedom in relationship to an acceptance of the relative as a human constraint, from within which one could recover a capacity to decide, to say yes or say no:

> The visibility of the invisible. The 'visual silence'. This experience tends towards the a-rational beyond the irrational and the rational ... With the work in the biennale (the 'whisper of the invisible') perhaps begins a phase of greater silence ... To listen (also silence). For this, for liberation. I know (today) that this life is not enough. Although life 'begins' with the 'knowledge' of liberation. I know that it is a path of liberation ... And our suffering is the result of ignorance. That which in space and time is nonnegotiable. For in space and time we are not free. For the 'I' (although its sovereignty is indispensable in this life) is limitation. All our effort at perfection in space and time is illusion. Nonacceptance of the relative. This is a bridge. We have to cross it ... Not run away from it nor dwell within it. In the relative – this is our liberty. To say yes or no. To love and not be attached, to take pleasure (if possible). Without 'losing' our 'heart' here.

15 Schendel's interest in Newman may well lie in its connection to the work of Wittgenstein, whose work she read far more consistently. There is a convergence of concern with between Newman's belief and Wittgenstein's later philosophy, particularly his *Uber Gewissheit* (*On Certainty*), in which he argues against the existence of absolute certainties; the first remark in *On Certainty* reads: 'When one says that such and such proposition cannot be proved of course one does not mean that it cannot be derived from other propositions; any proposition can be derived from other ones. But they may be no more certain than it is itself (On this a curious remark by H. Newman)'. Ludwig Wittgenstein, *On Certainty*, trans. G. Anscombe (New York: Harper & Rowe, 1969), p.1. Comparative studies of Newman and Wittgenstein include a publication by the Oxford scholar Cyril Barrett whom Schendel had met during her first visit to England in 1966. C. Barrett, 'Newman and Wittgenstein on the Rationality of Religious Belief', in *Newman and Conversion*, ed. Ian Ker (Edinburgh: T&T Clark, 1997), pp.89–99.

16 John Henry Newman, *An Essay in Aid of a Grammar of Assent* (Oxford: Clarendon, 1985), p.187.

17 In a letter to Guy Brett she had indicated her attraction to the term, and distinguished it from the idea of possibility: 'It is a question of probability rather than possibility, I would say. Unlimited possibility is in a certain sense a-historic, "meta-temporal". Or religious, in the worst sense of the word. When possibility is unlimited, art becomes also a means of exorcism', Mira Schendel, letter to Guy Brett, São Paulo, 12 April 1966 (archives of Guy Brett).

18 Flusser draws from his own reading of Gebser's 'transparency' in a May 1969 text on Schendel's work entitled *Diacronia e diafanidade* (Diachronicity and Transparency); for Flusser, 'transparency' implied a chronological complexity that visual art, in distinction to written discourse, was capable of making present or capturable: 'in reality, the conditions for capturing transparency are neither prohibitive nor an invitation to mysticism. To capture transparency it is enough that it is presented. Presented, not diachronically, as it is in explanatory discourse (like this essay) ... But that is presented literally – by art. We depend on art to capture transparency. This is the function of art: to make capturable.' Vilem Flusser, 'Diacronia e diafaneidade', *O Estado de S. Paulo*, 3 May 1969, p.4.

> To be faithfully of THIS world. And not to be of this world. With love and happiness and also the inevitable suffering with devotion and without illusions.[19]

In accepting the invitation to participate, Schendel took the risk of testing her own gut instincts and continuing to experiment with a capacity for relative freedom, a freedom that was her own, but also one that was created, through the work, as conditions by which others might be able to experience it. 'I do not care if they destroy it', she said of *Ondas paradas de probabilidade* in her letter to Gebser, 'It depends – on the possibility of seeing something in it or of there being nothing to detect. If someone leaves these thin strands of nylon intact – or cuts them in anger – or kicks them to the ground it would not have the slightest importance. This amuses me – without exaggerated seriousness as you'd say!'[20]

To boycott because to do otherwise would place you on the side of a repressive state is the type of decision that is programmatic, that already contains the knowledge of what is the right thing to do. Thus it is no type of decision at all. In relation to the demands of her time, the power of this work within the boycotted biennial lies in its affirmative capacity, its discovery of a reason to continue at a time when certainty was not easily apparent. The path of following rational ('perspectival') agreement with the boycott through to its logical conclusion would have required no such conviction, no such leap of faith. As her words to Gebser attest, Schendel's commitment to the transformative potential of what she was able to make symbolically present within the world was matched with the defence of a right to experience freedom, a capacity to say yes or no, a freedom for pleasure too (amusement, even). In relation to the political upheavals of her time, the position of maintaining a psychological resistance towards the psychic disciplines enforced by repression appears now to be no less radical, and no less hard-won than more ostensibly heroic or divisive forms of action. *Ondas paradas da probabilidade* also works now to establish a lasting position from which to reconsider the history of the boycott, and the wider history of the biennial's persistence among others sites for experimentation and intervention throughout the difficult decades that followed this event.[21]

Isobel Whitelegg specialised in Latin American Art at the University of Essex, where she completed a PhD on Mira Schendel and her critical milieu. Her post-doctoral work focused on the reception of Latin American art and artists in Britain during the 1960s and 1970s. She has an interest in the history of exhibitions and non-collecting institutions and has published widely on the critical history of the Bienal Internacional de São Paulo. She has curated a number of exhibitions on Brazilian artists including most recently the Geraldo de Barros retrospective *What Remains* (The Photographers' Gallery, London, 2012). She is Curator of the Public Programme at Nottingham Contemporary and was previously Director of MA Curating Programme at Chelsea College of Art & Design, UAL.

19 Mira Schendel unpublished diary entry; quoted in Souza Dias 2009, p.147.

20 Mira Schendel, letter to Jean Gebser, São Paulo, 26 June 1969; quoted in Souza Dias 2009, p.149.

21 For a study of the persistence of the Bienal de São Paulo as a site for experimentation and resistance in the post-boycott decade, see Isobel Whitelegg, 'The Bienal de São Paulo: Unseen/Undone (1969–81)', *Afterall*, no.22, Autumn/Winter 2009, pp.106–13.

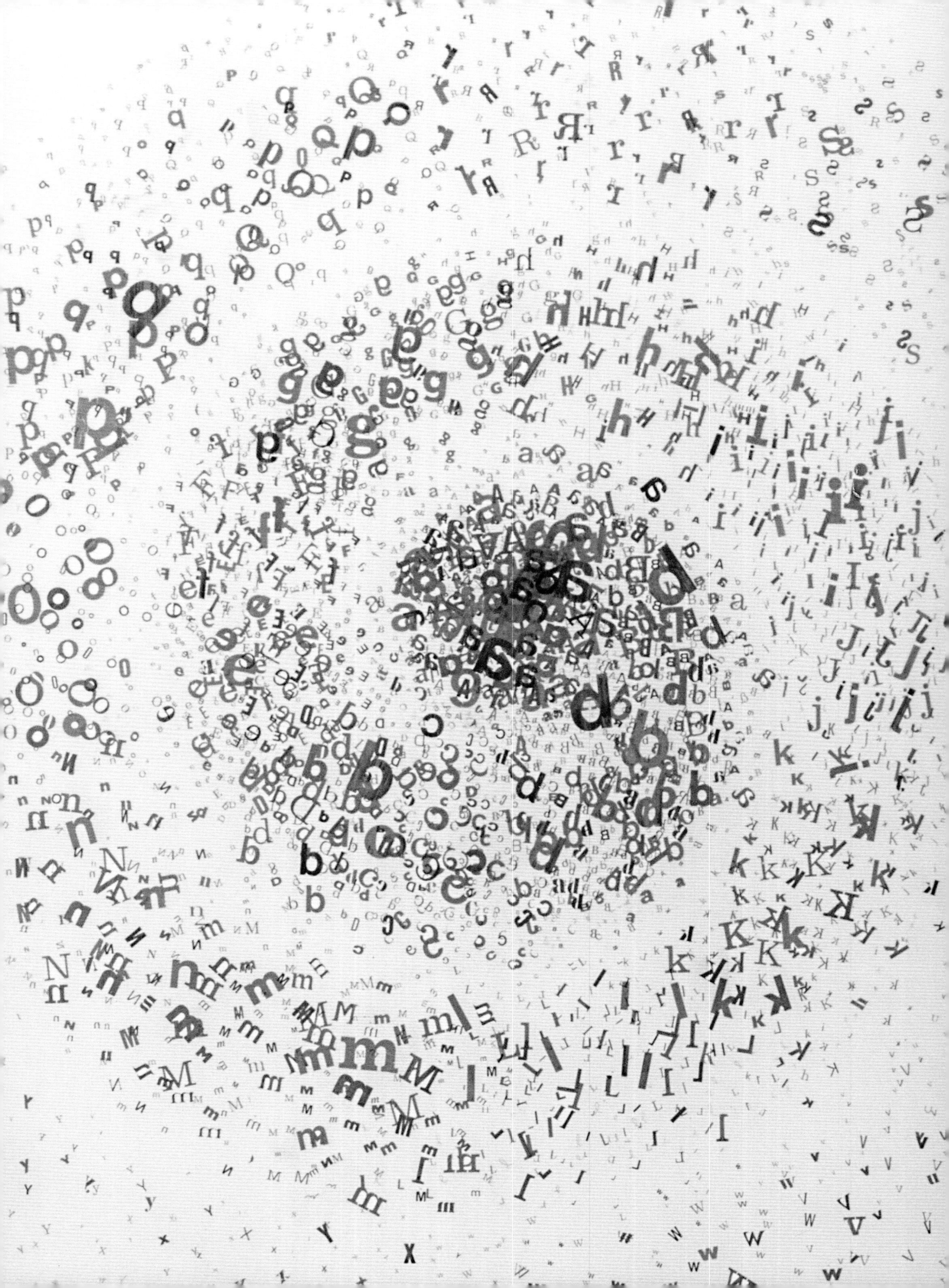

MIRA SCHENDEL'S IMMANENCE

John Rajchman

Detail of *Graphic Object*, 1972 [p.141]

The work of Mira Schendel was slow to be recognised in her own lifetime, its singularity and complexity emerging only after the fact, as if harbouring a potential or 'immanence', unfolding posthumously through a complex exhibition history in Brazil and out. At first bracketed with the work of the great neo-concretist artists, then situated in the larger postwar Latin field outside the confines of the 'Euro–American narrative', it now seems poised to raise yet new questions. Perhaps today we might view the difficulties in seeing and placing her work within given art-histories from another angle, close to the kind of search and research she herself felt she was carrying on in her invention of a new way of thinking in and through art. We might then look at her intense research in São Paulo as a singular and unnoticed episode in the larger, still unwritten story of the interconnections between philosophy and art and their fate across the cataclysm and displacements of the fraught and pitiless twentieth century. We might see Mira, in other words, working in deliberate isolation in São Paulo, and especially in her graphic works of the 1960s and 1970s, as reopening questions about writing, language, drawing, image, and the role of the body in thinking, the implications of which we are only starting to see today.

The evocations of all those who knew her already suggest such an approach. All speak, in various ways, of her strong philosophical desires, motivations, exigencies, carried on with a small circle of thinkers, in a new tropical setting, as a bodily practice of art – and of a 'metaphysical calligrapher', a 'thinking artist'. As Haroldo de Campos puts it, 'with Mira, thinking is more related to the thinking of the philosopher, the mystic' than concerned with art-critical theories.[1] Formed as she was in Zurich by German-language philosophy, with its strong Catholic theological bent, Mira nevertheless fell victim to Mussolini's anti-Jewish legislation, and was obliged to leave Europe. Coming to Brazil, eventually to São Paulo, she found a way to come back to philosophy, pursuing it in a 'nonexpert' or 'autodidactic' manner, explored in discussion with a small extra-disciplinary 'circle' through which her art-experimentation first took shape and became known. Whilst taking part in the new climate of artistic experimentation, she joined no group of constructivist or concrete artists. She kept a distance at once existential, intellectual, even geographical, in a kind of 'populated solitude' from which her work would emerge.[2]

1 Haroldo de Campos, 'Interview', in Sônia Salzstein (ed.), *No vazio do mundo: Mira Schendel*, (Exh. cat., Galeria de Arte do SESI, São Paulo, 1997), p.237. The interview is reproduced in this publication on p.208.

2 Ibid., p.229. Haroldo de Campos calls her an isolated artist, who never belonged to any of the groups of constructivist or concrete painters, and who 'lived away from things' in Santo Amaro, on the outskirts of São Paulo.

This partial independence from the Brazilian art-world from which she nevertheless drew in turn is reflected in a number of ways in her work. Her relative lack of formal art-school training; her expressed disinterest in seeing her work in terms of 'the history of art'; her close associations instead with Haroldo de Campos and concrete poetry; the nature of the intellectual circle in which her work germinated, and the ways, later, she sought to present it in her trips to Europe; her on-going readings, research, library, the many pages of her notebooks, sometimes incorporated in the works, even the controversies into which it led her, notably with her piece for the internationally boycotted Bienal de São Paulo in 1969 – all this suggests a certain 'philosophical' distance from the art-critical debates of the day, in particular those based on internalist stories of purely formal changes away from traditional conventions. In effect she took up this artistic experimentation from her own philosophical or mystical point of view, her own idea of the 'realm of symbols' on which such formalist views still relied. For, starting with the monotypes in the 1960s, her work, she said, was an attempt to capture the bodily 'origins' of this symbolic realm, to make it visible, palpable to others. Today we might more generally see the different overlapping series of graphic works in this light, as together forming a larger group that explores this question from different angles or in different ways. We might see the series of graphic works, in other words, as part of a single evolving research project, punctuated by the rise of the military dictatorship in Brazil, and carried on 'in between' art and philosophy, or in a new indistinct zone between the two, itself forming a kind of intense point from which her larger oeuvre spirals out, drawing her early still lifes (with domestic objects) or late *Sarrafos* (*Battens*) [pp.192–5] (defeating the 'phallic' character of vertical viewing) into its turbulence.

In Mira's own account of her project in the graphic works – 'the result of a hitherto frustrated attempt to capture discourse at its moment of origin'[3] – we then find the artistic-philosophical theme of 'immanence' in her work, put in a striking formula by Vilem Flusser in his essay on the monotypes in 1967. 'Her ephemeral and vulnerable strips of rice paper are covered with lines and footprints impressed on the snow of immanence', he wrote, their 'commotion of lines and dots, curves and figures' belonging to a 'discovery that can't be verbally stated, only described' in art, in *her* art.[4] The idea is echoed in Mira's own remarks just quoted above from an undated note in Portuguese, discovered after the fact, in the voluminous notebooks of her on-going research. In retrospect, we can see these two statements about 'origin' of language or discourse (published together first by Sônia Salzstein, then reprinted in *Tangled Alphabets*[5]) as a starting point for the question of immanence in her work – or in Salzstein's useful formula, its '*impersonal* immanence'. How then did the attempt to capture 'discourse at its moment of origin', in an extraordinarily intense and existentially fraught graphic artistic research carried on in postwar São Paulo, put Mira on an original path, at once artistic and philosophical, towards the great question of immanence?

3 Ibid., p.257.

4 Ibid., p.266.

5 *León Ferrari & Mira Schendel: Tangled Alphabets*, exh. cat., The Museum of Modern Art, New York, 2009.

What does it mean to suppose there exists a pre-linguistic, pre-discursive, pre-textual bodily *origin* of thinking and yet to show, explore, 'capture' it or its 'moment' in art? While Mira's work at the time is filled with the movement of many graphic and pictorial elements, it was not meant to assert or to declare; it was supposed rather to be and to remain at once 'opaque' and 'ephemeral'. For it came from a process which, on the contrary, attempts to reinsert the material codes (and related 'media', linguistic or pictorial) of saying and seeing things, back into a turbulent 'moment of origin', in which they seem to break up or spin out of control, discovering a new freedom, no longer simply objects presented to outside subjects to be seen in frontal vision or to be read in linear time. The word 'origin' (or 'moment of origin') is thus not used in a simple psychological sense, more a phenomenological one, following the development of the Kantian idea of conditions of experience (the principle of phenomenology being that the conditions or origins of appearance are to be found in the appearances themselves). In Heidegger's essay in the 1930s on 'The Origin of the Work of Art', we already find a picture of art and especially of poetry prior to the technological 'world picture' of art-exhibition culture. But in many ways Mira's own philosophical preoccupations were closer to Edmund Husserl's *Origin of Geometry* (1962), which, in roughly the same years as Mira's artistic experiments in Brazil, would play a key role in French philosophy, first in Maurice Merleau-Ponty's last courses, then in Jacques Derrida's translation and commentary, focused on the question of writing. For in this late work, Husserl was asking how we generate geometric figures (like circles) from everyday experiences (such as ordinary 'roundness') situated in the bodily life-world which is their 'origin', thus offsetting a positivist 'crisis in European science'. Derrida's starting point was then that writing (*écriture*) doesn't have an origin in this sense of an ideality generated from the bodily life-world and indeed points to something prior to it. For in the endless possibilities of 're-writing' we find a more 'original' sense of delay, or '*différence*' (as Derrida coined it) incompatible with the sense of immediacy on which Husserl relies. Derrida would, of course, go on to develop from this starting point a whole new idea of 'trace' and 'marking' (and technology, media, and much else), as part of a search for a new image of thinking itself.

In many ways Mira's attempt to capture the origin of discourse in her graphic works is close to this introduction of the question of writing – mixing, as they do, geometric figures with scriptural or graphic elements, words, letters inscriptions, often guided by diagrammatic indicators in a space freed from their discursive or linguistic (more generally symbolic) enclosure, opening rather to another temporality, close to film. But, at the same time, Mira had a more vitalist notion of the 'immediate life', the experience or *vivência* (bodily experience) at the origin of discourse and her attempt to 'capture' it thus in effect moved in the opposite direction from Husserl: not to ideal or abstract geometric figures from their origins in a situated or anchored consciousness, but rather from such a situated 'consciousness of objects' to a vital, ungrounded, a-cented, unfixed condition. It was, in her own words, 'an attempt to find an arstistic passage from immediate life, the kind I suffer and within which I act is mine alone, "incommunicable" into the realm of symbols, which seeks to capture that life' but which 'is anti-life, in the sense of being intersubjective, shared, emptied of emotion and suffering'. The problem, in other words, was how to render the singular experiences of her suffering body in a lifeless public, intersubjective, formal or formalist 'realm of symbols', without abolishing what makes it at once vital and singular ('mine alone'). It was then this supposition of a singular vital incommunicable bodily origin of thinking which made the attempt to capture it artistically a spiritual or ethical matter, concerned with question of immanence – an 'experimental exercise in freedom', involving a series of distinctions between inner and outer, private and public.

In particular, an idea of an *impersonal* immanence follows from it. What is 'original' comes from a zone before 'persons' are established in the life-killing realm of symbols – before, in other words, what Emile Benveniste called the 'apparatus of enunciation' in languages, or Foucault, the 'subject-positions' in a discursive (and by extension visual) field, or for that matter, the *Mitsein* of phenomenological views of intersubjectivity. That is why she felt her works could not be simple 'objects'. They had to reach out and affect others in a manner at once 'singular and impersonal', and so supposed 'radically passive', affective (rather than active, assertive) relations with others.[6] As we will see later, this attempt was at some distance from Hannah Arendt's dream of 'the public' (and of 'being at home' in philosophical German). But this idea of 'impersonal singularity' also moves, in a certain sense, in an opposite direction from Ludwig Wittgenstein's 'private language' argument, according to which there can be no language of just my sensations, since language in itself is always public ('introspection' being just one language-game among others), deriving its sense from a tacit or background 'forms of life'. For Mira's origin, while presented 'in public' or for an 'audience' is yet not a language; and the life from which it derives and to which it appeals is not a tacit background of a public practice (any more than a warm rich phenomenological life-world), but rather a singular, suffering *vivência*, incompatible with any such 'publicness'. Indeed, just what lends her graphic art its striking 'opacity' is the ways in which its materials have been withdrawn and withheld from such public uses and inserted instead into a swirling, vital or 'kinetic' zone, inviting other kinds of approach, other kinds of relation with others. That would then be the task of the 'metaphysical calligrapher', the aim of the 'thinking artist': to show or capture this original zone of thinking, prior to the otherwise lifeless realm of symbols, and to impart it affectively to others. It is what makes capturing the origin of discourse or language into a play with immanence in a sense very close to the one Gilles Deleuze was developing around the same time in philosophy, encapsulated, just before his death, in a last short essay called 'Immanence: A Life'.

6 See Isobel Whitelegg's thesis, *Mira Schendel: A Radical Passivity – Towards Another History of Art, Thought and Action in the Brazilian Sixties* (University of Essex, 2004).

If, then, we see Mira's graphic art as an attempt to explore and make visible such an origin of thought, what is the relation between visual and graphic elements in it? How is it related to thinking in poetry or writing, or to painting or pictorial practice? Why did Mira think of it all as a kind of 'drawing' before such divisions? In 1967, in an early exhibition called *Graphic Reduction*, Max Bense offered one answer.[7] The scattered letters of the monotypes would take over and assume the role of points, lines, surfaces in pictorial space and so be 'reduced' to them. The problem in this idea of reduction is that it preserves the idea of pictorial space as a kind of code lying in the 'realm of symbols', closer to Wassily Kandinsky's idea of 'the spiritual in art' than to Paul Klee's 'inflexional' (or 'folded') diagrammatic space, developed notably in the pedagogical sketchbooks.[8] Indeed, Mira's graphic works seem much closer to the kind of 'scattered space' prior to figure-ground relations that Roland Barthes saw in Cy Twombly, whose blackboards also use writing to get outside figure-ground relations, in a manner already to be found in Klee, in many ways the European artist closest to Mira's origin, before the divisions between poetry, painting, and music. Mira's visual space is thus not so much a 'graphic reduction' as a shift to a 'graphic immanence', in a sort of ungrounded space, with voids, points of inflexion, diagrammatic indicators and spatio-graphic games.

On the other hand, Haroldo de Campos views the swarm of what he amusingly called 'alphabees' more as a matter of concrete poetry. But such 'swarming' of the scattered letters is part of the way the letters spin or spiral out of control, breaking away from the 'calligraphic dream' still confined to the 'thickness' of the printed page as if the very alphabetic code of writing had undergone a kind of cataclysm, entering a new space beyond the linearity of even concrete-poetical reading. But if printed matter thus frees itself from the page, the installations in which it then figures are not quite 'printed sculpture' either, since they are presented not as objects, but rather as 'spaces', inviting a 'participation' closer to the singular bodily *vivência* from which they derive. Mira's graphic matter is thus not to be read either as 'text' or as 'image', the induced inability to simply do one or the other causing one to think – or have an affective sense of thinking 'at the origin'.

More precisely, Mira's graphic elements, in the words of Rodrigo Naves' suggestive analysis, seem to come 'from behind'.[9] Thus 'her lines emerge from the paper as if unguided by any external action', not as gesture marked by a subject but in a more impersonal manner, although in a very different sense than, for example, automatic writing. The process she developed – fingernails and sharp instruments applied to inked rice paper – was in itself a singular invention. It allowed her to treat different 'media' (drawing, printing, handwriting) all on the same footing, close to her hands, to her singular body, yet in a non-gestural impersonal way. For, from the start, the rice paper was treated not as 'blank surface' for an inscription or a picture but rather as a zone of immanence,

7 Max Bense in *No vazio do mundo*, p.263.

8 See Klee's inflexional space, in Bernard Cache, *Earth Moves: The Furnishing of Territories*, ed. Michael Sparks, trans. Anne Boyman (Cambridge, MA: The MIT Press, 1995).

9 Rodrigo Naves, 'From Behind', in *No vazio do mundo*, pp.66ff.

out of which markings seem to emerge, as through a new kind of drawing. Beyond the centrality of ink and rice paper (therefore of black and white) in her work, we thus find something close to Chinese (or 'East Asian') art, where painting, calligraphy, drawing are all thought to derive from the same source or origin, and where the act of painting is a 'spiritual' act, or a practice of thinking (or 'wisdom') involving a vital Taoist sense of immanence of a kind François Jullien explicitly contrasts with the sense of 'void' in Heidegger and Jacques Lacan, and their all-too-Christian sense of 'spirituality'.[10] Unlike the 'hand–eye–easal' technique in Western painting it would take Jackson Pollock to break away from, or the 'hand–wrist–scroll' procedures of Eastern ink painting Jullien thus rediscovers in Chinese pictorial practice, Mira's singular way of drawing with her fingernails on inked paper allowed her to become a new sort of 'metaphysical calligrapher', discovering an uncoded vital tropical immanence and spirituality all her own.

At the same time, in thus freeing drawing from hand–eye and print–eye 'media' arrangements, putting printed matter back into an uncoded space where it can no longer be read like book or seen like a picture, at the same time, Mira can be seen to participate in a series of debates deriving from notions of 'absence of work' or 'neutrality' Maurice Blanchot had introduced into literature, carried on in France during the same years as her vital experimentations in Brazil – for example, Foucault's essay 'This Is Not a Pipe' of 1968, in which there is an idea of 'void' already to be found in his study of Raymond Roussel, itself a kind of humorous underside of his theory of discourse and visuality.[11] The break with the 'calligraphic dream', taking off from Klee, was thus part of a new sense of the 'origins of discourse', characterised by the disjunction of word and image, ways of seeing and talking. Similarly, in his book *Discourse-Figure*, Jean-François Lyotard was looking at cases where the pictorial logic (the 'good Gestalt' of figure-ground, frontal-vision) was undone in a kind of 'formless space', at the same time as a break-up in the attributive and enunciative frame of discourse, leading to new kinds of relations between the two. Deleuze's general formula for such disjunctions of words and images (developed in his study of cinema) – 'break open things, break open words' – seems peculiarly well suited to Mira's intense graphic experimentation, undertaken independently in the same years.

But if we then see Mira's immanence in this way, as a zone before graphic and pictorial elements are brought together in the public realm of symbols, drawn instead from her impersonal, yet singular suffering body, we find another striking feature of her work of a kind to which Lyotard or Foucault paid scant attention in these essays – what might be called a 'multilingualism of the origin', found especially in the *Monotypes* called *Escritas* (*Writings*) [p.106] and *Objetos gráficos* (*Graphic Objects*) [pp.125–41] series. Into the swirling, ungrounded space opened up by the monotypes, Mira started to insert actual handwritten phrases of printed words, in several languages, as if they were no less a part of the suf-

10 François Jullien, *The Great Image Has No Form; or On the Nonobject through Painting*, trans. Jane Marie Todd (Chicago: The University of Chicago Press, 2009), chap. 6. The theme of immanence is a constant one in Jullien's approach to Chinese art and philosophy.

11 This theme is especially developed by Deleuze starting from his first essay on Foucault, 'Raymond Roussel Or the Horror of the Void' of 1963.

fering body, its existential distress, that she felt was hers alone. In this play, we find not only the several languages she knew or used – Portuguese, German and Italian, found also in her private diaries – but also others, notably French and English, part of a larger on going 'translingual' graphico-visual play. In particular, often using 'diagrammatic' markers, we find such often wonderfully humorous play 'at the origin' devoted to highly loaded German philosophical words like *Zeit* (time) or *Umwelt* (vital environs), almost like a private joke intersecting with her larger philosohical research [pp.111; 108]. It is this playful multilinguism which makes her art not simply ungrounded with respect to codes of writing, reading, depicting, but also 'deterritorialised' with respect to the predominance of any one national language, as if all national languages, withdrawn from their 'territories', had been thrown together into the cauldron, or the 'fire' of immanence [p.107].

But if the origin of discourse Mira was trying to capture was thus before any one language, it was before the Word (and Name) of God, as expressed in any one, especially the German-language theology of her philosophical formation, now exposed to the translingual fires. In this multilinguism of the origin – *at* the origin – (so difficult to read or see by monolingual audiences), we thus find in a very striking, concrete way questions which Derrida, for his part, would come to only later, first in a critical examination of nationalism (especially to be found in Heidegger's German-language philosophical nationalism), and then in a more autobiographical form in *Monolingualism of the Other; or, The Prosthesis of Origin*.[12]

For the cataclysm that had brought Mira to Brazil with her philosophical desires in her suitcase at the same time would help recast the geographies of philosophy in Europe after the war. Indeed, there is something pleasingly anachronistic and 'old European' about the autodidactic philosophical interests she continued to pursue in São Paulo, then later in her travels in Europe (notably with Herman Schmitz), in particular, the way she clung to phenomenological ideas of 'the origin', while yet submitting them to a new Brazilian artistic experimentation. We might thus see Mira's work in relation to the 'hypothetical typology' Derrida sketches in a long note on the different relations to the 'mother tongue' (French or German) given the 'event of Auschwitz' – and in particular to his two contrasting Jewish women thinkers, Hannah Arendt (who, in conversation with Günter Grass,[13] said 'the mother tongue is all that remains'), and Hélène Cixous, who, sharing the same situation in Algeria that had led Derrida himself to his own 'neurotic' relation to French, would weave together all the threads of his typology, in a 'miraculous' way, pointing to a 'future still without a name'. As with the case of Mira in Brazil, in the work of these two different woman thinkers, the question of the language, or 'realm of symbols' in which one thinks intersects with a series of questions about private and public, inner and outer, 'fatherland' and 'mother tongue'.

12 Jacques Derrida, *Monolingualism of the Other; or, the Prosthesis of Origin*, trans. Patrick Mensah (Stanford: Stanford University Press, 1998). See especially, note 9, pp.78ff.

13 '*Was bliebt? Es bliebt die Muttersprache*' was a talk Arendt had with Günter Grass, which aired on German television in 1964, won a prize, and was then published in Günter Grass, *Zur Person*.

If Mira then took up all these questions as a 'Brazilian artist', it was part of a larger situation there that included Flusser himself, but also, in another way, the great Brazilian writer Clarice Lispector.[14] But what then was the role of Brazil in this cataclysmic story of philosophical displacement at the 'origins' of Mira's work? The question of Brazil in postwar art is no doubt part of a more general debate, reflected in the exhibition history of Mira's work. In the important *Tangled Alphabets* exhibition in New York in 2009, for example, her graphic preoccupations were presented as part of a larger postwar 'Latin American' preoccupation with writing, drawing, image, seen in contrast to the Euro–American story of the 'dematerialization' of conceptual art as propounded, for example, by Sol LeWitt, involving instead a bodily engagement with the 'thickness' of language, philosophically closer to Derrida's idea of 'grammatology'.[15] But at the same time, the question of Brazil in Mira's work can be seen in relation to Derrida's story of philosophical and artistic displacement captured in a striking way by Haroldo de Campos, when he declared that 'Mira, while really a Swiss moving amongst three horizons – Portuguese, Italian and German – had a profoundly Brazilian mind, and lived here fully and intensely'.[16]

But Mira didn't like the all-too-Cartesian idea of 'mind', so perhaps it would be better to speak of a profoundly Brazilian *vivência* – an intense Brazilian way of being, or being an artist, shown even in her 'isolated' experimentations at home with inked rice paper, the resulting 'translingual play' involving not only these 'horizons', but also the larger role of European languages in the 'fires' of this new setting. For, as Rodrigo Naves suggests, in these years Brazil offered a sort of free zone for her artistic-philosophical experimentation just because it didn't have the more institutionally entrenched and sophisticated traditions that dominated European art or cultural life.[17] Indeed, that is what led Flusser to see in postwar Brazil, connected to the Portuguese language, the formation of a great new 'anthropophagic' site freed from the nationalist prejudices of European philosophy, part of a dream of creating a new Brazilian philosophy 'with the help of a few partners'. Raised in 'German culture' in Prague's Jewish circles that were later to be decimated ('all of the people to whom I was mysteriously bound in Prague were murdered. All of them'), Flusser found in São Paulo a sort of 'no-man's-land', where 'one was a pioneer in everything', in which European philosophical discourse could become part of a new free extra-disciplinary 'dialogue'.[18] But this dream of Brazil as 'home of a future society' in contrast to the 'closed-mindedness, fanaticism and prejudices of every European homeland' would not survive the rise of the military dictatorship and the new technocractic 'populist' idea of Brazil it brought with it. After 1964, Flusser's dream of Brazilian 'deterritorialization' would increasingly clash against political realities; and after 1972, he would give up his dream, retreating to an 'anti-Brazil' in the French countryside, there abandoning not only this dream of a new home, but also all ideas of 'homeland', in favour of circles, habits of

14 Clarice Lispector (1920–77) is internationally acclaimed as one of Brazil's most important writers. Born into a Jewish family in Podolia, Chechelynk, in what is today Ukraine, she was brought to Brazil as an infant when her family fled from the pogroms during the Russian civil war.

15 Luis Pérez-Oramas, 'Introduction' *León Ferrari & Mira Schendel: Tangled Alphabets*, pp.13ff.

16 Haroldo de Campos in *No vazio do mundo*, p.229.

17 Rodrigo Naves, 'Mira Schendel: The World as Generosity', in *León Ferrari & Mira Schendel: Tangled Alphabets*, pp.58ff.

18 Vilem Flusser, 'Taking Up Residence in Homelessness', in *Writings*, ed. Andreas Ströhl (Minneapolis and London: University of Minnesota Press, 2002), p.97.

reading and ethical responsibility of dialogue that cannot be contained in any one State or Territory or confused with 'philanthropy, cosmopolitanism, humanism'.[19]

It is not clear, however, whether Mira shared this vision (and related disappointment) in which she nevertheless was a dialogic 'partner'. For, in a sense, there was no place, even a 'lost' one in Europe for her to go back to (she chose to stay); and in the Swiss 'origin' of her peregrinations, there was nothing like the Jewish circles in Prague in which Flusser grew up. There was only the suppressed or silent family history.[20] Perhaps that is why, while Flusser could say he was 'at home in four languages', Mira's translingual play suggests she was at home in none, not even the ones which formed her 'horizons'; and perhaps why, at least in her work, rather than declaring herself as a 'citizen of São Paulo', she preferred to work in deliberate isolation, at some distance from the city, in her home, tracing strange lines, letters, phrases, with her fingernails on inked rice paper, in a frenzied experiment.

With this in mind, we can approach the question of 'femininity' (to use Cixous' term) in and of her work. In contrast to Hannah Arendt, Cixous called for a 'feminine writing' (*écriture féminine*) outside the Law or Word of the Father, and she would find it, perhaps in its strongest form, also in Brazil, in Lispector. We might see Mira, in other words, as taking up the question of the 'relation to language' in a search for a new 'feminine' way of thinking, though not as a writer, but as an artist – working on her own, yet exerting a fascination on the circle of male intellectuals, through whom her work would become known. For into this highly philosophical discussion about the origin of language or discourse, Mira was attempting to introduce something bodily which precisely cannot be said 'discursively' or 'publicly', only shown, at the cost of great existential risk, in and through her art. The nonassertive character of her work was thus reflected in her peculiar role in her circle – so different from the declarations of an avant-garde group with its 'pope' and its manifesto. Mira's circle instead tried to work out different ways of thinking about the unspeakable experience at the origin in her work. Indeed, in contrast to Arendt's dream of 'the public' freed from the household, Mira preferred to carry on her experimentations at home, rather even than in a separate studio. Only late in life with the *Sarrafos*, would she say she had 'learn[ed] to be aggressive'.[21] She was thus closer in many ways to Clarice, whose family, fleeing the Ukranian pogroms, had come to Brazil, thus making Portuguese her 'mother tongue'.

In Clarice's fiction, we find a new kind of female protagonist with strong philosophical desires. As Caetano Veloso puts it, in the 'humdrum concerns of normal life', a woman, on her own, unexpectedly encounters something extra-ordinary – an 'event, a Thing'

19 Ibid.

20 Cf. Chronology.

21 Quoted in Iole de Freitas, 'The Slats', in *No vazio do mundo*, p.226.

– the start of a long adventure in thinking 'near to the wild heart', which, whilst it cannot be understood by Professors or Husbands, nevetherless remains close to a kind of Spinozistic 'impersonal immanence'. For we now know that Clarice at a young age had been madly reading Spinoza, as if in search of a new kind of tropical Spinozism she would then pursue in her fiction.[22] Her question becomes how, at what cost, a woman can attain this vital zone that can't be understood, leading her, in Caetano's words, to a new relationship between thinking and writing: 'It's not a story that leads the reader to philosophical thoughts. And it's not a philosophical treatise that needs a story to convey them. Instead it is a vivifying experience that leads a person to the most ambitious philosophical discoveries.'[23] With this reference to 'vivifying experience', we are thus not far from Mira, even if she took up the problem not in fiction, but in terms of a new kind of graphic art, a new way of being a 'thinking artist'. Indeed, if we look at the last lines of Lispector's *The Passion According to G.H.* – 'how could I speak without the word lying for me? how could I speak except timidly like this: life is just for me. Life is just for me, and I don't understand what I'm saying. And so I adore it.'[24] – we find something akin to Mira's sense of her own vital singular *vivência* in relation to language, and more generally to the 'realm of symbols'. But if Portuguese (which she came to only in her thirties) could not be a 'home' (even one to be inhabited like a foreign 'guest'), nevertheless, as an artist, Mira developed her own kind of 'immanence', even if, unlike Clarice, she gave the place of honour to Heidegger rather than to Spinoza in her library.

If Clarice's protagonists find a path to a 'pre-linguistic' immanence that no one can quite understand, it is thus in a Spinozistic vein: the 'passion' in question is not an ascetic mysticism or a 'negative theology' (as with mimimalist 'reduction'), but rather a vital bodily experience, carried on by a new kind of woman thinker, leading to an ecstatic solitude, often fascinating to the men unable to see it. We might see Mira's immanence along such lines, as if she shared with Clarice the attempt as a woman, alone in Brazil, to invent a new vital way of thinking. Indeed, in many ways Mira shared with the 'Marrano' Spinoza, the great philosopher of immanence, the complex multilingual situation of a silent inheritance irreducible to any one language. Writing in Latin, yet for a nonacademic public, as shown in his refusal of any public university professorship, preferring to polish lenses and talk with a small circle of friends, excommunicated in Portuguese, carrying on discussions in the local Dutch of a new globalising Amsterdam, like Mira, Spinoza was at home in no one language. For Deleuze, this indeed is part of his strange attraction 'for us' – especially us 'writers, musicians, filmmakers, even painters' drawn to the 'new Spinoza' emerging in French philosophy at the time, taken up notably by Toni Negri.

In a complex commentary, Deleuze had tried to extract the idea of immanence itself from prior Substance or given Totality, seeing it instead as a kind of 'plan' or 'plane',

22 On Clarice's relations with Spinoza, see Benjamin Moser, *Why This World: A Biography of Clarice Lispector* (Oxford: Oxford University Press), p.109ff.

23 Caetano Veloso, 'Introduction' to Clarice Lispector's *The Passion According to G.H.*, trans. Idra Novey (New York: New Directions, 2012), p.ix.

24 'The Passion According to G.H.', in Lispector 2012, p.189.

shown through its 'expressions'. To attain such a plane one must find a way to enter it, constructing it, composing it with others, in a kind of experimental freedom. Only then does immanence become 'pure' or 'absolute' – not immanence *to* anything, subjective or objective, in particular not to the sort of centred situated consciousness Husserl ('and many of his followers') had sought. If Spinoza is the 'prince of philosophers', it is just because his immanence was always yet to be constructed in new vital formations; and that is why, in a manner unique among philosophers, the purest metaphysical speculation offers the most intense zone for a nonphilosophical understanding of philosophy by writers or artists. Such in any case is precisely his appeal 'for us', Deleuze would declare in the 1970s, at the same moment when Mira was carrying on her graphic experimentations in São Paulo.[25]

If in our inherited religions, we can distinguish two poles, 'spirituality' and 'theology', Spinoza is perhaps the philosopher who went the furthest to make the first prior to the second, seeing the 'Word of God' as deriving only from a bodily 'experience of God', theology being in effect only a necessary superstition or fiction for attaining it. 'God or Nature', Spinoza would say ('God or Chaos', Nietzsche would say after him). If in Mira's philosophico-theological artistic experimentations (as in Clarice's fictions), we rediscover something like this priority of a singular, impersonal body to the Word of God or the Father, it is from an original angle, all her own. Developed in extra-disciplinary circles of discussion in the peculiar conditions of postwar São Paulo, drawing on the techniques and resources of neo-concretist art and concrete poety, in the 'anthropophagic' conditions in which Flusser dreamt of a new home for European philosophies beyond the geography of their fanatical divisions, in her graphic works, Mira invented a new immanence, at once 'feminine' and 'homeless', close to the wild heart, and so took up, in her own way, the great question Deleuze saw as the intense point of Spinoza's *Ethics*: 'What can a body do?' Such then is perhaps Mira Schendel's singular immanence for us today.

John Rajchman is a philosopher and a professor of Art History at Columbia University (New York). A contributing editor at *Artforum*, he was a founder editor of *Semiotexte*, a member of the editorial board of *October* (in the 1980s), and the only non-architect on the board of ANY, an itinerant global architectural symposium of the 1990s. His books and articles have been translated into many languages. His most recent publication, co-edited with Etienne Balibar, is *French Philosophy since 1945: Problems, Concepts, Inventions* (New York: The New Press, 2011). Forthcoming is *Art and Theory in a Global Context*

25 Gilles Deleuze, *Spinoza: Practical Philosophy*, (San Francisco: City Lights Books, 1988), Cf. especially chap. 6, 'Spinoza and Us'.

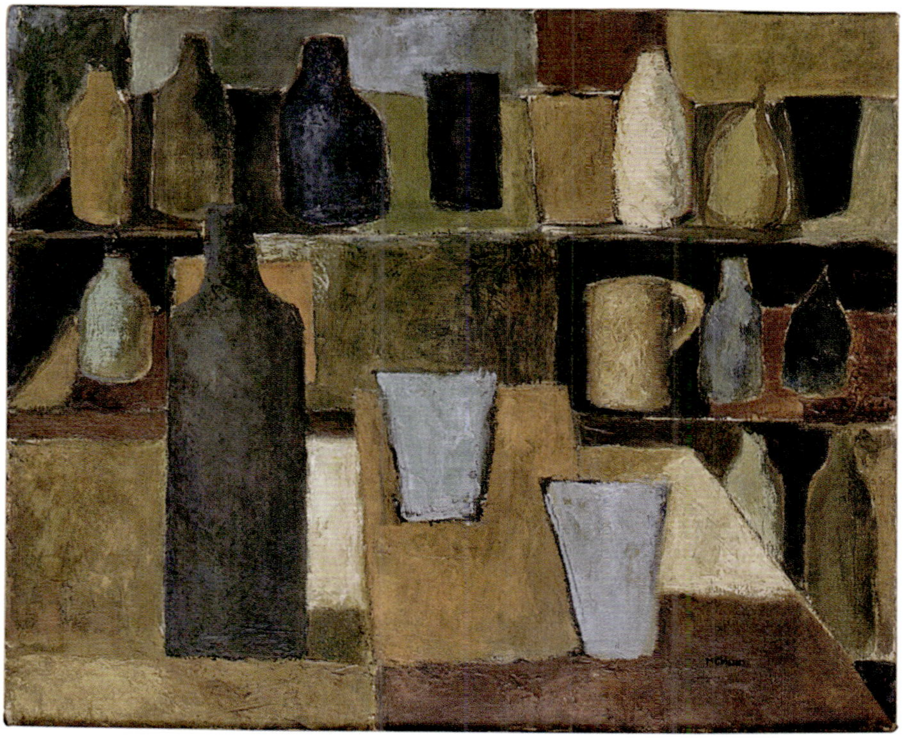

Untitled
Sem título
1953
Oil on canvas
53.3 x 64.6 cm
Museu de Arte Contemporânea
da Universidade de São Paulo,
São Paulo, Brazil

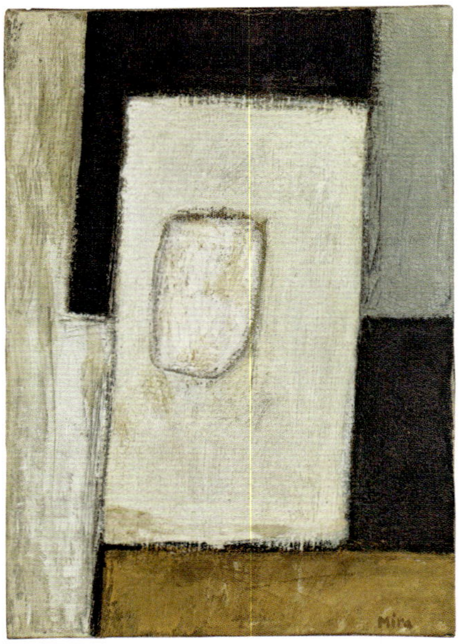

Untitled
Sem título
c.1954–5
Tempera on canvas
26.8 x 19 cm
Eduardo Duvivier Neto

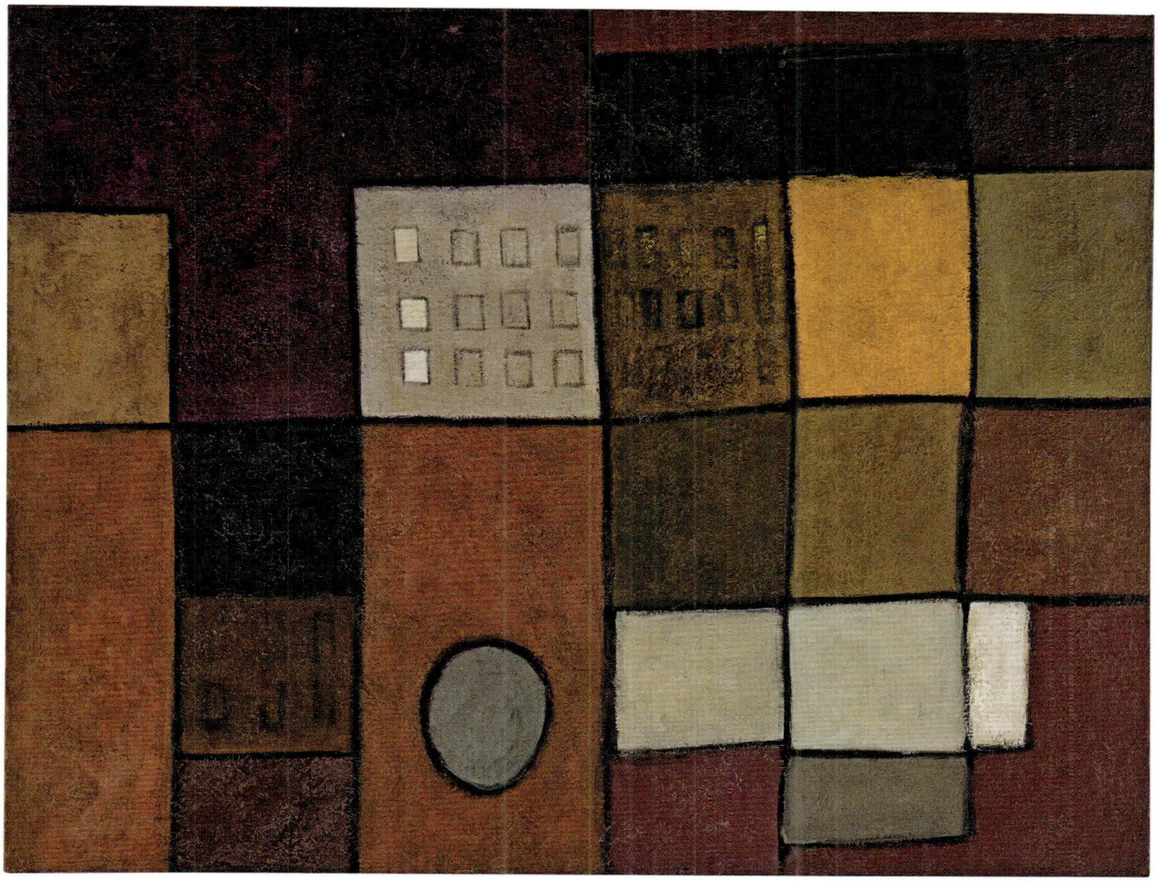

Untitled
Sem título
1950s
Tempera on jute
96.5 x 130 cm
Luiz Paulo Montenegro

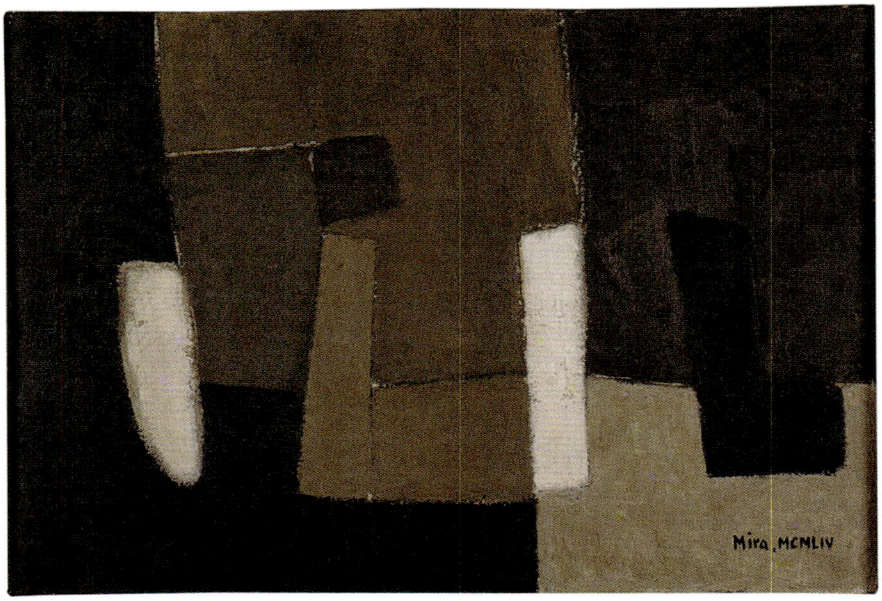

Composition
Composição
1954
Oil on wood
24.3 x 35.6 cm
Museu de Arte Contemporânea
da Universidade de São Paulo,
São Paulo, Brazil

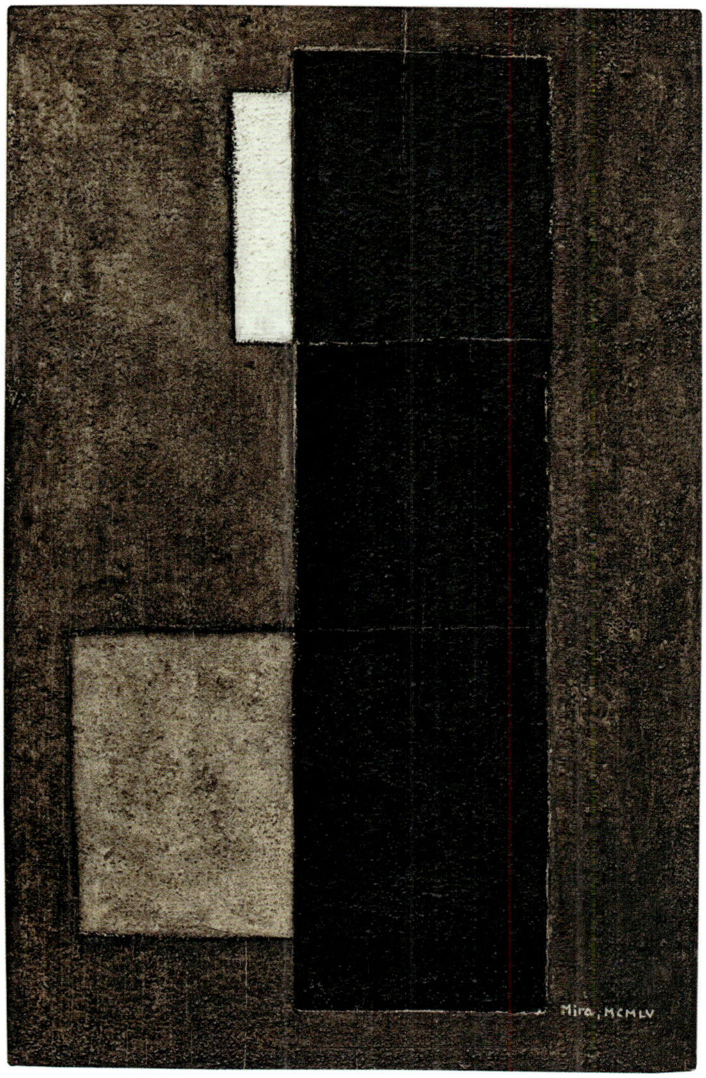

Untitled
Sem título
1955
Tempera and sand on wood
60 x 40 cm
Private collection

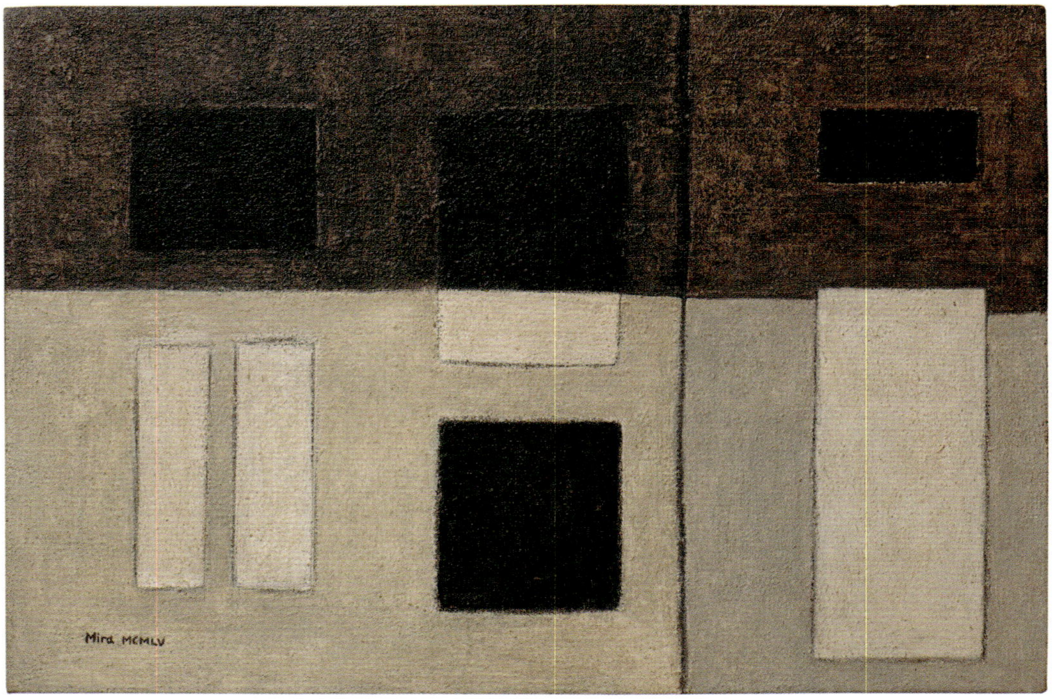

Untitled
Sem título
1955
Tempera on wood
40 x 60 cm
Private collection

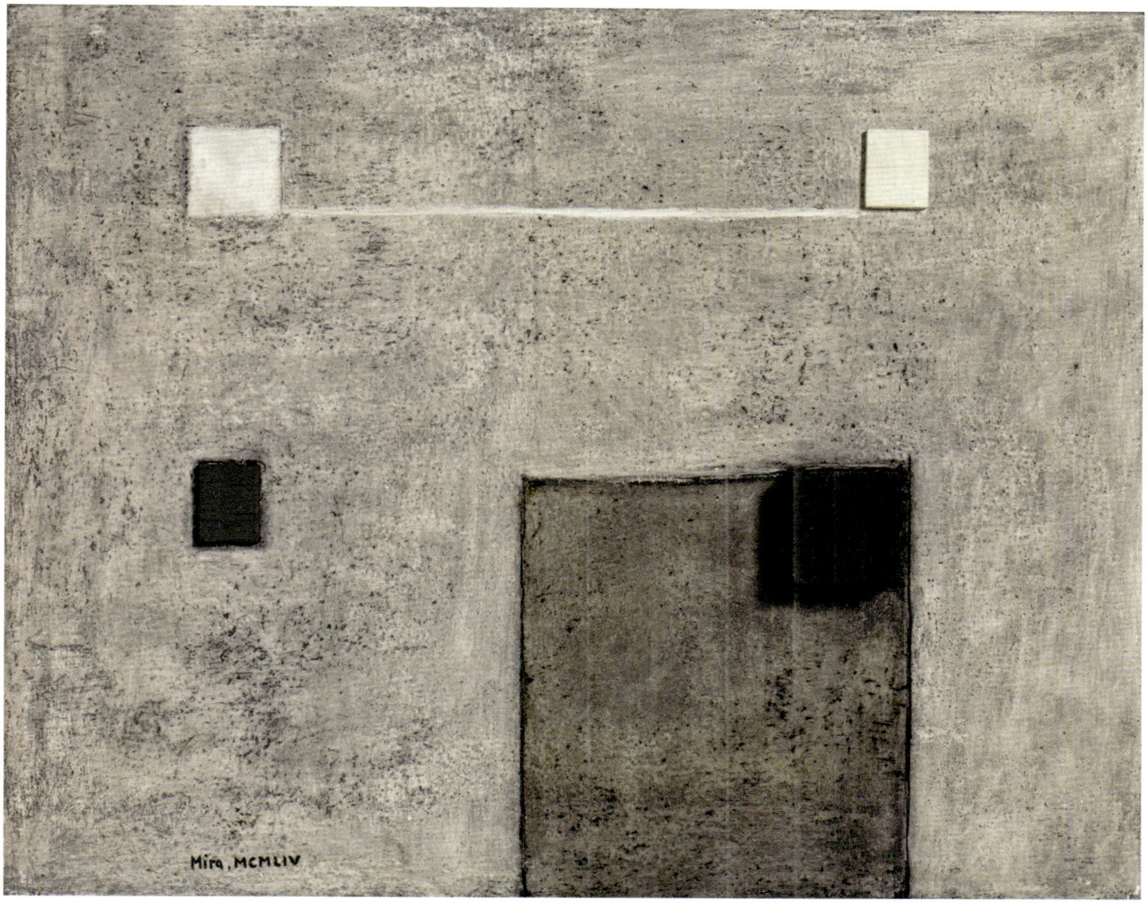

Untitled
Sem título
1954
Tempera and gesso on wood
51 x 66 cm
The Museum of Fine Arts, Houston, The Adolpho Leirner Collection of Brazilian Constructive Art, museum purchase with funds provided by the Caroline Wiess Law Accessions Endowment Fund

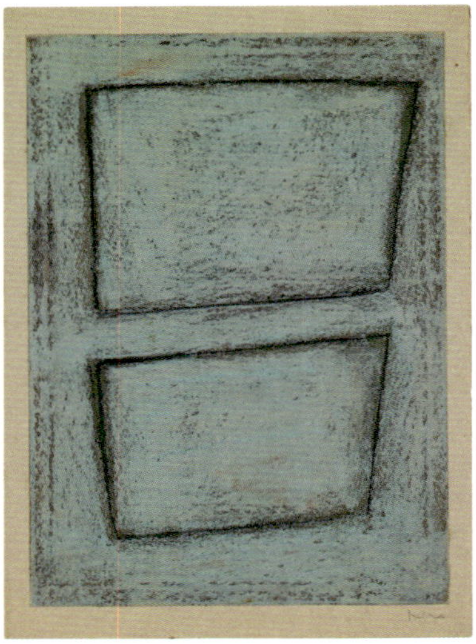

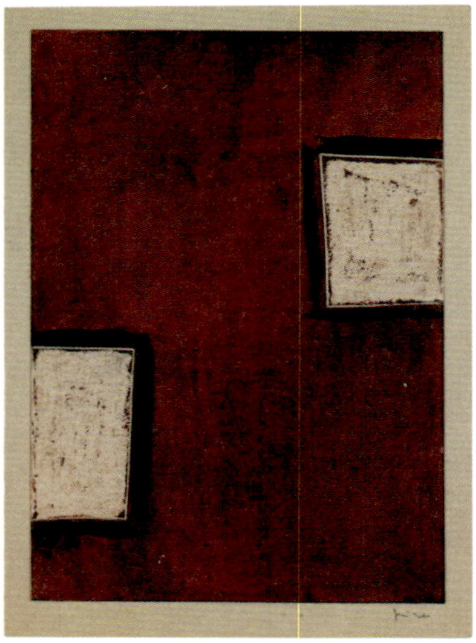

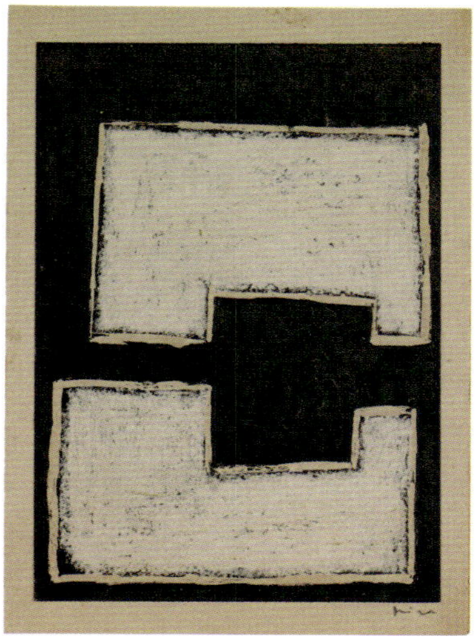

Untitled
Sem título
early 1960s
Oil stick and gouache on paper
each 21 x 16 cm
mira schendel estate

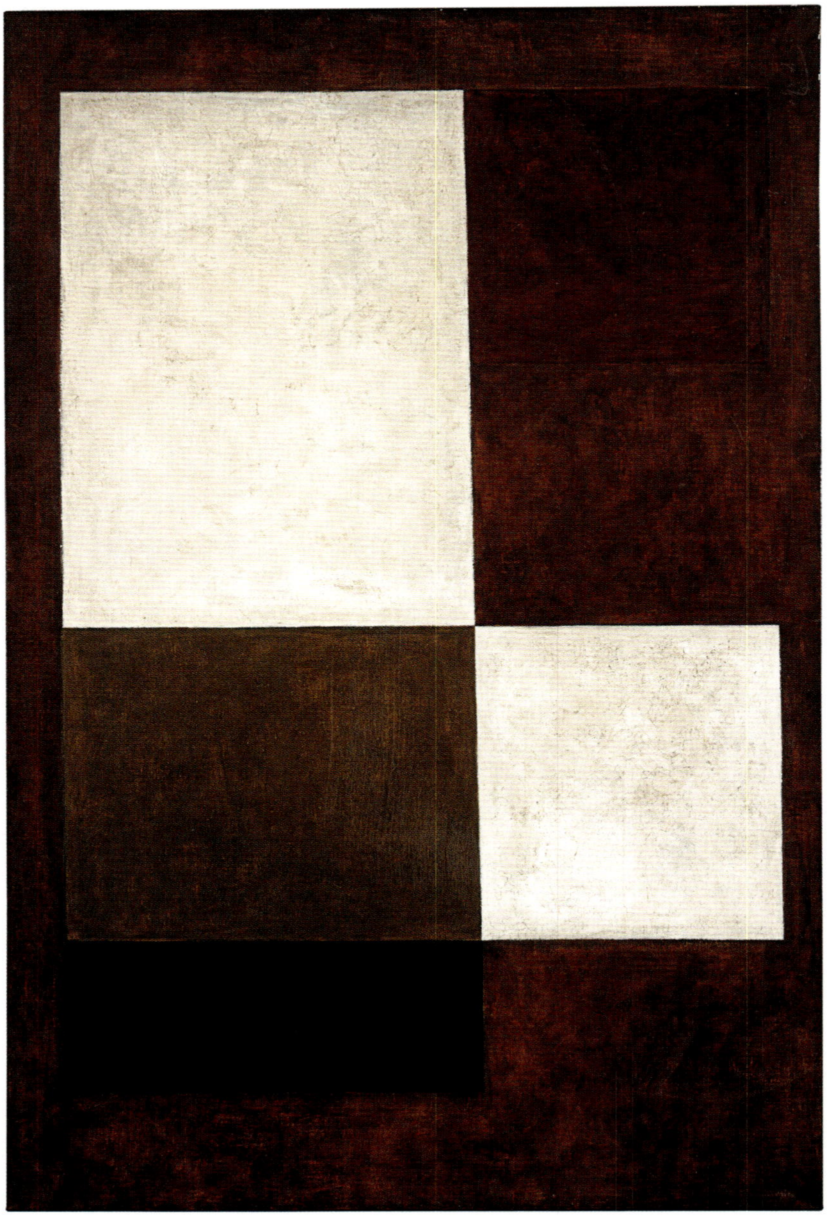

Untitled (Rectangles on a Brown Ground)
Sem título (Rectangulos sobre fundo marrom)
1960s
Oil on canvas
119.4 x 80 cm
Colección Patricia Phelps de Cisneros

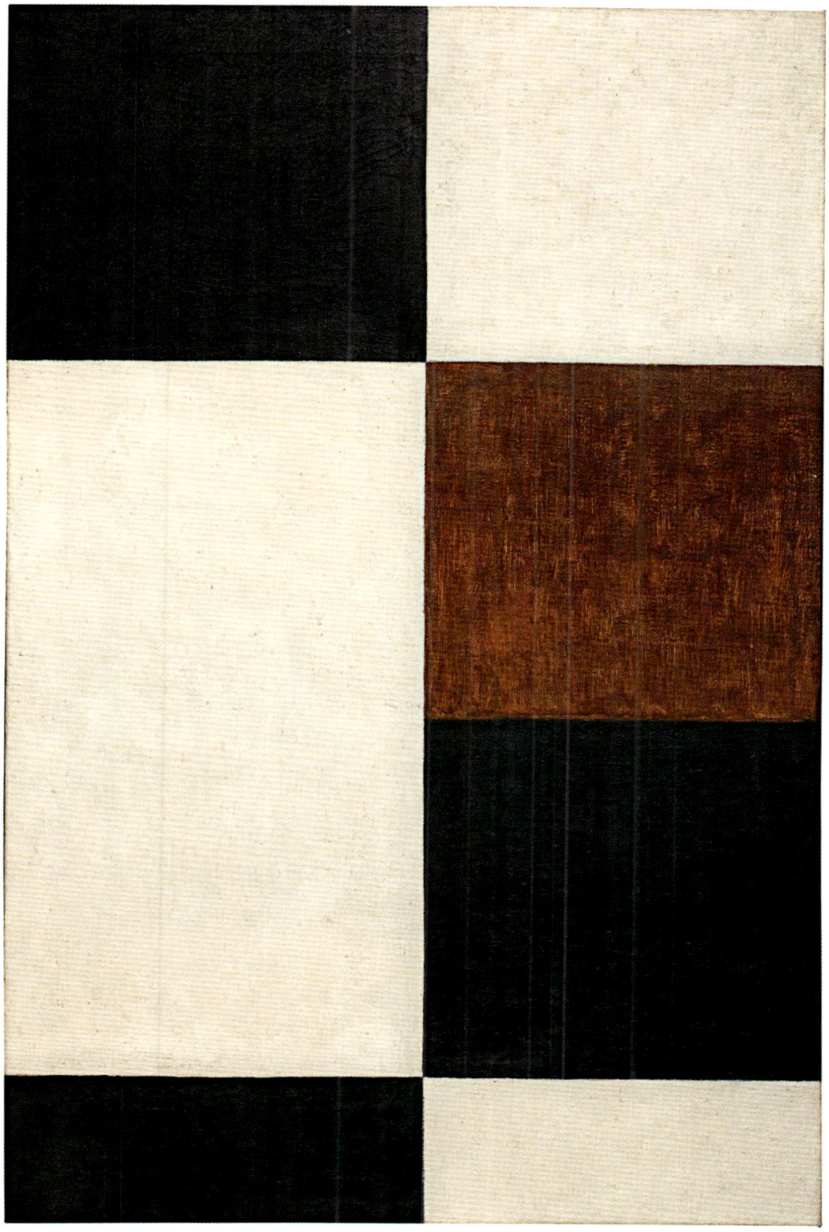

Untitled
Sem título
c.1960–5
Tempera on canvas
120 x 80 cm
Private collection

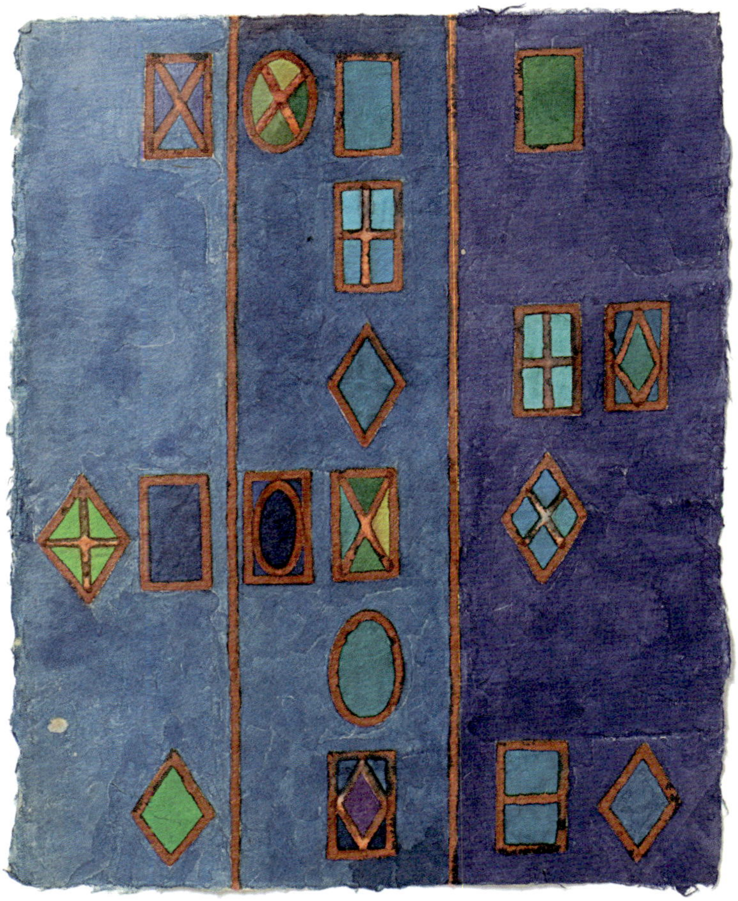

Untitled, from the series *Embroideries*
Sem título, da série *Bordados*
1960s
Watercolour on paper
35 x 28.7 cm
Museu de Arte Moderna de São Paulo,
donation of Zurich Brazil Seguros S.A.

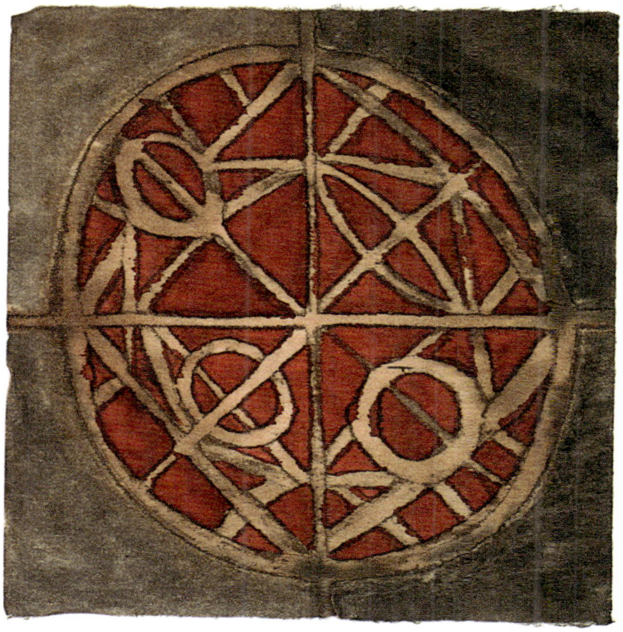

Untitled, from the series *Embroideries*
Sem título, da série *Bordados*
1960s
Watercolour on rice paper
15.3 x 15.3 cm
mira schendel estate

Untitled (Facade)
Sem título (Fachada)
1960s
Oil on jute
91 x 91 cm
Luisa Malzoni Strina

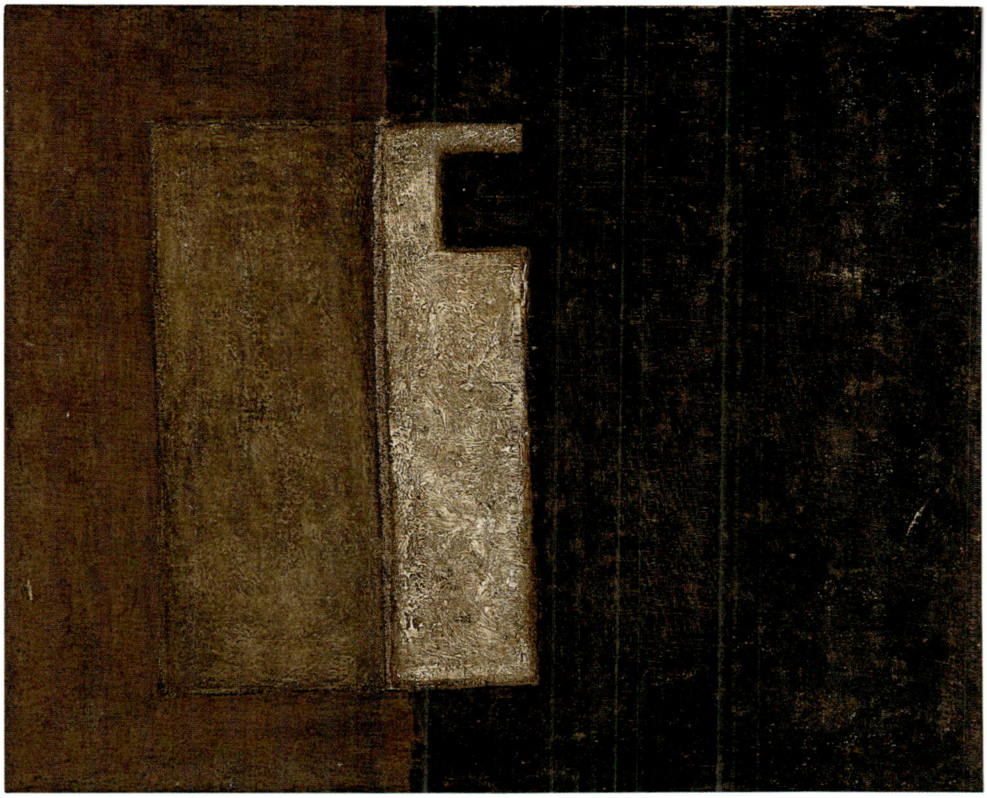

Untitled
Sem título
1963
Tempera on canvas
81 x 101 cm
Private collection

Untitled
Sem título
1964
Tempera on canvas
100 x 50 cm
Marcos Ribeiro Simon Collection

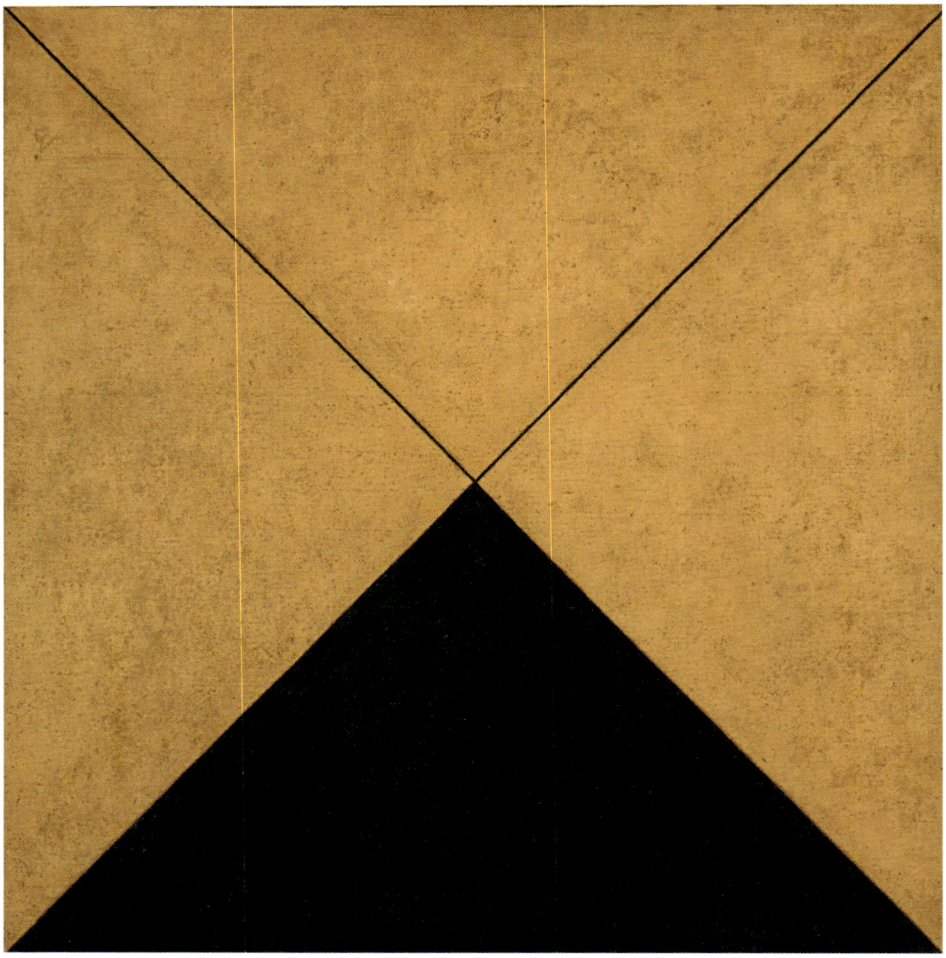

Untitled
Sem título
1962
Oil on canvas
74.9 x 74.7 cm
The Museum of Fine Arts, Houston,
The Adolpho Leirner Collection
of Brazilian Constructive Art,
museum purchase

Untitled (Abstract)
Sem título (Abstração)
1962
Tempera on canvas
75 x 75 cm
Private collection

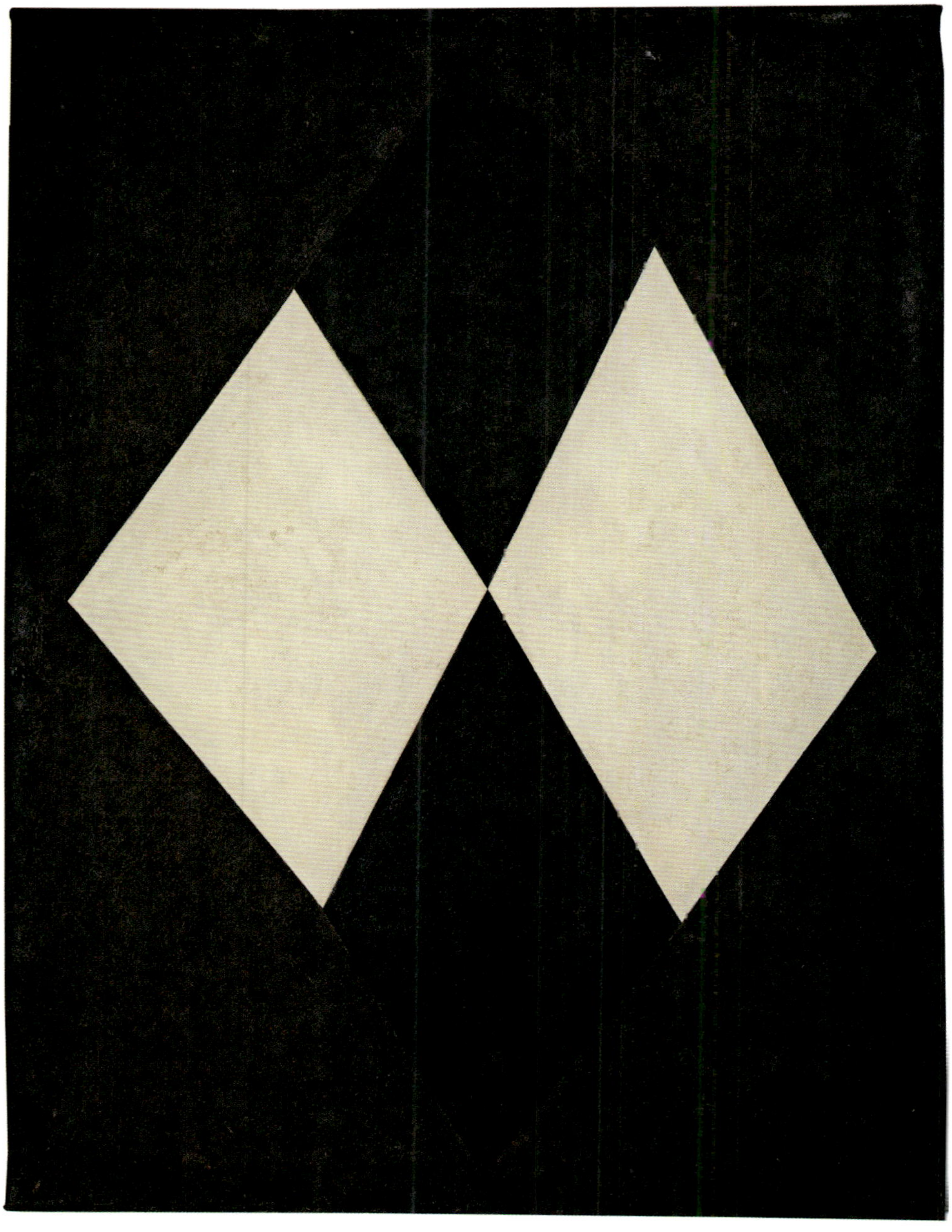

Untitled
Sem título
1963
Oil on canvas
145.9 x 114 cm
Tate. Presented by Tate Members 2006

Untitled
Sem título
1960s
Latex and sand on canvas
79.8 x 99.8 cm
Museu de Arte Contemporânea
da Universidade de São Paulo,
São Paulo, Brazil

Untitled (Landscape)
Sem título (Paisagem)
1963
Tempera on canvas
76 x 150.5 cm
Orandi Momesso Collection

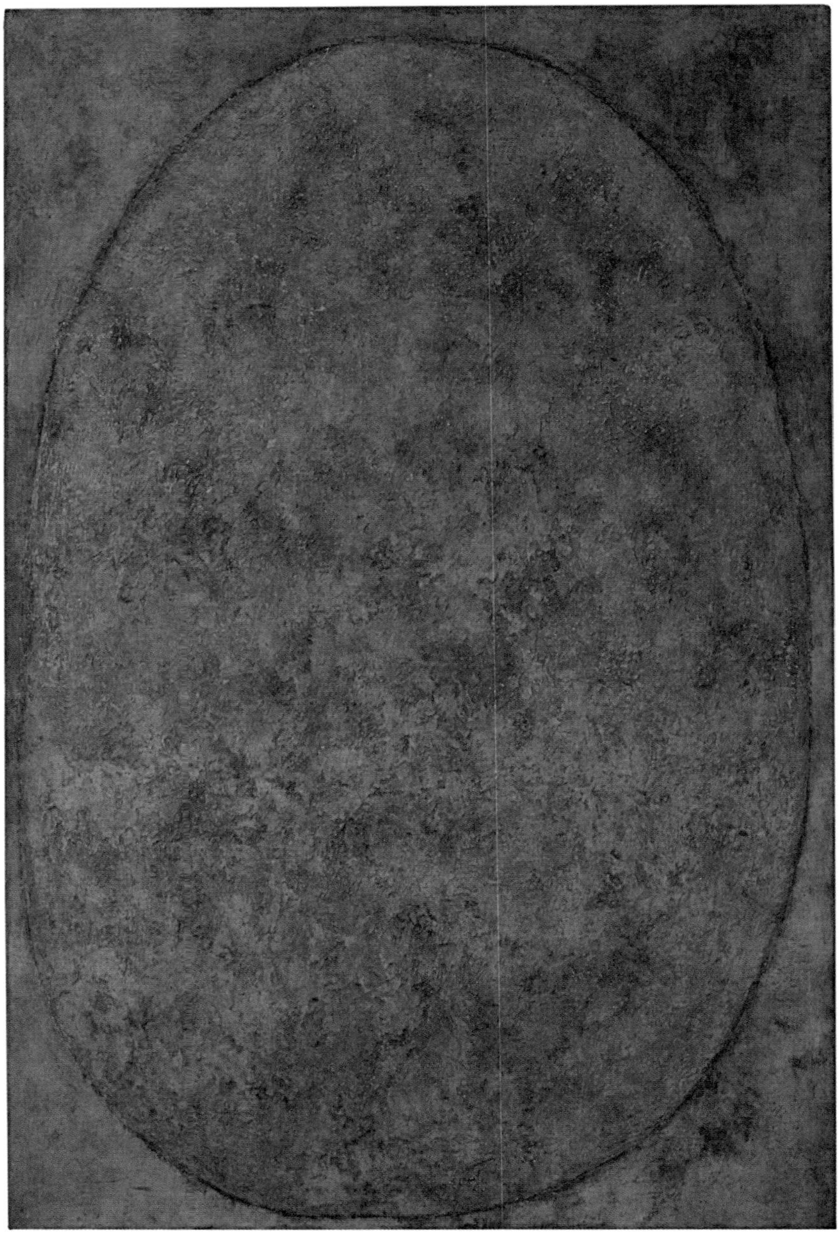

Untitled (Egg)
Sem título (Ovo)
1963
Tempera and plaster on wood
132 x 90 cm
Private collection

Untitled
Sem título
1963
Tempera and plaster on canvas
100 x 100 cm
Hecilda and Sergio Fadel

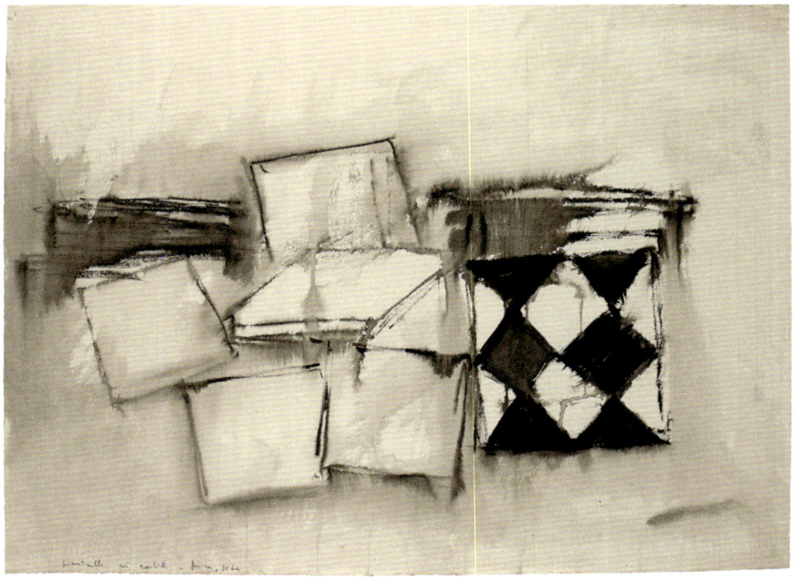

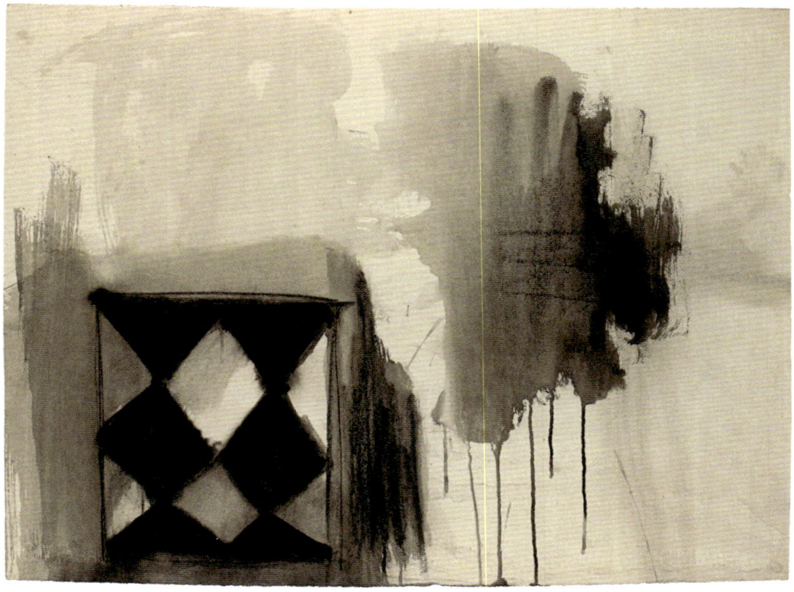

Untitled
Sem título
1964
Ink on paper
each 48 x 66.3 cm
mira schendel estate

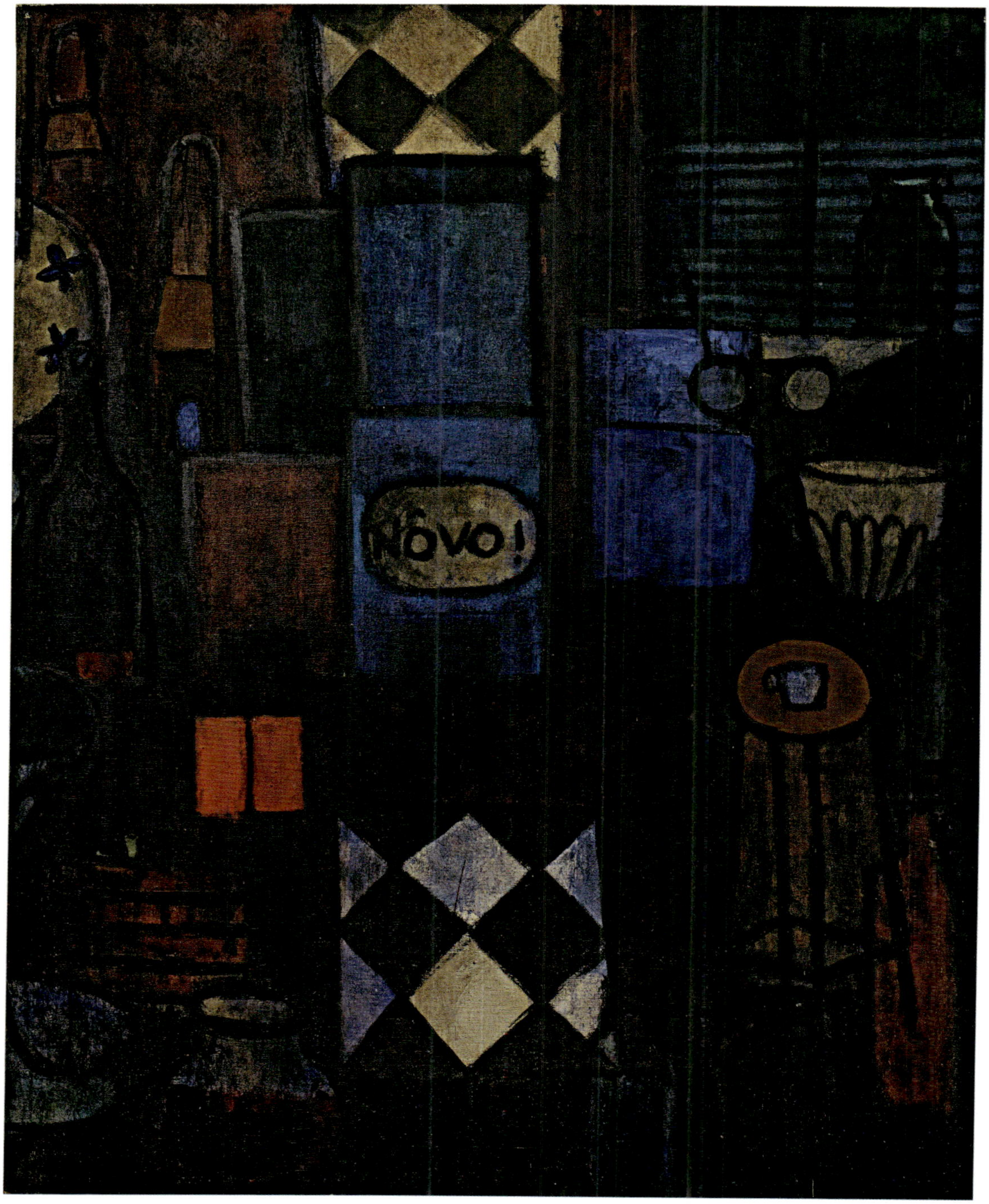

Untitled
Sem título
c.1964
Oil on canvas
115.8 x 94.8 cm
mira schendel estate

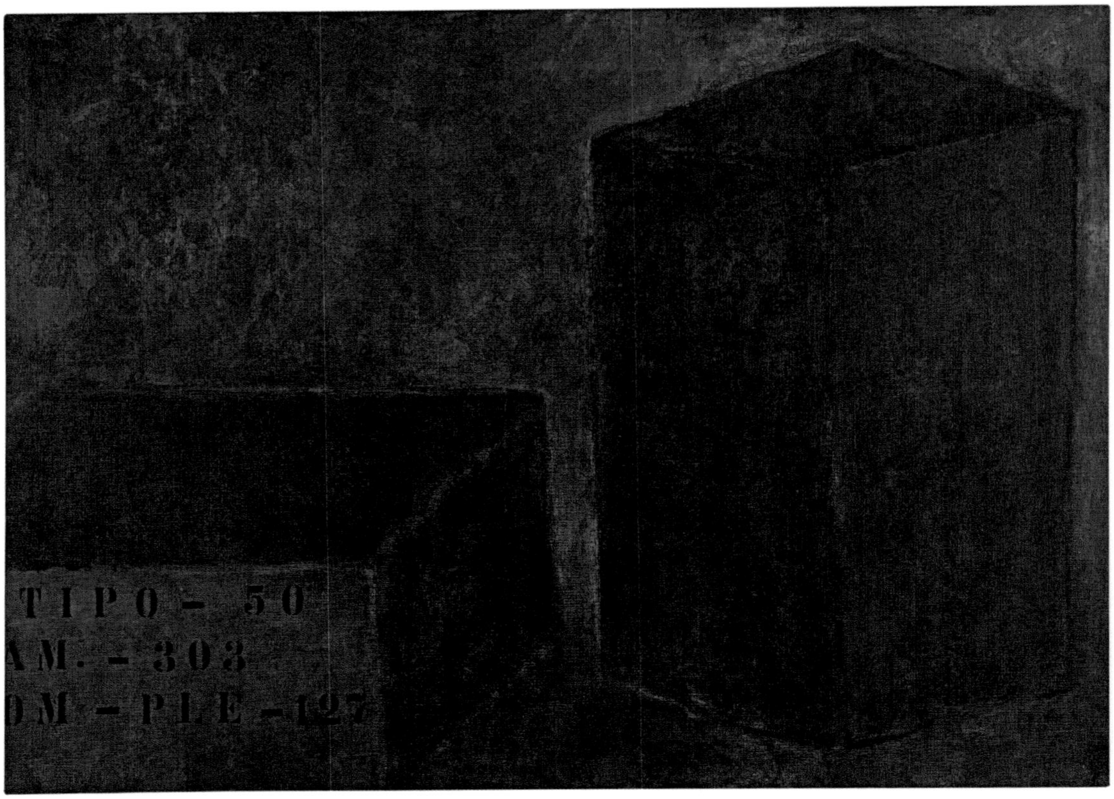

Untitled
Sem título
c.1964
Oil on canvas
92 x 130 cm
Marta and Marcio Lobão Collection

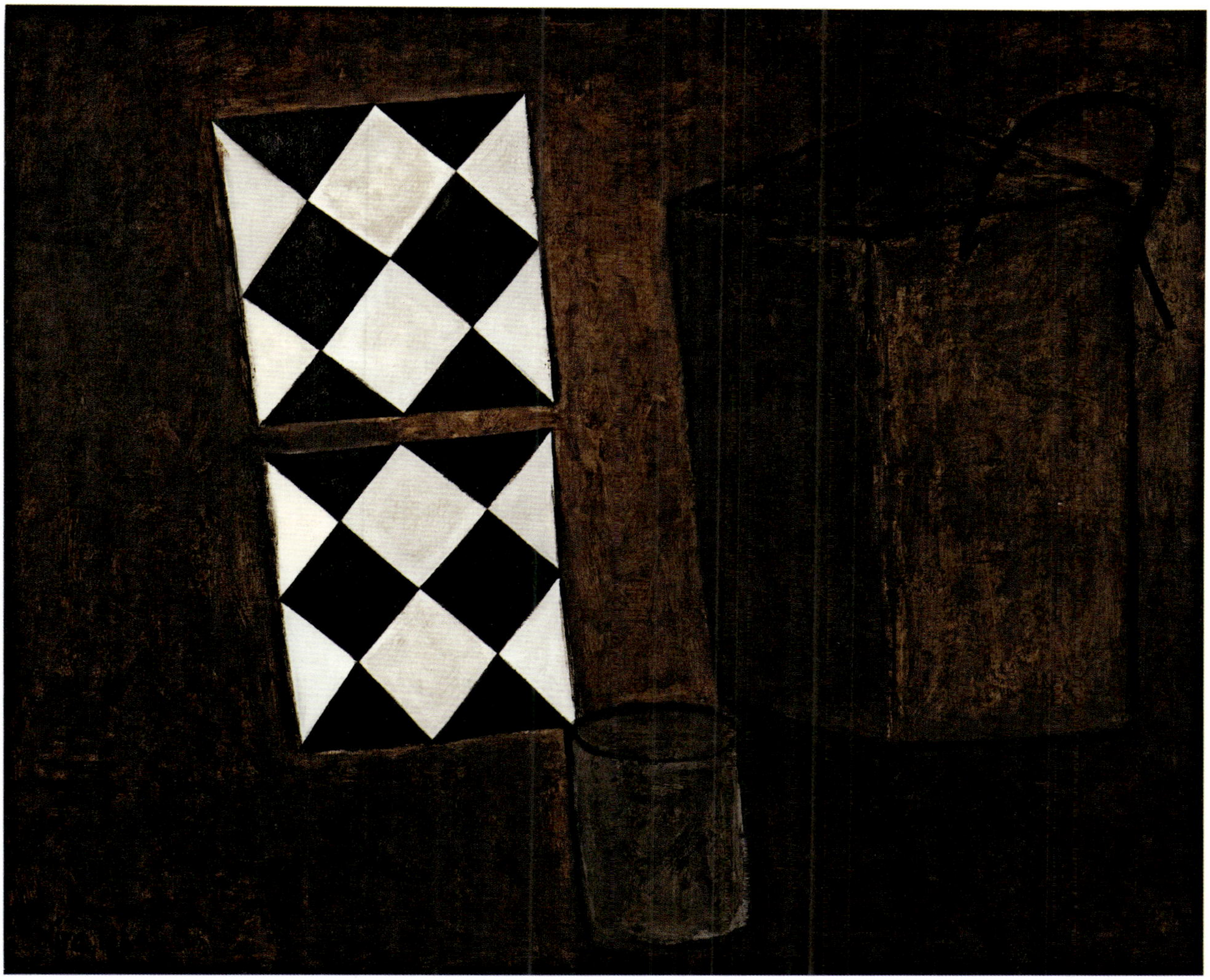

Untitled
Sem título
1964
Oil on canvas
130 x 162 cm
Orandi Momesso Collection

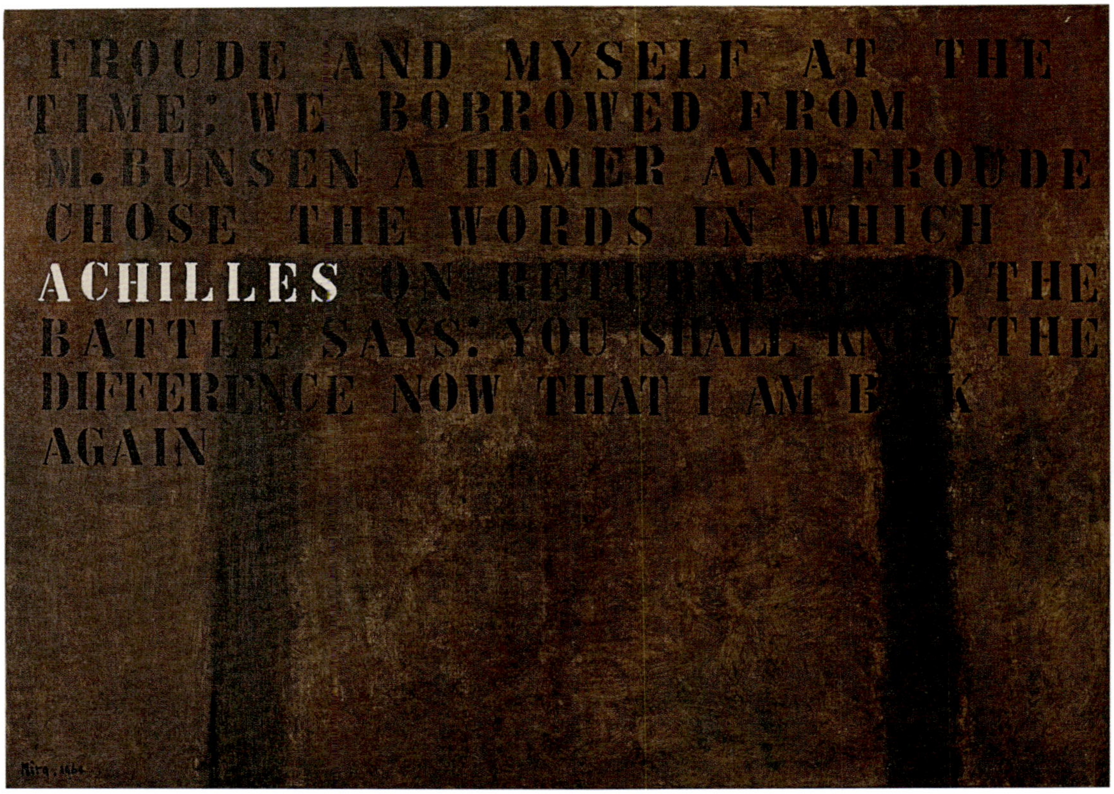

The Return of Achilles I
O Retorno de Aquiles I
1964
Oil on canvas
93 x 132 cm
Private collection

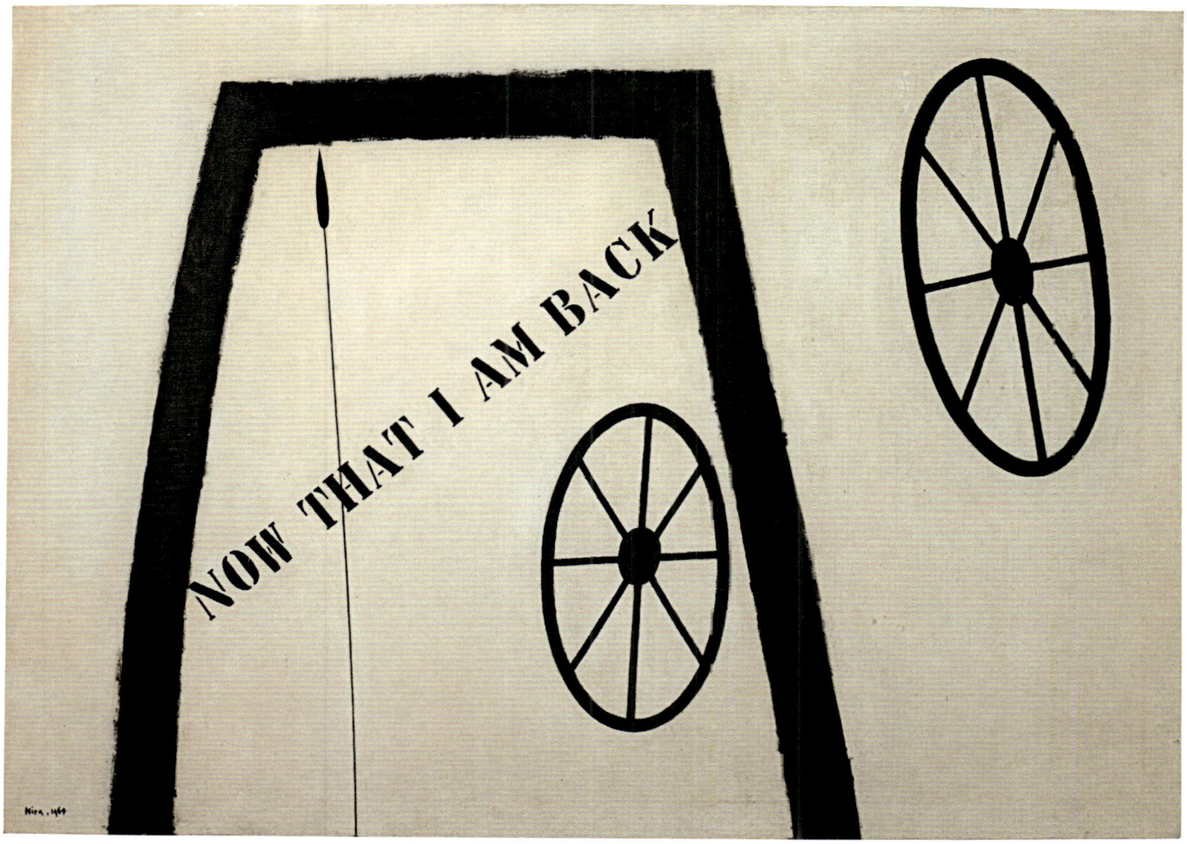

The Return of Achilles
O Retorno de Aquiles
1964
Oil on canvas
93.4 x 130 cm
mira schendel estate

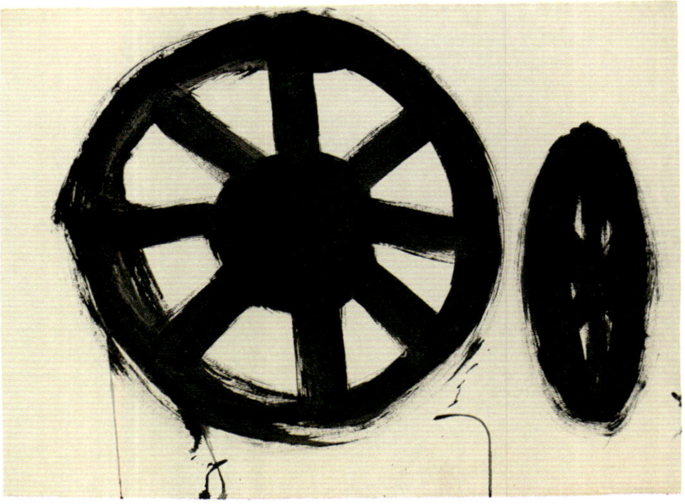

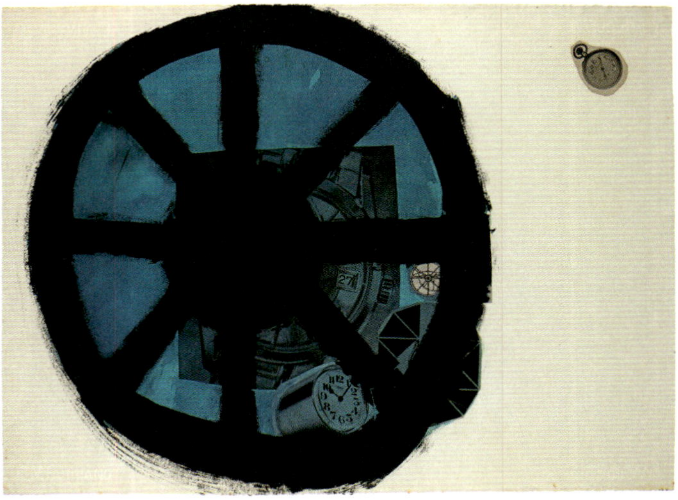

Untitled
Sem título
c.1963–4
Ink and collage on paper
each 48.4 x 66.5 cm
mira schendel estate

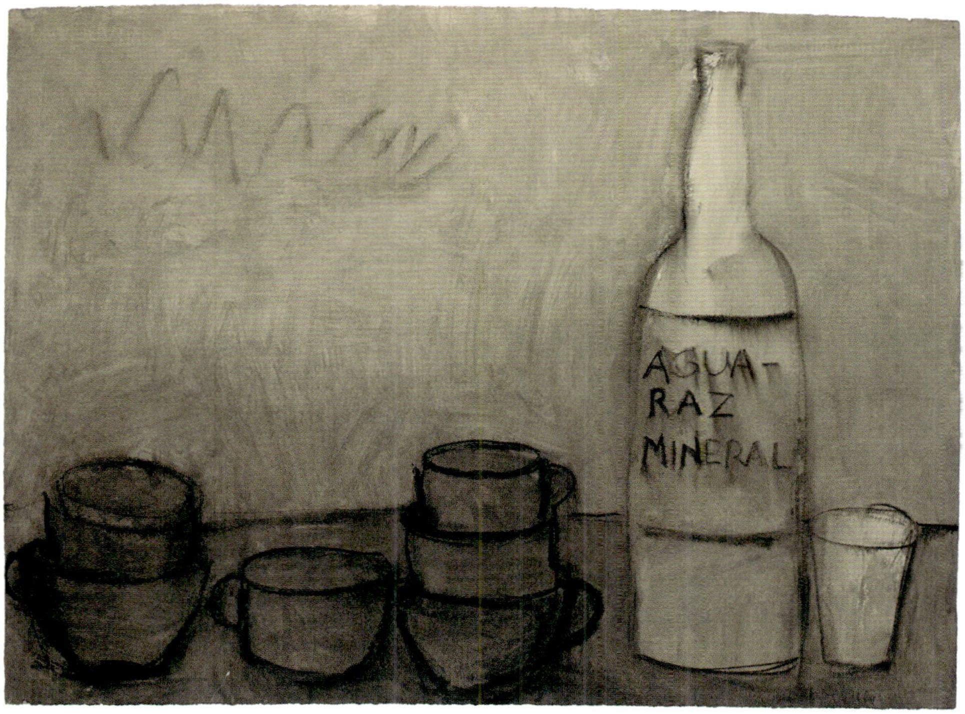

Untitled
Sem título
1964
Ink on paper
48.5 x 66.5 cm
mira schendel estate

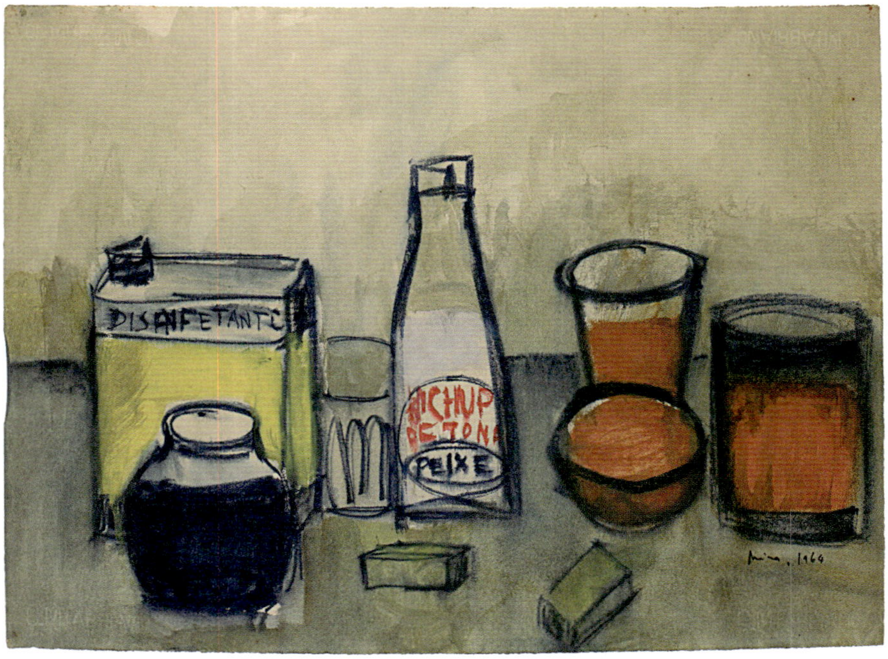

Untitled
Sem título
1964
Watercolour on paper
48.7 x 66.5 cm
mira schendel estate

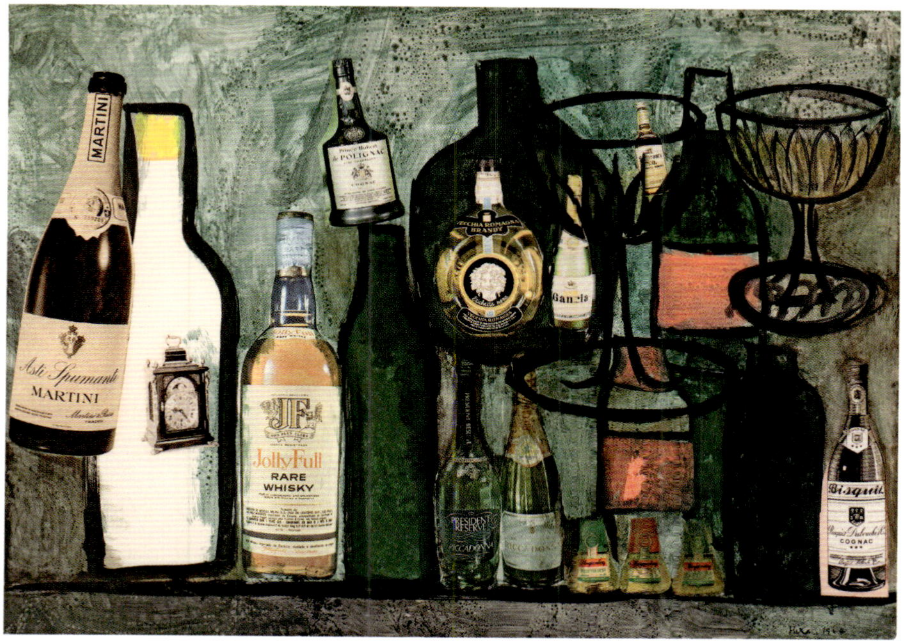

Untitled
Sem título
1960s
Collage, watercolour and ink on paper
50 x 70 cm
Private collection

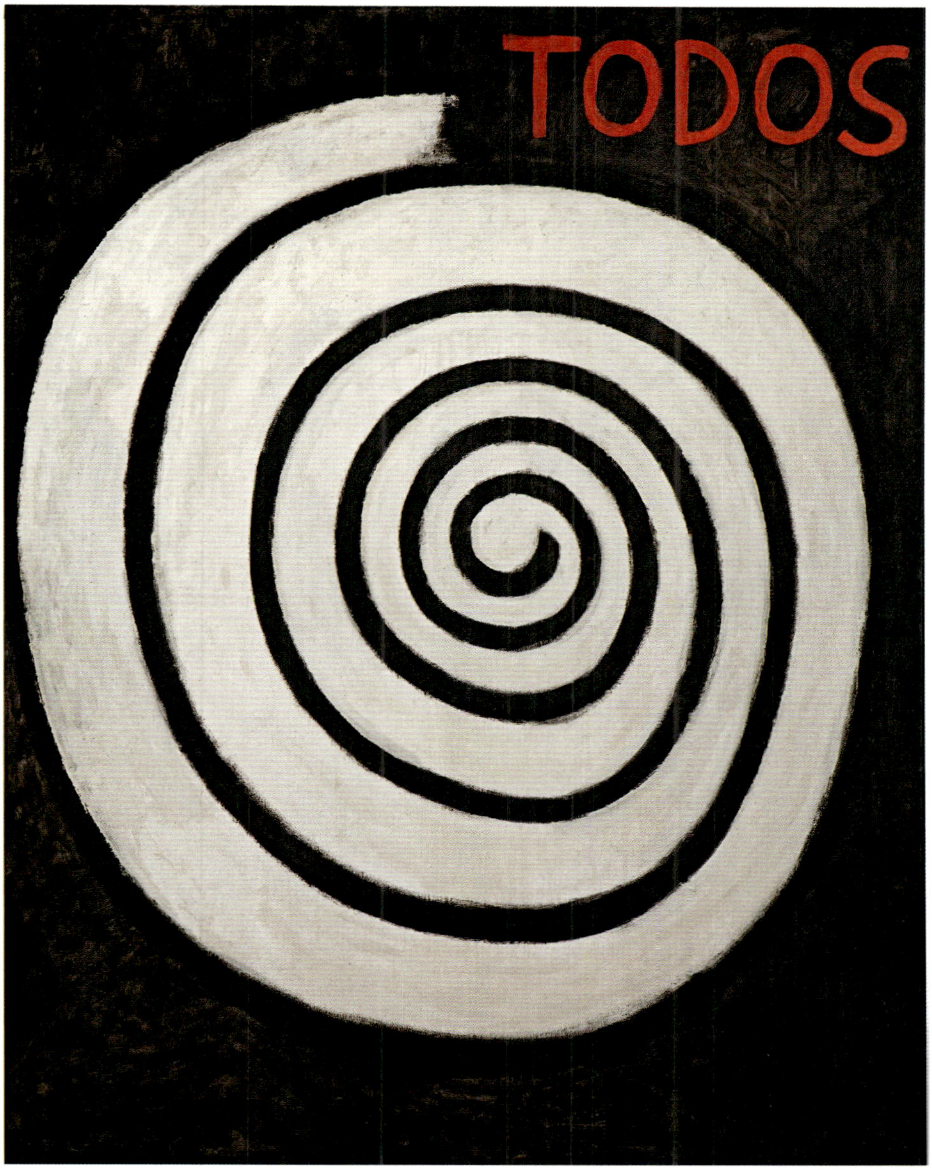

Untitled (All)
Sem título (Todos)
c.1964
Oil on canvas
162 x 132 cm
Jones Bergamin

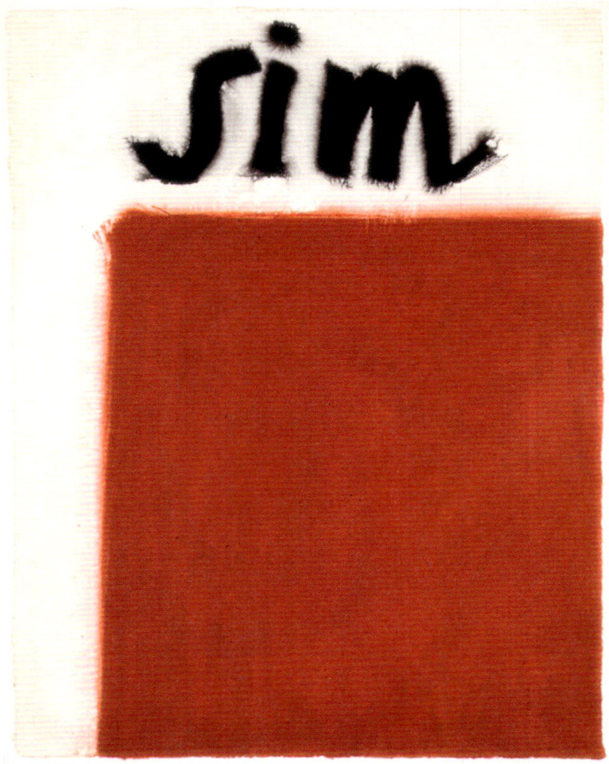

Untitled (Yes)
Sem título (Sim)
1960s
Watercolour and oil stick on paper
48 x 38 cm
Private collection

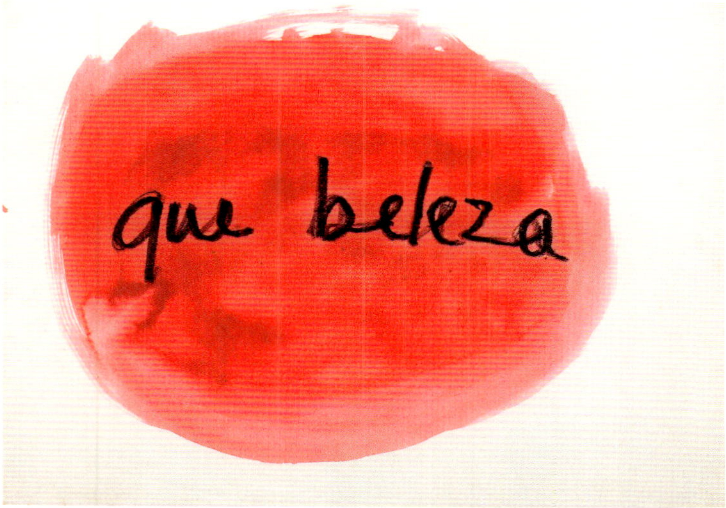

Untitled (How Beautiful)
Sem título (Que beleza)
1966
Watercolour and oil stick on paper
43 x 61.5 cm
Private collection

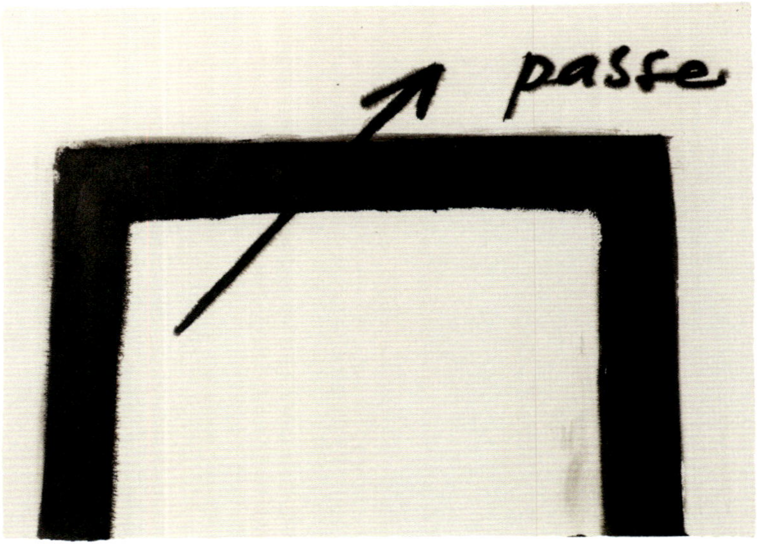

Untitled (Pass)
Sem título (Passe)
1965
Ink on paper
48 x 66 cm
Esther Faingold

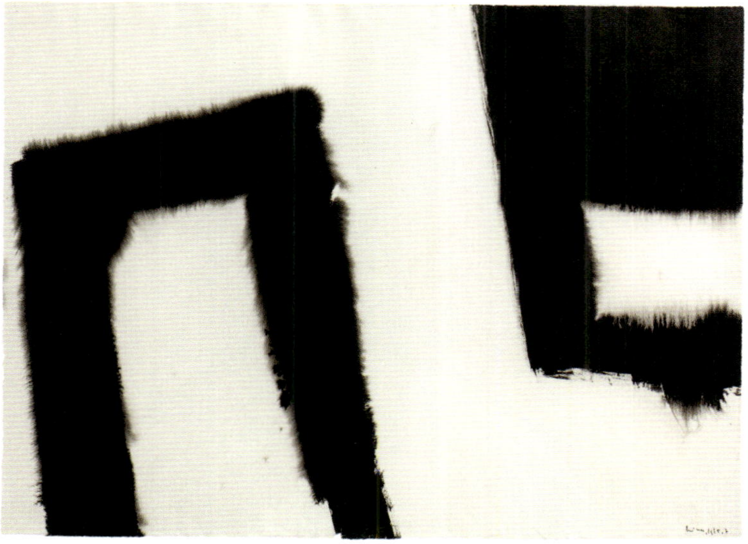

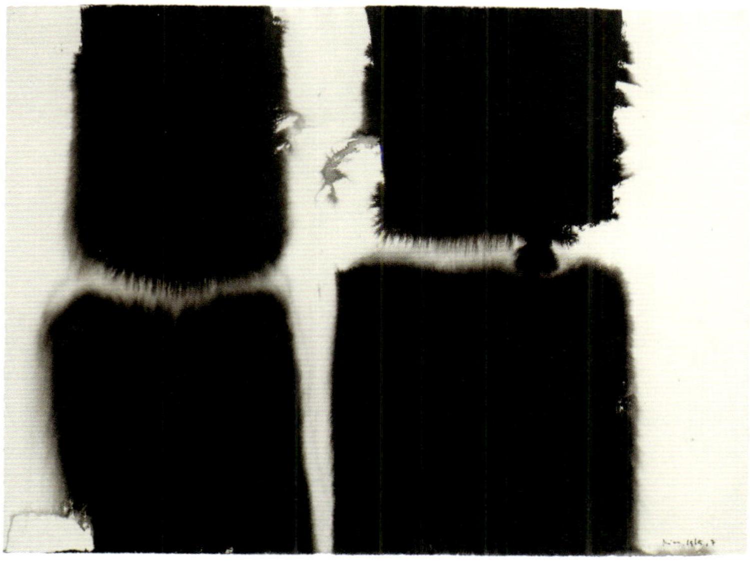

Untitled, from the series *Bombs*
Sem título, da série *Bombas*
1965
Ink on paper
each 48 x 66 cm
BBM Collection

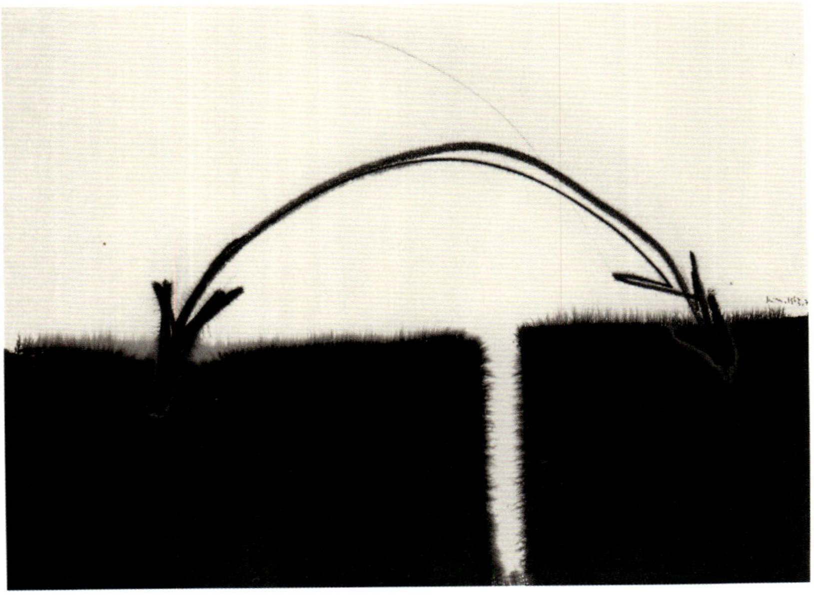

Untitled, from the series *Bombs*
Sem título, da série *Bombas*
1965
Ink on paper
47.9 x 65.4 cm
Colección Patricia Phelps de Cisneros

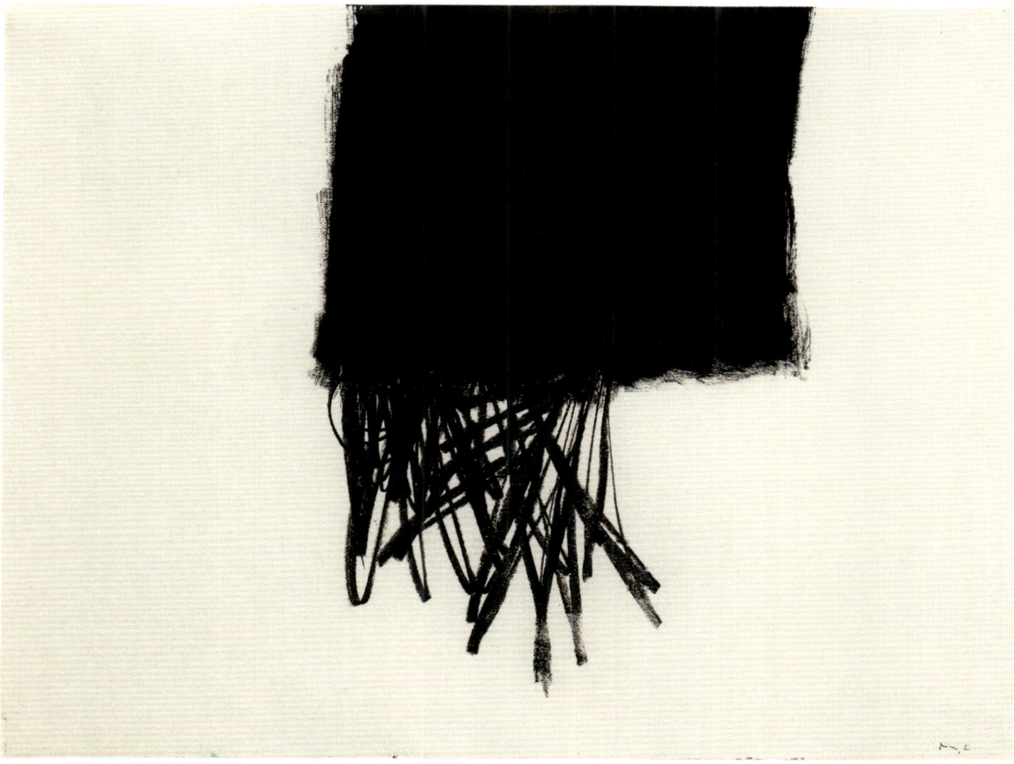

Untitled
Sem título
1965
Ink and crayon on paper
65.8 x 88.2 cm
Daros Latinamerica Collection, Zürich

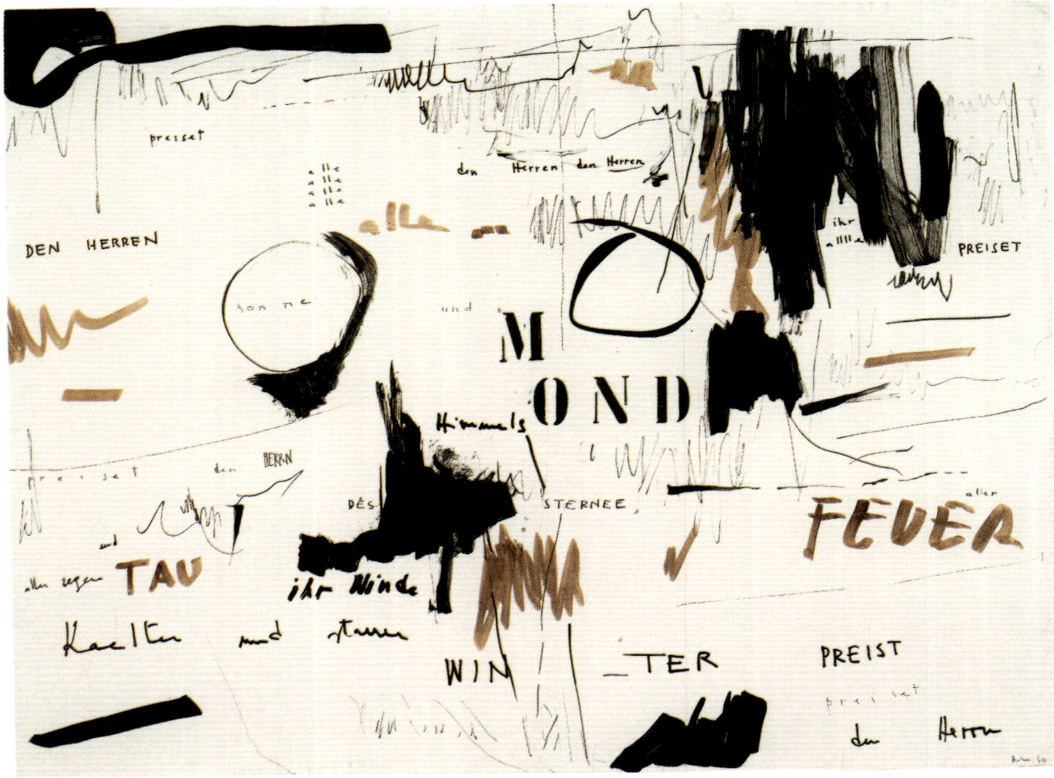

Untitled
Sem título
1964
Ink, gouache and graphite on paper
58 x 77 cm
Estrellita B. and Daniel Brodsky Collection

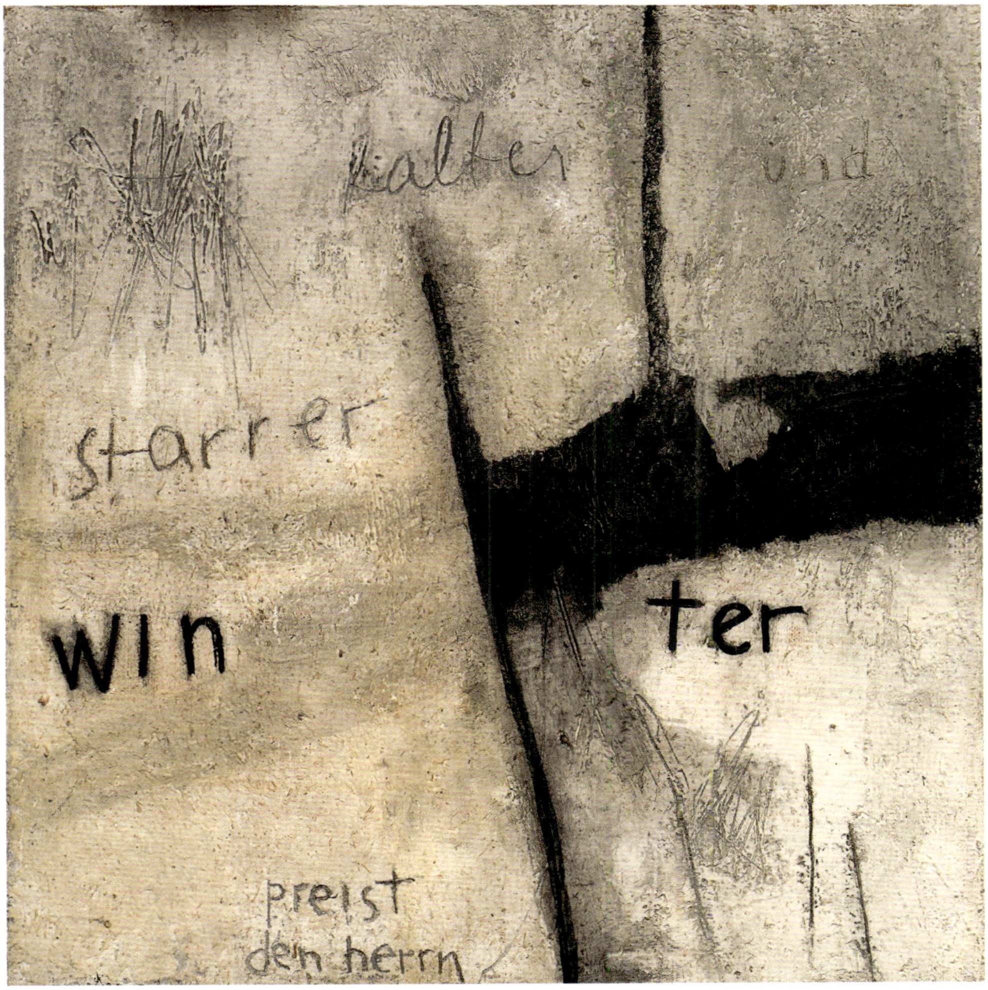

Untitled
Sem título
c.1963–5
Tempera on jute
50.5 x 50.5 cm
Private collection

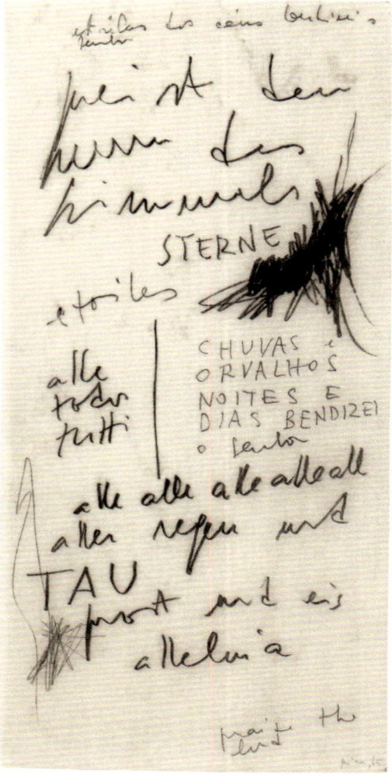
STERNE
CHUVAS e
ORVALHOS
NOITES E
DIAS BENDIZEI
TAU
alleluia

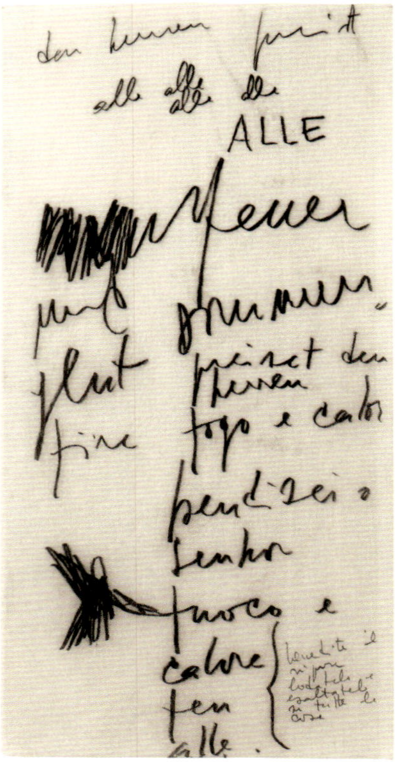
ALLE

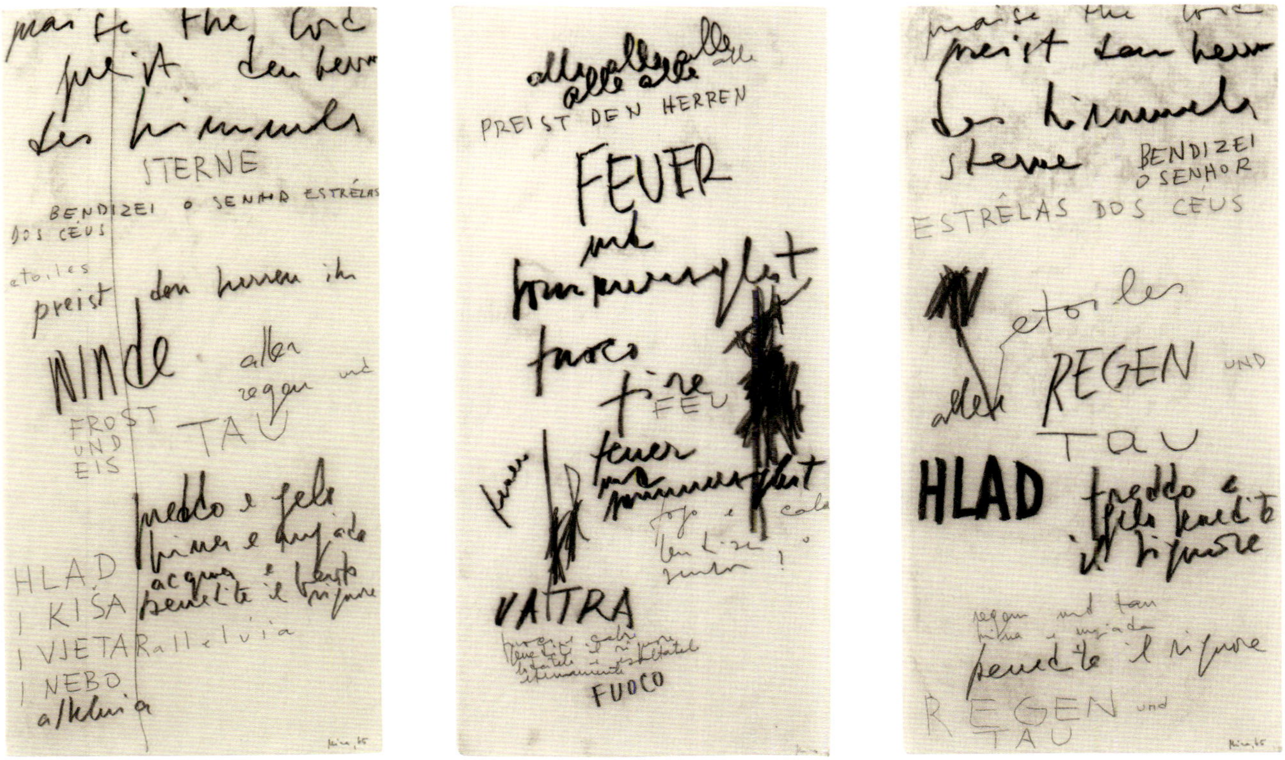

Untitled, from the series *Monotypes*
Sem título, da série *Monotipias*
1965
Oil on rice paper
5 parts: each 45 x 23 cm
Marcela and Israel Furmanovich

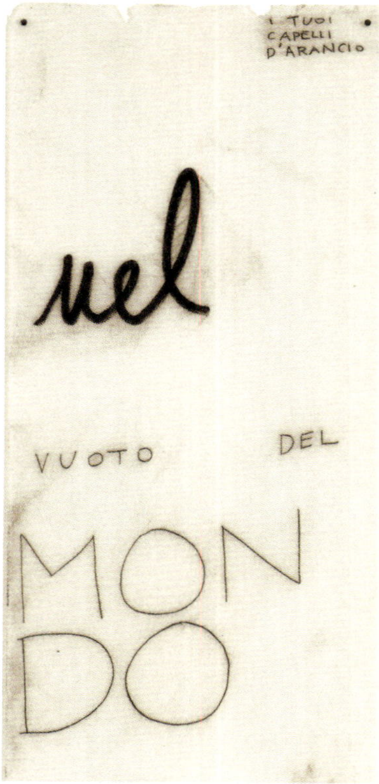
I TUOI
CAPELLI
D'ARANCIO
uel
VUOTO DEL
MON
DO

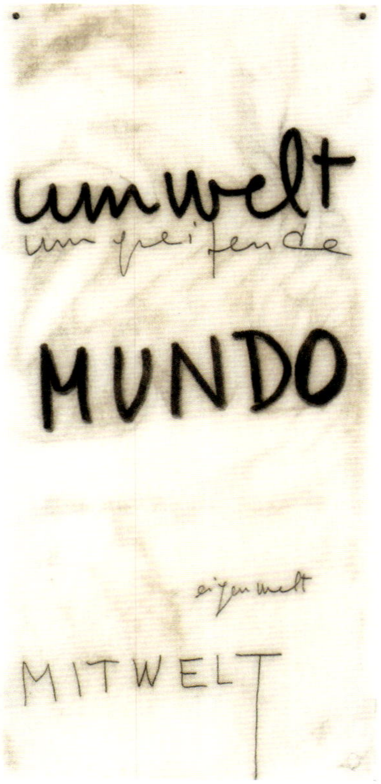
umwelt
umgreifende
MUNDO
eigenwelt
MITWELT

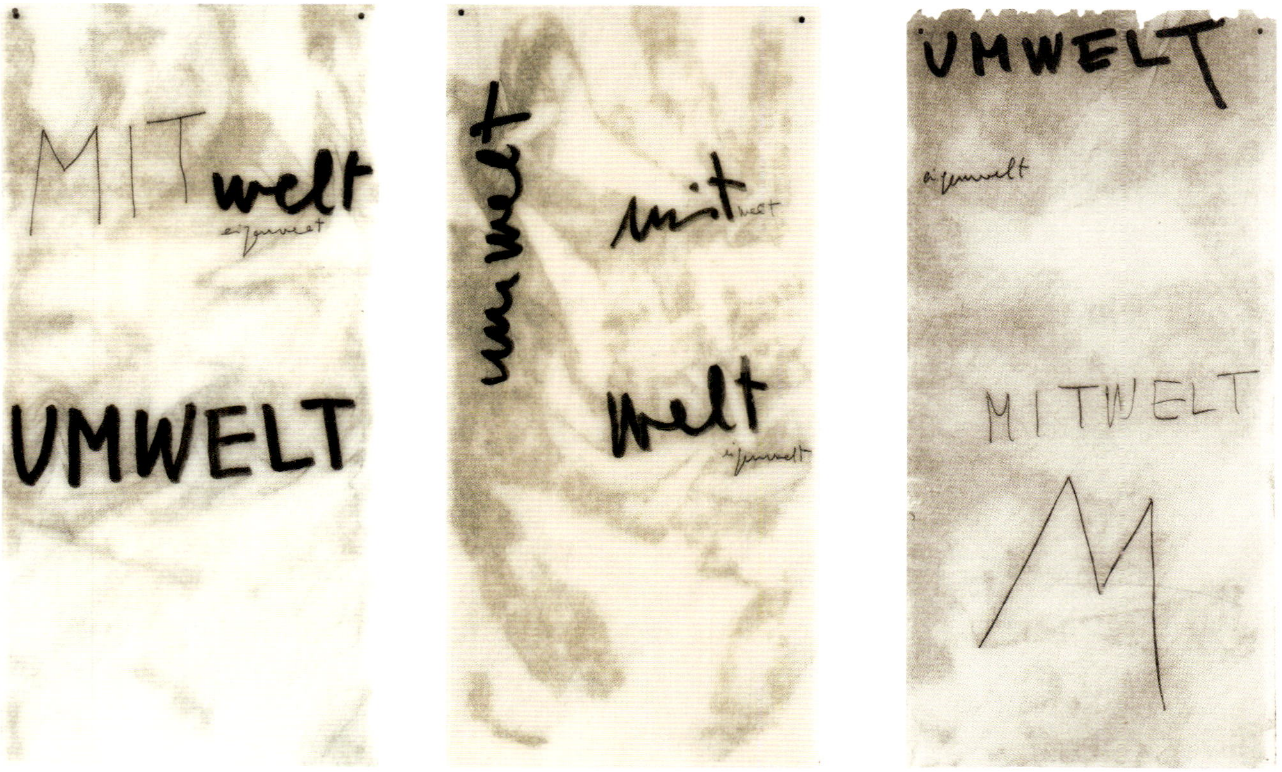

Untitled, from the series *Monotypes*
Sem título, da série *Monotipias*
1965
Oil on rice paper
5 parts: each 46 x 23 cm
Collection G. and J. Fainas

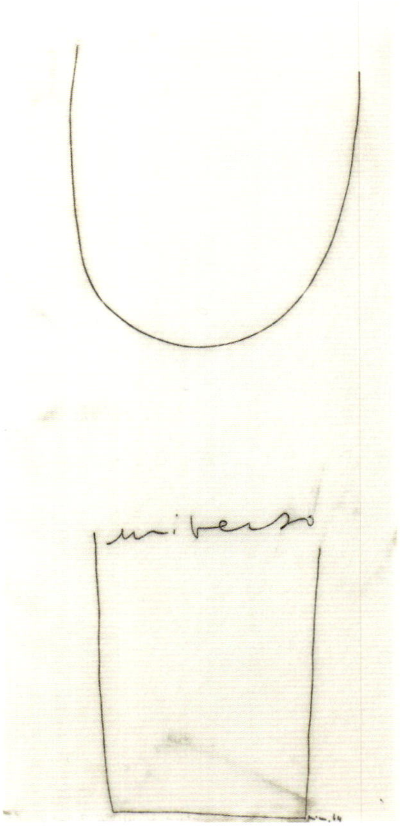

Untitled (Universe), from the series *Monotypes*
Sem título (Universo), da série *Monotipias*
1964
Oil on rice paper
47 x 23 cm
Museu de Arte Moderna de São Paulo,
donation of Paulo Figueiredo

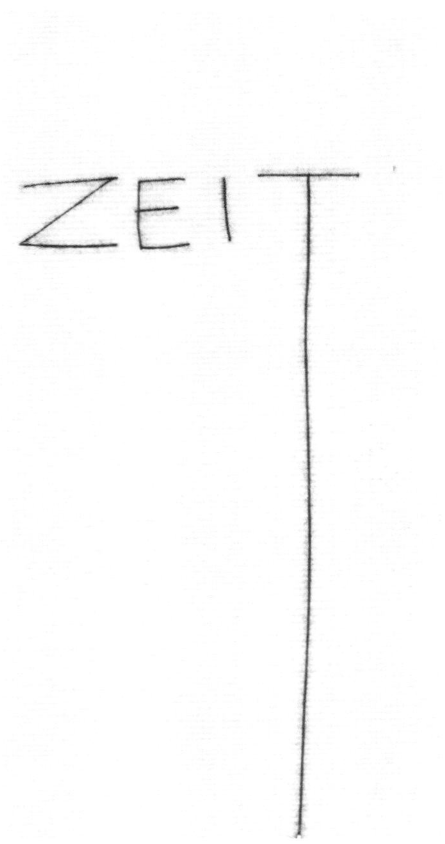

Untitled (Time), from the series *Monotypes*
Sem título (Zeit), da série *Monotipias*
1965
Oil on rice paper
47.4 x 23 cm
Inhotim Collection, Brazil

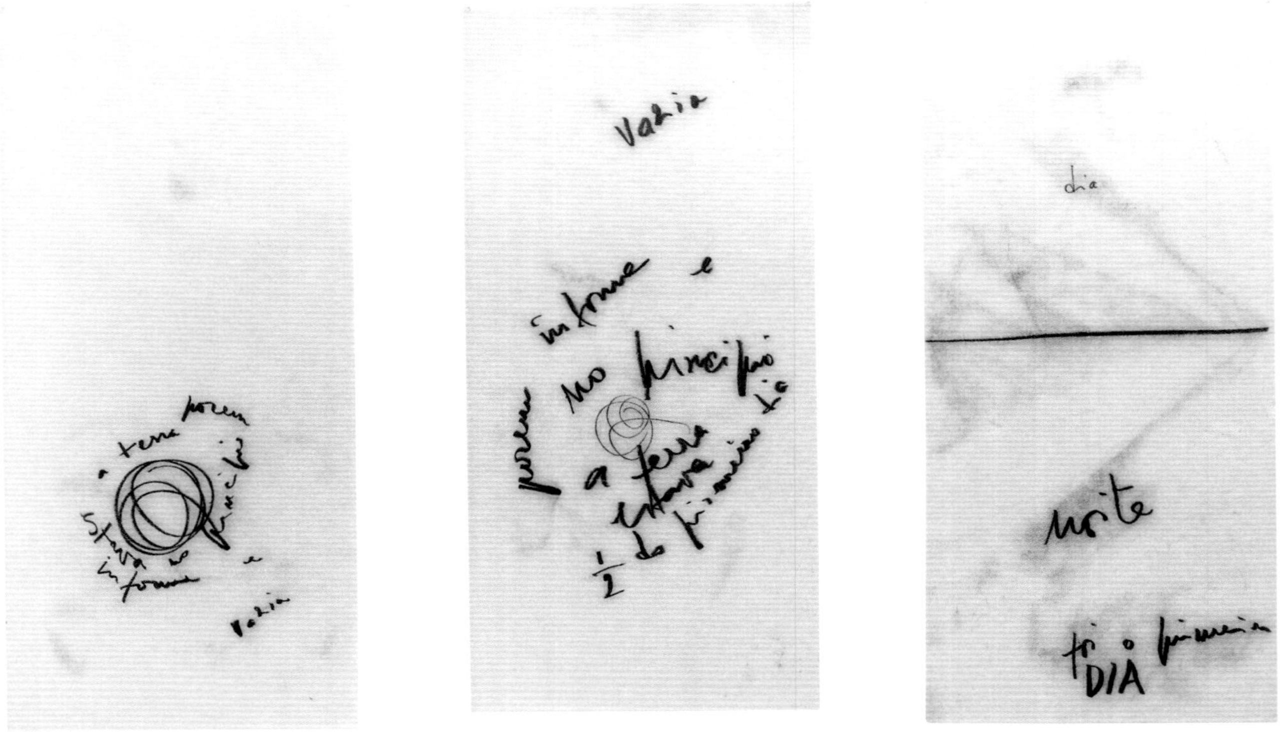

Genesis
Gênesis
1965
Oil on rice paper
9 parts: each 46.5 x 22.9 cm
Tate. Presented by the Tate Americas Foundation 2012

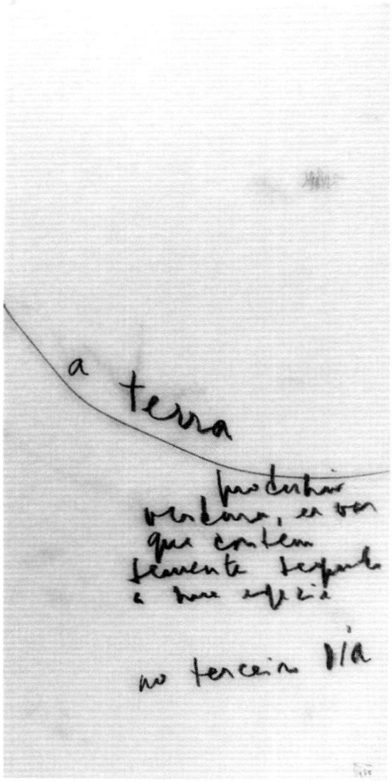
a terra
no terceiro DIA

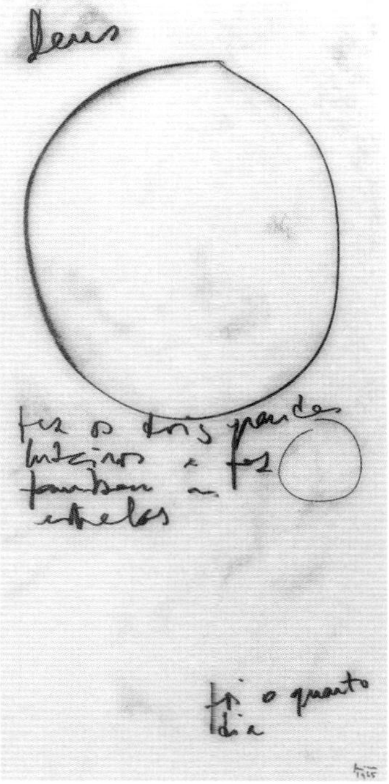
Deus
foi o quarto dia

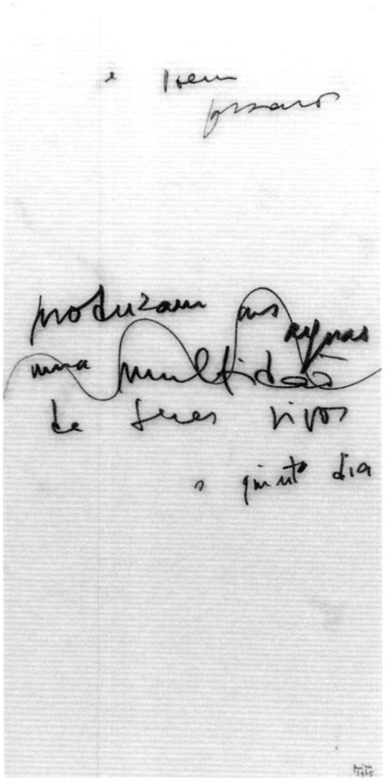
de seres vivos
o quinto dia

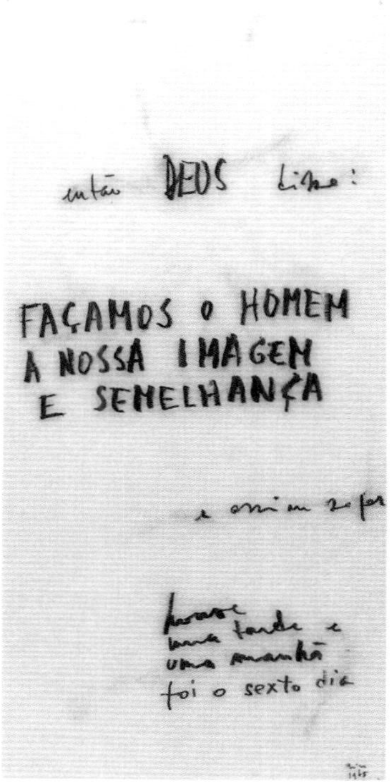
então DEUS disse:
FAÇAMOS O HOMEM
A NOSSA IMAGEM
E SEMELHANÇA
uma tarde e
uma manhã
foi o sexto dia

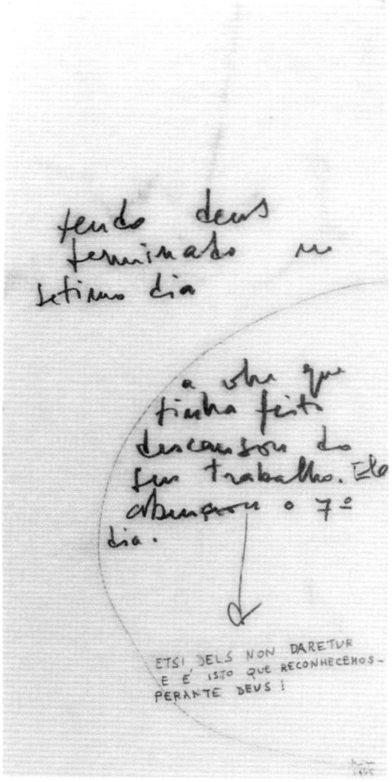
tendo deus
terminado no
sétimo dia
a obra que
tinha feito
descansou do
seu trabalho. Ele
abençoou o 7º
dia.
ETSI DEUS NON DARETUR
E É ISTO QUE RECONHECEMOS -
PERANTE DEUS !

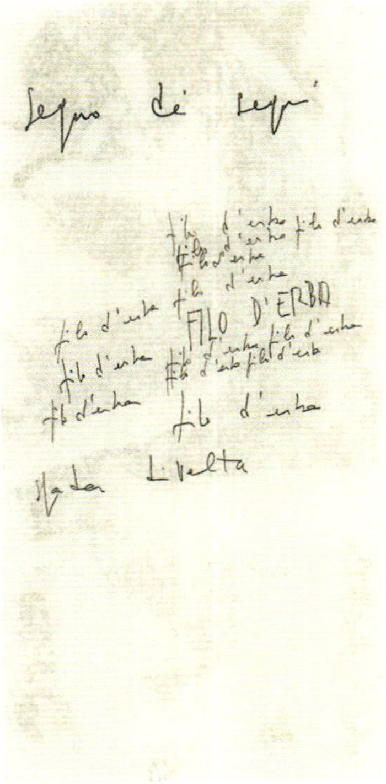
Segno dei segni
FILO D'ERBA

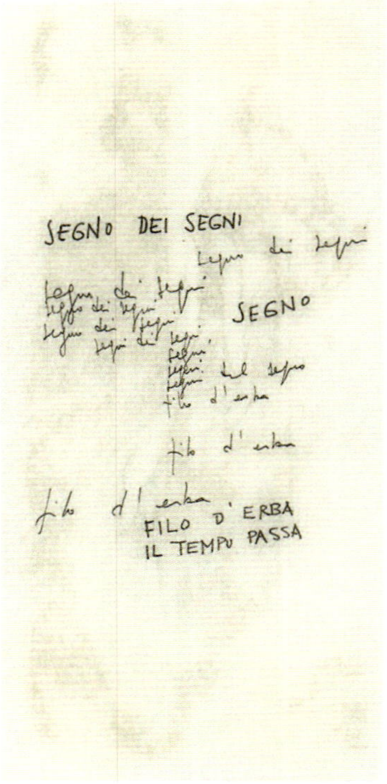
SEGNO DEI SEGNI
SEGNO
FILO D'ERBA
IL TEMPO PASSA

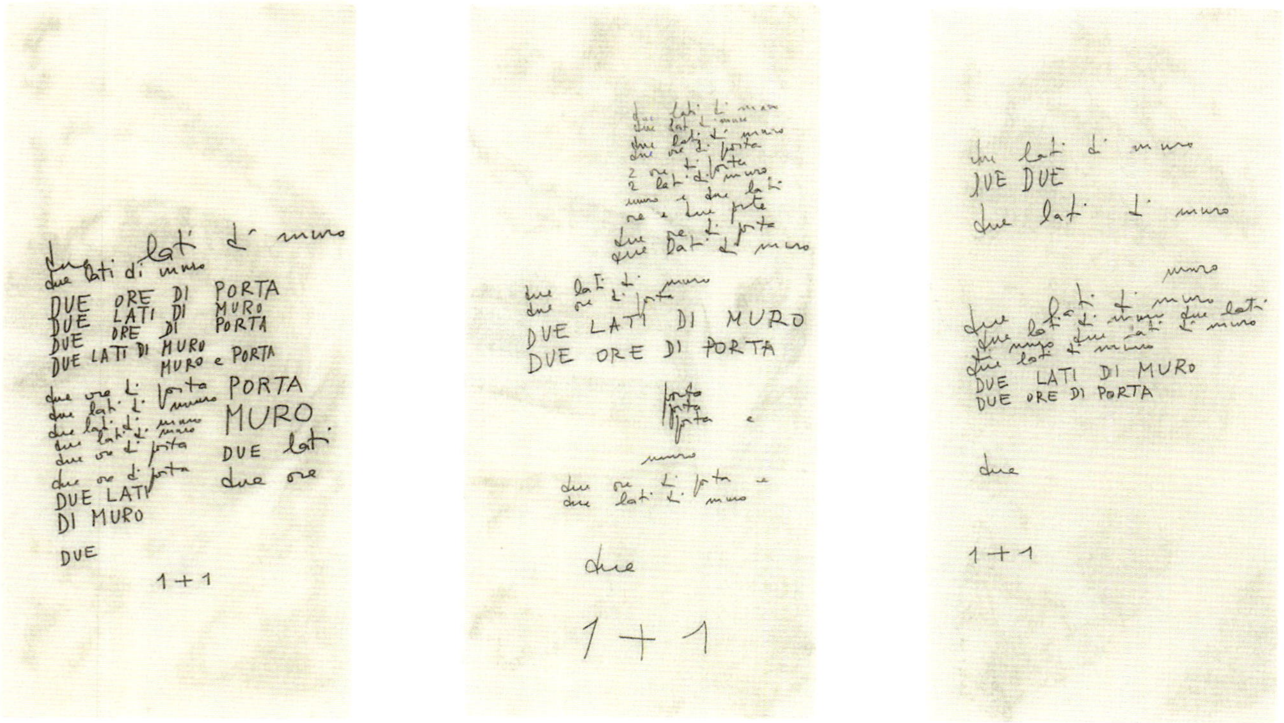

Sign of Signs
Segno dei Segni
1964–5
Oil on rice paper
5 parts: each 46 x 23 cm
The Museum of Modern Art, New York.
Latin American and Caribbean Fund, 2008

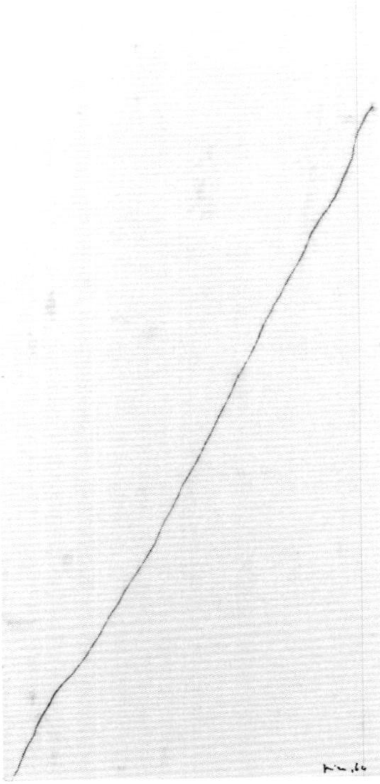

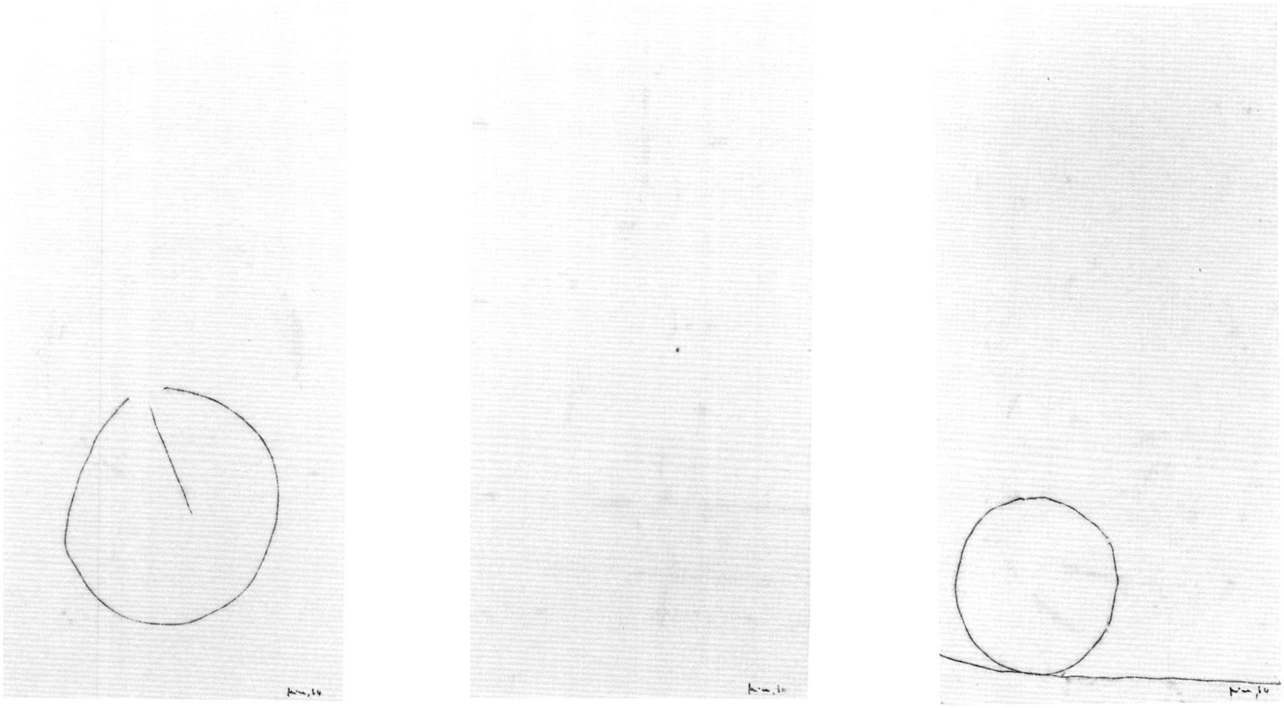

Untitled, from the series *Monotypes*
Sem título, da série *Monotipias*
1964
Oil on rice paper
each 47 x 23 cm
Instituto de Arte Contemporânea (IAC), São Paulo

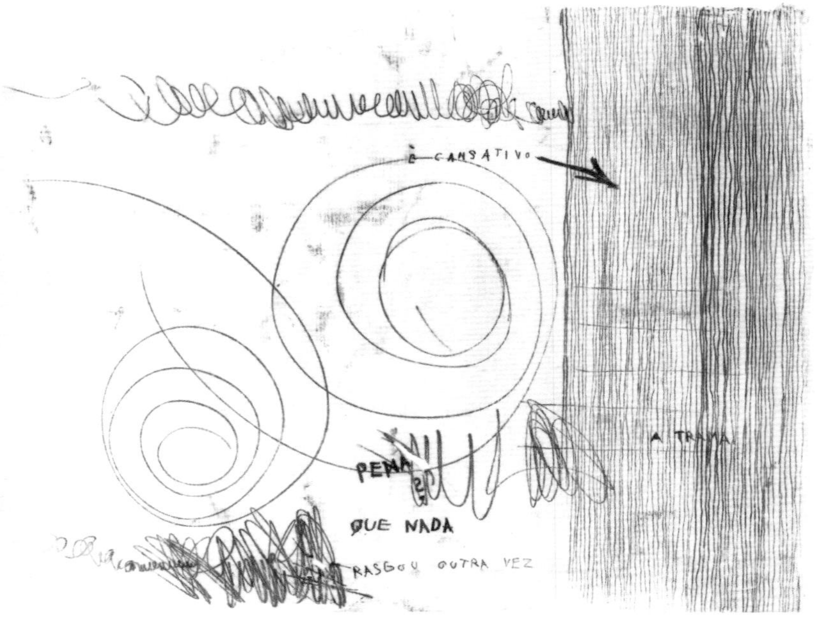

A Fabric Net
A trama
1960s
Oil on rice paper
45.1 x 62.2 cm
The Museum of Modern Art, New York.
Gift of Ada Schendel and the Latin American and Caribbean Fund, 2008

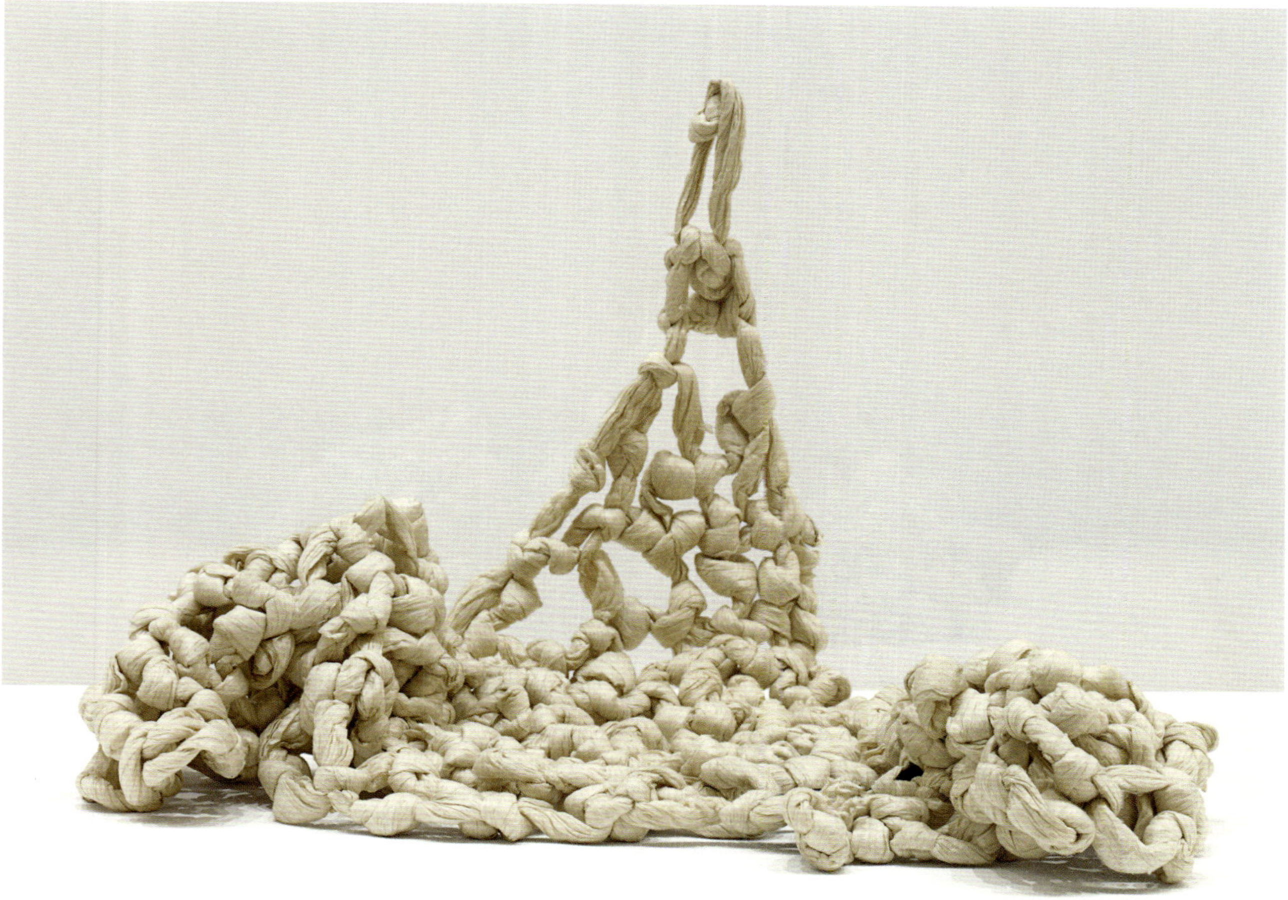

Untitled, from the series *Little Nothings*
Sem título, da série *Droguinhas*
c.1965–6
Rice paper
Dimensions variable, approx. 90 x 70 cm
The Museum of Modern Art, New York.
Scott Burton Fund, 2005

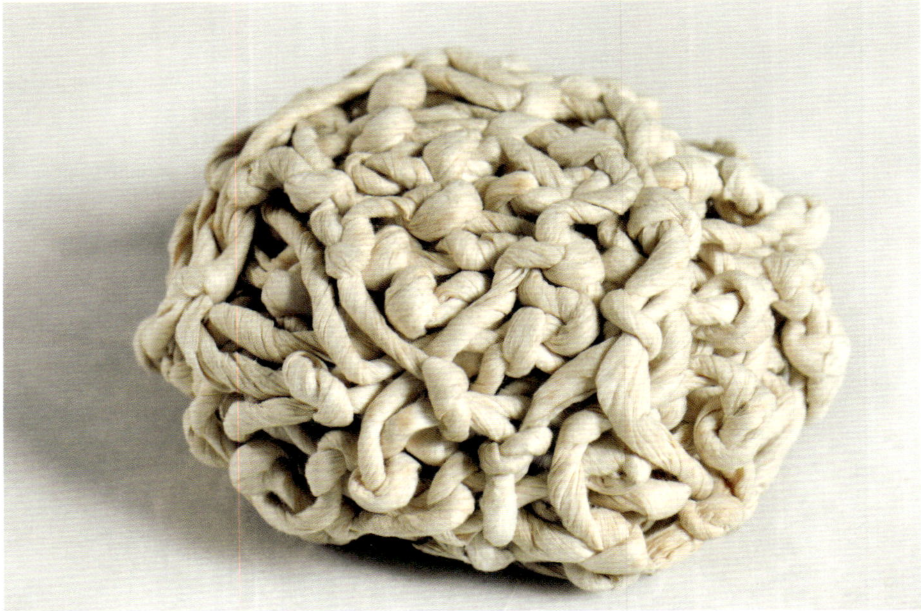

Untitled, from the series *Little Nothings*
Sem título, da série *Droguinhas*
1965
Rice paper
20 cm diameter
Private collection

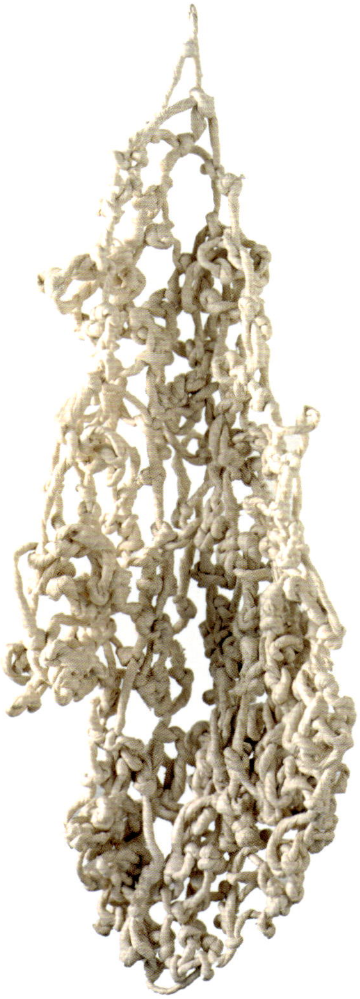

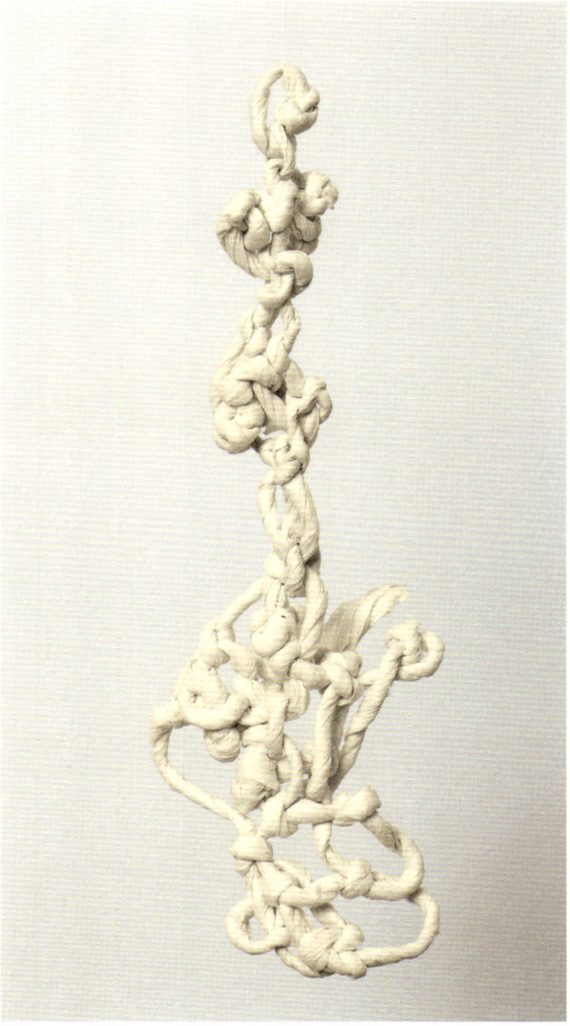

Untitled, from the series *Little Nothings*
Sem título, da série *Droguinhas*
1966
Rice paper
66.6 x 26 x 15.7 cm
Colección Patricia Phelps de Cisneros

Untitled, from the series *Little Nothings*
Sem título, da série *Droguinhas*
c.1965–6
Rice paper
Dimensions variable
Private collection

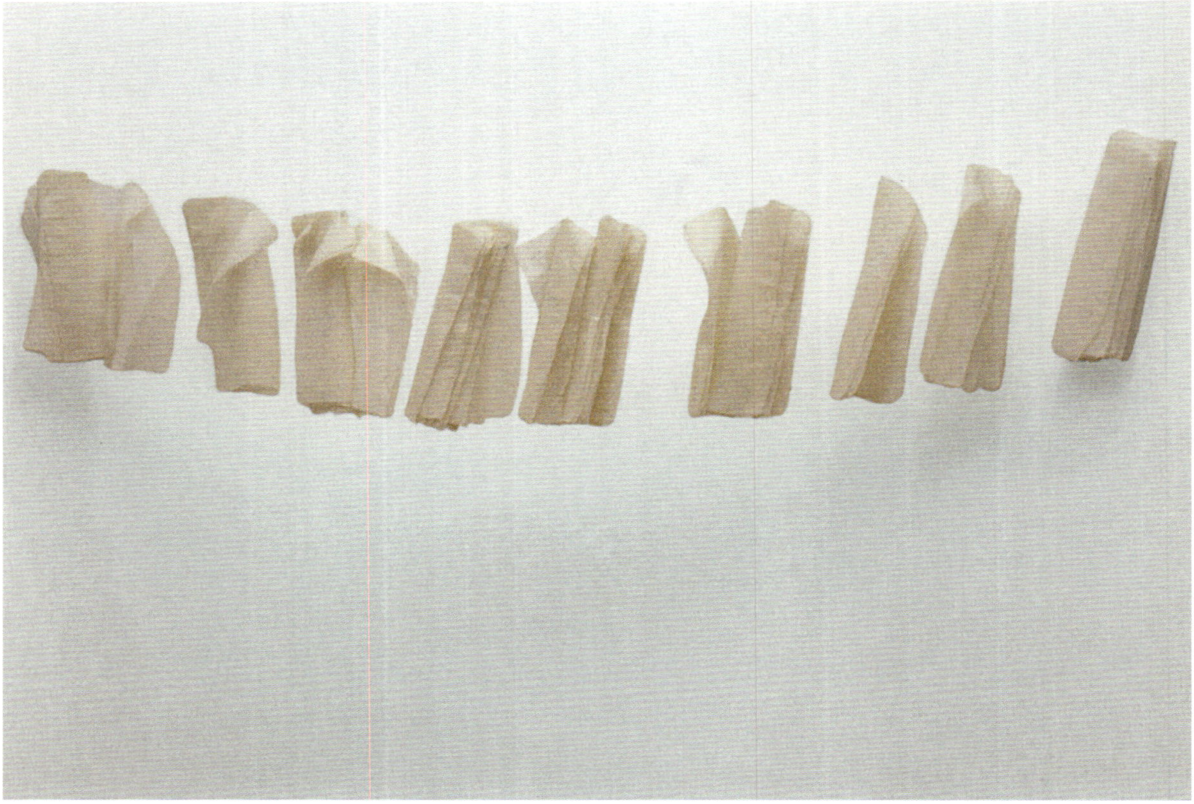

Little Train
Trenzinho
c.1965
114 sheets of rice paper and cotton thread
Dimensions variable
mira schendel estate

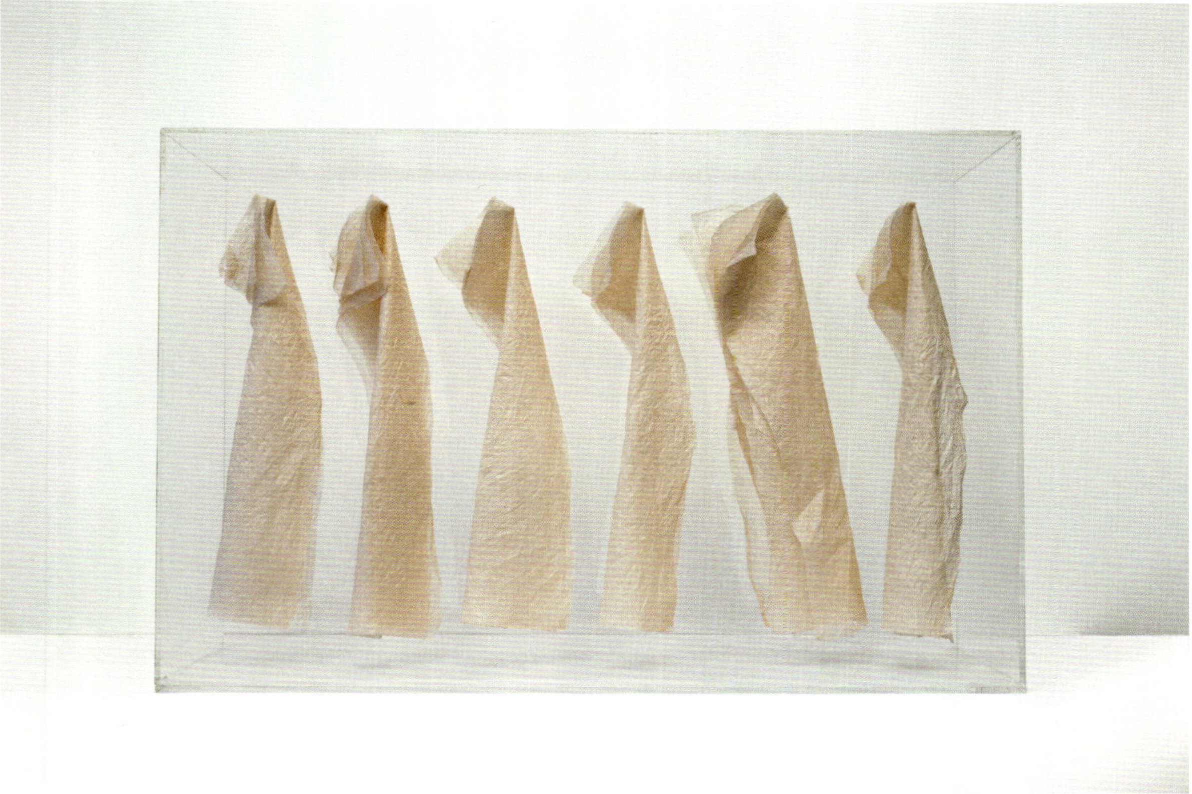

Little Train
Trenzinho
c.1965
Rice paper and cotton thread
46 x 65 x 15 cm
Collection Antonio Dias

Graphic Object
Objeto gráfico
1967–8
Oil on rice paper with acrylic
100 x 100 cm
Ernesto and Cecilia Poma Collection

Graphic Object
Objeto gráfico
1967–8
Oil on rice paper with acrylic
100 x 100 cm
Rose and Alfredo Setubal Collection

Graphic Object
Objeto gráfico
1967–8
Oil on rice paper with acrylic
100 x 100 cm
Marta and Paulo Kuczynski Collection

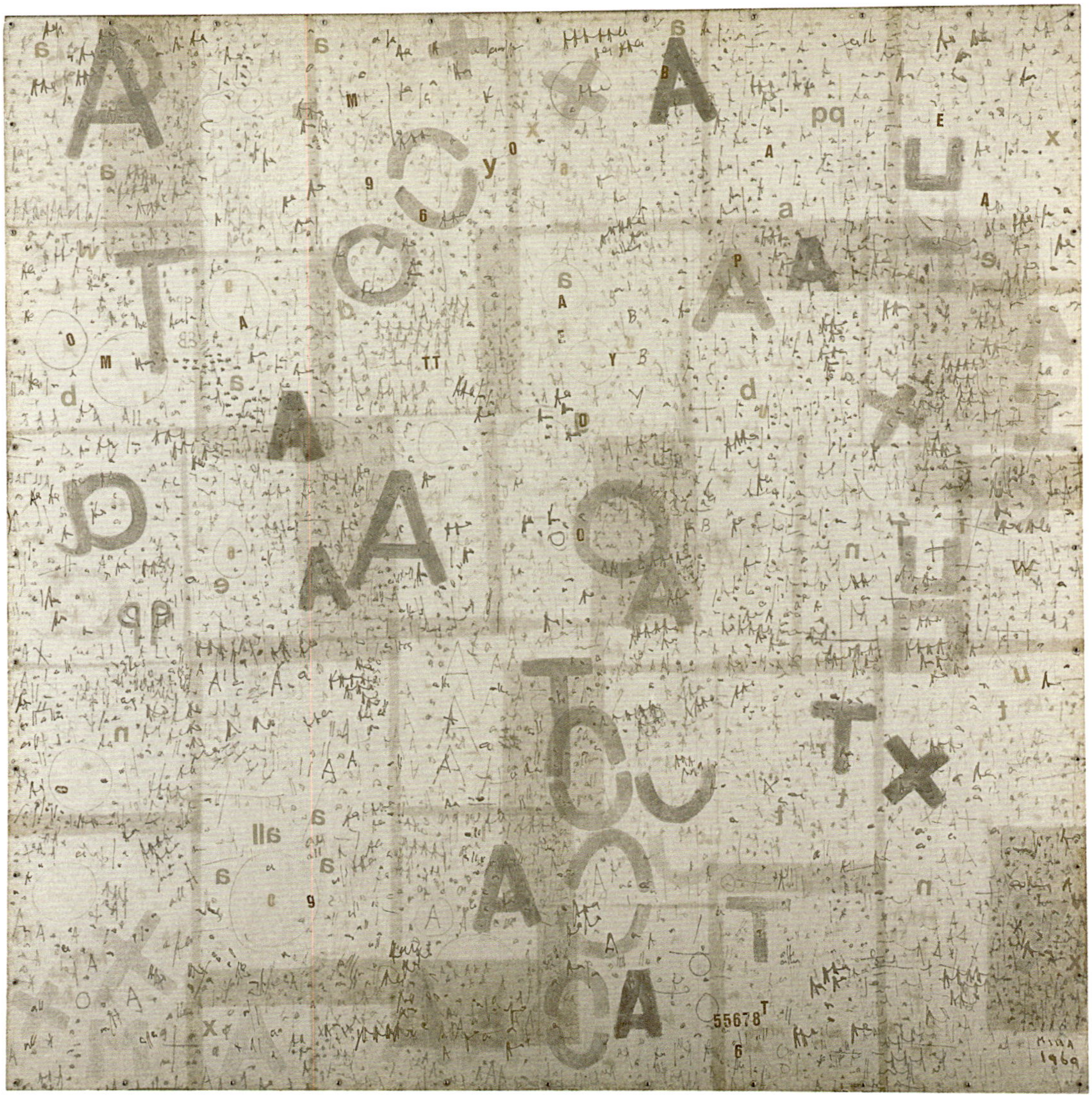

Graphic Object
Objeto gráfico
1969
Oil and transfer lettering on rice paper with acrylic
100 x 100 cm
Private collection

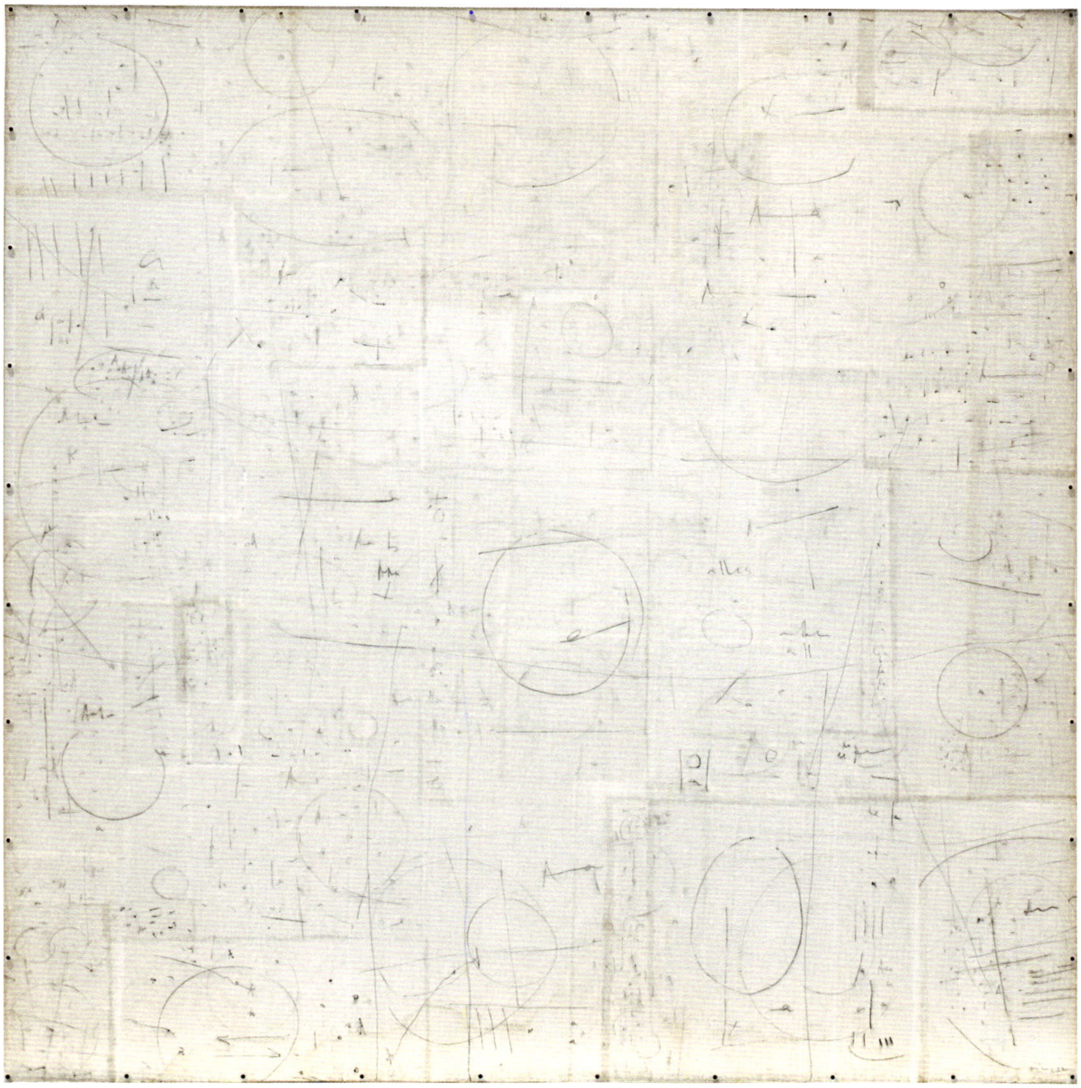

Graphic Object
Objeto gráfico
1972
Graphite on rice paper with acrylic
97.8 x 97.8 cm
FEMSA Collection

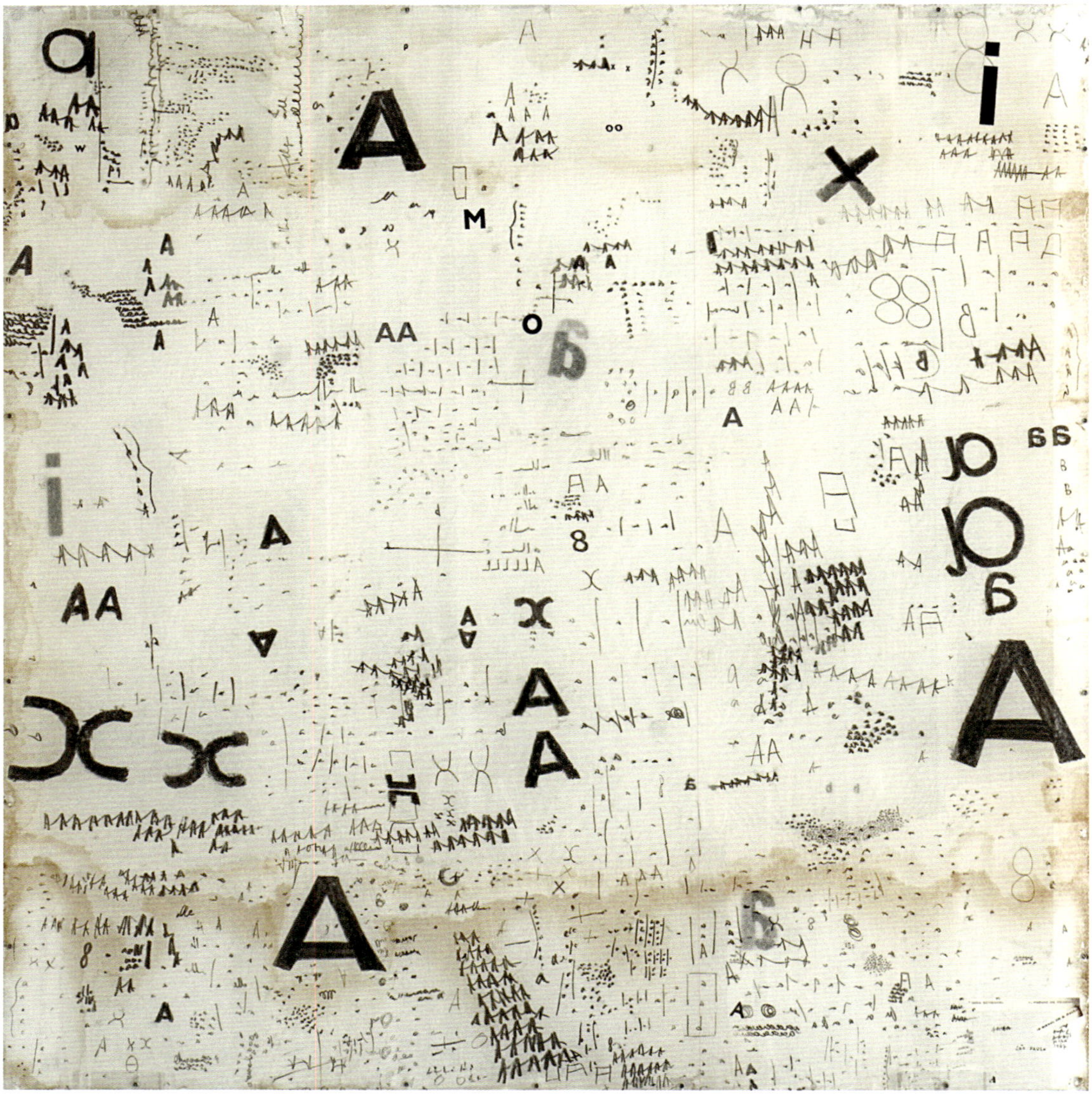

Graphic Object
Objeto gráfico
1967
Oil and transfer lettering on rice paper with acrylic
99.7 x 99.7 cm
The Ella Fontanals-Cisneros Collection

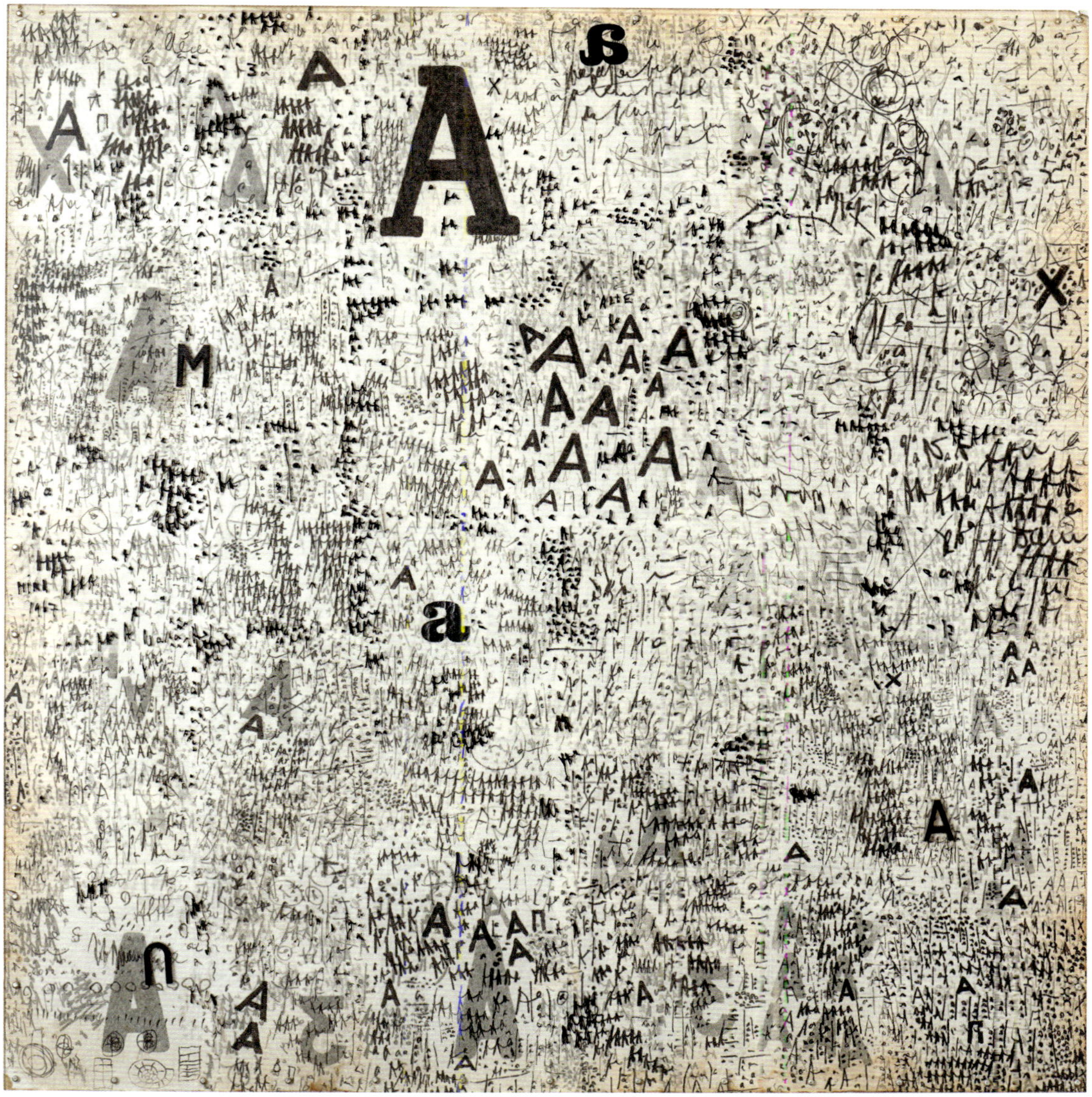

Graphic Object
Objeto gráfico
1967–8
Oil and transfer lettering on rice paper with acrylic
100 x 100 cm
Fernanda Feitosa and Heitor Martins Collection

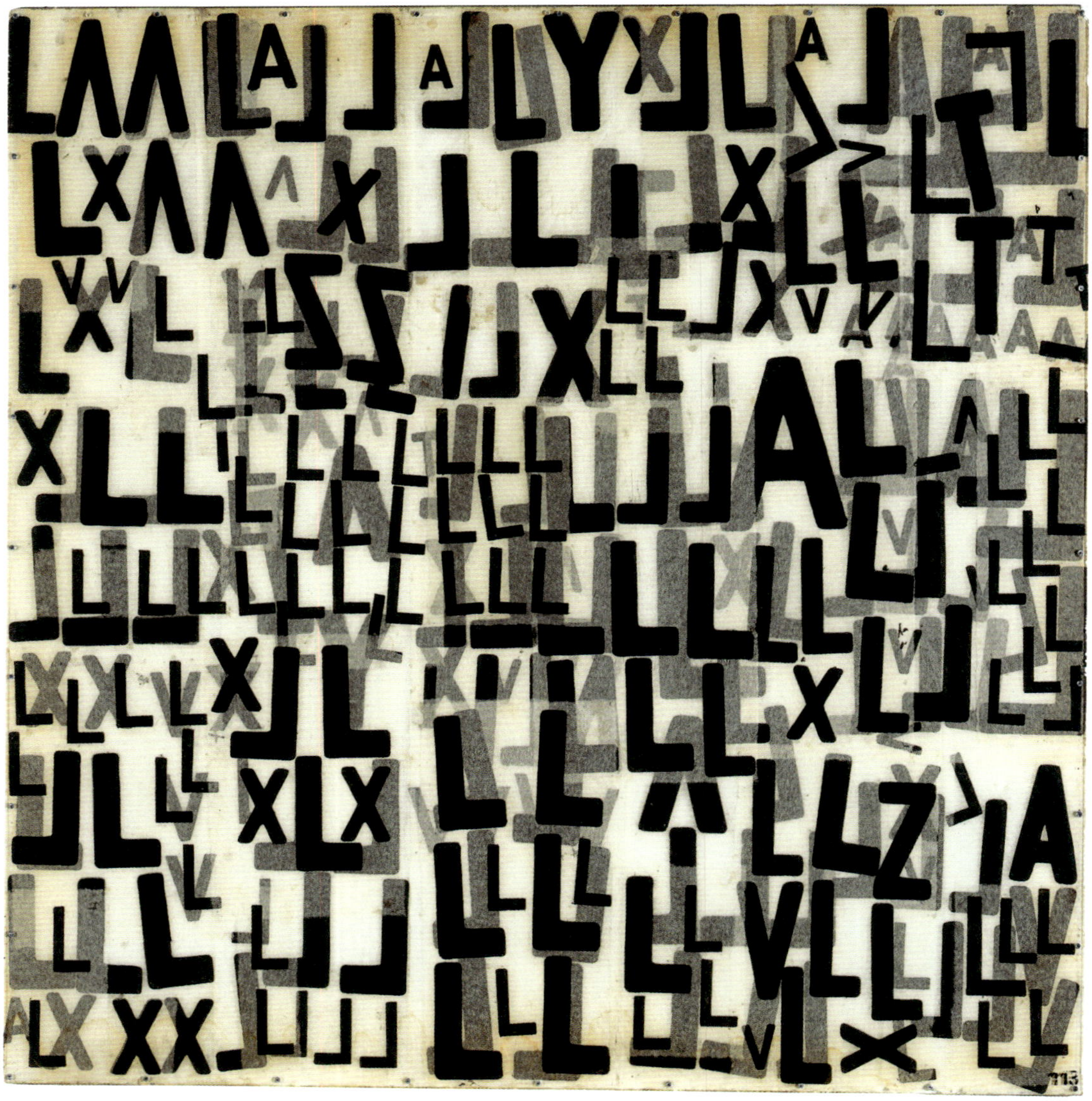

Graphic object
Objeto gráfico
1967–8
Oil on rice paper with acrylic
100 x 100 cm
Daros Latinamerica Collection, Zürich

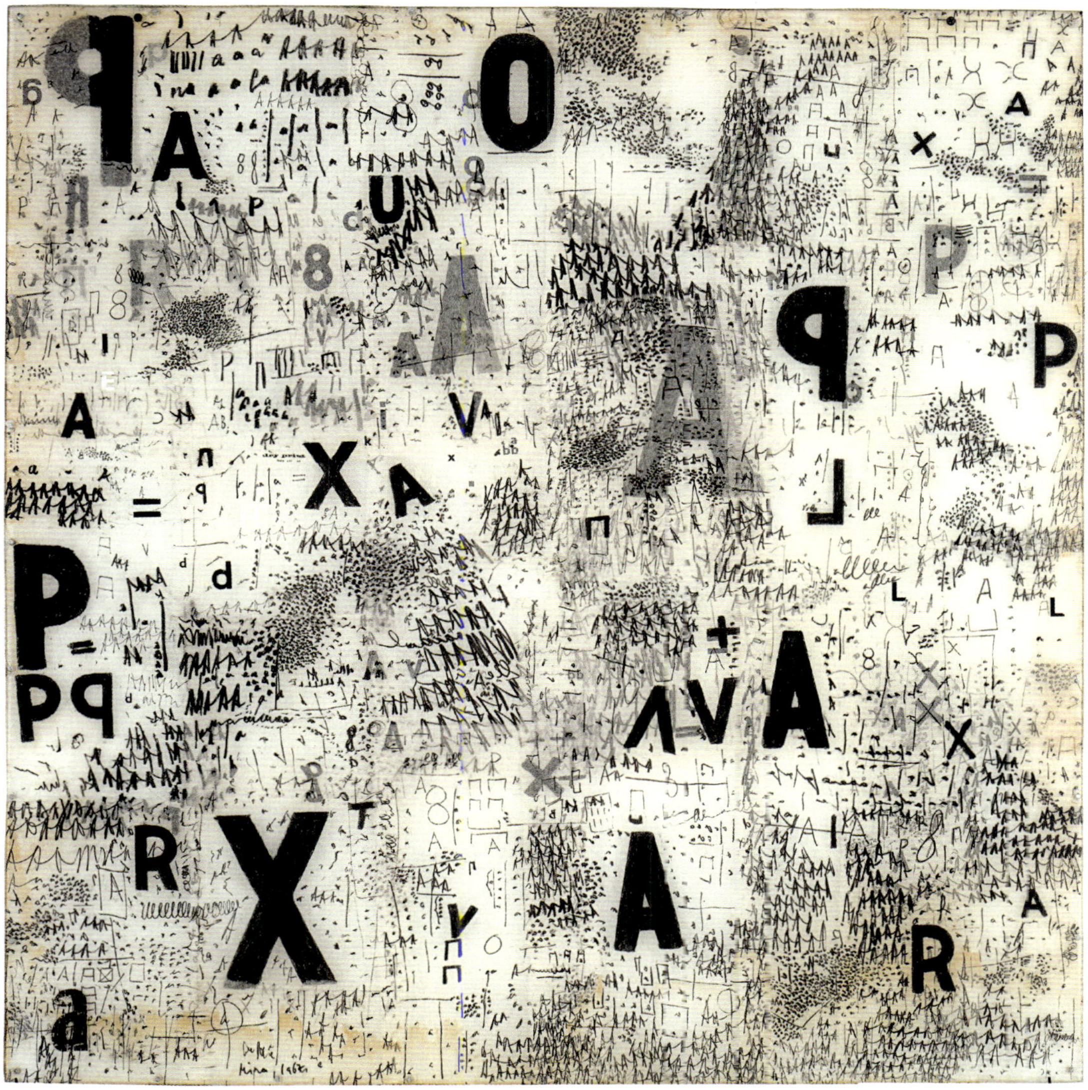

Graphic Object
Objeto gráfico
1967
Graphite, transfer lettering and oil on rice paper with acrylic
99.8 x 99.8 cm
Colección Patricia Phelps de Cisneros

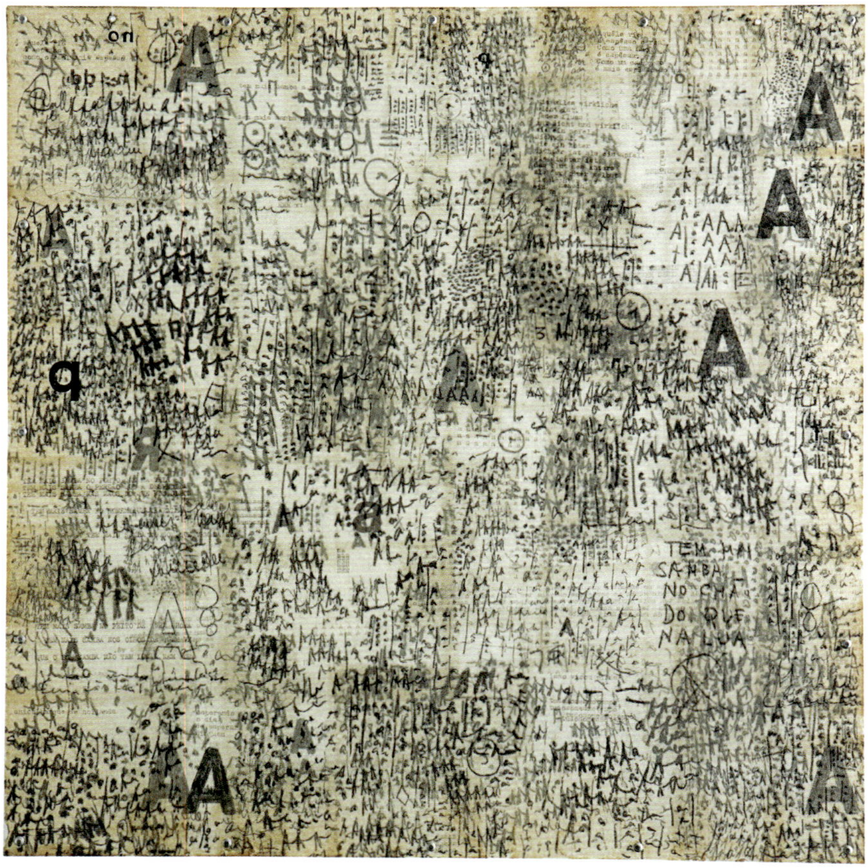

Graphic Object
Objeto gráfico
c.1967–8
Oil and transfer lettering on rice paper with acrylic
50.3 x 50 cm
Private collection

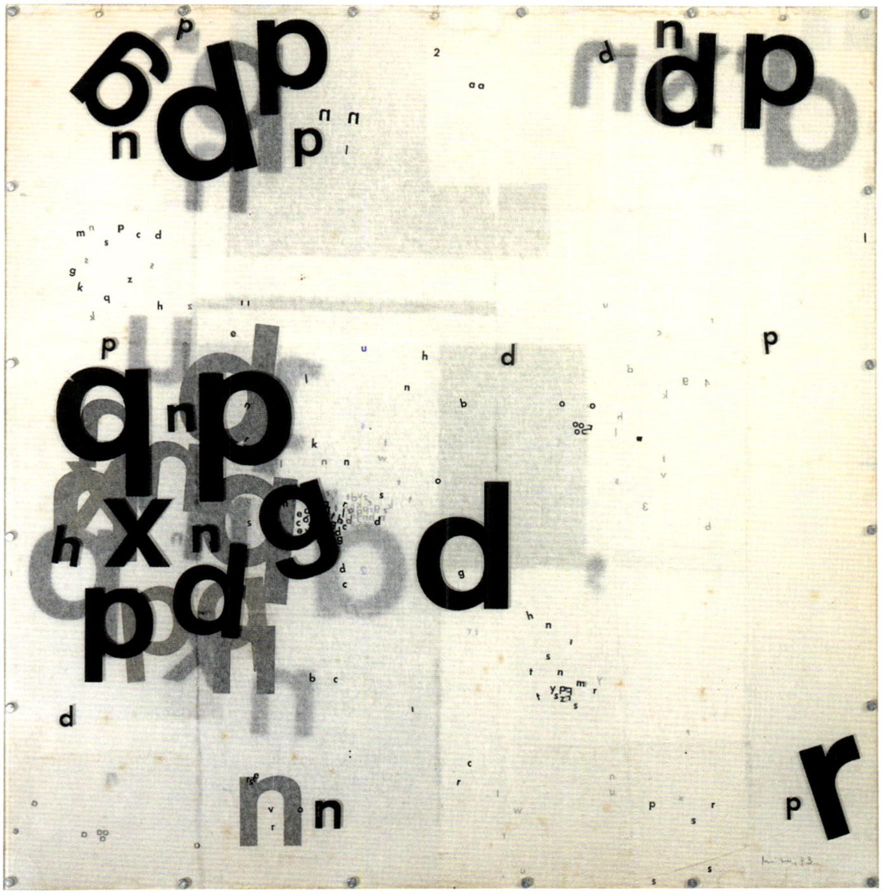

Graphic Object
Objeto gráfico
1973
Transfer lettering on paper with acrylic
55.9 x 55.9 cm
Colección Patricia Phelps de Cisneros

Graphic Object
Objeto gráfico
1967
Oil and ink on rice paper
with acrylic
100 x 100 cm
mira schendel estate

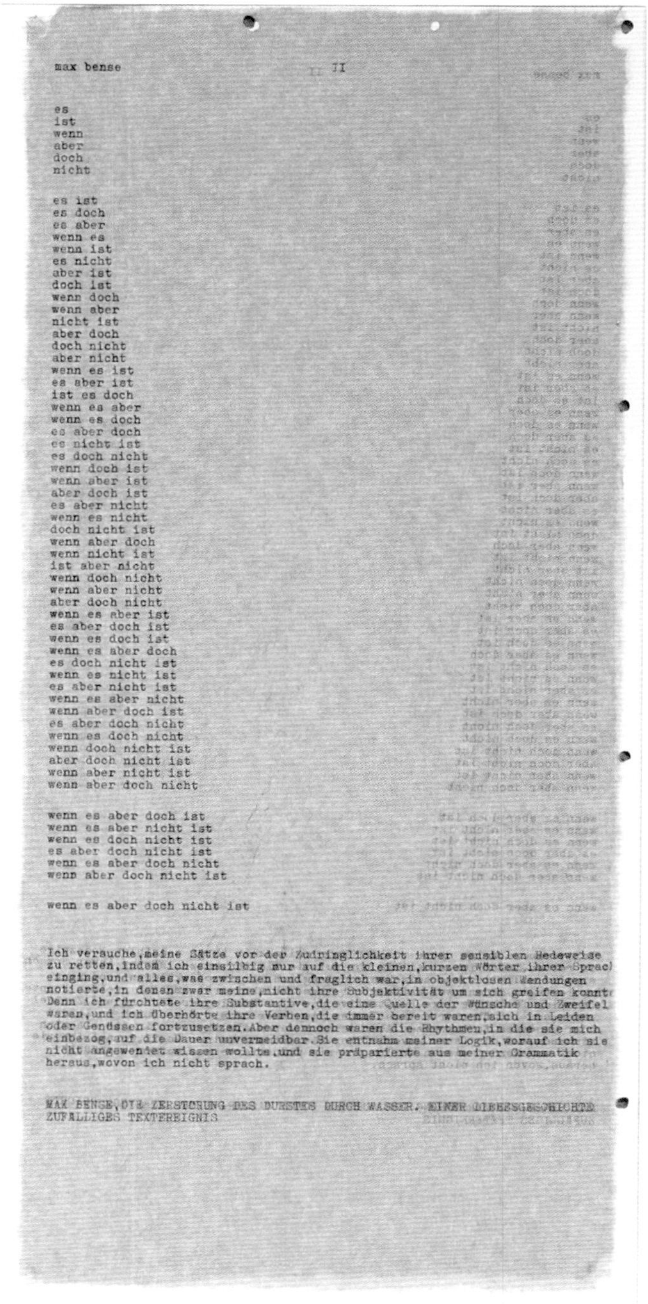

Graphic Object [details]
Objeto gráfico
1967
Oil and ink on rice paper
with acrylic
100 x 100 cm
mira schendel estate

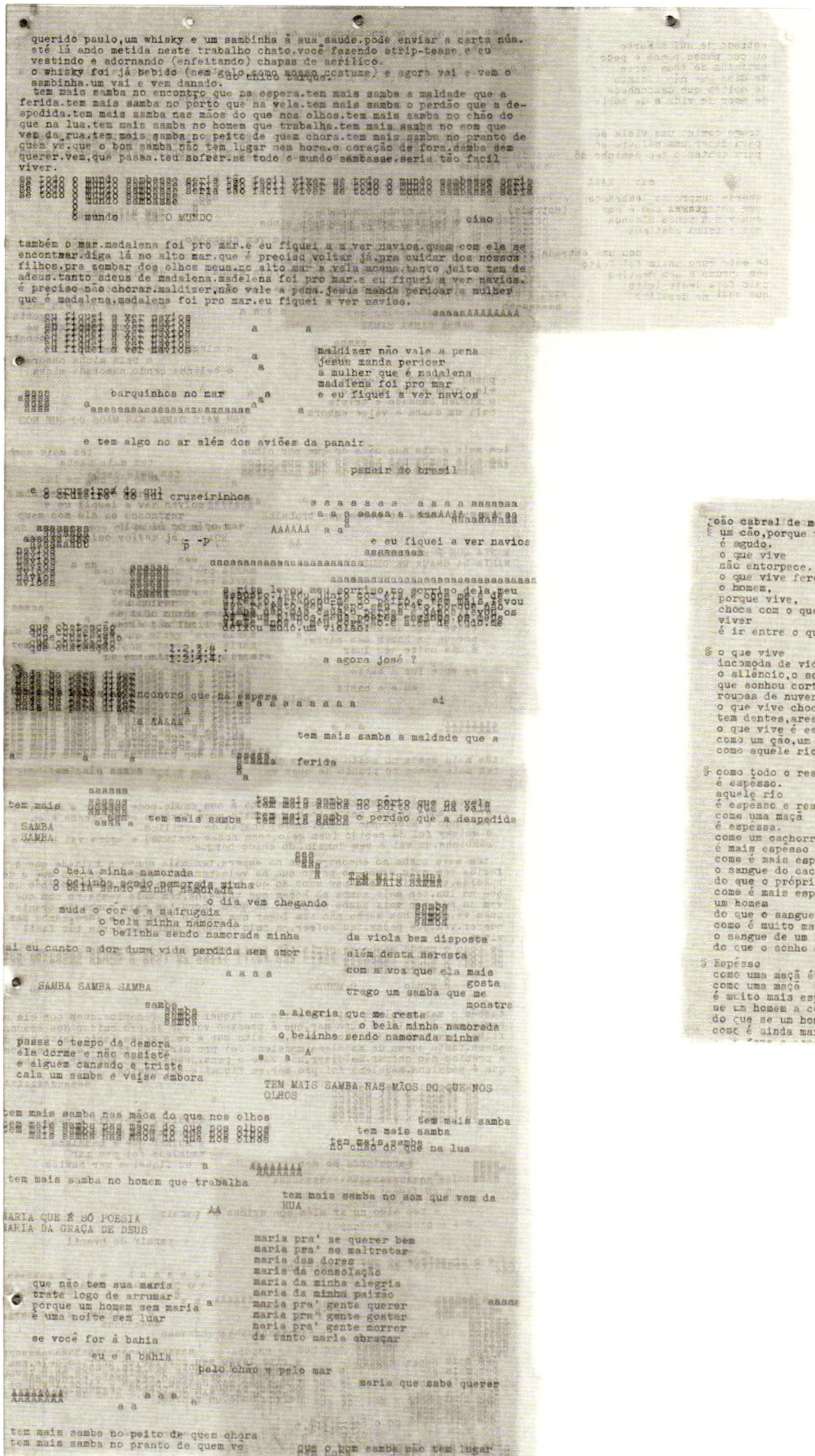
querido paulo,um whisky e um sambinha à sua saude.pode enviar a carta núa. até lá ando metida neste trabalho chato.você fazendo strip-tease e eu vestindo e adornando (enfeitando) chapas de acrilico.
o whisky foi já bebido (nem galo como nosso costume) e agora vai e vem o sambinha.um vai e vem danado.
do chico barque.
tem mais samba no encontro que na espera.tem mais samba a maldade que a ferida.tem mais samba no porto que na vela.tem mais samba o perdão que a despedida.tem mais samba nas mãos do que nos olhos.tem mais samba no chão do que na lua.tem mais samba no homem que trabalha.tem mais samba no som que vem da rua.tem mais samba no peito de quem chora.tem mais samba no pranto de quem vê.que o bom samba não tem lugar nem hora.o coração de fora.samba sem querer.vem,que passa.teu sofrer.se todo o mundo sambasse.seria tão facil viver.
se todo o mundo sambasse seria tão facil viver se todo o mundo sambasse seria
o mundo
ciao
também o mar.madalena foi pro mar.e eu fiquei a a ver navios.quem com ela se encontmar.diga lá no alto mar.que é preciso voltar já.pra cuidar dos nossos filhos.pra zombar dos olhos meus.no alto mar a vela acena.tanto jeito tem de adeus.tanto adeus de madalena.madelena foi pro mar.e eu fiquei a ver navios. é preciso não chorar.maldizer,não vale a pena.jesus manda perdoar a mulher que é madalena.madalena foi pro mar.eu fiquei a ver navios.
aaaaaAAAAAAAA
eu fiquei a ver navios
maldizer não vale a pena
jesus manda perdoar
a mulher que é madalena
madalena foi pro mar
e eu fiquei a ver navios
barquinhos no mar
aaaaaaaaaaaaaaaaaaaaaaaa
e tem algo no ar além dos aviões da panair
panair do brasil
e o cruzeiro do sul cruzeirinhos
e eu fiquei a ver navios
a agora josé ?
encontro que na espera
ai
tem mais samba a maldade que a
ferida
tem mais
tem mais samba no pôrto que na vela
tem mais samba
SAMBA
SAMBA
tem mais samba o perdão que a despedida
o bela minha namorada
o belinha sendo namorada minha
TEM MAIS SAMBA
o dia vem chegando
muda o cor e a madrugada
o bela minha namorada
o belinha sendo namorada minha
da viola bem disposta
ai eu canto a dor duma vida perdida sem amor
além desta seresta
com a voz que ela mais gosta
SAMBA SAMBA SAMBA
trago um samba que me monstra
samba
a alegria que me resta
o bela minha namorada
o belinha sendo namorada minha
passa o tempo da demora
ela dorme e não assiste
e alguem cansado e triste
cala um samba e vaise embora
TEM MAIS SAMBA NAS MÃOS DO QUE NOS OLHOS
tem mais samba nas mãos do que nos olhos
tem mais samba
tem mais samba
tem mais samba no chão do que na lua
tem mais samba no homem que trabalha
tem mais samba no som que vem da RUA
MARIA QUE É SÓ POESIA
MARIA DA GRAÇA DE DEUS
maria pra' se querer bem
maria pra' se maltratar
maria das dores
maria da consolação
maria da minha alegria
maria da minha paixão
maria pra' gente querer
maria pra' gente gostar
maria pra' gente morrer
de tanto maria abraçar
que não tem sua maria
trate logo de arrumar
porque um homem sem maria
é uma noite sem luar
se você for à bahia
eu e a bahia
pelo chão e pelo mar
maria que sabe querer
tem mais samba no peito de quem chora
tem mais samba no pranto de quem vê
que o bom samba não tem lugar
nem hora

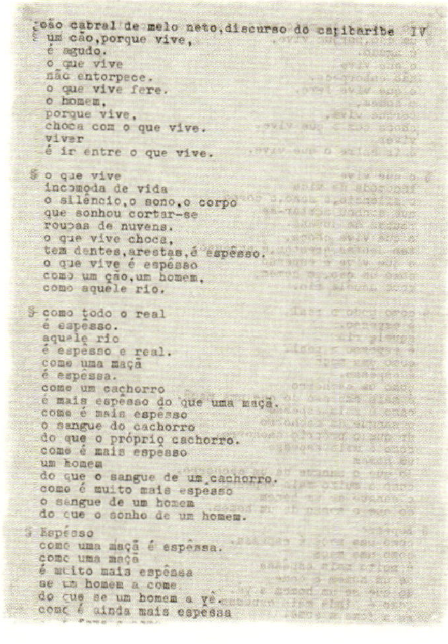
joão cabral de melo neto,discurso do capibaribe IV
um cão,porque vive,
é agudo.
o que vive
não entorpece.
o que vive fere.
o homem,
porque vive,
choca com o que vive.
viver
é ir entre o que vive.
§ o que vive
incomoda de vida
o silêncio,o sono,o corpo
que sonhou cortar-se
roupas de nuvens.
o que vive choca,
tem dentes,arestas,é espêsso.
o que vive é espêsso
como um cão,um homem,
como aquele rio.
§ como todo o real
é espêsso.
aquele rio
é espêsso e real.
como uma maçã
é espêssa.
como um cachorro
é mais espêsso do que uma maçã.
como é mais espêsso
o sangue do cachorro
do que o próprio cachorro.
como é mais espêsso
um homem
do que o sangue de um cachorro.
como é muito mais espêsso
o sangue de um homem
do que o sonho de um homem.
§ Espêsso
como uma maçã é espêssa.
como uma maçã
é muito mais espêssa
se um homem a come
do que se um homem a vê.
como é ainda mais espêssa

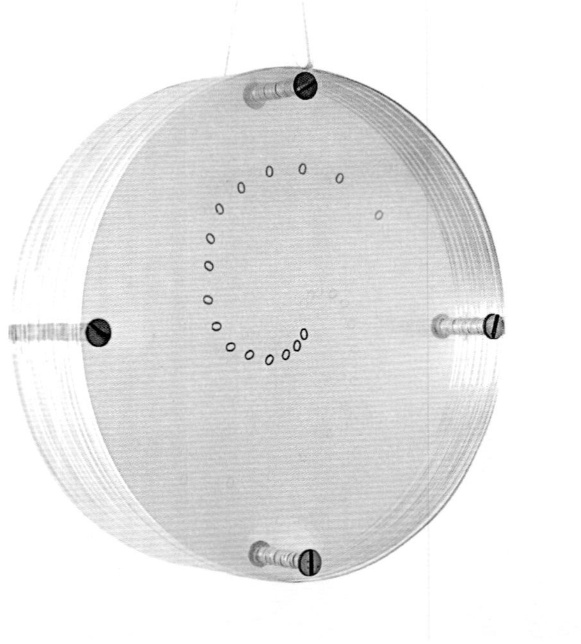

Untitled, from the series *Discs*
Sem título, da série *Discos*
1972
Transfer lettering with acrylic
18.5 diameter x 5.2 cm
Marta and Paulo Kuczynski Collection

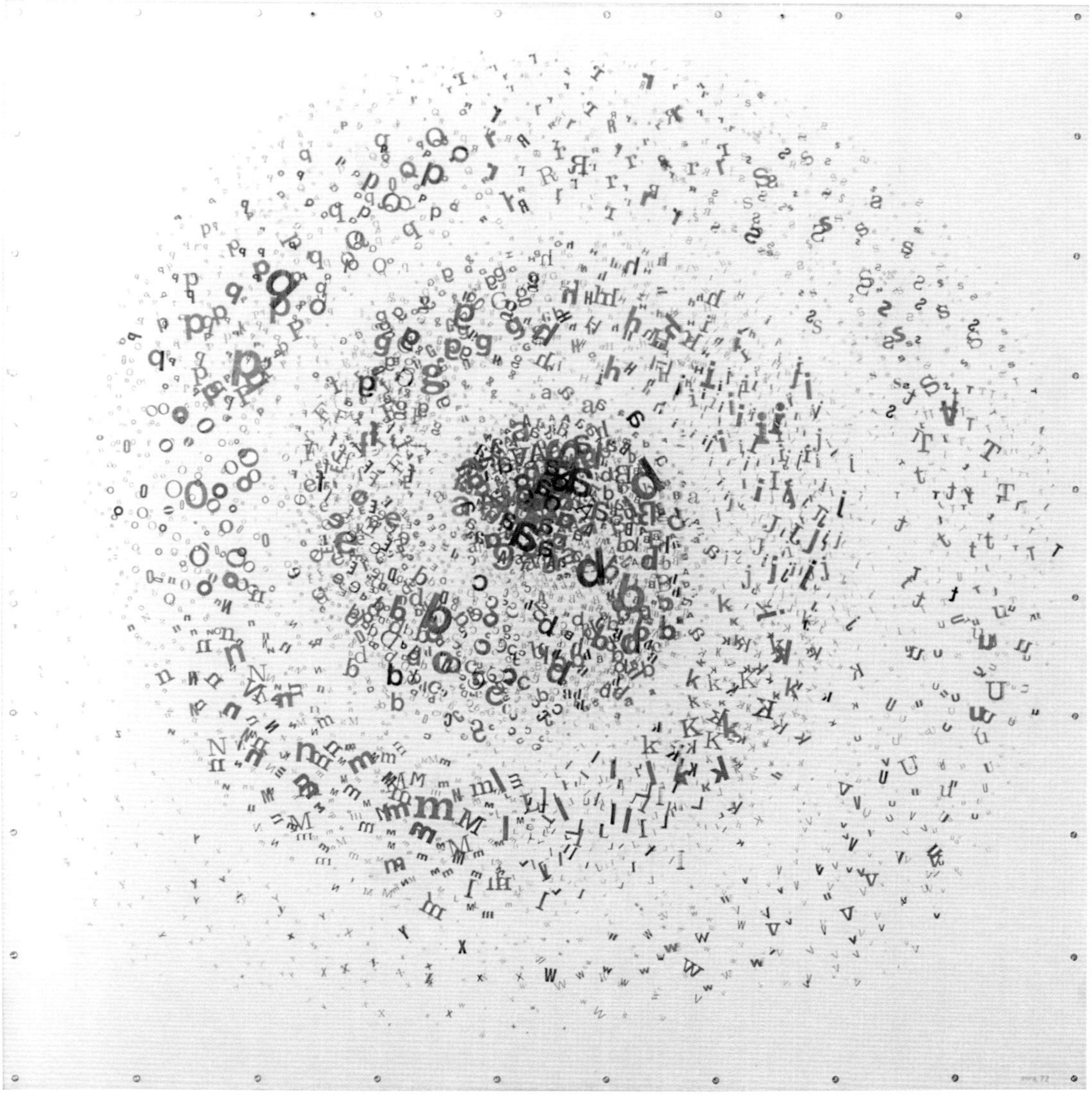

Graphic Object
Objeto gráfico
1972
Transfer lettering on rice paper with acrylic
95 x 95 cm
Collection Clara Sancovsky

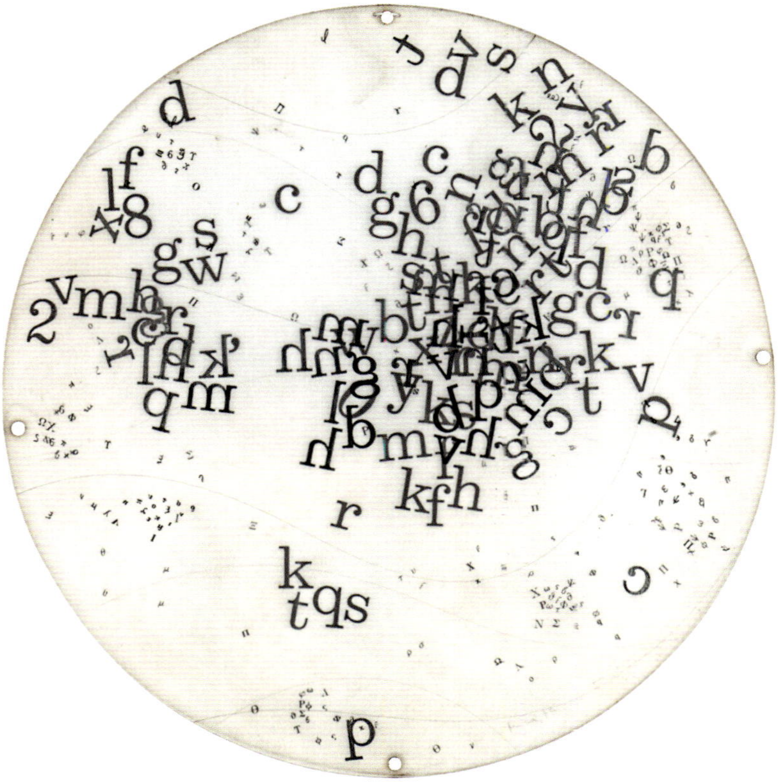

Untitled, from the series *Discs*
Sem título, da série *Discos*
1972
Transfer lettering and graphite with acrylic
27 cm diameter x 0.7 cm
Tate. Presented by Tate Americas
Foundation 2012

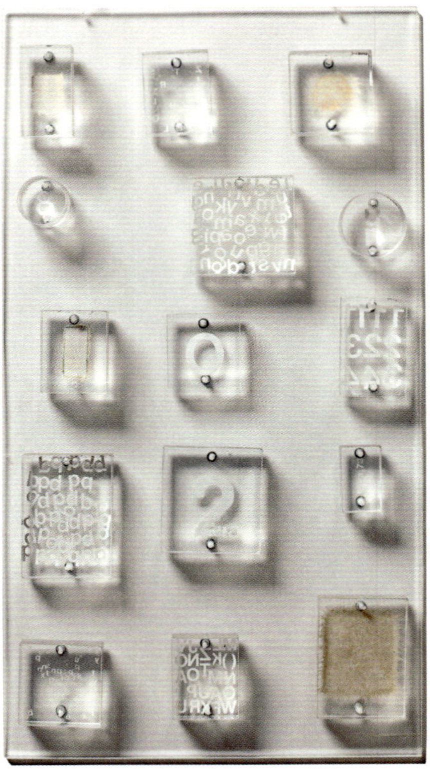

Untitled, from the series *Little Stubs*
Sem título, da série *Toquinhos*
1973
Transfer lettering and acrylic
47 x 26 x 3.5 cm
Private collection

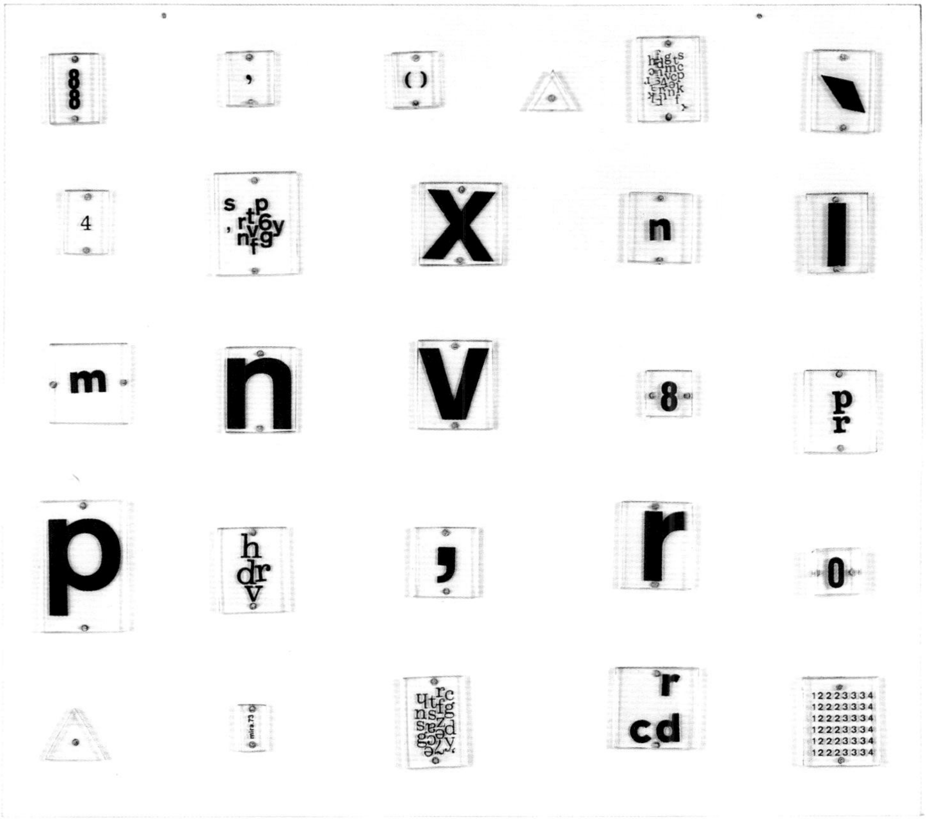

Untitled, from the series *Little Stubs*
Sem título, da série *Toquinhos*
1973
Transfer lettering and acrylic
50 x 58 cm
Luiz Paulo Montenegro

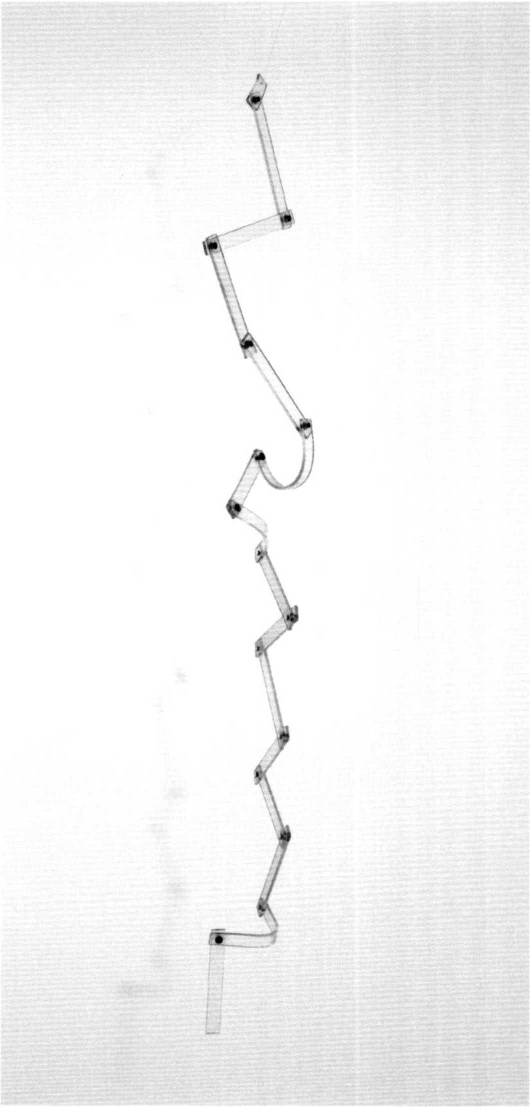

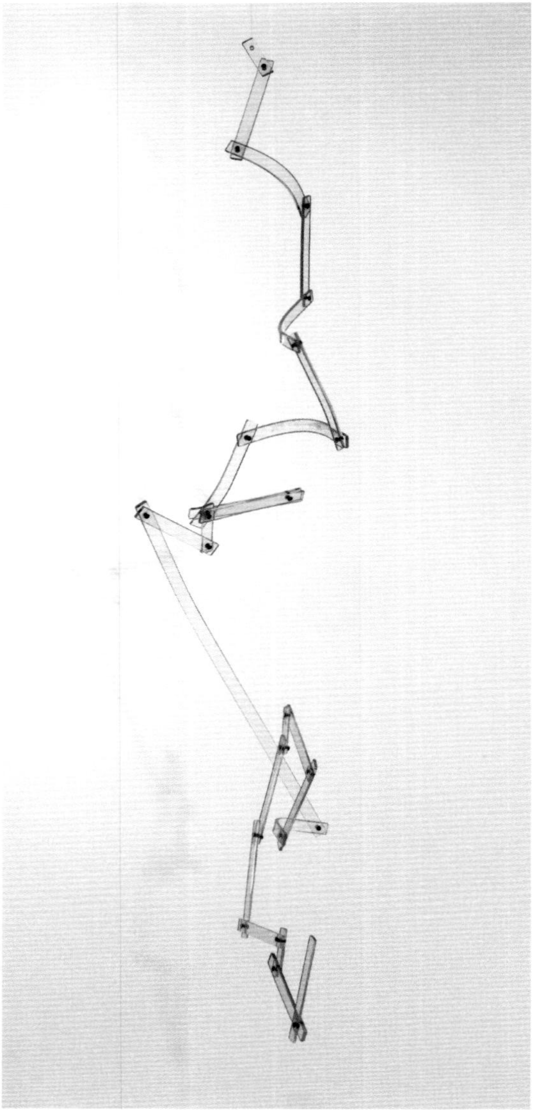

Untitled, from the series *Transformables*
Sem título, da série *Transformáveis*
early 1970s
Riveted acrylic
Dimensions variable
Marcela and Israel Furmanovich

Untitled, from the series *Transformables*
Sem título, da série *Transformáveis*
early 1970s
Riveted acrylic
Dimensions variable
Luisa Malzoni Strina

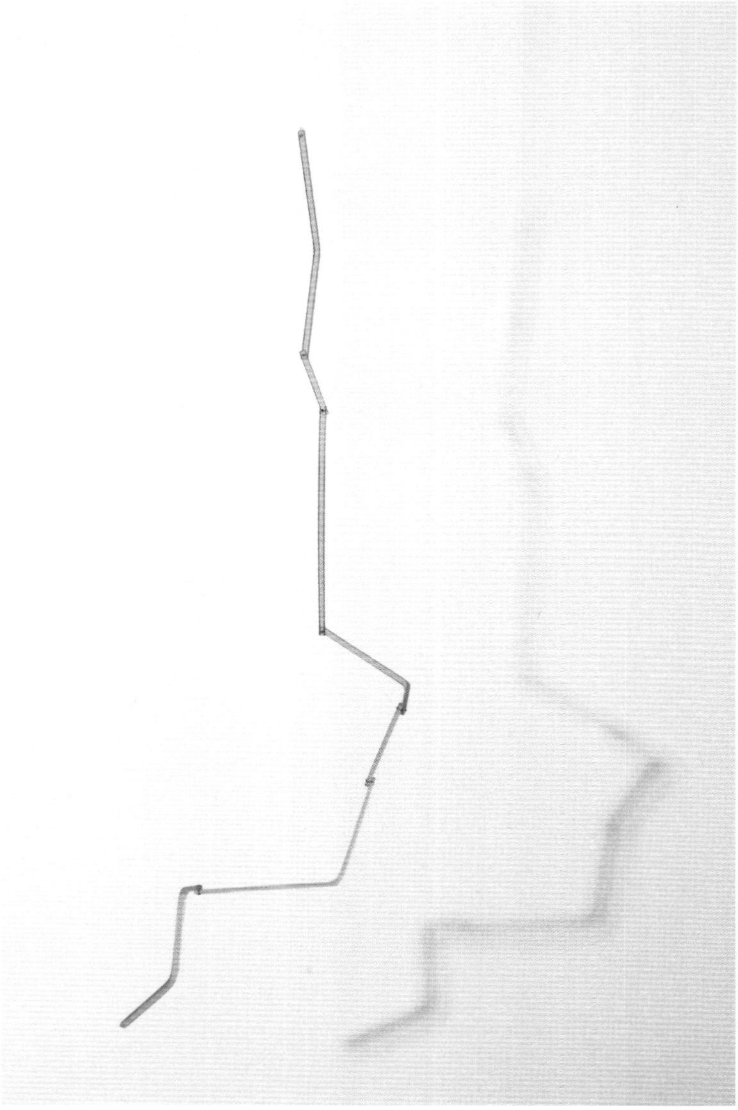

Untitled, from the series *Transformables*
Sem título, da série *Transformáveis*
1970
Riveted acrylic
Dimensions variable
Private collection

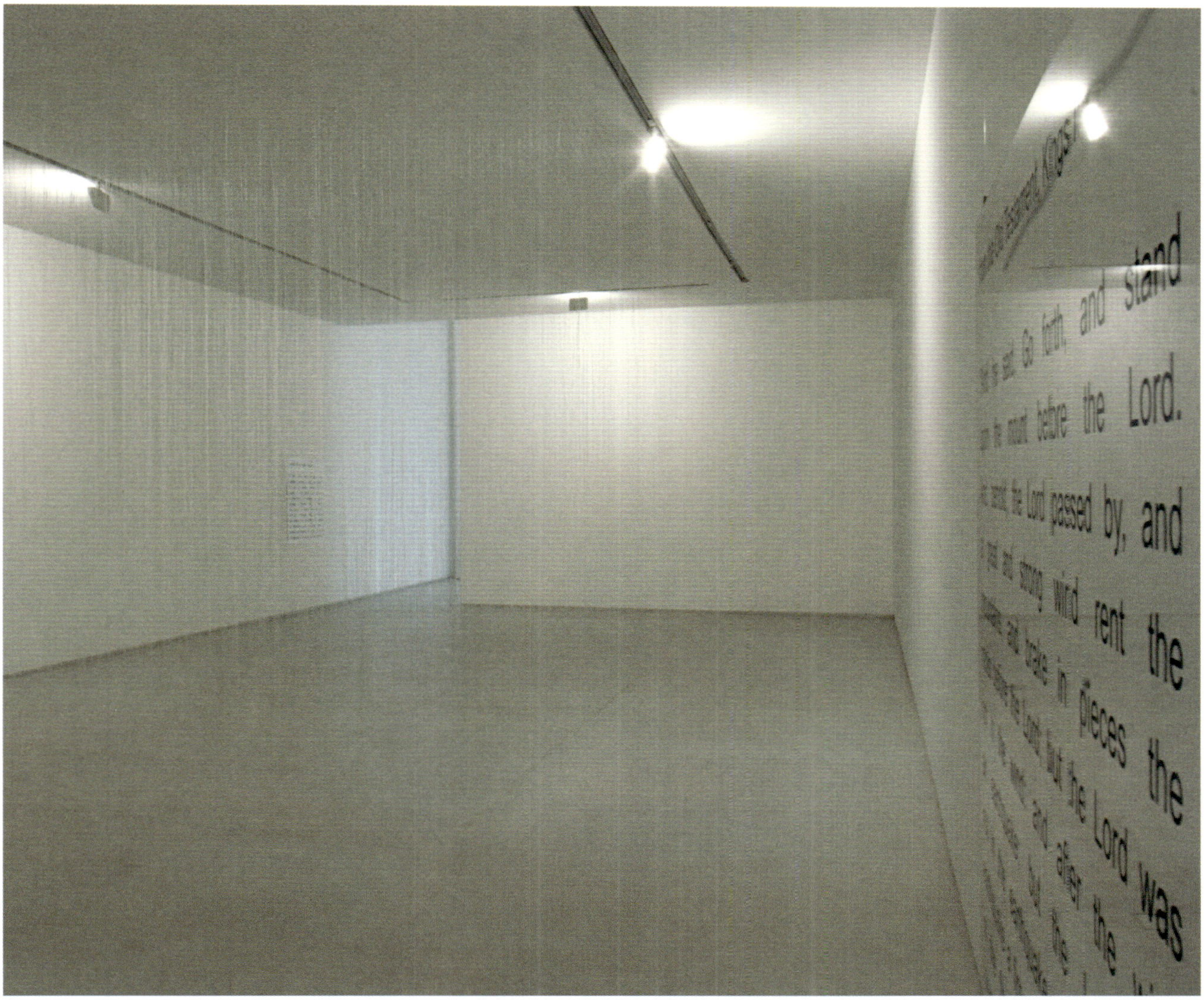

Still Waves of Probability
Ondas paradas de probabilidade
1969/2006
Nylon thread with text on acrylic
Dimensions variable
mira schendel estate
[Installation view at Galeria Millan, São Paulo, 2006]

Variants
Variantes
1977
Oil on rice paper with acrylic
93 parts, dimensions variable
The Museum of Fine Arts, Houston,
Museum purchase with funds provided
by the Caroline Wiess Law Accessions
Endowment Fund

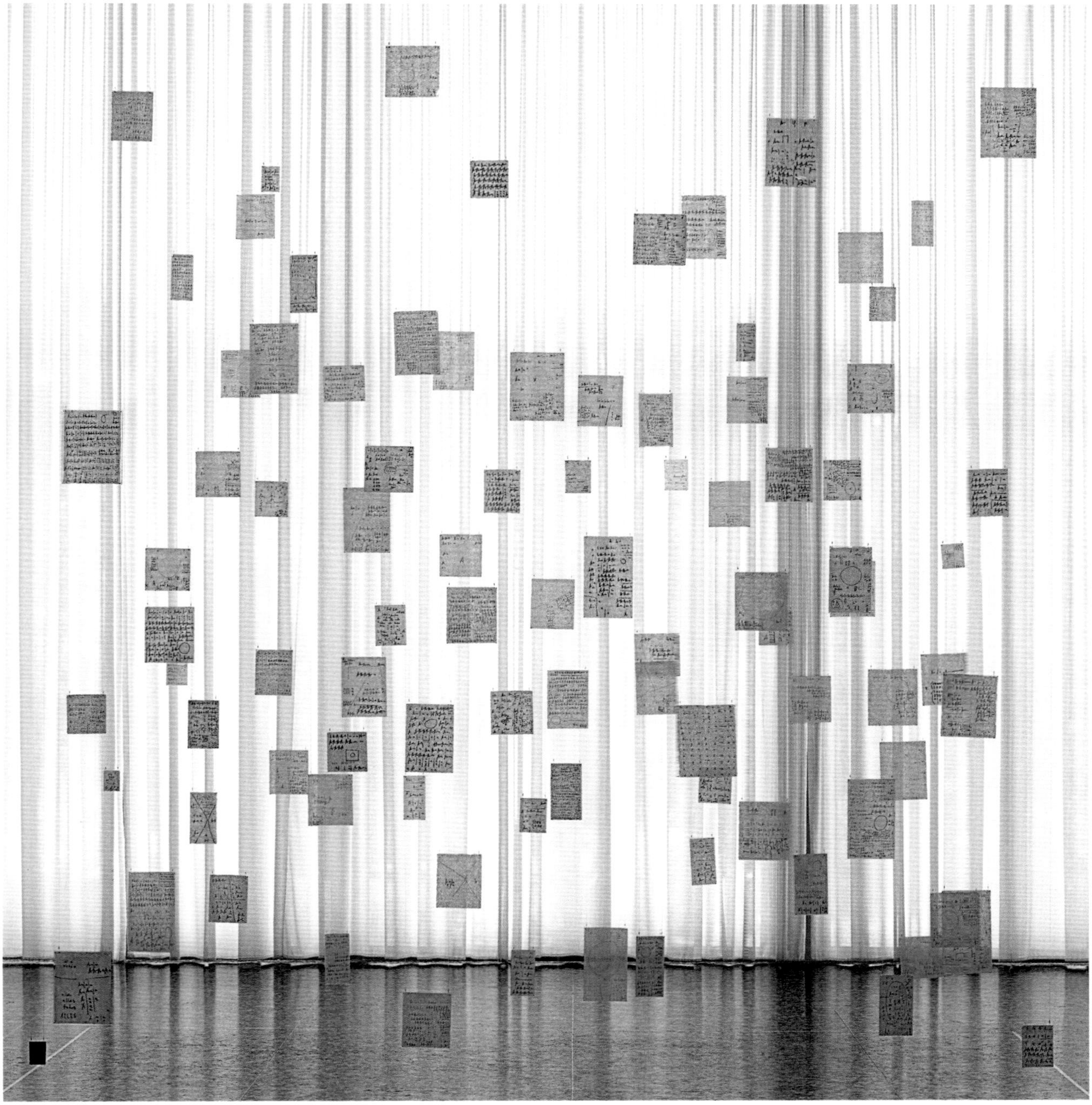

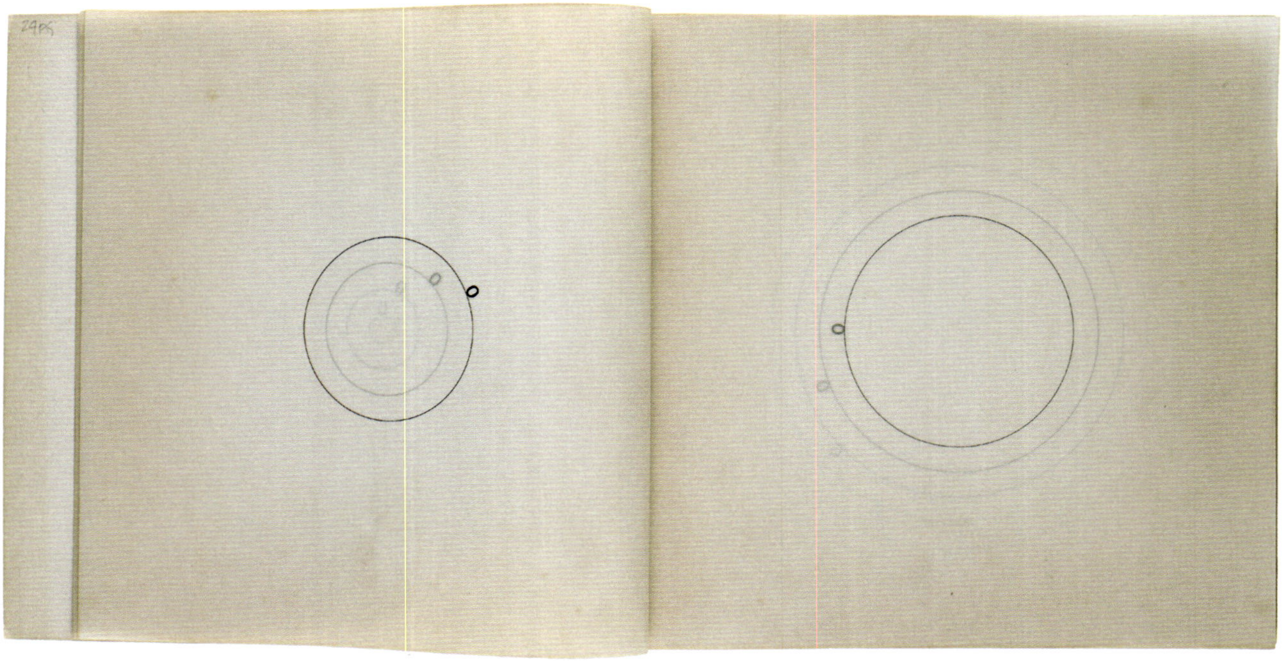

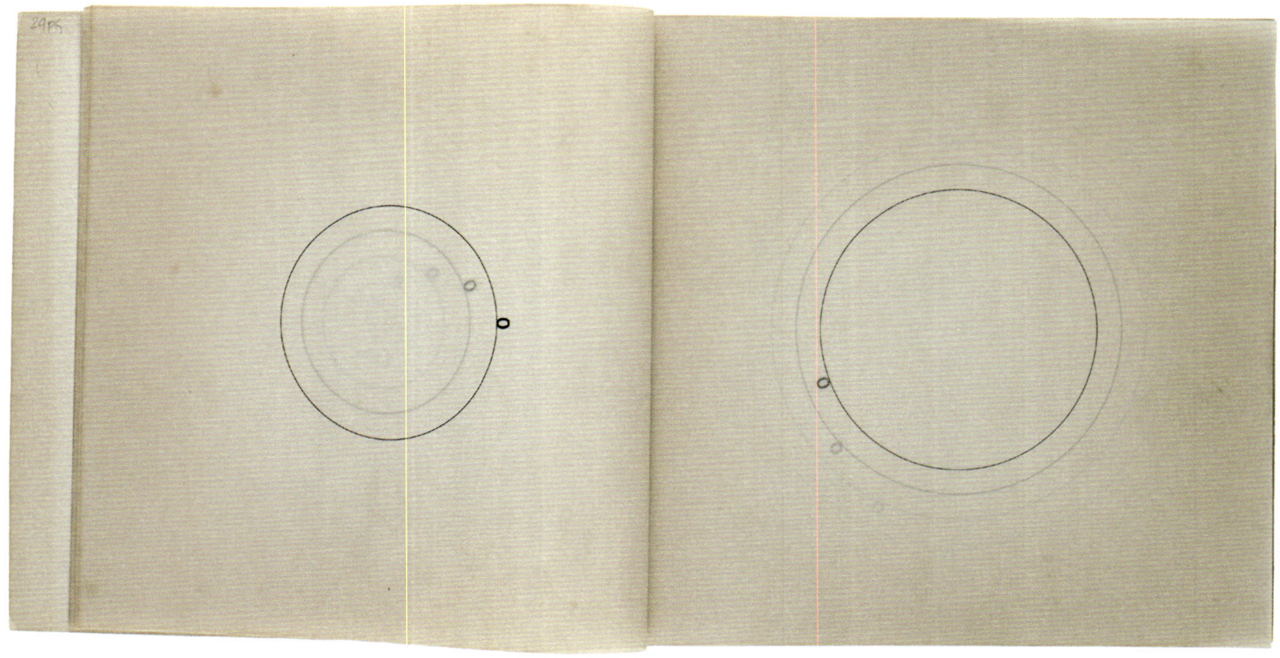

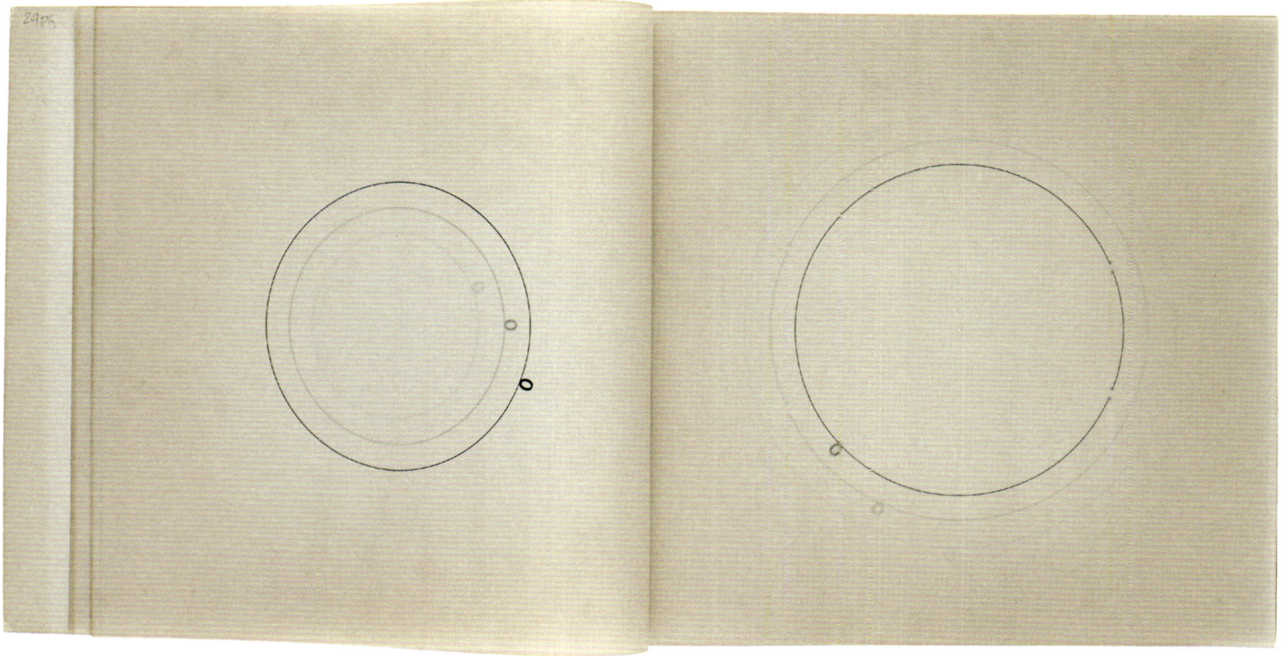

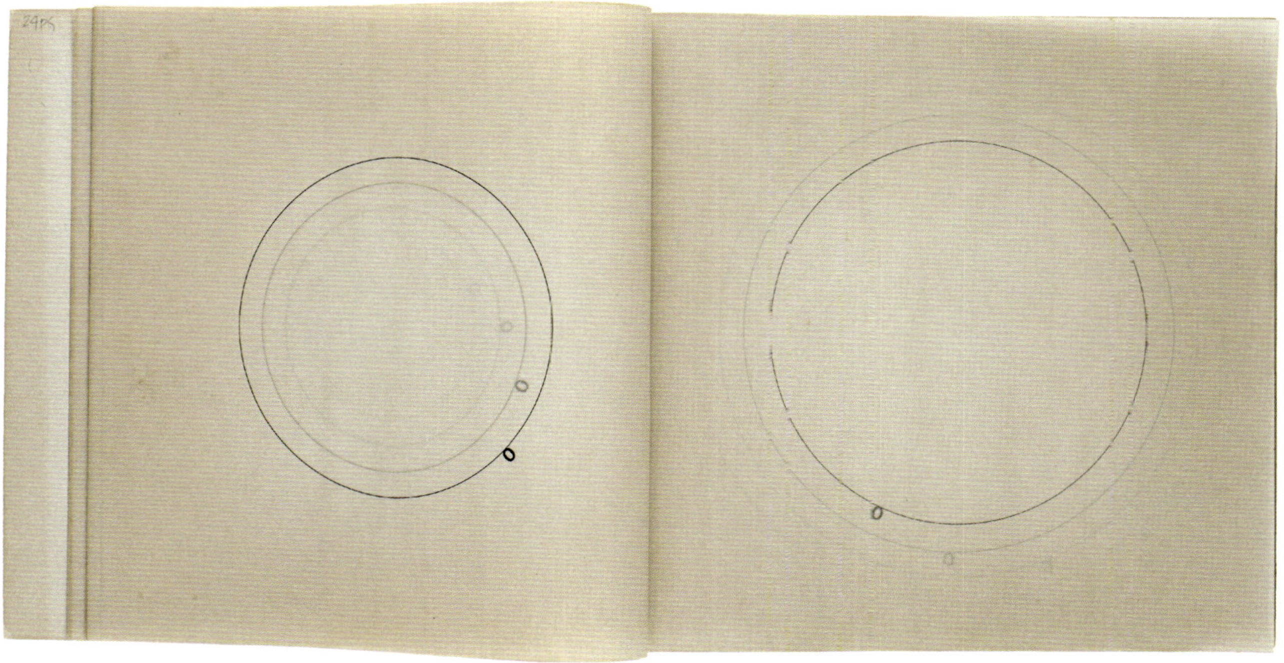

Untitled, from the series *Notebooks*
Sem título, da série *Cadernos*
1971
Transfer lettering and graphite on paper
19.5 x 21.8 cm
mira schendel estate

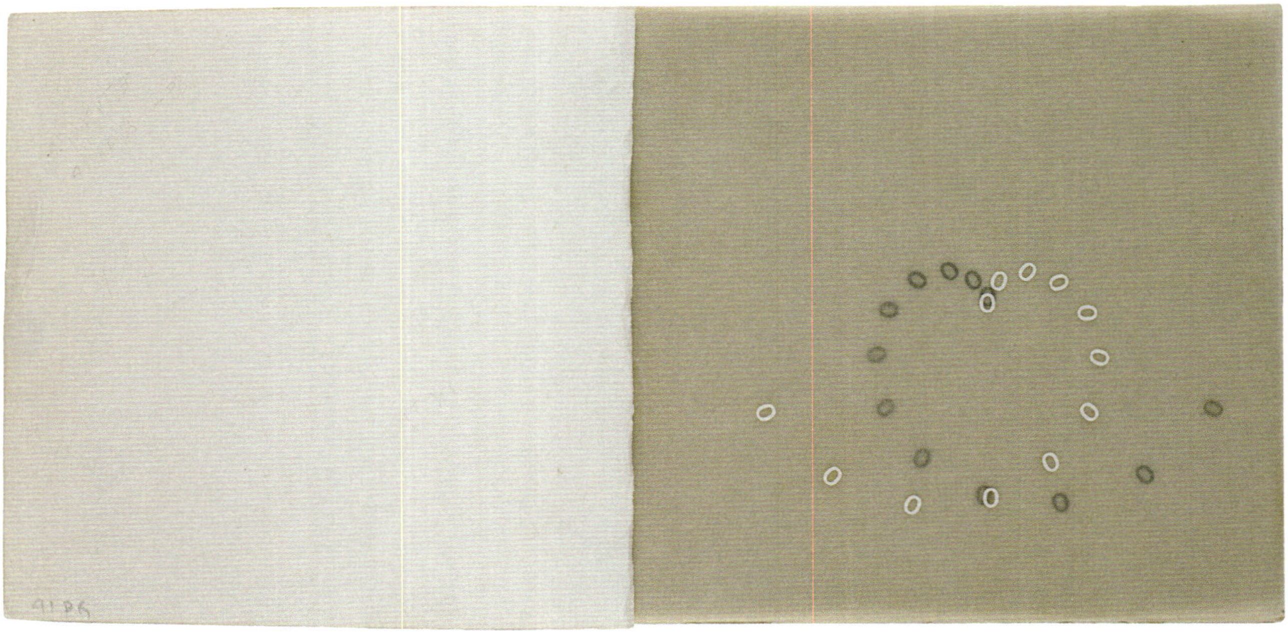

Untitled, from the series *Notebooks*
Sem título, da série *Cadernos*
1971
Transfer lettering on paper
13 x 15.3 cm
mira schendel estate

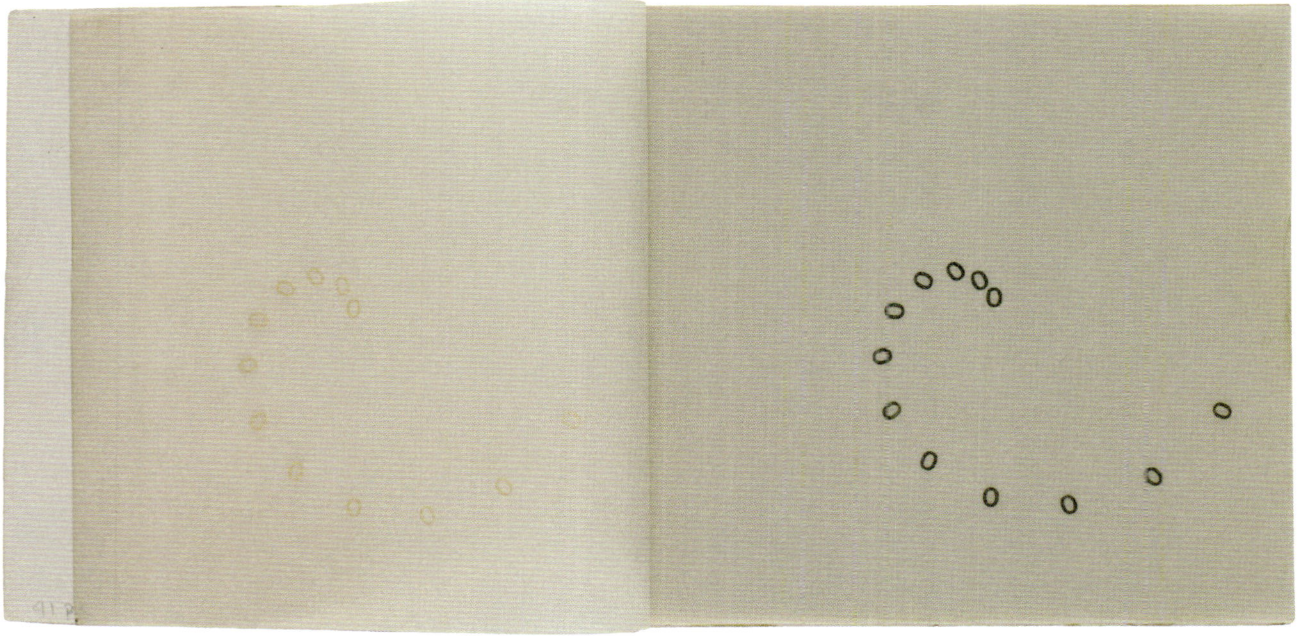

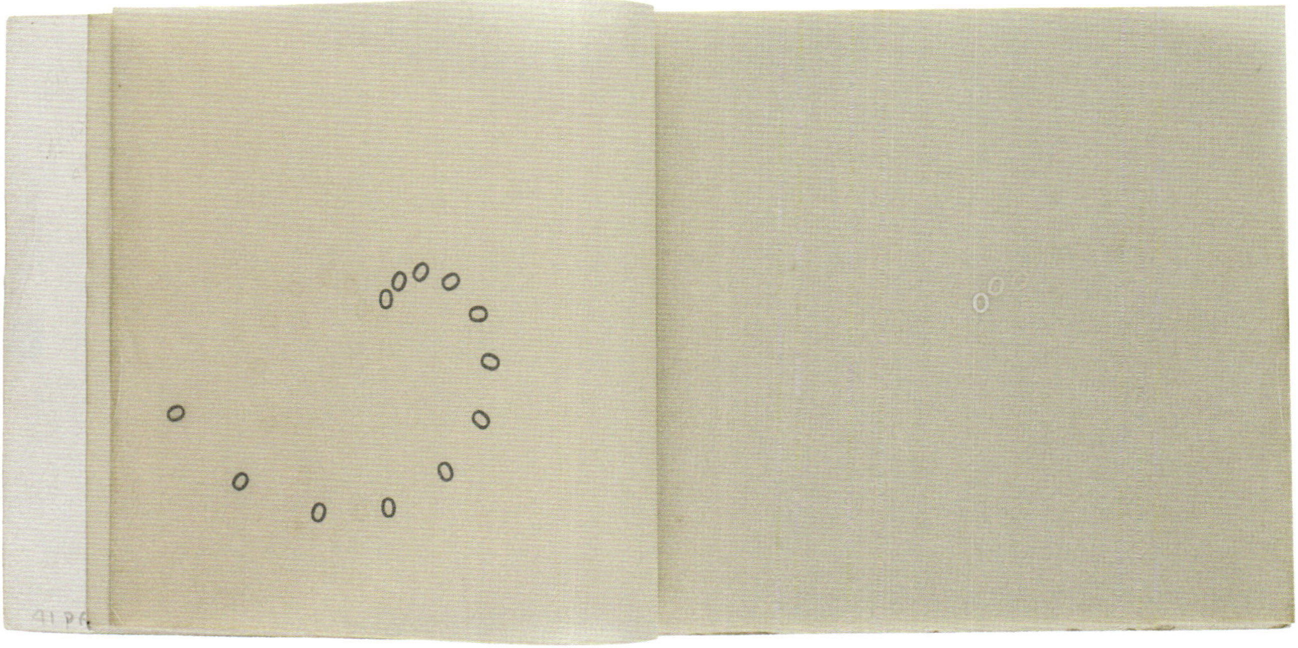

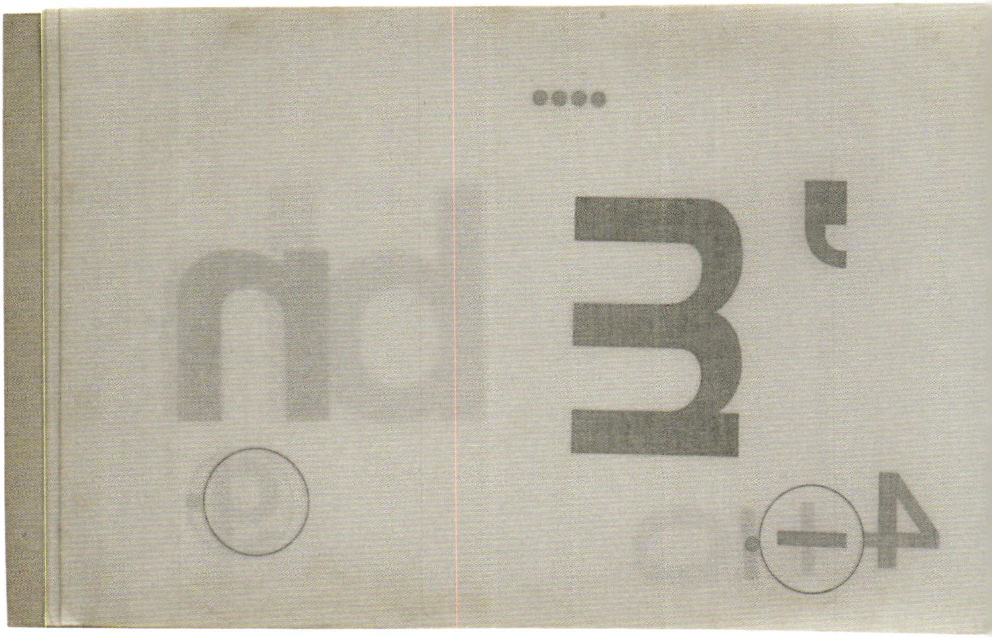

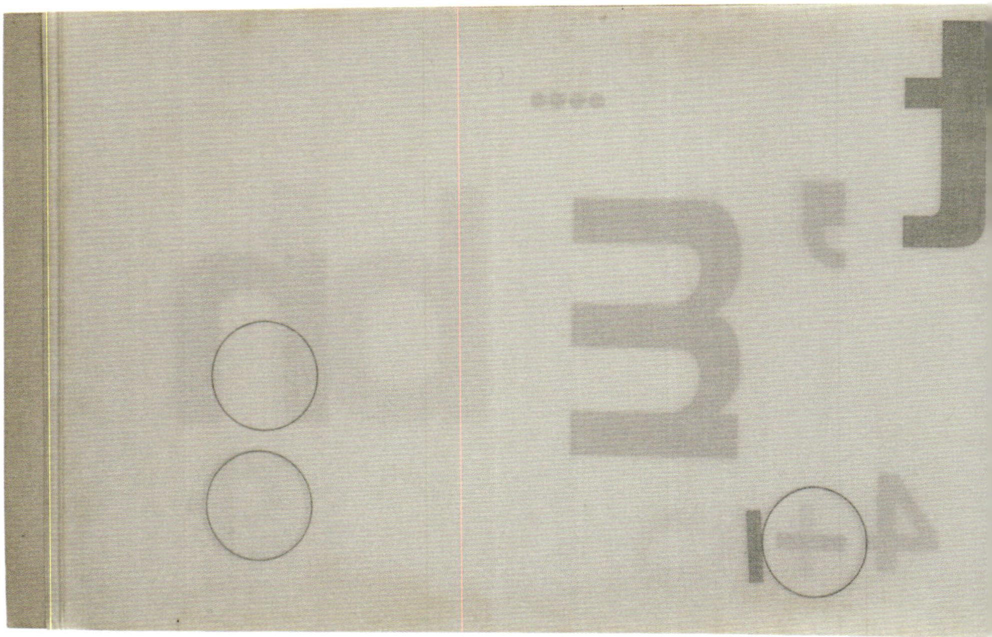

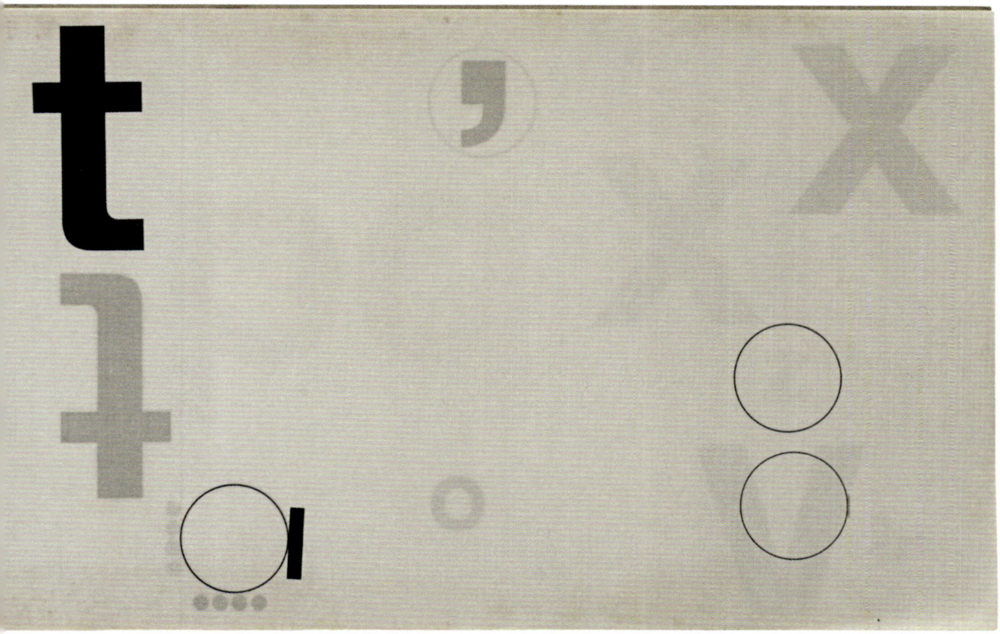

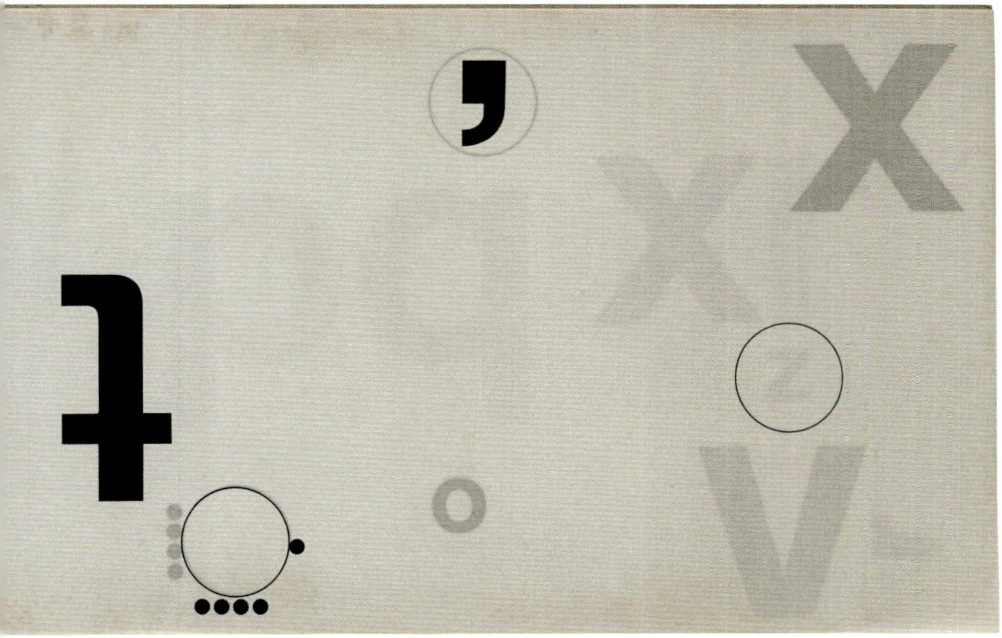

Untitled, from the series *Notebooks*
Sem título, da série *Cadernos*
1971
Ink and transfer lettering on paper
16 x 30 cm
mira schendel estate

Untitled, from the series *Notebooks*
Sem título, da série *Cadernos*
1971
Ink and transfer lettering on paper
23 x 31 cm
mira schendel estate

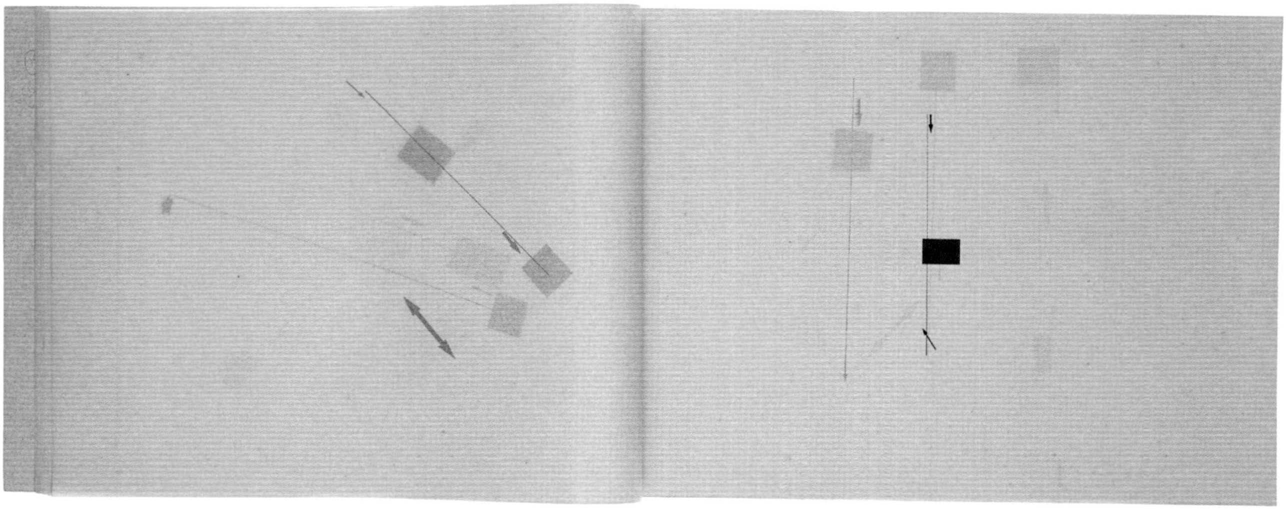

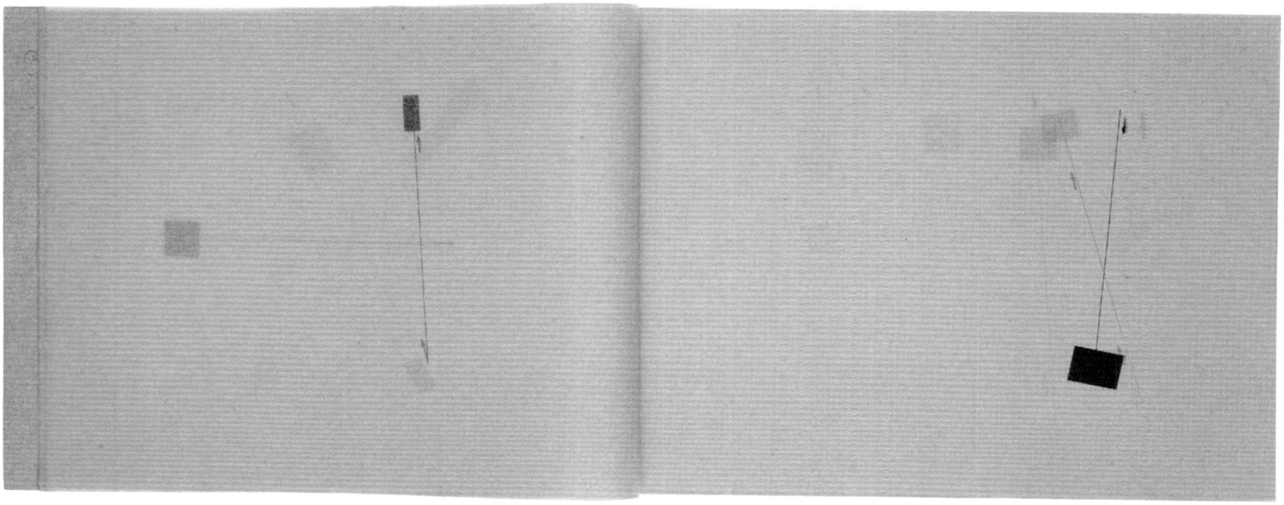

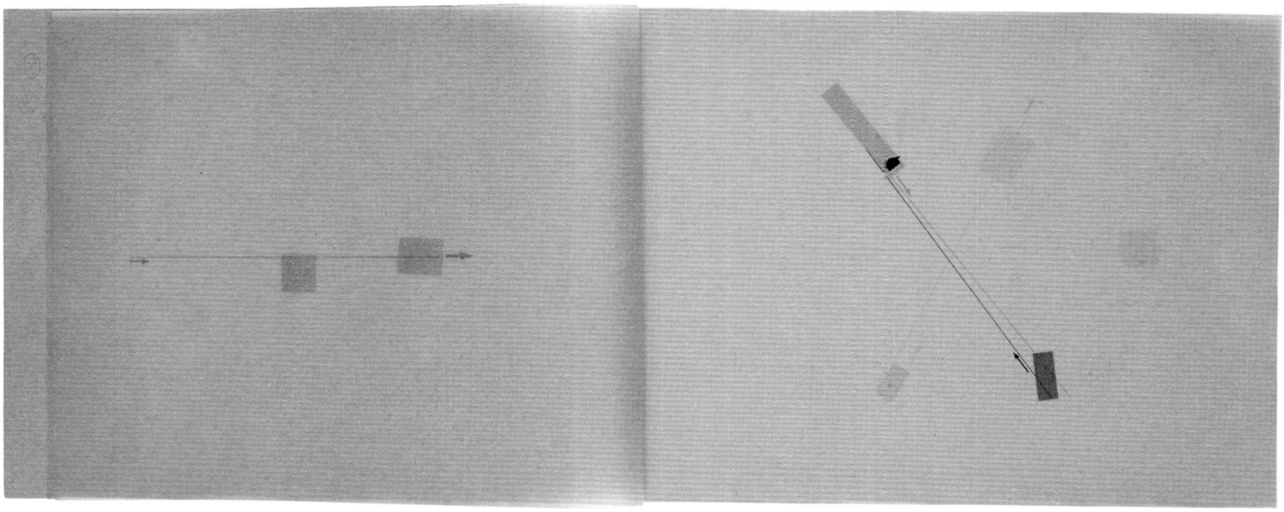

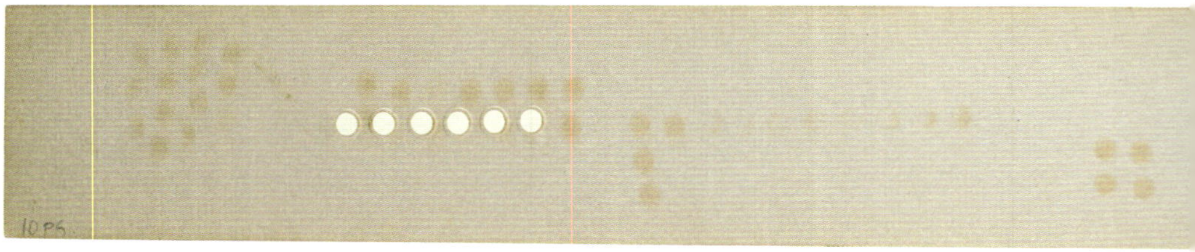

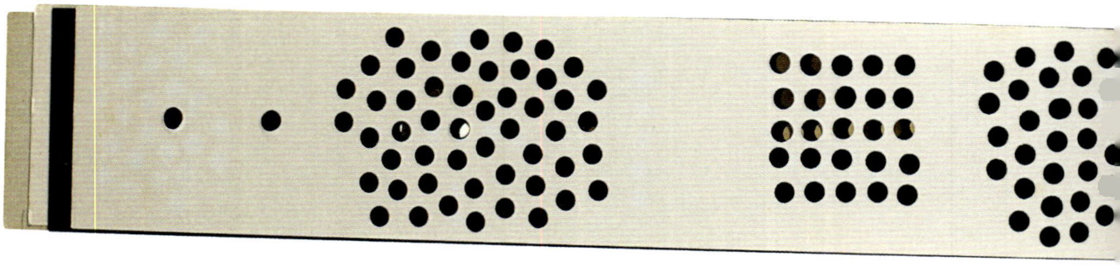

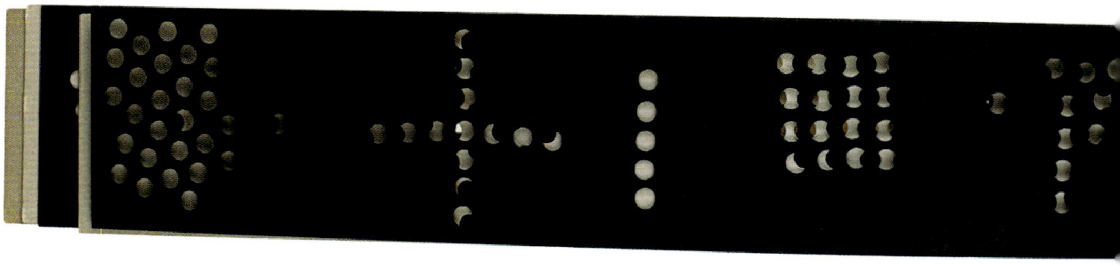

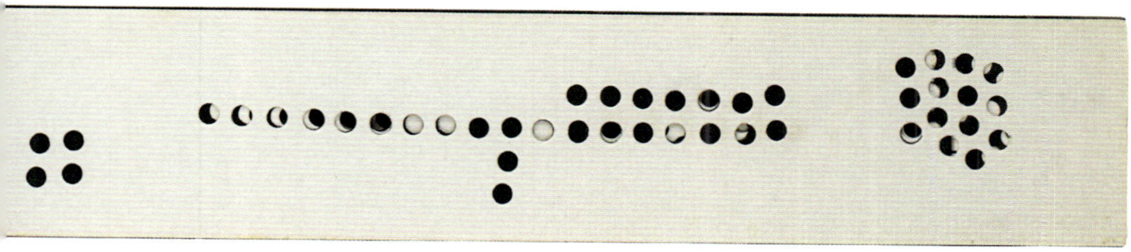

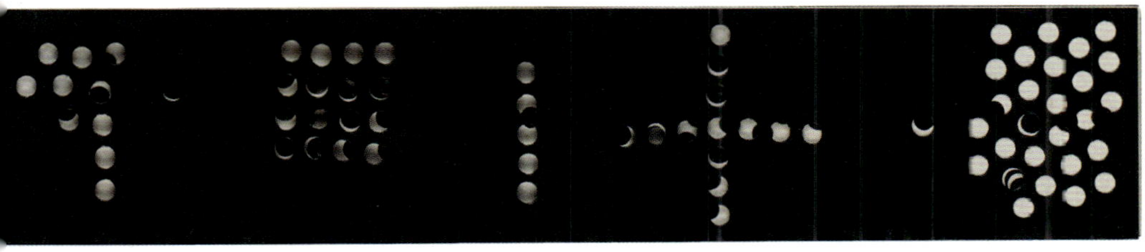

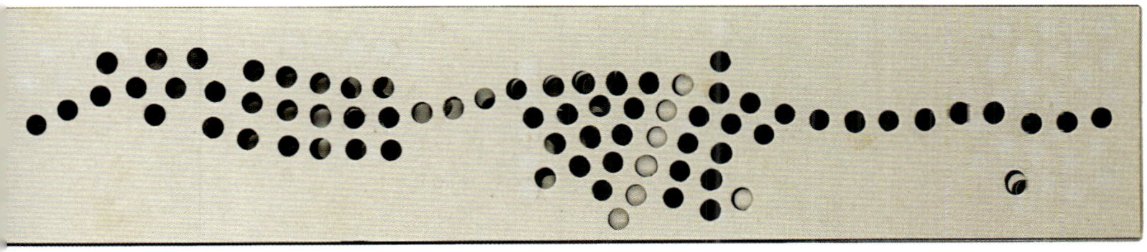

Untitled, from the series *Notebooks*
Sem título, da série *Cadernos*
1971
Perforated paper
5.5 x 32 cm
mira schendel estate

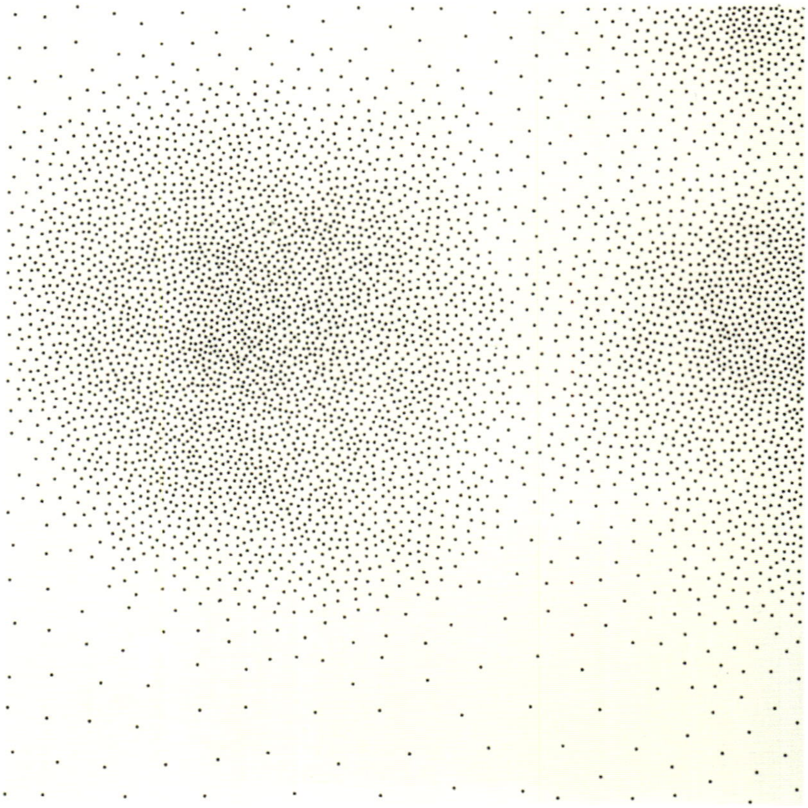

Perforated I
Perfurados I
1970s
Perforated paper
31.8 x 31.8 cm
Colección Patricia Phelps de Cisneros

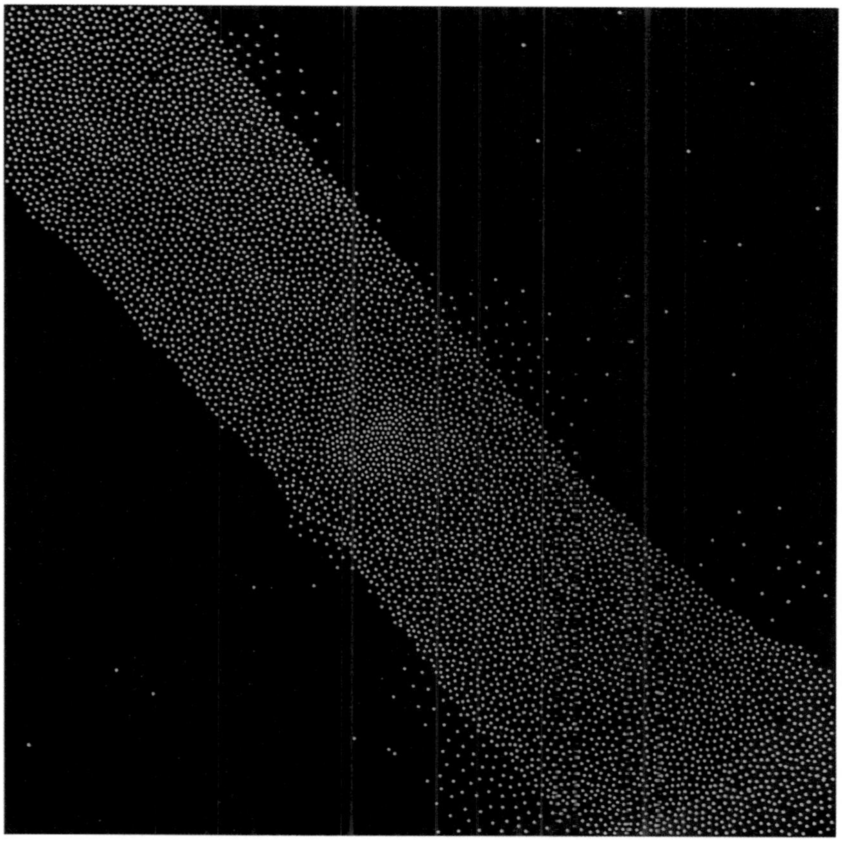

Perforated II
Perfurados II
1970s
Perforated paper
32 x 32 cm
The Museum of Modern Art, New York.
Purchase, 2005

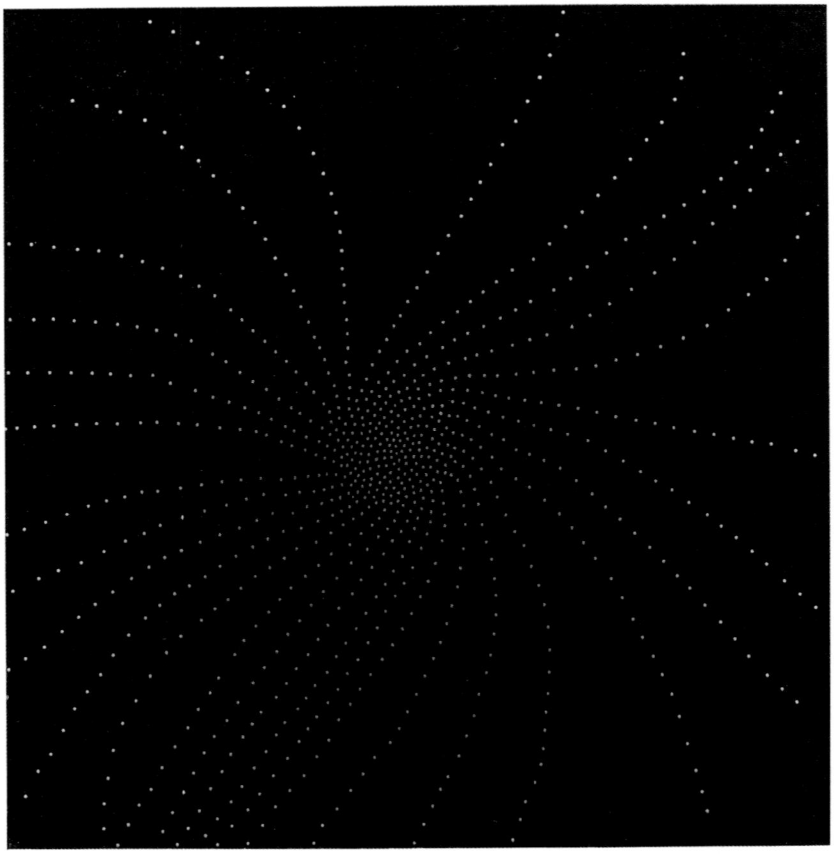

Perforated III
Perfurados III
1970s
Perforated paper
32 x 32 cm
The Museum of Modern Art, New York.
Purchase, 2005

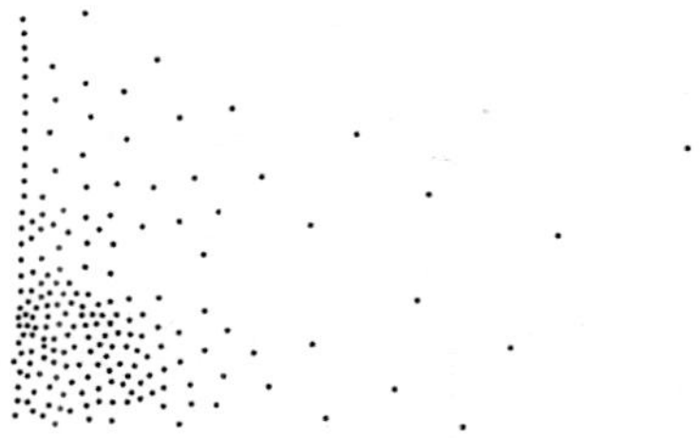

Perforated V
Perfurados V
1970s
Perforated paper
32 x 32 cm
The Museum of Modern Art, New York.
Purchase, 2005

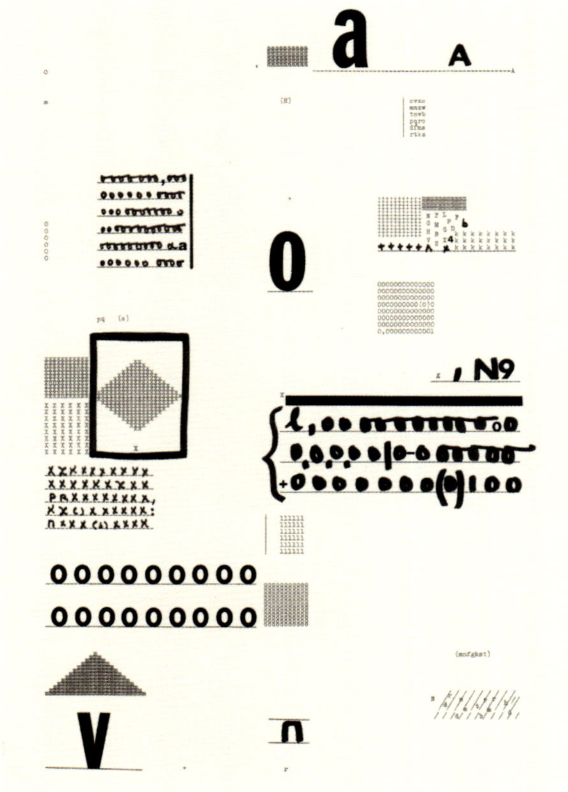

Untitled, from the series *Typed Writings*
Sem título, da série *Datiloscritos*
1974
Ink and transfer lettering on paper
50 x 36 cm
Estrellita B. and Daniel Brodsky Collection

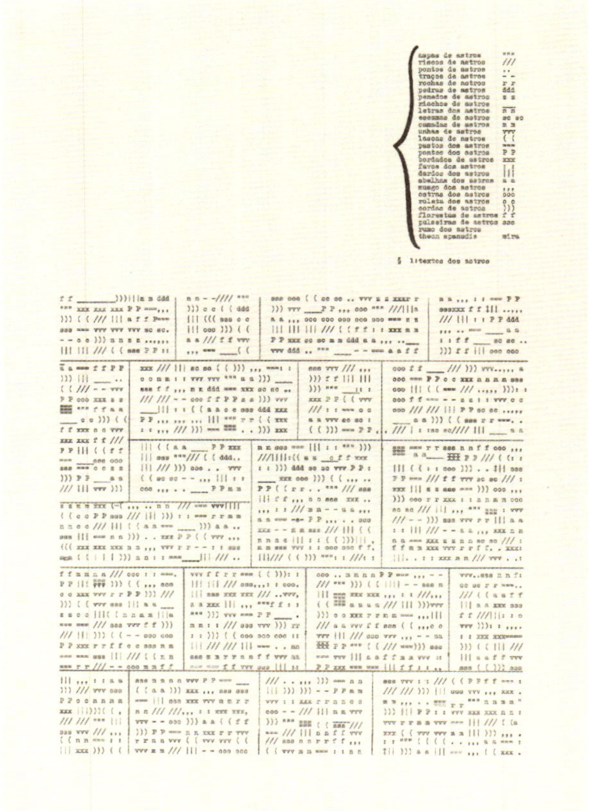

Untitled, from the series *Typed Writings*
Sem título, da série *Datiloscritos*
1970
Ink on paper
50.2 x 36.2 cm
The Museum of Modern Art, New York.
Committee on Drawings Funds, 2008

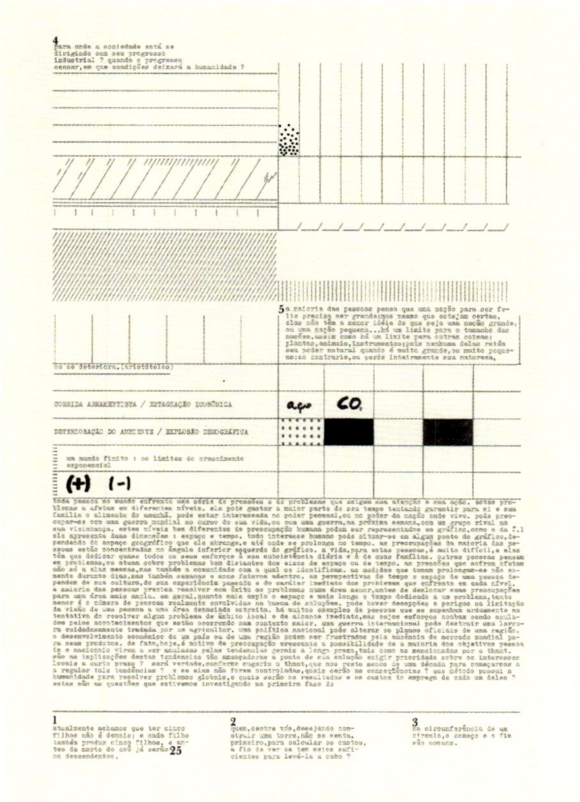

Untitled, from the series *Typed Writings*
Sem título, da série *Datiloscritos*
1974
Ink on paper
50.2 x 36.2 cm
The Museum of Modern Art, New York.
Committee on Drawings Funds, 2008

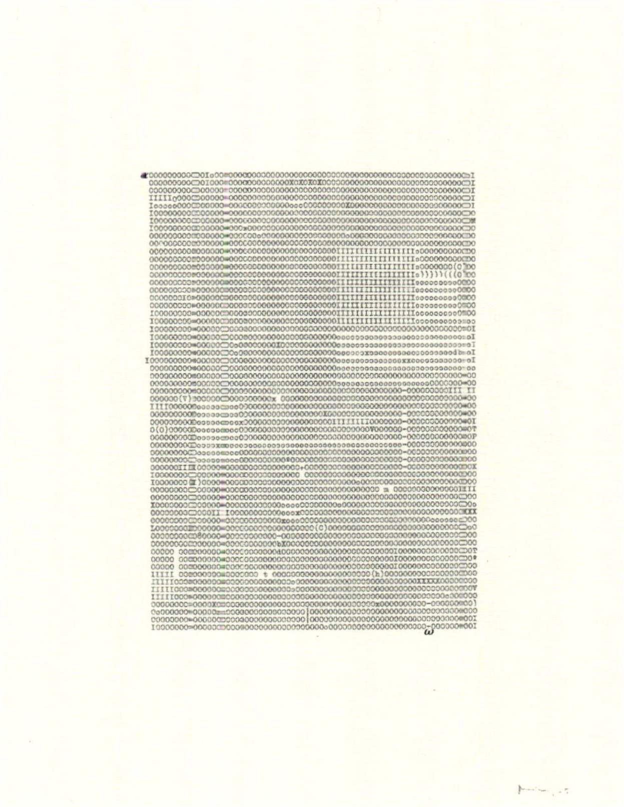

Untitled, from the series *Typed Writings*
Sem título, da série *Datiloscritos*
1974
Ink and transfer lettering on paper
50 x 37 cm
Private collection

Untitled, from the series *Typed Writings*
Sem título, da série *Datiloscritos*
1974
Ink on paper
50.8 x 36 cm
Private collection

hermann schmitz:system der philosophie
7 kapitel : zur geschichte der verdeckung und entdeckung des leibes,1965

§ 1 : die Gegenwart
§ 2 :
§ 3 :
§ 4 :
§ 5 :
§ 6 :
§ 7 :
§ 8 :
§ 9 :
§ 10 :
§ 11 :
§ 12 :
§ 13 :
§ 14 :
§ 15 :
§ 16 :
§ 17 :
§ 18 :
§ 19 :
§ 20 :
§ 21 :
§ 22 :
§ 23 :
§ 24 :
§ 25 :
§ 26 :
§ 27 :
§ 28 :
§ 29 :
§ 30 :
§ 31 :
§ 32 :
§ 33 :
§ 34 :
§ 35 :
§ 36 :
§ 37 :
§ 38 :
§ 39 :
§ 40 :
§ 41 :
§ 42 :
§ 43 : der Leib
§ 44 :
§ 45 :
§ 46 : die Überwindung des anthropologischen Dualismus
§ 47 :
§ 48 : Enge und Weite
§ 49 : Spannung und Schwellung
§ 50 : die Richtung
§ 51 : die Intensität und der Rhythmus
§ 52 : Privative Weitung
§ 53 : Protopathische und epikritische Tendenz
§ 54 : Leibinselbildung und Leibinselschwund
§ 55 : das Alphabet der Leiblichkeit
§ 56 : der Schreck
§ 58 : Mystische Techniken der Leibbemeisterung
§ 59 : Traum und Erwachen
§ 60: Die Wollust
§ 61 : Der Hunger
§ 62 : Der Durst
§ 63 : Der Ekel
§ 64 : Die Frische
§ 65 : Die Müdigkeit

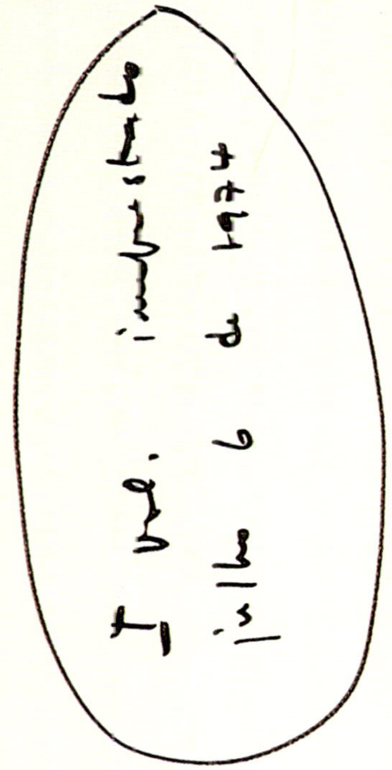

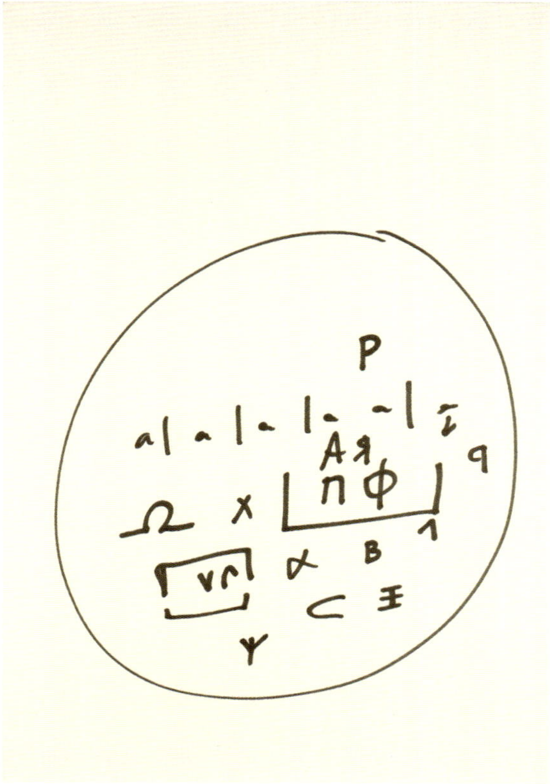

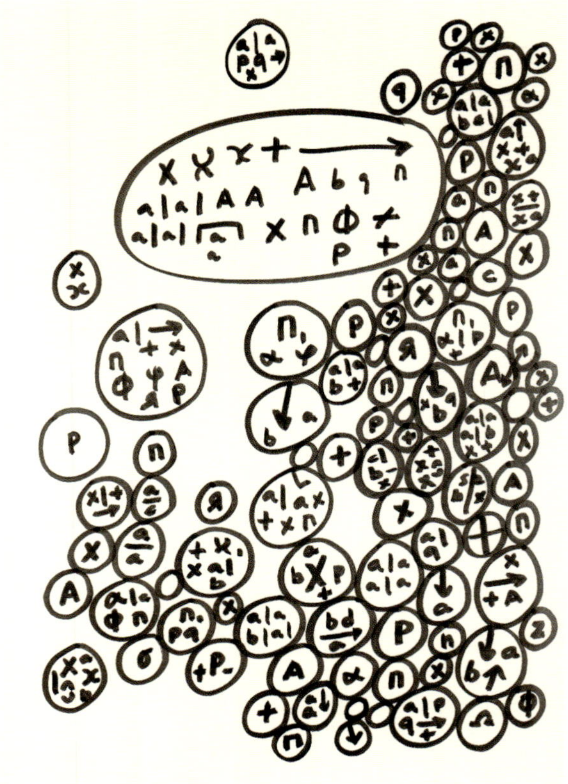

Untitled, from the series *Calculations*
Sem título, da série *Cálculos*
1970s
Ink on paper
49.8 x 34.7 cm
mira schendel estate

Untitled, from the series *Calculations*
Sem título, da série *Cálculos*
1970s
Ink on paper
50.2 x 36.2 cm
mira schendel estate

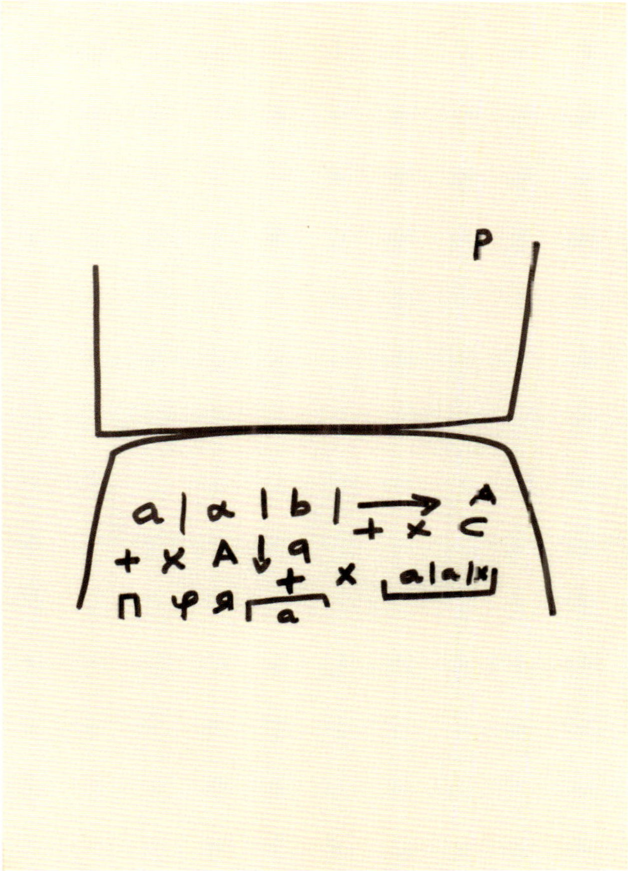

Untitled, from the series *Calculations*
Sem título, da série *Cálculos*
1974
Ink on paper
50 x 36 cm
Museu de Arte Moderna de São Paulo,
donation of Paulo Figueiredo

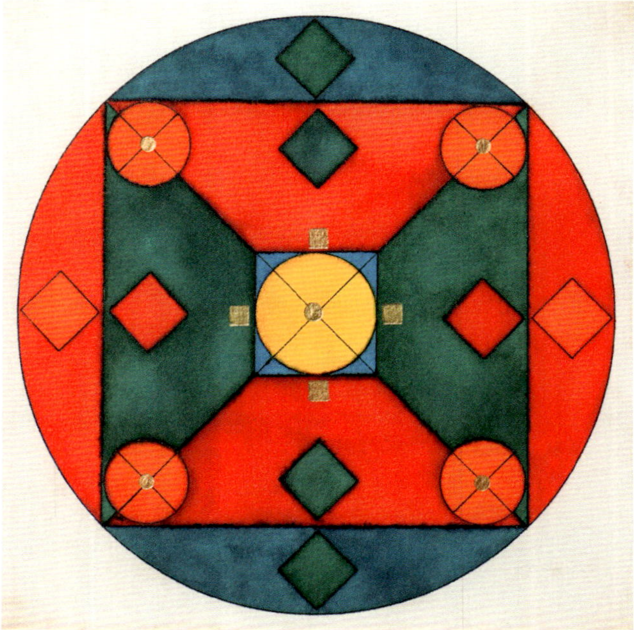

Untitled, from the series *Mandalas*
Sem título, da série *Mandalas*
1975
Ink and watercolour on paper
17.9 x 17.8 cm
Museu de Arte Moderna de São Paulo,
donation of Paulo Figueiredo

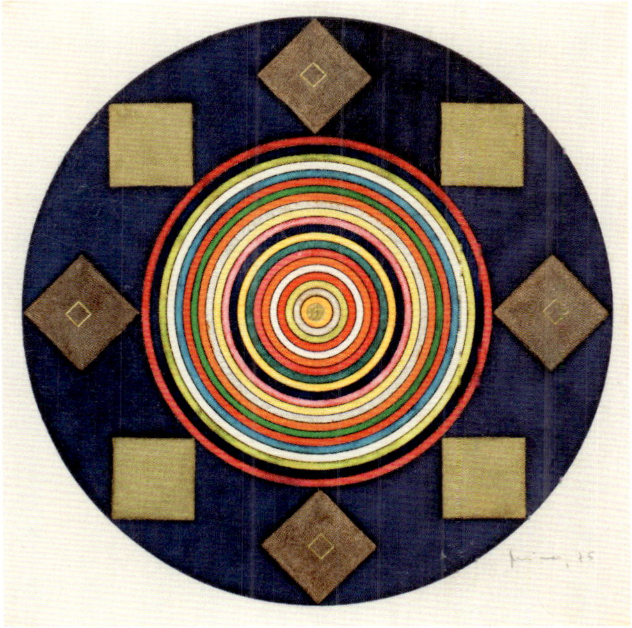

Untitled, from the series *Mandalas*
Sem título, da série *Mandalas*
1975
Ink and watercolour on paper
17.7 x 17.7 cm
Private collection

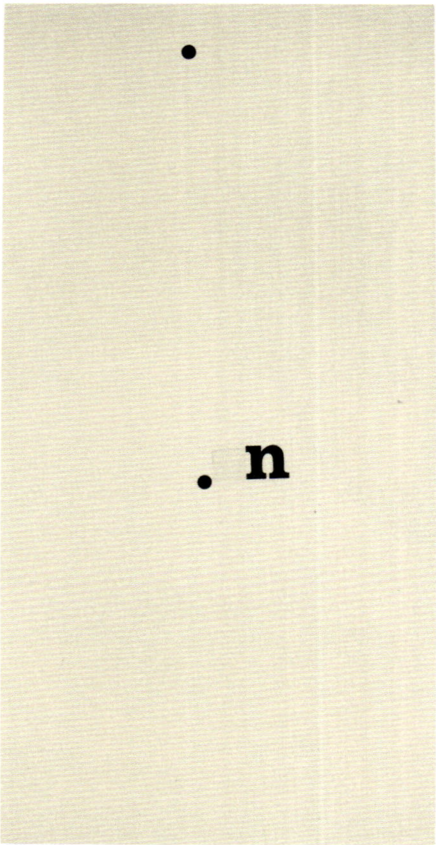
n

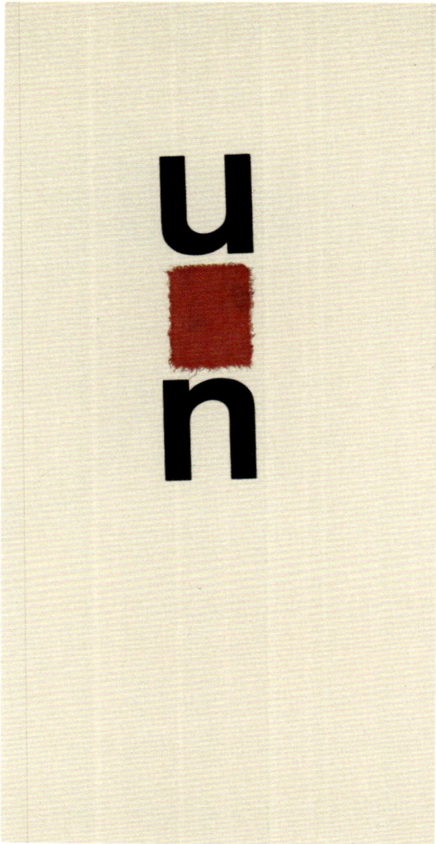
u
n

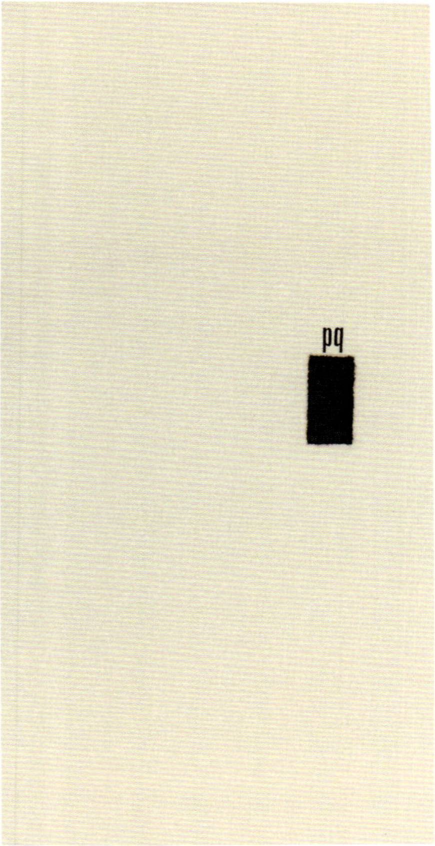

Untitled, from the series *Little Stubs*
Sem título, da série *Toquinhos*
1972–3
Transfer lettering and dyed paper on paper
each 49.3 x 25.5 cm
mira schendel estate

1 Homage | to God – Father of the West

2 Be glad Mount Zion | exult daughters of Judea | because of your judgments

3 And the spirit of God | moved over | the waters

4 The Just will rejoice | when vengeance comes; | their feet will bathe in impious blood. | Then it will be said: in truth there is | reward for the righteous – there is a God, in effect, | who judges the earth.

5 Your right hand will seize | those who hate you. | Will banish their seed from the land | Aim at their faces | with your bow. | Be exalted, oh Lord, in | your strength! We will sing and praise your power.

6 Do not punish me in your | wrath.

Homage to God – Father of the West
Homenagem a Deus – Pai do Ocidente
1975
Transfer lettering and ink on paper
16 parts: each 50.2 x 26 cm
Private collection

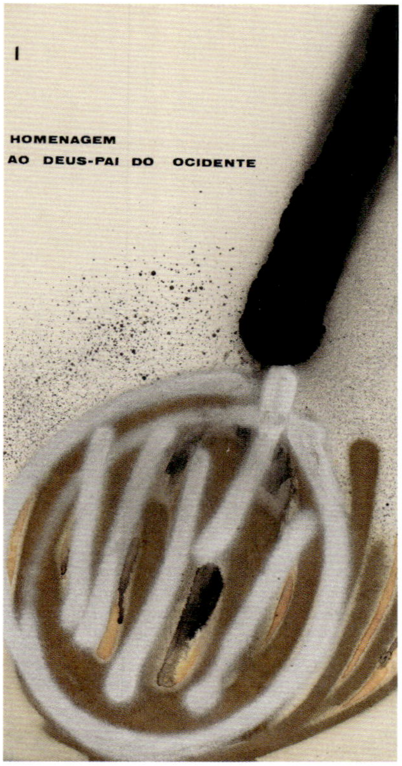
1
HOMENAGEM
AO DEUS-PAI DO OCIDENTE

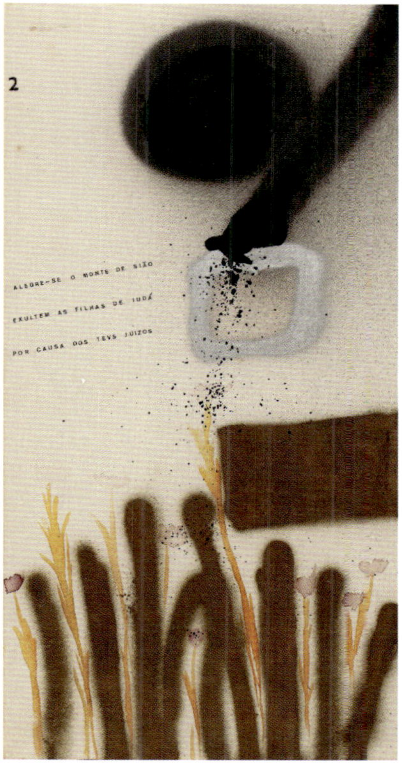
2
ALEGRE-SE O MONTE DE SIÃO
EXULTEM AS FILHAS DE IUDÁ
POR CAUSA DOS TEUS JUIZOS

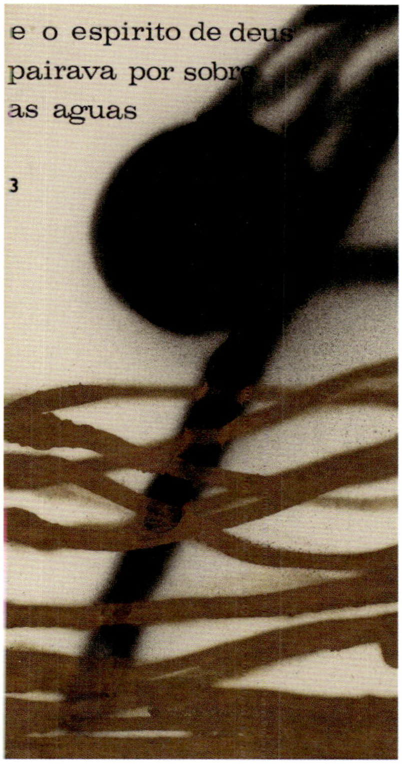
e o espirito de deus
pairava por sobre
as aguas
3

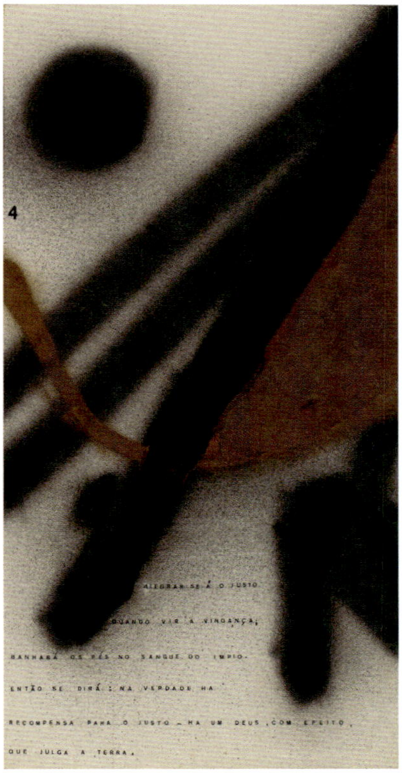
4
ALEGRAR-SE-Á O JUSTO
QUANDO VIR A VINGANÇA;
BANHARÁ OS PÉS NO SANGUE DO IMPIO.
ENTÃO SE DIRÁ: NA VERDADE HA
RECOMPENSA PARA O JUSTO – HA UM DEUS, COM EFEITO,
QUE JULGA A TERRA.

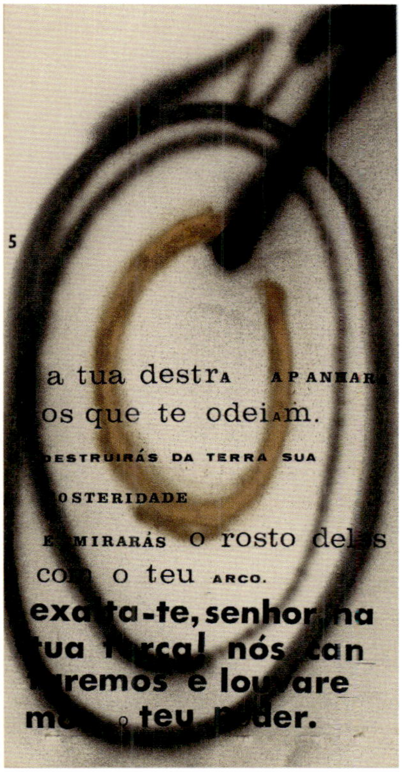
5
a tua destra APANHARÁ
os que te odeiam.
DESTRUIRÁS DA TERRA SUA
OSTERIDADE
MIRARÁS o rosto del
o teu ARCO.
exa ta-te, senhor, na
tua nós can
remos e lou are
o teu der.

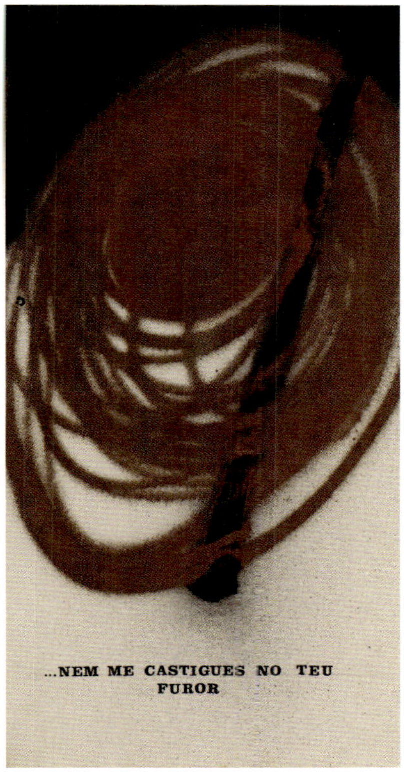
...NEM ME CASTIGUES NO TEU
FUROR

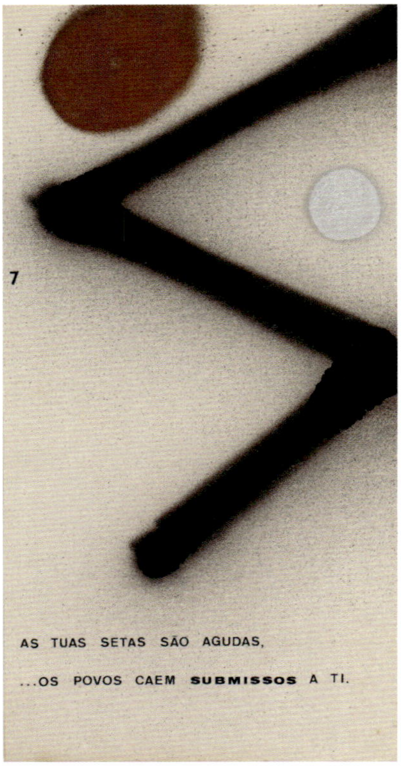
AS TUAS SETAS SÃO AGUDAS,
...OS POVOS CAEM SUBMISSOS A TI.
7

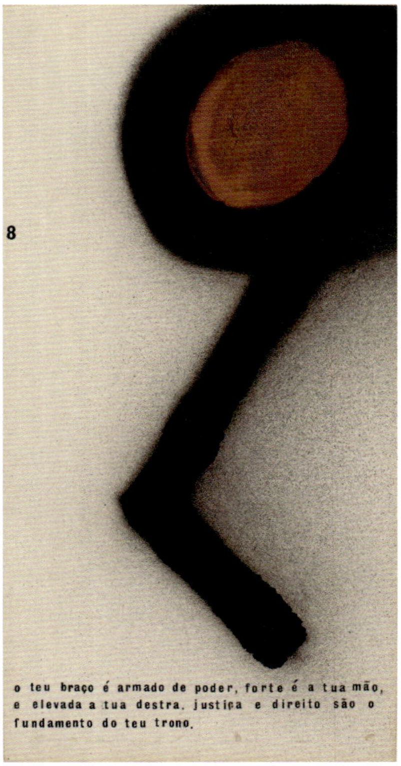
o teu braço é armado de poder, forte é a tua mão,
e elevada a tua destra, justiça e direito são o
fundamento do teu trono.
8

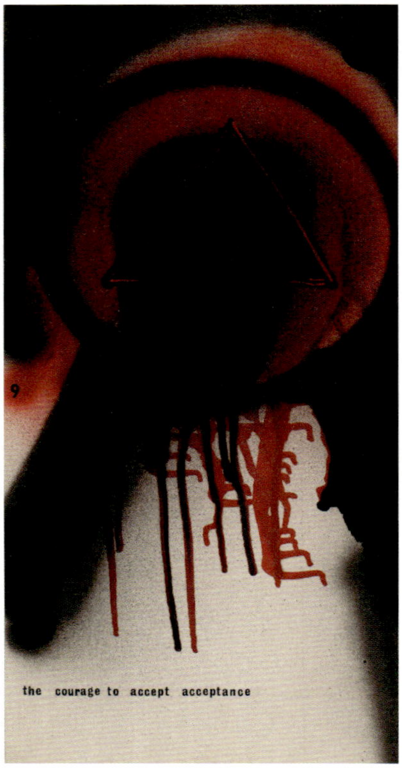
the courage to accept acceptance
9

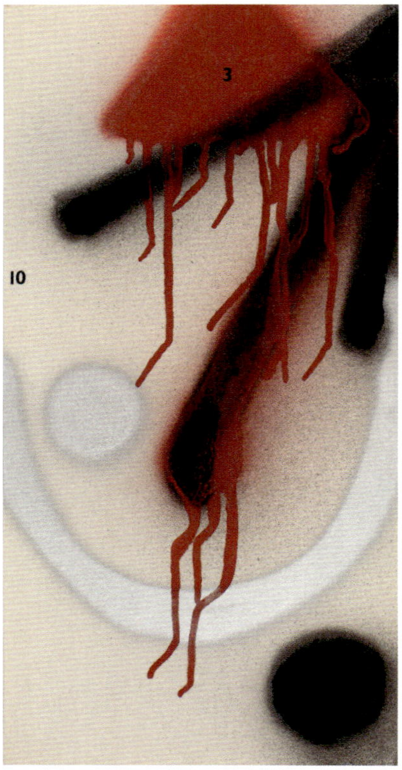
3
10

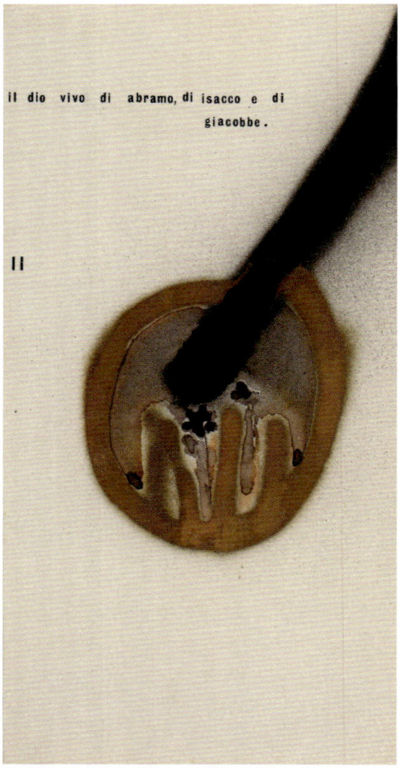
il dio vivo di abramo, di isacco e di
giacobbe.
11

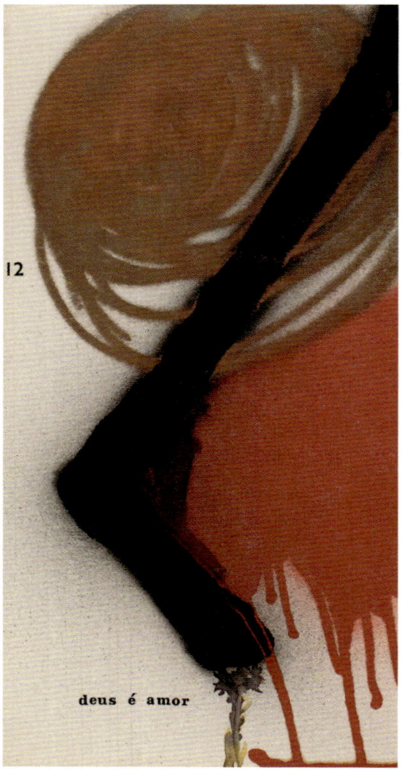
deus é amor
12

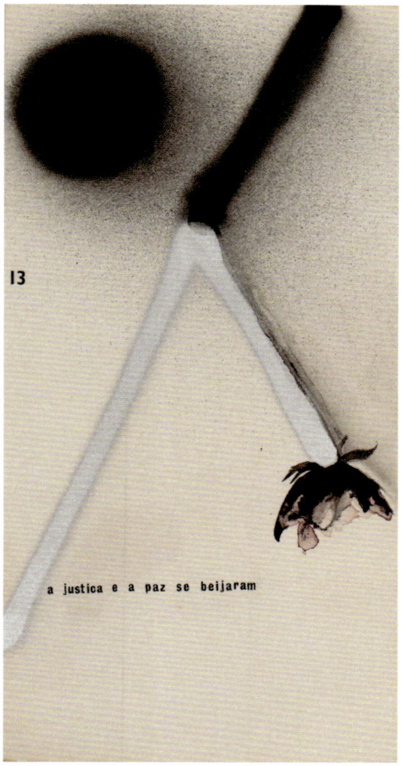

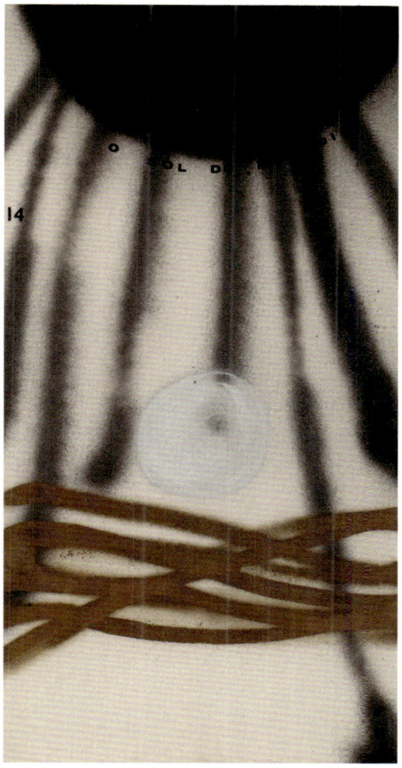

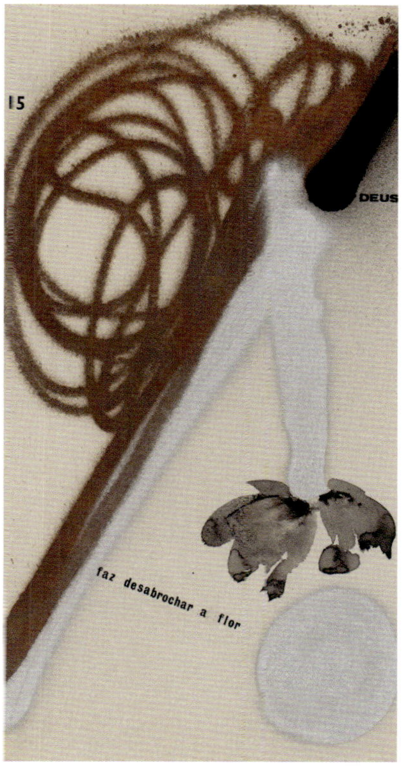

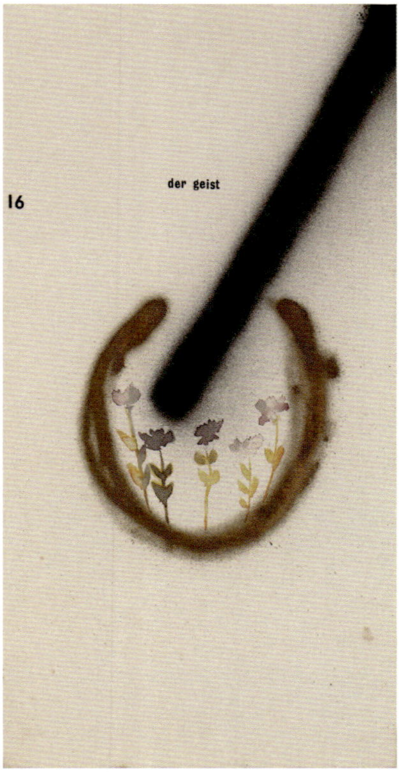

7 Your arrows are sharp. | ...the people submit to You.

8 your arm is full of power, strong is your hand, | raised high is your right hand righteousness and justice are | the foundation of your throne

9 the courage to accept acceptance (in English)

10 3

11 the living God of Abraham, Isaac and Jacob (in Italian)

12 God is love

13 justice and peace have kissed

14 the sun at noon

15 God | makes the flower bloom

16 the ghost (in German)

I Ching
I Ching
1970
Watercolour on paper
6 parts: each 45 x 23 cm
Private collection

I Ching
I Ching
1970
Watercolour on paper
6 parts: each 46 x 24 cm
mira schendel estate

Untitled
Sem título
c.1985
Tempera and gold leaf on wood
140.6 x 90.5 cm
Collection of Paulo Joppert (in Memoriam)

Untitled
Sem título
1987
Tempera, gesso and graphite on wood
90 x 180 cm
Collection Raquel Arnaud

Untitled
Sem título
1985
Tempera, gesso and gold leaf on wood
89 x 159 cm
Andrea and José Olympio Pereira Collection

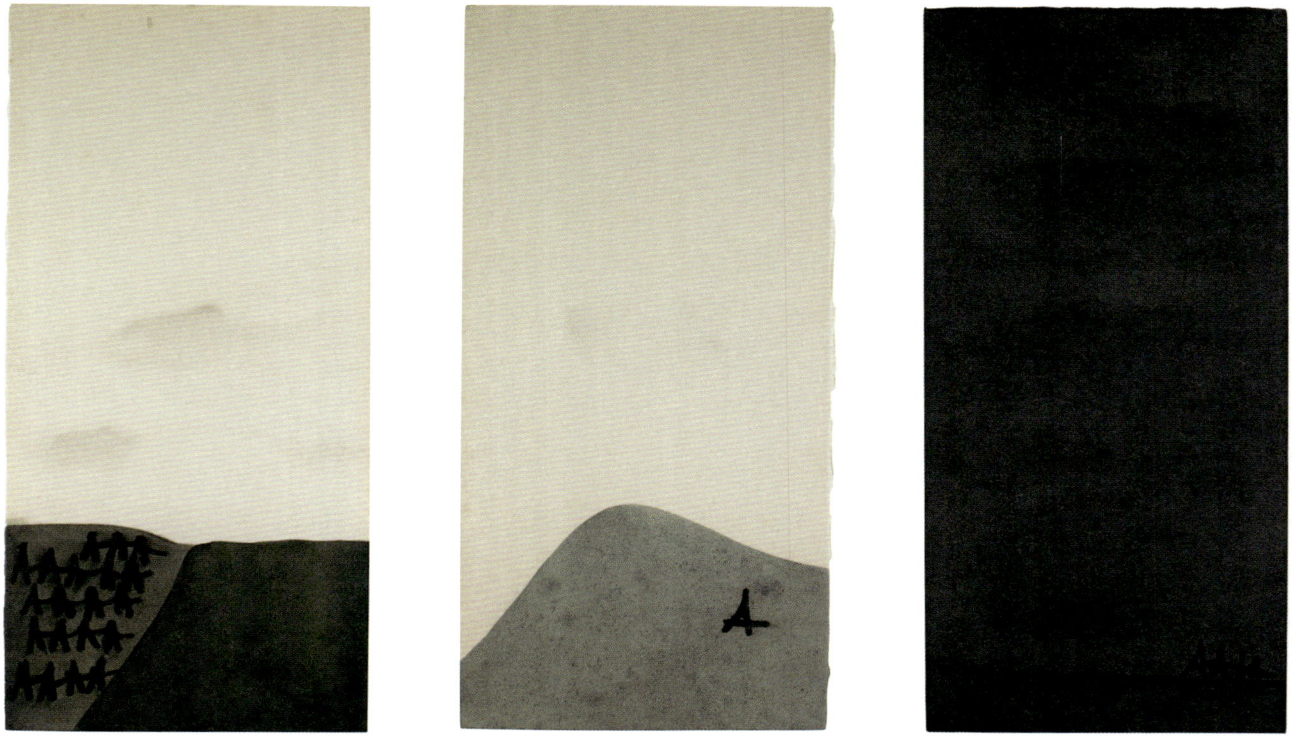

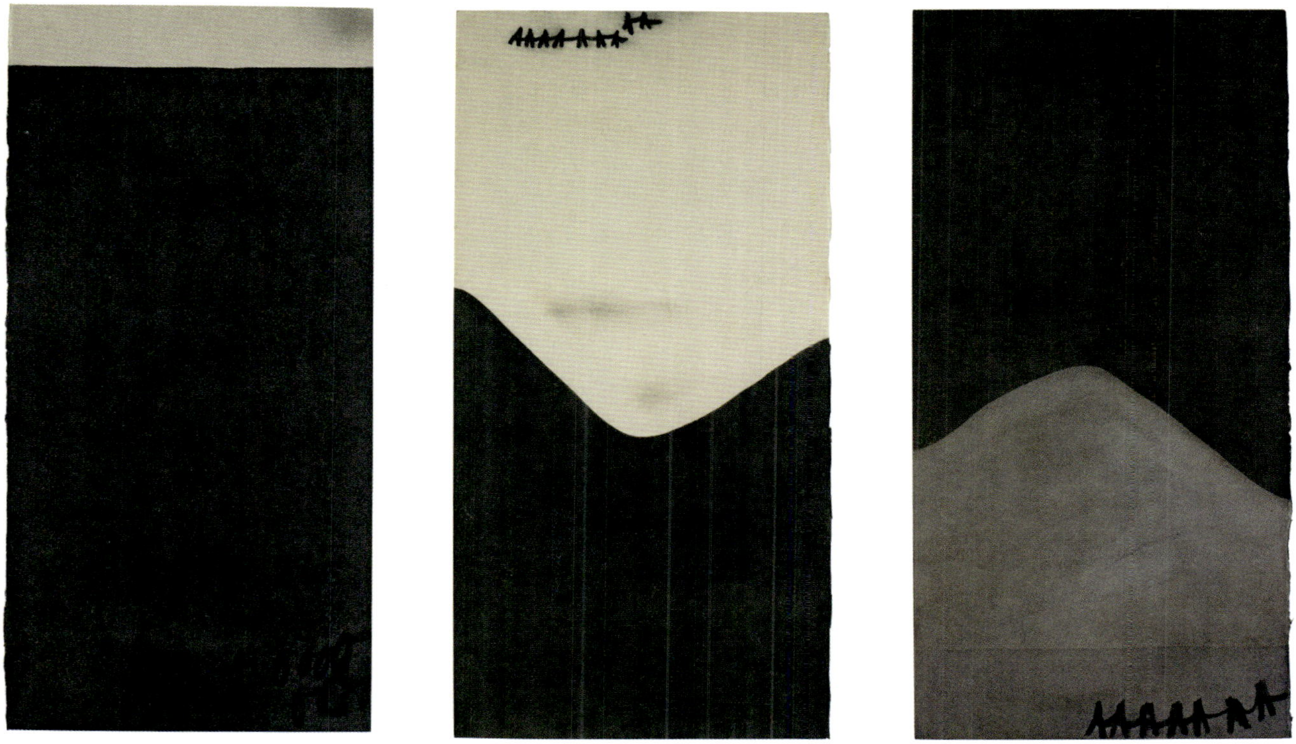

Untitled, from the series *Itatiaia Landscape*
Sem título, da série *Paisagem de Itatiaia*
1978
Tempera on paper
each 46 x 23.5 cm
mira schendel estate

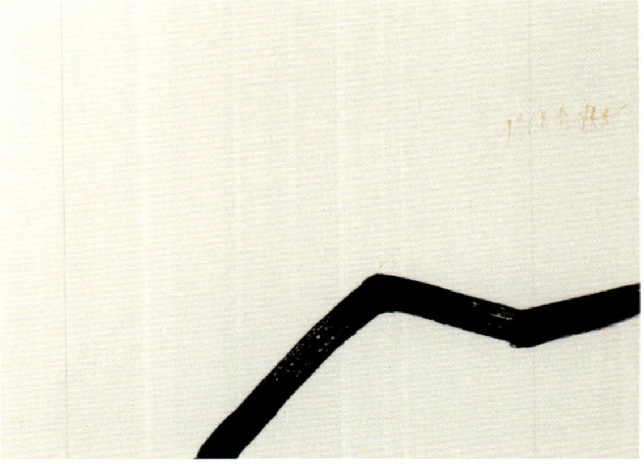

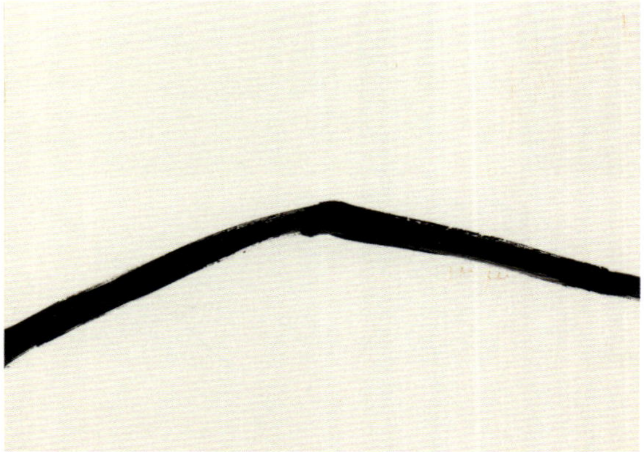

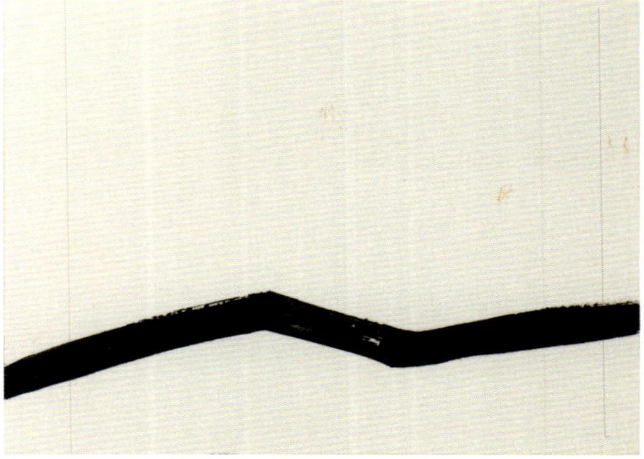

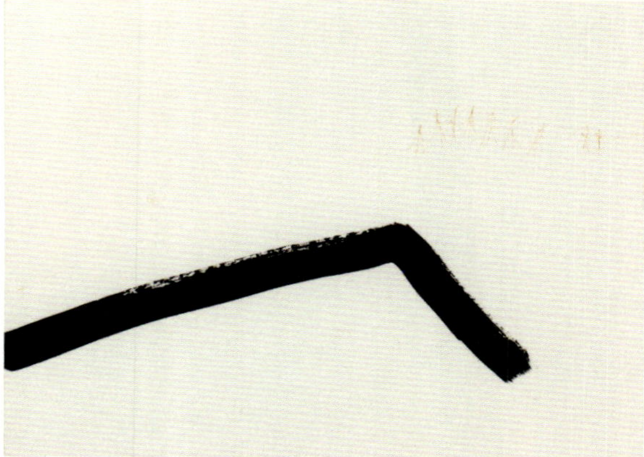
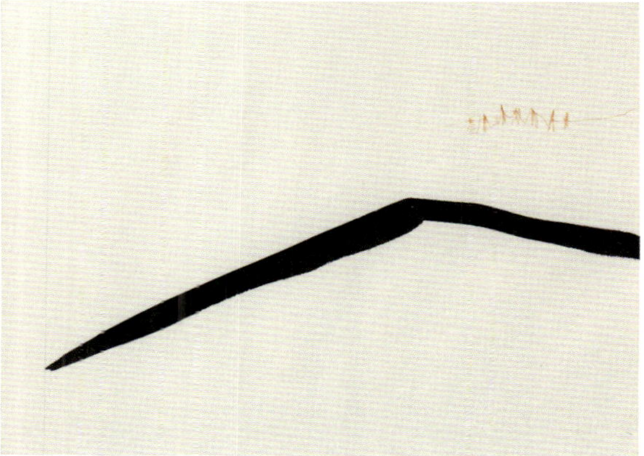
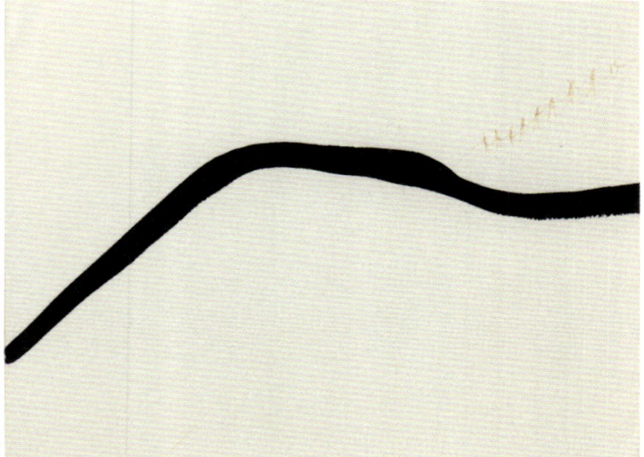
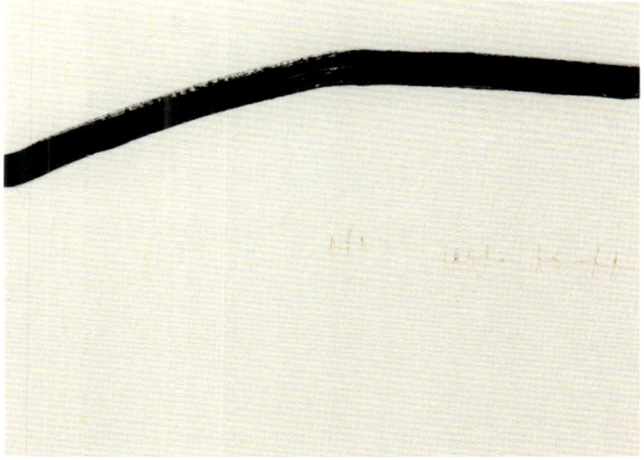

Untitled, from the series *Chinese Landscape*
Sem título, da série *Paisagem Chinesa*
1980s
Ink on paper
each 25 x 35 cm
Collection Ivo Vel Kos

Batten
Sarrafo
1987
Tempera and gesso on wood
198 x 180 x 9.2 cm
Colección Patricia Phelps de Cisneros

Batten
Sarrafo
1987
Tempera and gesso on wood
96 x 180 x 47.5 cm
Jones Bergamin

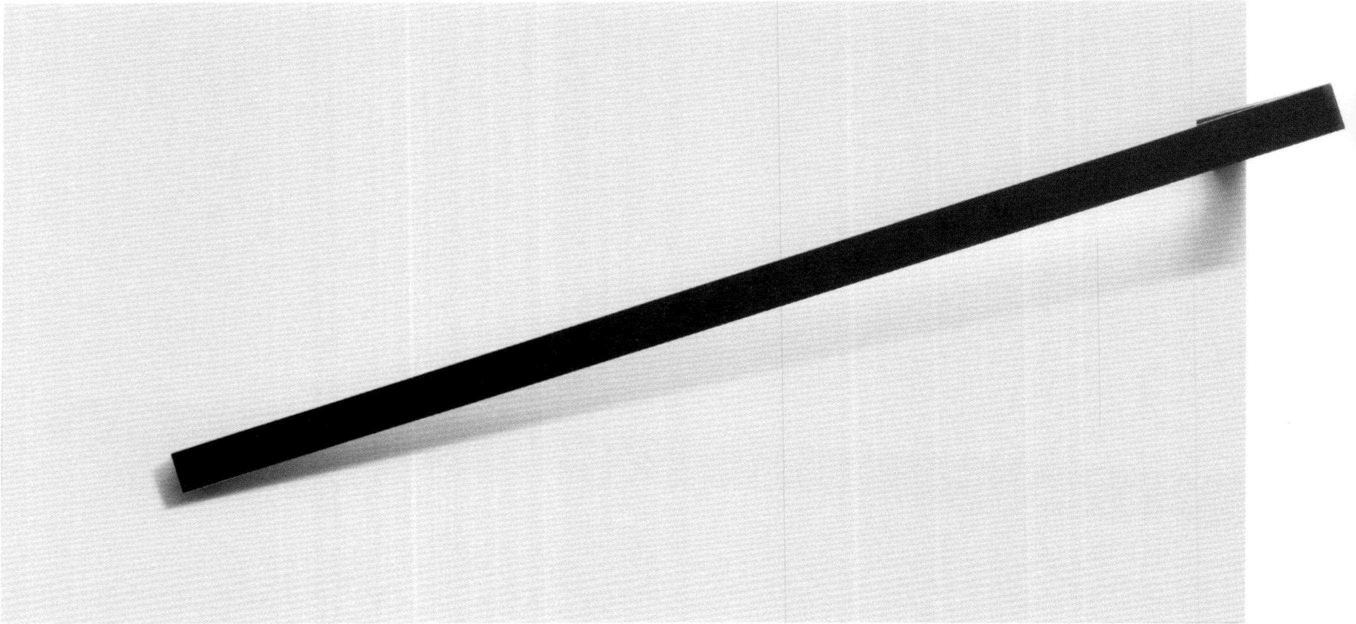

Batten
Sarrafo
1987
Tempera and gesso on wood
90 x 180 x 54
mira schendel estate

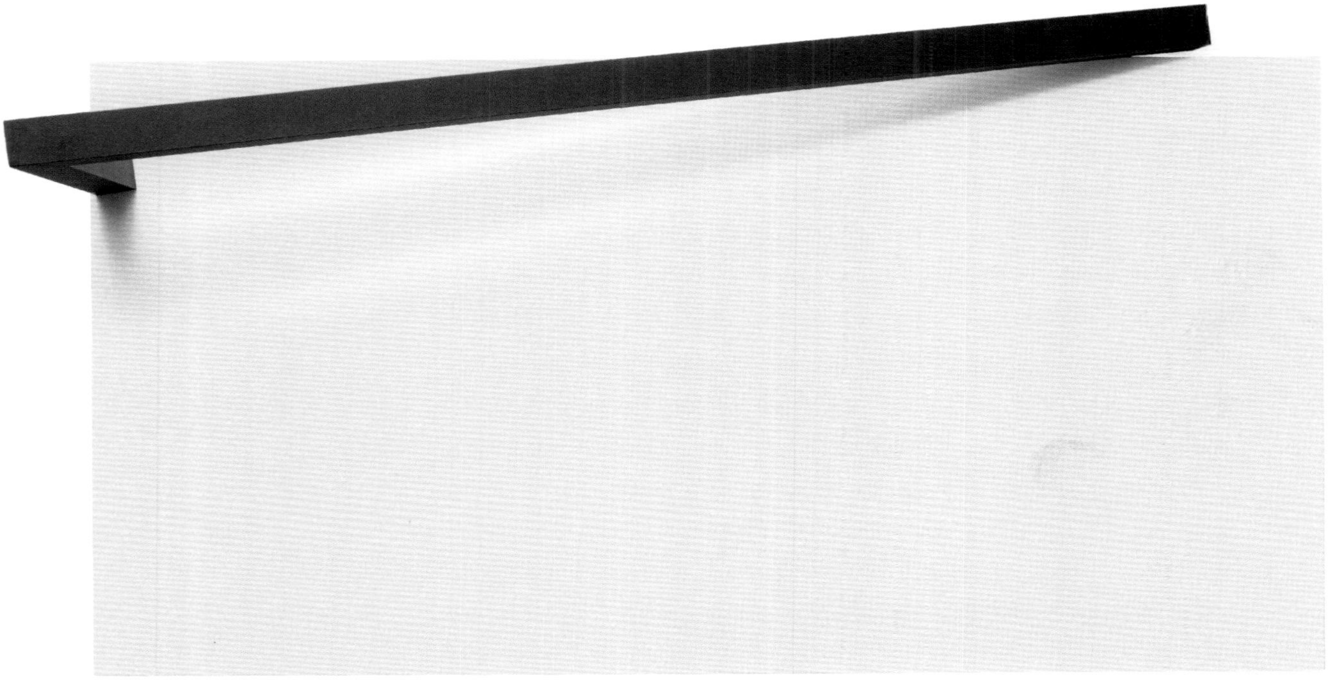

Batten
Sarrafo
1987
Tempera and gesso on wood
97 x 180 x 52 cm
mira schendel estate
Gift of José Resende and Sofia Telles

Mira Schendel Statement*

The works curently on display have resulted from a hitherto frustrated attempt to catch the discourse right at the moment of its birth. My concern is with capturing the transfer of the instant living experience, full of empirical vigour, onto the symbol imbued with memorability and relative eternity. I know that, in fact, I have a problem in that the immediate life, i.e. the life I live and within which I act, is solely, incommunicably mine, and, for this reason, senseless and without purpose. On the other hand, the realm of symbols which seeks to seize this life (the realm of languages), is an anti-life–in the sense of being something intersubjective, ordinary, devoid of emotion and suffering. If only I could match these two realms, I would combine the richness of this living experience with the relative immortality of the symbol. In other words, my work constitutes an attempt to immortalise fleeting moments and confer meaning to ephemeral things. Obviously, therefore, for this endeavor I must seize the very instant in which the living experience seeps onto the symbol, which in this case is the letter.

Initially I believed that for this purpose all I must do was identify within myself the living experience's urge for articulation; in other words, I should sit and wait for the letter to form itself, to take shape on paper and to connect itself with other letters into a pre-literal, pre-discursive writing. However, from the beginning I felt that to ensure a successful accomplishment I should use transparent paper. Now I am in a position to make a better assessment of the reason why, back in those days, I had this impression. To be itself, the character has to have its sides as exposed as possible during its shaping up.

A second problem is the fact that the set of characters on paper imitate time, though it cannot actually represent it. These characters simulate the time past but do not seize the unretrievable living experience that characterised this time. Anyone can read and reread my scribbles on paper, but no one can read time. The scribbles denote, but do not immortalise, the fluidity of time. For this reason I have quit trying.

I gave up because I have discovered acrylic, that seemingly offers the following possibilities: a. it shows the reverse side of the plane, thus denying the plane surface of

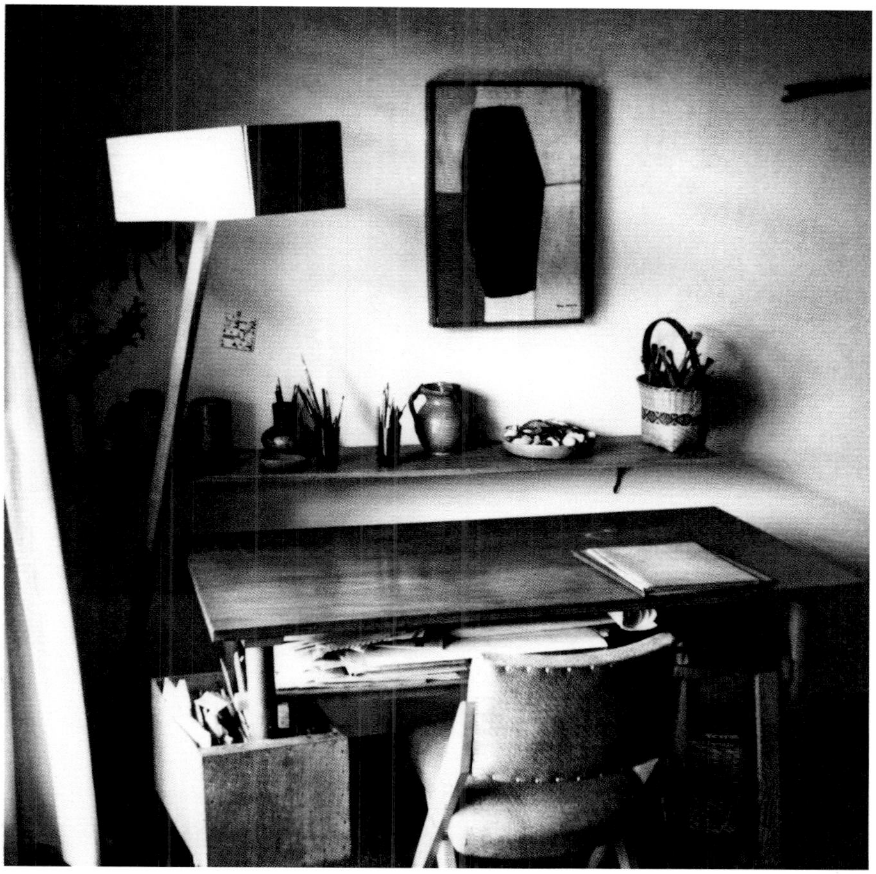

Mira Schendel's studio, 1960s
mira schendel estate archive

the plane; b. it confers legibility to the reverse side of the characters, thus transforming text into anti-text; c. it allows a circular reading, where the lettering constitutes a fixed centre around which the viewer moves. Thus time is transferred from artwork to viewer as it is bounced back from symbol to life; d. the characteristic transparency of acrylic is that false transparency of explained meanings not the clear, flat transparency of glass, but the mysterious transparency of the clarification of problems.

I am still not satisfied. I do not believe acrylic is the wisdom stone, and for this reason I have begun to experiment with film, simultaneously. But if the work presently being exhibited has any worth, it comes from denoting a station on one of the multiple potential roads to the aggregation of value onto life's goal.

* Translation by Izabel Burbridge.

Excerpt from undated and unsigned typed text found among the artist's papers, mira schendel estate archive

Interview with Mira Schendel
Mira Schendel, Painter: Empty Space Moves Me Deeply*
Jorge Guinle

Mira's sunny apartment looks like a Bauhaus refuge: Spartan, albeit simple and comfortable. One breathes an atmosphere of logic and, at the same time, affability. We talked for a long time before starting our interview. As the interview progressed, Mira retrieved several folders containing drawings and prints from different phases of her career. In the end, always affectionate, she laughed a lot with the new-born grandson who had recently arrived.

Jorge Guinle>> Mira, this interview, following our conversation, aims to better understand your work. I was very lucky because one day in 1966, while visiting the Museu de Arte Moderna do Rio de Janeiro, I entered a room and saw a line with various sheets of rice paper hanging from one side to the other. On the wall there were about thirty very fragile drawings, lines tenuously traced. I had never seen work like that. It made a great impact on me. After that I spent many years, ten to fifteen, without seeing your work, Mira. But the visual experience engraved in my memory was that of seeing something very fragile and tenuous, blurring the border between being and non-being.

Mira Schendel>> Something ambiguous, Jorge.

JG>> Ambiguous. It was a very strong visual experience during my adolescence, one that I can remember very well. It is wonderful for us to meet here, years later, in São Paulo, and begin again to enter your world, to see new works and older pieces, and draw up an inventory, a profile of your entire artistic and poetic world; feel all the diverse influences, cultures, different eras that intersect in your work. This energy that comes as much from Tantric art as from a drawing by an inspired Zen monk, from concrete art, from Klee. And this accumulation of experiences is arranged in abstract space in the simplest possible way.

MS>> Well, I wanted to ask you a question. When you – I don't know if you can remember because you were very young at the time – when you entered the room, was the room empty? There was no one there, right?

JG>> Yes, it was empty.

* Interview held in July 1981 for *Interview* magazine. Translated by Oswaldo Corrêa da Costa.

MS>> Because that was a bit of a joke, that exhibition at MAM in Rio in 1966. When I arrived at the exhibition, after having installed it, there was not a living soul; it was empty, everybody had run to another room nearby, where there was another exhibition being held. Mine was empty. All that whiteness. It was like that. Something amazing. It was all white, all empty. Then I received, from a friend here in São Paulo, a bouquet of red roses. For me, the hope was that those red roses, set against the whiteness, would make someone appear. Indeed, every now and then someone did appear. But deep down it was as if I had presented a red rose to that whiteness. A most impressive thing.

JG>> Well, talking of that, when you speak of a red flower on white, it is curious, this whole series of collage-drawings that you're showing me; the concrete, material flowers, pasted against this abstract, infinite background, are truly a mental landscape that is being handled here as in your exhibition. Indeed, the exhibitions could be called mental landscapes.

MS>> That was very strange, the low attendance [at MAM] that somehow suited the work itself. Now, it was completely different in London. I remember, in London, in 1966, it was a time of great ferment, of change; it was a very important moment. I remember the gallery.[1] It was full. There was coming and going. There were people everywhere. A completely different atmosphere. The English must have a different mentality. They were not startled by the work. On the contrary, it was much better received. There was a more resounding effect in England than in Rio de Janeiro. But, in Rio, the absent people did nothing but reinforce all that emptiness that was in the drawing itself, both in the line and on the sheets. I find this experience of the work very interesting. Because an idea also depends very much on the appreciation of others. How they see it, face it, consider it art or not. In the most fragile way possible, at its most precarious, on the threshold of existence, it presents itself to the world. It is interesting that, surrounding the work in Rio de Janeiro, the atmosphere created by this absence, this emptiness, was almost the atmosphere of the drawing itself. The exhibition did not disappoint me. It was a spiritual experience, so to speak. It touched me from both sides. I did not take it as a slight.

JG>> And maybe the experience that you drew from the exhibition gave you the courage to continue working. This conviction of the importance of the work itself made you want to continue along those lines.

MS>> Ah, I guess. Because people fleeing that emptiness, after all, strengthened it too, and that was very interesting indeed.

JG>> Were there reviews at the time?

1 This refers to her solo show held at Signals, London, a gallery devoted to experimental art. [Editor's note].

MS>> I think something came out. There must be reviews that I haven't even read yet. Now, in England a review came out in the *Times*, by Guy Brett, who also did a book on kinetic art.

JG>> Including you, Lygia Clark and Hélio Oiticica.

MS>> Hélio, Lygia, Sergio Camargo.

JG>> Funny how Brazilian art has an ascetic, rigorous side that means it deviates from a tropical register. One thinks, for example, of Antonio Dias, from the state of Paraíba, what rigorous, ascetic work he makes. All, or almost all, Brazilian visual avant-garde art has this cleanness.

MS>> I don't know.

JG>> But it is also a legacy of 1950s concretism.

MS>> I don't know. The ascetic is so dangerous. It is possible to have an asceticism overturning the extremely sensorial. Now, asceticism is always presented to us as something disconnected from the world, but there can be other types of asceticism, like Tantric asceticism, for example, which is extremely sensorial and sensual, so, as you see, asceticism does not necessarily mean an absence of the sensorial or sensual.

JG>> Often it is contained energy.

MS>> Contained. In other words, ready to break out. I find a good example in the ascetic music of certain works by Stockhausen from a decade ago, or more; I think there is this extraordinary restraint in order to generate an almost cosmic explosion at the end. Now, as far as the avant-garde, I am somewhat out of touch. It is a very difficult topic for me; I cannot describe what avant-garde is. When I lived near Oxford, there was a beautiful windmill on a country road with an exhibition of concrete poetry. It was on the way to Oxford, and there were many Brazilian artists. There are people out there saying that Brazilians import fashions, that Brazilians were colonised. I think Brazilians have done much that has been exported, but few have realised that. I think that there may be moments of greater give-and-take, but artists from different countries have always influenced each other.

JG>> Yes, like the French fauves. Matisse and Derain influenced the German fauves Schmidt-Rottluff or Kirchner. I think that's great. The opposite would have been terrible. Cultures would be closed off, tied down. I find it curious, though, the way even cultures of the past that were unaware of each other, like those of Egypt, or of China, how similar they are, how they have things in common. I have always liked this osmosis between different cultures. If we had Indian or Chinese influences here in

Brazil, it would be amazing. The Japanese influence is very strong here in São Paulo, for example, and I think that's great. All this enriches art. In the early days of modern painting, impressionism was greatly influenced by Japanese prints: the lack of shading, the flatness of the image, the bird's-eye perspective instead of Renaissance perspective. Matisse also stated that the idea of black as a colour like any other, rather than the opposite of white, to a great extent derived from Japanese prints. Much of modern gesturalism derives from Far Eastern calligraphy. Therefore, I too find it simplistic to view Brazilian art as the art of a colonised country, instead of part of a worldwide give-and-take. Now, returning to your work, nowadays it has a simplicity, a restraint, a very pronounced rigour; volume, line, opaque light, bright light are all translated in the simplest possible way on paper.

MS>> Well, this simplicity allows for thousands of variations. As a matter of fact, for me, the sense of space touches me subjectively but, objectively, for me, places that are physically small can also be large spaces. The large empty space is something that moves me deeply, touches me deeply, but I can also paint other types of space. In these collages [*Mira reaches for collages*], for example, I use a more psychological space, less timeless. I also have to accept that these things ultimately came from me, more or less intentionally, made me laugh or even have fun, but do not move me so deeply.

JG>> Are they your psychological side?

MS>> Yes, but they are important things, lived through, evoked from my memory. Phenomena like these also lend validity to other, more abstract ones.

JG>> In all your works, Mira, I feel this junction of different cultures, of different styles. In the recent exhibition at Galeria Luisa Strina, for example, in the thirty-five drawings shown there, I felt two movements in opposite directions: the static part represented by the well-delineated geometric shape and the temporal part that is experienced (when this geometric form, originally well traced and delineated, is rubbed and blurred, indicating movement and texture). Here we find two worlds: the temporal and the timeless. Two different styles intersect. At first glance, hastily, it would be a work of concrete art. Looked at longer, the sketched part, erased or in movement, creates an almost expressionistic emotional aura. These oppositions define your work and give it strength.

MS>> Indeed, today, even in painting, no matter how much I use geometric shapes, the sensory element of the brushstroke, the texture is always there; for me this is very important. I would never make a completely smooth painting.

JG>> It's very funny. Because in Mondrian this aspect is also very important, the brushstroke and texture are very beautiful. It is hard to grasp that in reproductions. But painting is alive, the directions of the brushstrokes and the slightly pasty texture contrasting with a certain rigidity of composition; and the black lines, dense from being reworked so often, are like a relic of the difficulty in creating a composition. This dialogue between the sensual side of matter and the rigidity of construction, all of this is very significant.

MS>> For me, according to my way of seeing things, I think that we can never escape this aspect of perception and corporeality. And that is because, in whatever kind of art, even the most abstract, or in architecture, we always have this second category of corporeality that will engage the disposition of each person's body, isn't that right? Art that completely covers this texture, this movement of the hand is extremely wrong. I give the utmost importance to it being manual like this, that it be handmade, that it be experienced, that it come out this way from the womb. I think this is of utmost importance.

JG>> We feel that in your work.

MS>> Now, there are people saying that my work is very intellectual. I don't think so.

JG>> Yes, I used to think that way. Nowadays less so.

MS>> I do not agree, do not agree.

JG>> Funny. Now I see things in a different way, but that is because I have seen so many examples. My first impression was that it was very intellectualised, very rarefied, but, little by little, the more sensitive, the more poetic side is emerging.

MS>> Because even intellectual life, let's say, even it assumes a specific, corporeal disposition; in other words, we can never withdraw ourselves from corporeality.

JG>> You mean the body in relation to the work.

MS>> The work, the world, the way of being, of living, artists have always had this sense of the body within space. It is a very strong concern. It is the dimension of the work. And they happen simultaneously. Where there is the void, there is also the individualisation of the full. They are simultaneous; they cannot be separated from each other.

JG>> You see, Corbusier himself used to measure the size of the habitat in relation to the human body.

MS>> Indeed, a human measure.

JG>> When you think about North American abstractionists – Pollock, Newman – they wanted pictures that would fully envelop the person looking at them, a bit like the walls of the caves where painting was born; a desire to rediscover the mythical space of total involvement. Except that Pollock indicates this space without any associative or symbolic connotation.

MS>> Concrete.

JG>> Pollock was concrete, not symbolic. In his case, it is energy without any philosophical connotation. The very phenomenon of looking, the thing itself without any separation. Then this frees the mind from all the past, from all symbolism, it proposes fantastic paths, cleansing the human mind of all the accretions of civilisation or rather, it easily encompasses these accretions because it is an open structure. Now, going back to your work, Mira, I keep thinking about this canvas[2] that I picked up in the hall and that is partially illustrated in the photograph in this magazine; these few symbols that you use in the work, this black stain, either door or territory, a delimitation, the arrows, the two wheels and the phrase 'NOW THAT I AM BACK', how do all these symbols relate to your later work?

MS>> Well, this is a picture from 1964; there were two works with this title, actually. They contain texts from *Iliad*. I made only two pictures along those lines. One was text only. This one here has only a tiny excerpt, and this image of the wheel, the spear, the door, the gate, the defence, the space, the territory, something like that. Yes, but these are the only pictures along those lines that I made. I know that many people liked this picture, were interested in it, but, it's funny, I never made anything quite like that again; it was a random work of sorts.

JG>> And the drawings incorporating letters from the alphabet?

MS>> Well, they were already there in the Japanese paper works that I also began in 1964; it was then that I started to use letters. Later I made transparent acrylics for the Venice Biennale.

JG>> Except that, unlike concrete poetry, these drawings contain such a complexity of signs that they contradict the random meaning that one might draw from them. It's almost a dialogue between two schools: the concrete in the presentation of the text, and a more intimate poetry stemming from the tangle of meanings that would defy their elucidation. [*Turning to another group of drawings in a different folder*] Now, let's talk about colour here in this latest series. These watercolours are bathed in colour, there is a saturation of colour. You stain the paper to the limit, something reminiscent of Nolde watercolours or Rothko canvases, something crepuscular, and the last ray of sunshine appears to land on the golden arrows, Achilles' farewell. You create an individual space for

2 He is referring to the work *O Retorno de Aquiles* (*The Return of Achilles*) [p.91]. [Editor's note]

each series of drawings, always working with oppositions; oppositions that endure, nonetheless, that allow for immediate visibility; which might even hinder a more complex reading of the work. But this may well be the fate of most works of art, simple in presentation but rich in ideas. In order to apprehend your message, a person needs to possess a certain cultural baggage; let's say, be familiar with Japanese culture, for example.

MS>> Now, it is very difficult for me to talk about my work, because really, if I could speak or write, I think I would not paint or draw. Really, for me, talking about my work is very difficult, finding the right words to express it in its entirety.

JG>> Would you like the work to be difficult for others to talk about?

MS>> No, on the contrary, I give credit to them; also, because, being further removed than me, they can speak much better than I, through certain intuitions – as you had yesterday about the endless space in Japanese prints. I give a vote of confidence to the intelligence and sensitivity of the other person. It is not only the artist who did the work who is omniscient; none of that, the other may very well enter the fray. Now, as for the threshold, the fact that the threshold is, in this manner, also a situation of limit is something difficult to express. But that does not mean that the other is happier than I in verbalising certain aspects of my work.

JG>> [*Moving on to another folder of drawings*] There is always a reflective side to your work, even in the still lifes that I'm looking at, dated 1961–2. For example, in these still lifes, which are very strong, the traces are very assertive, very vigorous, whilst the light that bathes them is simultaneously very dark, crepuscular, creating considerable opposition between the object drawn aggressively and violated by the crepuscular light.

MS>> But there I advocate creative aggressiveness, as some say; I defend the aggressive side for being active. Aggressiveness is part of corporeal unity.

JG>> I remember having seen a series of collages made of blue cloth that seem ready to explode.

MS>> It's not cloth, it's handmade Japanese paper.

JG>> In Japanese drawing, there is a more unified side, let's say, without the exposures found in your work. For example, in Japanese drawing, the writing is united with the object represented, it has the same texture, the mark is the same. In your work, in contrast, the saturation, which is considerable due to the colour of the paper, contrasts with the incisive golden trace that wounds the surface. On the other hand, the mark by which the arrow is inscribed is very hesitant, delicate.

MS>> There it has to be very incisive; because it has this strength, it cannot be drawn slowly, otherwise it loses direction; it has to have a certain velocity in space; that is how I feel it, intuitively and theoretically. It has to be dry, very incisive; but the drawing can be very delicate, with a slow mark, in fact. There are, let's say, drawings that are quick, others that are slower; some are drier, others softer, but the arrow is always very strong, sharp, localised, fine, directed.

JG>> You use, for example, the texture of the paper in order to dye the volume, the matter, upon it; you even use colour saturation to capture the sensation of endless volume. Now, the arrow would be the representation of human energy, crossed through the eye that sees and identifies with this energy. It would be the human point of view within the vastness without reference point.

MS>> Indeed, the arrow is actually a very firm individualisation, in contrast to an extremely diffuse world.

JG>> It's very psychological, a heroic impulse within abstract space.

MS>> You might as well call it psychological, but not necessarily; I think it is closer to a corporeal disposition within a diffuse situation.

JG>> Now, the arrow would be the focus of the eye upon a certain detail, hence the energy that emanates from it.

MS>> You like a white wall, with nothing?

JG>> I often need a white wall. The other day, you mentioned that you hated symmetry, and symmetry is really something that shuts down the field.

MS>> Well, I think that asymmetry is one of the great lessons of the people from the East. I think it came from the East, this great asymmetry lesson; I think the West has always understood symmetry better. It is rare for a drawing of mine to be symmetrical. In general, intuitively, I run from symmetry.

JG>> Symmetry also eliminates ambiguity, restrains the level of ideas.

MS>> I moved towards asymmetry, but I know that is very important. Eastern extremes almost ignore symmetry. You look at Chinese houses, Japanese houses, they are not symmetrical, the tea room is not symmetrical, the disposition of objects is not symmetrical. Only when they become Westernised do they begin to arrange things symmetrically.

JG>> You lived in Milan, were you born in Milan?

MS>> No, I was born in Switzerland. I went to Milan as a child, already a little older.

JG>> During the era of Fascism?

MS>> Yes, during Fascism.

JG>> So, it was a time of terrible repression.

MS>> I don't know if was so terrible with respect to art. After all, there was De Chirico, Morandi.

JG>> You used to draw a lot?

MS>> From the age of four or five, I drew furiously. If anyone gave me a gift, it had to be coloured pencils and graph paper. I drew figures. And in adolescence, I remember, on the tram to school I drew figures, people. The school was quite far away, I think that more or less each way was half the return. The school was in the outskirts, so I drew all the way there. I always carried a notepad around with me, and a black pencil, so that I could draw. I drew, and people would stare at me drawing furiously.

JG>> Did you fill in the figures?

MS>> A bit, but not much. Of course I could not draw well, but I drew passionately. After the war, I began to paint, drawing came later. In practice, I started painting in Brazil. Life was very hard, I had no money to pay for paint, but I bought cheap materials and painted passionately. It was a matter of life and death. I submitted work to the first Bienal de São Paulo. I was that daring. The courage of youth, of madness. I was accepted. I set up an exhibition. Two colleagues came up to me and said, 'Look, you have no talent. Drop it, because it won't do, it's not for you'. So I quit for three years.[3] Then I broke down. And that memory is very important for me. When a young person shows me something, even if I don't think much of it, I prefer to say that it is very good, because later the person can do excellent things. This experience taught me a lot, but it was a terrible thing.

JG>> Were they critics?

MS>> This happened twice. The first time, in Europe, the second time here in Brazil. We all need encouragement. But we have to be very demanding of ourselves.

3 From c.1951 to c.1954. [Editor's note]

JG>> What about the acrylic works? [*Pointing to several works in acrylic. One shows a line in space, another, an acrylic pane with letters on both sides, the third a circular form in space, made of acrylic panes, where the letter O or Zero fades from pane to pane*]

MS>> This one I sent to the 1968 Venice Biennale, the other to the 1967 Bienal de São Paulo. Here [*pointing to the circlular work*], there is the issue of transparency, of inside and outside; inside and outside at the same time, in the same way that object and subject are the same; the concave and the convex together; in this way, one can feel the transparency theme. This was a theme that I fell in love with because transparency is not a mirror. The mirror is symmetrical whilst transparency is not. There are three phases in my work: first is the actual happening of the thing as it happens to me, then there is a moment that the work meets another, and then the third moment that, when I was younger, was not important, but which has become more important because I have become more realistic, which is the work of circulating in economic terms, in order to support the work itself.

JG>> A problem of cultural acceptance.

MS>> Because it is not just an economic acceptance, it is also a cultural acceptance. If a person spends Cr$35,000[4] on this drawing that is on display, in addition to liking the work, to the work meaning something to that person, that person is also willing to surrender something, rather than just enjoy it without giving anything in return.

JG>> Then it becomes acceptance. People put in an effort to own what you put in an effort to make. It is a conjunction of interests, there is something beautiful about it.

MS>> In the past, art had to be free, like the grace of God, i.e. the artist had to distribute the work and not ask anything for himself; give, just give; but then I noticed that if the work is not economically conquered by the other, it is not loved by the other, it is not understood by the other, it is only accepted.

4 Cr$ indicates Cruzeiros, the currency of Brazil at the time [Editor's note]

Interview with Haroldo de Campos*

Sônia Salzstein

Sônia Salzstein >> I would like you to tell us about your first contact with Mira, how you developed this network of contacts involving Max Bense, Elizabeth Walther and the University of Stuttgart.

Haroldo de Campos >> I met Mira in the 1960s through Mario Schenberg, our great physicist and art critic; and a truly great supporter, perhaps the greatest in Mira's career. When she was still almost unknown, he called me to his home to show me examples of Mira's work and through him I came to know Mira personally. We became friends, she gave me some of those drawings on rice paper, and later other works.

Mira was an extremely fragile person; she showed she had a philosophical inclination and great metaphysical turmoil. I say fragile in the sense that she felt little understood because she made very refined work I say fragile in the sense that she felt little understood owing to the great subtlety of her work. And Mario Schenberg, a really extraordinary figure in our culture, soon perceived the importance of her work.

Although a militant Marxist, he was, in my definition, a Zen Marxist, because, by principle, he was anti-Stalinist by vocation, that is to say, he did not comprehend restrictions regarding artistic expression and had an extremely broad field of interest from the primitives to the most refined constructivists. He always gave his support to vanguard tendencies and also to the primitives, who, at times, had no access to the Bienal. It was really Mira Schendel, along with others such as Alfredo Volpi, who made up part of this cast of artists that received Schenberg's great encouragement here in São Paulo.

In 1959 I met Max Bense and his assistant Professor Elizabeth Walther, a teacher of philosophy and semiotics. Both worked in the department of Theory of Aesthetics and Philosophy of the Sciences of the old technical school, later the University of Stuttgart, in Germany. Bense was the main theoretician, a scholar of semiotics educated in philosophy and mathematics. He also gave classes at at the Ulm School of Design at the invitation of Max Bill, the school's chancellor and a great friend. Bense was very interested in Brazil. He visited us three times, wrote a book on Brazilian intelligence, and, through me, contacted Mira early on. That contact turned out to be very important because it resulted in an exhibition for her in Germany, for which he wrote an article and for which I also did. Bense also published a small volume with Mira's work, in the *rot* collection, edited together with Walther in Stuttgart (in one of these he also published fragments of my *Galáxias* [*Galaxies*]).

* Interview held in June 1996 on the occasion of the exhibition *In the Void of the World*, organised by critic Sônia Salzstein at the SESI Art Gallery in São Paulo. It was published in the exhibition catalogue and revised for this edition. Translated by Carolina Berringer. Edition in 2013 by Oswaldo Corrêa da Costa.

SS >> Were Mira's relations with Bense and Walther lasting?

HC >> I think so. She went to Europe more than once and was always in contact with them. They were very generous people, with a high regard for Brazil. In his book, *Brasilianische Intelligenz: Eine Cartesianische Reflexion* [1964], Bense considers tropical intelligence to be an ejaculatory intelligence, capable of impregnating. And Mira, while really a Swiss moving among three horizons – Portuguese, Italian and German – had a profoundly Brazilian mind and lived here fully and intensely.
In short, little by little her work became better known even though it was difficult, very subtle, close to the verbal. Indeed it has a touch that comes from concrete poetry, from the verbal elements summoned by concrete poetry and the real machinery of the text. Mira uses textual elements – alphabets, lettering – and creates veritable 'poem-paintings', even if what she is doing is a painting rooted in constructivism.

SS >> What was the climate of discussion at that time in which some of the interlocutors included you and Mario Schenberg?

HC >> I think Mira was a very isolated artist; for example, she never belonged to any group of constructivist or concrete painters in São Paulo. Perhaps there was contact, but she was by nature an isolated person. She lived away from things in Santo Amaro; she didn't live in the heart of São Paulo, but on its outskirts. Her temperament needed a certain isolation, not to be part of a group: she wasn't gregarious, she lived rather away from things.
Years later, she phoned me once in a while, late at night (it seems she slept very little). They were long calls, and she felt very rejected even during the phase when she was gaining recognition, had participated in international exhibitions and was considered an important artist, a great artist. She revealed that she doubted the communicability of the work she was doing.
I raised the idea with her that this was common in art in general. (I reminded her, for example, of Stéphane Mallarmé, who, at the end of his life, after publishing his great work *Un Coup de dés* (*A Throw of the Dice*), in 1897, was attacked by one of the major Parisian newspapers). But she was not to be consoled until one day I said: 'Mira, it's not possible for you not to be recognised by the younger generations. That is the best indication of the contribution of your work'.
That was shortly before she died; it was the last time I spoke to her. These phone calls happened repeatedly over time, though not regularly, and always ended up grappling with this great difficulty of being that she felt, of existing, and also with what she saw as the difficulty of her work being accepted on a broader scale, even if it brought her success and collective prestige from a more select group.

SS >> Perhaps a risk that work has from the moment it springs forth, for there is an obliqueness inherent to it.

HC >> It is highly refined work. At times it is just the white of the paper with light touches of a brush or pen. That last time, I asked her a question: 'Do you really not think that young people are paying attention to you? They are, after all, the best guarantors of the future of a work'. 'In fact they come to see me', she said, referring to artists such as Marco Giannotti and Nuno Ramos. Then the contribution of her work became clear; after Mira's death, one notes that an increasing number of artists are aware of it.

SS >> I think Mira had the gift of arousing a climate of intellectual curiosity.

HC >> Her work had something of the future that even she did not discern, did not suspect, owing to her concern with immediate communication, to living in isolation, to not taking part in the artistic world, to not being a worldly person.
She was profoundly concerned with existential questions. She read widely about phenomenology and felt that which the Argentinian novelist Julio Cortázar called 'the difficulty of being', of integrating with the whole: she felt rather exiled and, naturally, would like – every artist does – to be more warmly received; after all, there is the aspect of the way in which a work of art is received, even though the artist knows that this is at times the bottle thrown into the sea that will one day roll onto some beach. But in Mira's case, it was this way: after she died, her artistic reputation began to grow. There were large exhibitions, among them the Bienal de São Paulo[1], and, above all, the surge of interest among young artists and others.

SS >> How would you interpret the idea of the materiality of the sign in Mira's work and in that of the concrete artists?

HC >> Mira's view of work was different from that of the concrete artists – although I think this talk about the antagonism between the concrete and neo-concrete is outdated and there is no reason to bring it to the discussion today (I think Hélio Oiticica defined this question very well when he said that in Brazil all these various artists were constructivists but had different attitudes towards the construction. What they had in common was a 'new objectivity').
Mira came along after this debate, when there was a group of young painters, her contemporaries, who also had a constructivist grounding but who now practised other media – Antonio Dias or Rubens Gerchman, for example. Today I see that Antonio Dias has much affinity with Mira, which does not mean that there was any contact between them.
Although there were, at that time, many optical influences in the notion of construction– neo-figurative and ultrarealistic aspects etc.– there was a process of decantation in the art of Antonio Dias, especially in certain works that he has done lately, very Eastern, that, to a certain extent, is close to that of Mira's...

SS >> He also would be interested in an idea of the void that is relevant to Mira's work ...

1 1994 Bienal de São Paulo where Schendel's work was included in a special solo section. [Editor's note]

HC >> ... the idea of the void – I have the impression that it is what makes the works converse with each other. I am not talking of the direct influence but in dialogue. I have the impression that, if you held an exhibition of Antonio Dias's and Mira's work together, it would be harmonious, although one cannot say that one has influenced the other. I mean to say neither on the part of Dias influencing Mira – that would really be improbable since he was younger and Mira by then had already consolidated the physiognomy of her work – nor on the part of Mira directly affecting Antonio Dias, although one would suppose that he knew her work.

SS >> It seems to me that *The Illustration of Art*[2] series transmits Mira's work very well ... A moment ago you referred to an idea that I believe stirs one to ruminate about her work: the idea that it is constructive. For it is also very negative.

HC >> But construction and deconstruction are part of the same process from the historical point of view, an artist whom I think extremely important, perhaps the most important among the so-called dada artists, is Kurt Schwitters. He is a dada constructivist because he destroys all those fragments; works with what others throw away and with it builds his own home, the Merzbau, not to speak of what else he builds from thrown-away matter, in the Merz paintings (exhibited in one of the first Bienais de São Paulo) and in his poetry that is done in cut-up, reassembled, fragmented phrases, etc. Therefore, construction and deconstruction are, dialectically speaking, brothers; and Mira constructed by deconstructing. Her work reveals this aspect of the void, an Eastern aspect. I do not know to what extent she was acquainted with Buddhist aesthetics (I believe she was, because she read widely) about the void, the zero signifier, Sunyata. The signified zero is also related to the Hebrew world of the kabbalah, in which it is referred to, kabbalistically, as Ein Sof (endless). This has to do with negativity and in kabbalah and in certain Hebraic mysticism it deals with the theory of emanation, of the creation of the universe as a great retraction that later propels into an existential yes, a void that retracts and then bursts out in completeness.

SS >> This image of productive void reveals a lot about Mira's work because she subtracts nothing; in fact, she adds with great discretion.

HC >> Exactly. Indeed, I did write two texts about Mira. One was a kind of metapoem that was printed in the Stuttgart catalogue and is in Bense's *Pequena estética* [2009], published by Perspectiva [publishing house]; the other was a text that I wrote for an exhibition of hers, which was really a poem without further commentary. In the first, I commented on the calligraphic aspect: I think she is a metaphysical calligraphist. She reveals, first off, her fascination with material: for her, material is everything, the paper, its grain; and when she is not working with rice paper, she is working with other things, special supports. Look at this object I have of hers made of perforations on a quadric surface. These tiny holes

2 *The Illustration of Art* is a series of works by Antonio Dias from 1970s.

produce on one side a kind of black galaxy and, on the other, a white one that appears when we whirl it. This effect is created by the delicately made holes; they are like expansions of galactic nebulosities. It is a piece to be touched, moved by the wind, a true mobile.
She has, then, on the one hand, this great respect for the material, for the elements that she 'calls into' her work; on the other hand, she has a fondness for script. This script is not always letters; at times it is neither letters nor words. At other times words arise, and her painting immediately becomes a poem, a 'poem-painting', a 'painting-poem'. Certain writings are strokes, are residue, are vestiges, are leftovers that she leaves on the paper, allows to bloom on the paper, frees to run across it, as if they were existential ontological traces. There is a phase in which Mira used a lot of gold leaf, a very Chinese phase, with contrasting chromatic surfaces...

SS >> ... from the mid-1970s...

HC >> ... but there is always a golden sign, like a Chinese signature stamp, always that calligraphic touch. Early on I spoke about the words, the letters that she uses like veritable beehives. I kidded, saying that the 'a-b' in abelha [Portuguese for bee] work like bees because she makes a zigzag along the page, lending the work its calligraphic and material aspect.
The other aspect relative to the void I tried to emblematise in the second poem, 'Via Chuan-Tsé', Chuan-Tsé being the name of the famous Chinese philosopher who dreamed he was a butterfly and, after he woke up, did not know if he had dreamed of the butterfly or if the butterfly had dreamed of him.
I wrote two poems based on his aphorism and in one of them, published in a small catalogue, which I dedicated to Mira, I debated the zero, the zero signifier called the Buddhist Sunyata. In it I take the Chinese ideogram for zero; in its primary form, it is shaped by a roof with drops of rain sliding down it and has, below, three drops that quickly became stylised as a line in a most abstract manner. Then we have the rain falling in lines and the raindrops, something similar to Apollinaire's calligram 'Il pleut' (It Rains), a kind of rain 'pictogram'. In the Chinese concept, we have the idea of something very tenuous; the ideogram pronounced *ling* in the second tone of Chinese, reveals the content of residue, of something that has remained, of something very fine, very subtle, almost evanescent. But, in Japanese, this ended up assuming the idea of the zero, due perhaps to this Buddhist and Zen perspective.
This poem is linked to my earlier poetic work, previous to the phase I was in when I met Mira. It goes back to a group of five poems written in 1955 and 1956, brought together under the title of *O âmago do ômega ou a fenomenologia da composição* (*The core of the omega or the phenomenology of composition*). They show a great affinity with Mira, because, since she was a phenomenological artist, she used to peel off the layers of reality, words, and was moved by the idea of deconstruction to arrive at the essence, the eidos. She strove for this quest of essence.

SS >> Which, on the other hand, cannot be in any work...

HC >> But it is a quest. It is more quest than encounter. The essence is a tension, a shoot; it involves that philosophical idea of placing things between parentheses, to reach phenomenological reduction, which she often did, as if she were looking for a way to reduce intellectual interference to a minimum.
I wrote a poem that was printed in white on a black background, totally visual, and it ended with a large letter 'z'; 'zero to the zenith nitescendo ex nihilo' (I used 'nitescendo', which comes from the Latin and means 'to shine', because it regains the zenith). I evoked the idea of this zero signifier, which shines from the void, which retracts to then emanate and appear in the void.
Obviously, when I first saw Mira's work, my mind made this connection and motivated by that sign I wrote the poem. For me, the poetic act and the act of painting are neither rational nor sensitive; they are the two things: sensitive and rational, dialectically and concomitantly.

SS >> In an immanent way.

HC >> The poetic act and that of painting are immanent to sensibility and rationality. This idea has been present in Eastern thought and is very important to Mario Schenberg. One of the reasons he was interested in Mira doubtlessly lies in this Eastern horizon of his thinking, highly influenced by the Eastern philosophies, the Chinese and Hindu, in the 'Tao of Physics'. This is the reason why Mario sought to confront, translate contemporary physics concepts in Eastern thought, and Mira fits into this plane.
Chinese thought, and Japanese also, has this: not to separate the heart from the mind (in fact, in Japanese, there is one single ideogram, *kokoro*, for both the mind and the heart). Heart and mind are the same thing for the Japanese. At times, you don't know how to translate heart or mind. For instance, 'think' has the ideogram for the heart in its lower part and the cranium, the head with its cerebral circumvolutions, in the upper. It's a sort of cranium above the heart, as if the vital fluid, at the moment of thought, would rise from the heart to the mind, forming this interconnection between the sensorial and the rational. I find this beautiful. It is something that governed Mira's attitude. Or as Fernando Pessoa said so well: 'Everything that feels in me thinks'.
Mira was a thinking artist, not a very common thing. There are Hélio Oiticica and Lygia Clark; there is also the artist-theoretician, such as Waldemar Cordeiro, but he is more the theoretician in terms of the methodological and rational explanation of his ideas than the thinker in the sense of reflection. With Mira, thinking is more related to the thinking of the philosopher, the mystic, to a certain mysticism leaning toward essence...

SS >> I think that Mira's theoretical inquiry – I don't know what you think about this – would tend not to specialise in an artistic language.

HC >> Not only that, she was not a person who was proposing methods or theories, or one that wrote manifestos. She reflected because her way of being was to think while feeling. In truth, doing was foremost in her work. By the way, I saw a marvelous thing she did that I had not seen before.

At the Casa das Rosas exhibition, whose curator was Aguilar,[3] there is a Mondrianesque piece of Mira's obtained by turning the canvas backward. That is, she takes the structure of the canvas, its rectangular structure, and turns it around. An intervention in the realm of painting that results in a type of brutalist Mondrian, the opposite of Mondrian. Or, for a bit of horseplay, it would be a neo-plastic painting from its raw side, its reverse side, the side where the material is almost raw. Or even a script viewed from its ontic layers. Had I not seen it, had I not known that it was Mira's and had to think a little, I would say: 'Well, this could only be Mira's'. It has a simplicity, a constructivist discipline, something between neo-plasticism and suprematism, something that had no descriptive touches. And, suddenly, that took on the idea of construction so profoundly essential, and material-oriented (in the sense of raw materialness) as all the work she does.

SS >> It is curious that you made this comparison with Mondrian, for Mira, at that time, did several canvases that had a horizontal and a vertical axis. Evidently, she is a very material-oriented Mondrian.

HC >> Very much so, reduced to the common denominator, to the minimum trace of painterly interference – which is her inquiry. It's as if she were doing a strip-tease of form. It is as if she had got to a suprematism that was at the same time brutalist. Malevich's white on white, or black on black, are the colour reduction side, zero colour; in Mira's work, the background of the canvas is between a grey or brownish colour. It is really a material-like colour, almost a colour of the material. If the material itself had a colour, you would imagine that it would be between clay and certain tones of paper.

SS >> What you are saying suggests to me that Mira would be a 'nonoptical' Mondrian.

HC >> Absolutely, this specific work – you told me that there are others with these vertical and horizontal axes – is quite significant to me. There are also larger-sized works that she did at the end of her life, in which she maintains the same rigour, the same economy of means, and where she was less calligraphic...

SS >> But, on the other hand, it is the same question.

HC >> The problem is the same, except that the approach is not calligraphic, it is one having a more particular geometry, a geometry of absences. Let's look at Mondrian's Boogie Woogie composition, a marvellous painting opening a kind of dynamic, kinetic portrayal of New York in movement, the structure of Manhattan with its streets, cars...

SS >> Being noncompositive.

3 Campos refers to *The World of Mario Schenberg* exhibition at Casa das Rosas, in São Paulo, between 28 March and 16 June, 1996, curated by José Roberto Aguilar. [Editor's note]

HC >> Being noncompositive. There is a dynamic kinetic aspect. It is able to force its way out of the static and reach movement. Mira's case is different. She does not seek this dynamic, kinetic ostentation. Her work is extremely austere, a work that tends toward placidity, contemplation and Buddhist reflection, but which, at times, resorts to geometry. And resorts to this geometry less due to a geometric ostensibility but as geometry to circumscribe absence. Thus geometry serves as a support or a reference point that contains the absence the void. They are geometric stems or trails that imprison segments of a void. It is not therefore a geometry of ostensibility found in the concrete painting, where there is the manifestation of primary colours, where the optical element predominates. It is not that I criticise, I truly appreciate this type of work. But in her case, instead of being optic, it is more cosa mentale, that is to say, a geometry to be perceived not only for its optical ostensibility but for the inner reflection. Mira strives for erasure, for a consideration of the void, much more than for ostentation through the contrasting intervention of colours, which is characteristic of the optic work as much of the concrete artists of São Paulo as of Rio de Janeiro.

SS >> Do you think that, in spite of the fact that all her work has a strongly affirmative strain (she says things like 'I enjoy myself' and other lyrical phrases that clearly give the measure of this affirmative sense), that we could also see, in this materialistic view of things, some element, which I wouldn't call pessimistic, but some sceptical element? You used the term to refer to Mira's work.

HC >> I would not say that she was sceptic. Scepticism implies a question of ontological doubt. I don't know if Mira had this position of doubt; that would be virtually an agnostic posture. I really don't know. That would be another existential theme. There would be a mystical dimension, and I don't know to what extent that could be considered orthodox; but it is certain that she had the perception of something beyond.

In Buddhism, this beyond exists. I have the impression that she was mystical, that some horizon would transcend that preoccupation with her fascination with material (evident in her work). However, I think there was, yes, a touch of pessimism in her But it alternated with moments of joy, with that which was the pleasure of doing.

Her pessimistic side showed intensely in the conversations I had with her. It was always connected with a certain doubt she had regarding the relevance, the durability, the ultimate meaning of her work. It was such that she often felt fragile, despite being surrounded by the comprehension of extremely refined persons such as Mario Schenberg

SS >> As you yourself said, Mira worked quite set apart from others. How can we situate her in the recent history of art in Brazil?

HC >> I think that the people with whom Mira would be more closely related are Hélio Oiticica, for specific reasons that relate to the painting he did, and Lygia Clark, due to a certain emptying of form. The three make up a constellation.

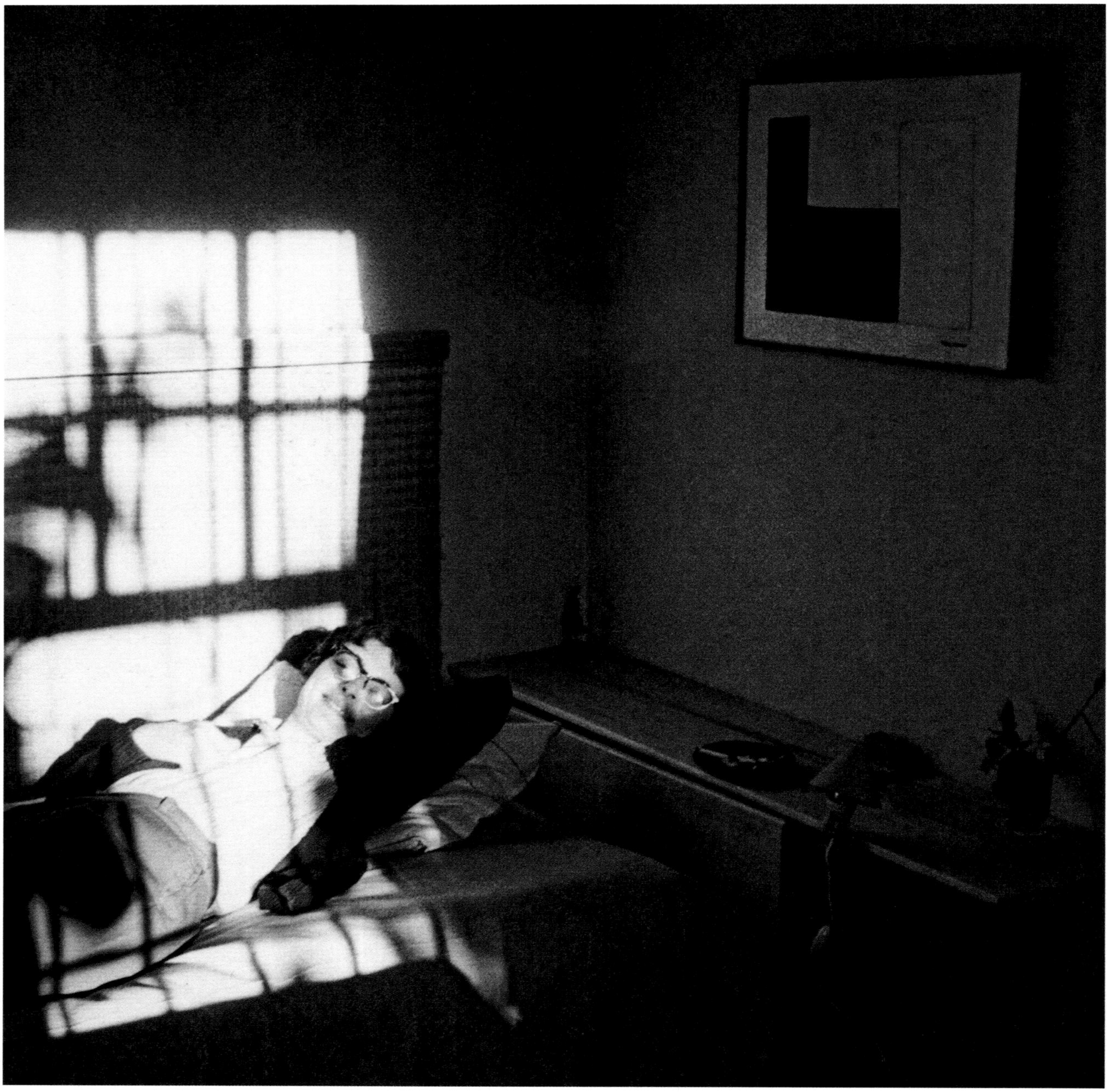

Mira Schendel at home, 1960s. mira schendel estate archive

Mira Schendel: Chronology*

Ana Cândida de Avelar

1919 Myrrha Dagmar Dub is born on 7 June 1919, in Zurich, Switzerland, the daughter of Karl Leo Dub and Ada Saveria. Her father, who works in the textile industry, comes from a German-speaking Jewish family of Czech descent. Her mother is the daughter of Max Büttner, a German Jew, and Amelia Muggia, an Italian from a Jewish family converted to Catholicism. Mira's mother has her baptised at the Catholic Church of Saint Peter and Saint Paul in Zurich

1919–22 Mira lives in Zurich and Berlin until 1922, when her parents separate and divorce, and she moves to Milan with her mother. She will never hear from her father again, who by all accounts emigrates to Argentina, though she does maintain a good relationship with her paternal grandparents, at whose home in Bohemia she frequently spends the school holidays.

1930–6 Mira studies art at a free school in Milan.

1937 Mira's mother Ada Saveria marries Count Tomaso Gnoli, a poet, librarian and director of the Biblioteca Nazionale Braidense. The Braidense library is located in the same building as the School of Fine Arts and the the Palazzo di Brera museum. Mira lives in an apartment in this building with her mother and stepfather when not away at boarding school. During her childhood and adolescence, Mira receives a strict religious upbringing and is introduced to the Count's contacts among the high clergy, including the future Pope Paul VI.

Mira begins her studies in philosophy at Università Cattolica del Sacro Cuore (Catholic University of the Sacred Heart) in Milan.

1938 Mira is forced to discontinue her studies, when a decree is issued stripping Jews of Italian citizenship and, among other measures, forbidding their attendance at Italian universities. Though baptised and raised a Catholic, under this decree she is still considered Jewish by origin.

1939–44 Between 1939 and 1944, Mira's movements are uncertain, however it seems that probably in 1939 she heeded her mother's advice and departs for Sofia, Bulgaria, to stay with

* Translated by Anthony Doyle.

an aunt. While in Vienna, en route to Sofia, Mira joins a group of refugees bound for what was then Yugoslavia. In Sarajevo, she meets a Catholic Croat of Austrian descent, Jossip Hargesheimer, whom she marries in April 1941. She receives a Yugoslav passport and papers under her married name to replace her revoked Italian citizenship.

1945–9 The couple returns to Italy when the war ends, and remain there until 1949. They live first in Milan and later in Rome. Between May 1948 and July 1949, Mira, a 'displaced person'[1] herself, works for the International Refugee Organisation (IRO). It is at this time that she begins her correspondence with the Italian priest, writer and theologian Ferdinando Tartaglia (1916–87), with whom she discusses philosophic-religious subjects and who must have introduced her to the writings of the English theologian Cardinal John Henry Newman (1801–1890). It is a friendship that will last for most of her life.

Given the economic hardships in postwar Europe, the couple decides to emigrate. Though their destinations of choice are Argentina, Canada or the United States, the Brazilian Immigration Bureau is the first to accept their application, so they set sail for Rio de Janeiro from Naples in July 1949, with Mira working as a typist aboard ship during the month-long crossing. In Brazil, she registers under her married name, Mira Hargesheimer, and is listed as a Yugoslav national. The couple immediately travel south, to Porto Alegre, a frequent destination for German-speaking immigrants.

1949–53 In Porto Alegre, Mira starts to paint and produce ceramics. She visits exhibitions, reads philosophy, writes and publishes poetry. She also begins life-drawing and sculpture classes at the Fine Arts School in Porto Alegre. She takes a job as a drafter at a printer's shop, Tipografia Mercantil.

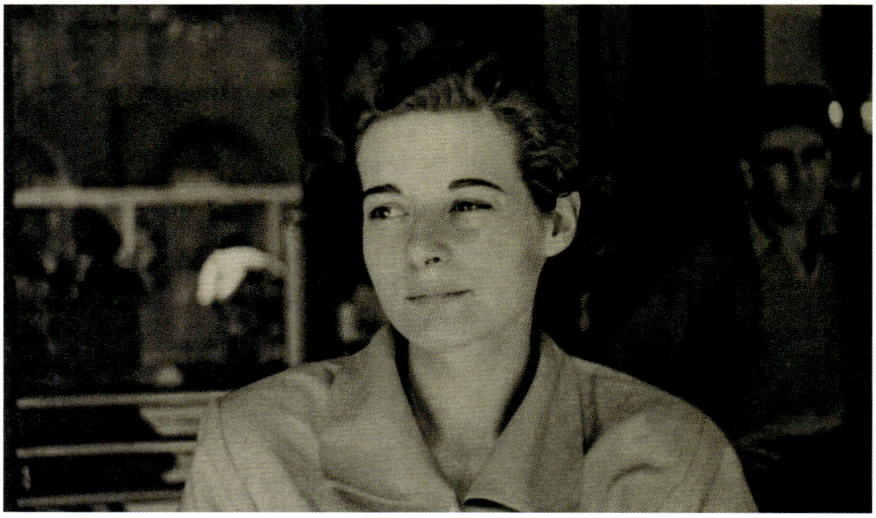

Mira Schendel, c.1950. mira schendel estate archive

1 The term used in postwar Europe for all those who had been forced to leave their home countries.

On 6 January 1950, the newspaper *Correio do Povo* runs an article entitled 'The Drama of European Immigrants'. The story is so inaccurate that Mira writes an open letter to the newspaper, published the following day, in which she describes what she feels are the actual conditions and experiences that European emigrés have to face in the 'New World'. It is one of the few public pronouncements the artist will ever make on the subject.

Her first solo exhibition – of portraits, landscapes and still lifes – is held in October 1950 at the auditorium of the same newspaper and is reviewed by the critic Aldo Obino in the article 'Pintora italiana que surge' (An up-and-coming Italian painter) (*Correio do Povo*, Porto Alegre, 17 Oct. 1950). Obino presents Mira as a self-taught painter whose work stands out for its melancholic realism.

After the positive reception of her first exhibition, Mira feels encouraged enough to submit work to the selection panel for the 1st São Paulo Modern Art Biennial.[2] Her *Paisagem* (*Landscape*), a work in oil on cardboard, is exhibited in the painting section under her married name, Mira Hargesheimer.[3]

Mira does not travel to São Paulo to see the exhibition in person, though she does write to her friend, the theologian Tartaglia, criticising the international jury for overlooking 'such major Brazilian names as Candido Portinari, Lasar Segall and Emiliano Di Cavalcanti' in awarding prizes only to works of an abstract persuasion.In the same letter, she confesses to Tartaglia,

> Art is nostalgia for God, you don't have to paint what you see not even what you feel, but only what lives inside us ... So much pain led me to a medium of expression. I don't know if my painting is great, I just know that it's art.[4]

When she reads the exhibition catalogue and sees that the painter Ennio Morlotti, a colleague from her student days in Milan, is exhibiting as part of the Italian delegation, she writes to him, saying,

> I started painting in April 1950; during our school days I had done nothing, absolutely nothing. It took me nearly twenty years to unlearn the nothing I knew and forget that environment ... So, for me, painting spent years and years as this distant thing; I preoccupied rather than occupied myself with it. Now I work like mad, with no contact with the world, without visiting exhibitions or galleries ..

2 After 1959, the Bienal de São Paulo.

3 Cf. *Catálogo da I Bienal do Museu de Arte Moderna de São Paulo* (São Paulo, October 1951), p.66.

4 Schendel, quoted in Knut Schendel, 'Mira', undated typewritten text from the mira schendel estate archive, p.7. The grand prize at the 1st edition of the Bienal de São Paulo was awarded to the Swiss concrete artist Max Bill for his sculpture *Unidade tripartida* (*Tripartite Unity*) 1948–9, which consolidated geometric abstraction as the hegemonic stylistic tendency in Brazilian contemporary art and put an end to the figuration vs. abstraction debate that raged among the Brazilian milieu in the late 1940s.

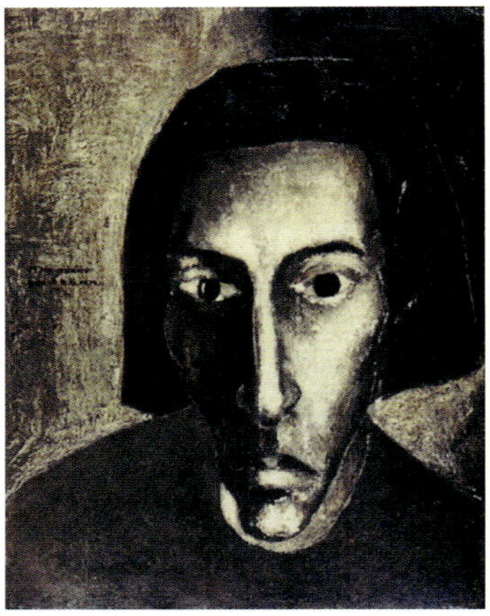

Untitled
Sem título
1952
Oil on chipboard
100 x 80 cm
Private collection

She continues,

> I don't know what to say of my painting, other than that it is not 'abstract', though it is abstract, as I believe all art to be.[5]

In a letter to Tartaglia that same year, she reflects on the Russian expressionist painter Von Jawlensky, a member of the German Blue Rider group, in questioning the separation between figurative and abstract art:

> I got into painting by error and by error I mean to go on, even though we cannot be so rationalist about art. Alexey von Jawlensky painted little 'abstract heads'. He thought this would free him from the death of time. So now I feel I must present Jawlensky with a most rigorous no. I say No to Jawlensky and to all those like him, to all we call art. That art (erroneously) called figurative, (erroneously) called abstract. Different, yes, but equally unreal.[6]

Between 1951 and 1953 she wins prizes at the salons of Bahia and Rio Grande do Sul, and holds another solo exhibition in 1952. During this period, in Porto Alegre, she visits an exhibition by the Uruguayan delegation showing at the Bienal de São Paulo, including Joaquín Torres Garcia, an artist who becomes a reference in her early work.

Despite her relative success, her letters to family and friends contain complaints about the isolation she feels in Porto Alegre and her desire to move to Rio de Janeiro or São Paulo.[7]

1953

Mira moves to São Paulo alone. She and Jossip never live together again. She begins to sign her works simply 'Mira'.

She visits exhibitions, attends conferences, concerts and cinema screenings, becomes a member of the Museu de Arte Moderna and a regular at the Mário de Andrade Library.[8] She gets to know a number of artists, including Antonio Bandeira, Bruno Giorgi, Fayga Ostrower and Paolo Rissone.

She is particularly impressed with the conferences 'Aleijadinho'[9] and 'Existentialism and Abstract Art' by the German art historian Georg Hoeltje at the Museu de Arte Moderna de São Paulo. In a letter, she mentions a visit to the professor's home, where they talk about major names in modern art: Picasso, Braque and Klee. She shows him some of her paintings and drawings, but is not happy with his comments on them. She tells friends in Porto Alegre that she is going through a 'frightful crisis'

5 Mira Schendel, letter to Ennio Morlotti, 22 January 1952 (mira schendel estate archive).

6 Mira Hargesheimer, 'Carta a caro A.', 28 May 1952 (mira schendel estate archive).

7 According to Schendel, Porto Alegre was overrun with an 'indecent academicism' and an 'imbecilic verism' and during the three years she spent there she only saw one decent exhibition, 'by the Uruguayans who took part in the Bienal'. (Knut Schendel, pp.7–10).

8 In charge of the library since 1943, the poet and art critic Sergio Milliet turns it into one of the city's main cultural hubs through courses, lectures, exhibitions and the Arts Department.

9 Antonio Francisco Lisboa (c.1730–1814), aka Aleijadinho (The Little Cripple), architect and sculptor from the state of Minas Gerais, considered the master of Brazilian baroque art.

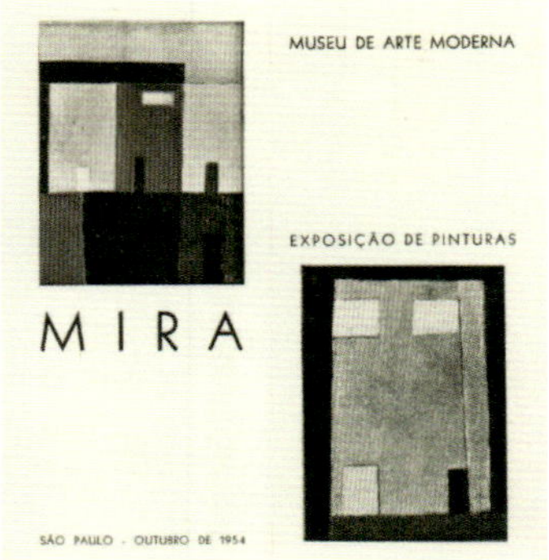

Brochure of the exhibition *Mira*, Museu de Arte Moderna de São Paulo, 1954. Archive MAM-SP

in relation to painting.[10] She signs up for the second edition of the Bienal in 1953, but withdraws out of dissatisfaction with her own work. She also writes to a friend, saying that she wants to start some new work: '... maybe abstract (or constructivist, or concrete: the terminology really doesn't matter)'.[11]

She produces posters for the Vera Cruz Film Company and illustrates some short stories. She joins Editora Companhia Melhoramentos as a graphic designer. This same year, 1953, she meets her future husband, Knut Schendel. About moving to Brazil, she says,

> It's been four years to the day since I arrived here. It was a sunny day like today, but a sad one, as I did not want to come here. But now it's different.[12]

1954

Due to the crisis mentioned in her letters, it is not until October 1954 that she exhibits again, at a solo show at the Museu de Arte Moderna de São Paulo – MAM SP. Of particular note is way the paintings are mounted perpendicularly to the wall, as

Untitled
Sem título
1954
Gouache and watercolour on paper
26 x 20 cm
Private Collection

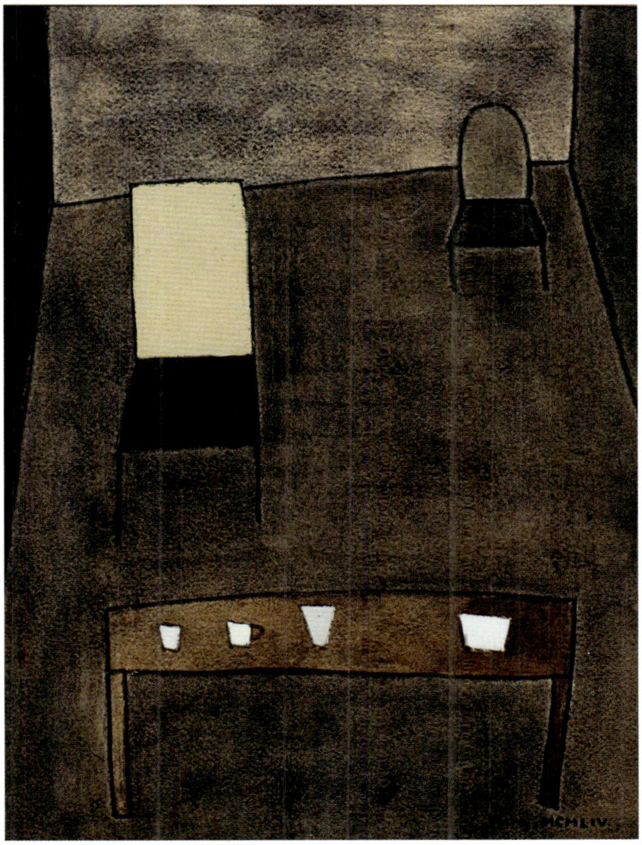

10 In a letter to Vaucuccio (Vauco) (8 August 1953), Mira writes, 'I wrote you before saying that I was still in the orange/blue phase, but I've blended that with the earlier phase. I think I'll have started a new canvas early next week, maybe something abstract. I think about painting a lot, and I really, really doubt I'll ever be any good at it' (typewritten letter, mira schendel estate archive).

11 'Letter to Dear Vauco', São Paulo, 12–13 August 1953 (mira schendel estate archive).

12 Letter to Vauco, 13 June 1953 (mira schendel estate archive).

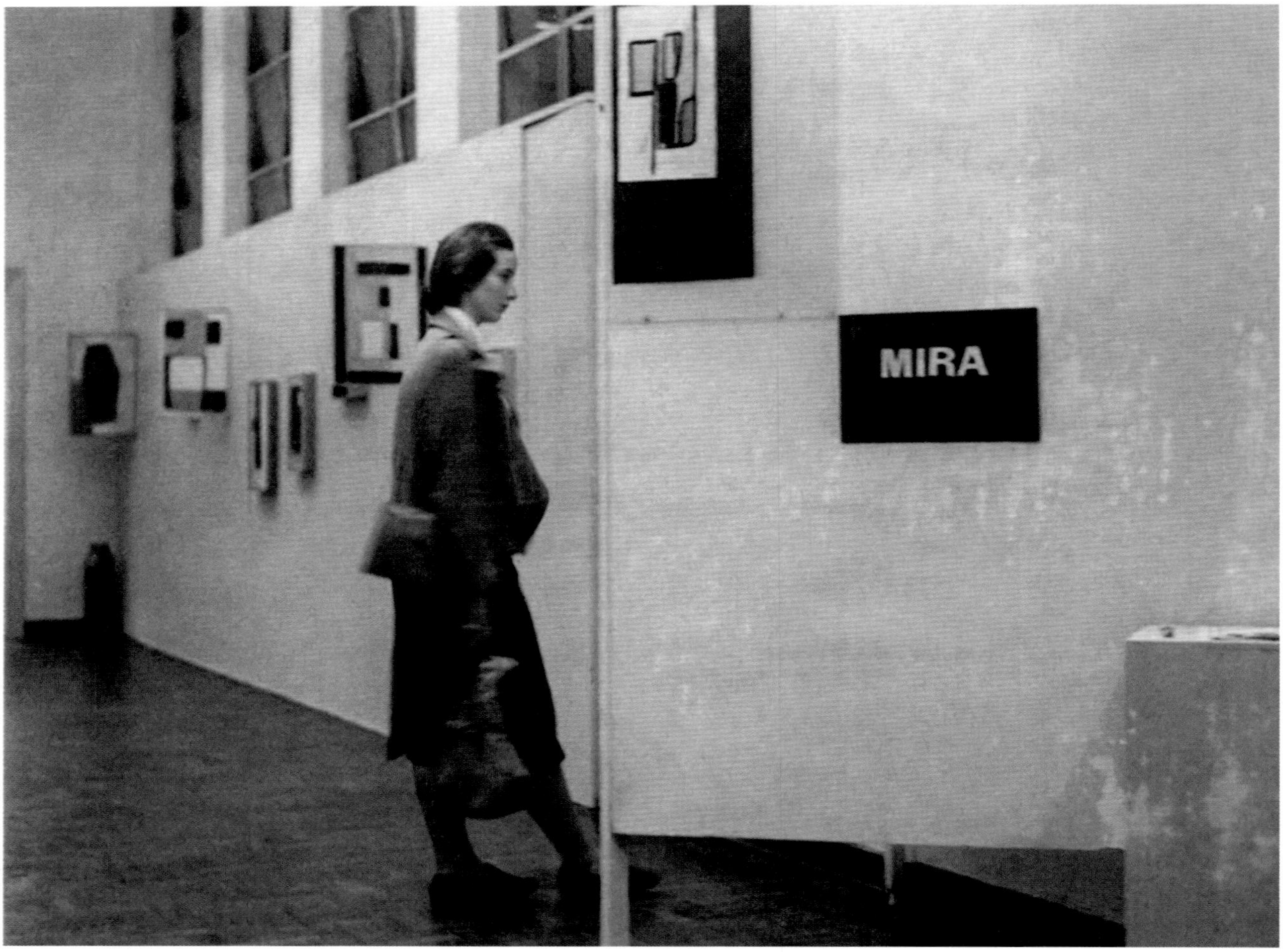

View of the Mira Schendel exhibition at the Museu de Arte Moderna de São Paulo, 1954

objects rather than flat surfaces. This group of works is known as *Geladeiras* (*Fridges*) and *Fachadas* (*Facades*), abstract-geometric paintings in which fields of colour are arranged according to an asymmetric geometry, the lines evidently drawn by hand or sometimes even scratched into the paint.

1955 Still using the name of Mira Hargesheimer, she shows at the 3rd Bienal do Museu de Arte Moderna. On this occasion, she presents two paintings in tempera entitled *Composição nº 4* (*Composition no.4*) and *Composição nº 5* (*Composition no.5*).

This new output launches her definitively onto the São Paulo art scene. This period coincides with her burgeoning friendships with the physicist and art critic Mario Schenberg; the psychoanalyst, poet, translator and art critic Theon Spanudis; and the philosopher Vilem Flusser.

1956 Mira and Knut move in together, and their only daughter, Ada Clara, is born the following year.

1957–62 Between 1957 and 1962 Mira produces and exhibits very little. The only known exhibition during this period is that of her greetings cards, held at a store in Rio de Janeiro in 1960. It is the first time that she works in a set and serialised format and scale. Mira and Knut marry in 1960, and the artist takes the surname Schendel.

Mira starts producing intensely again in 1962. Her work consists of drawings and paintings and various book illustrations for Herder, a publishing house in São Paulo. To mark her return, she exhibits the *Bordados* (*Embroideries*), a series of drawings, at Galeria Selearte. This is the first time she uses rice paper as a support, in this case for drawings in watercolour, a paint whose transparent texture signals some of the directions her work will take from that time on.

1963–4 Mira stages another exhibition, this time at the Galeria de Arte São Luiz in São Paulo, at which she presents paintings in dark, earthy tones with abstract divisions which the critics interpret as indicative of a transition in her work towards concretism. In his opening text to the exhibition, the art critic Mario Pedrosa remarks,

> [In her earlier work], the same lines that divided the rectangle into multiple or sequential regular forms, into repetitions, also divided the canvas into figure

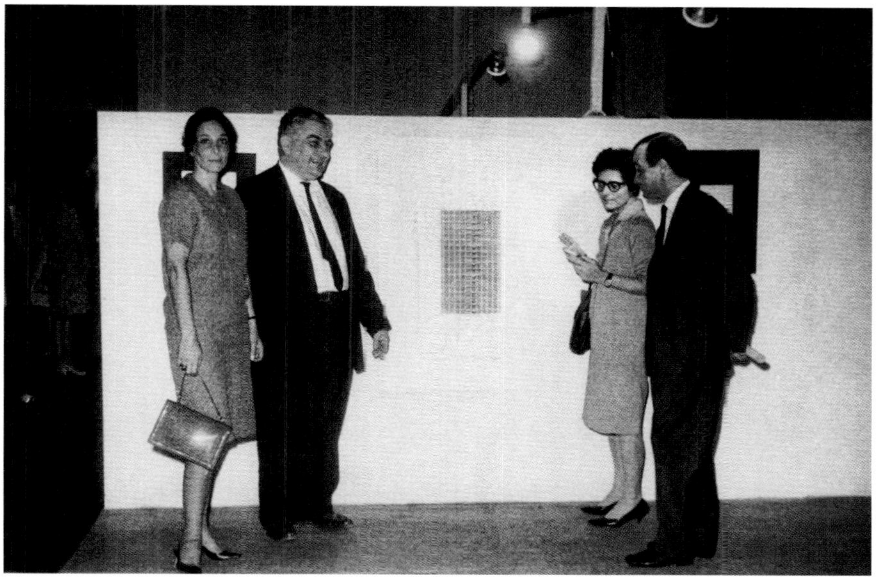

Ely Bueno, Mario Schenberg, Mira Schendel, unidentified man, 1960s. mira schendel estate archive

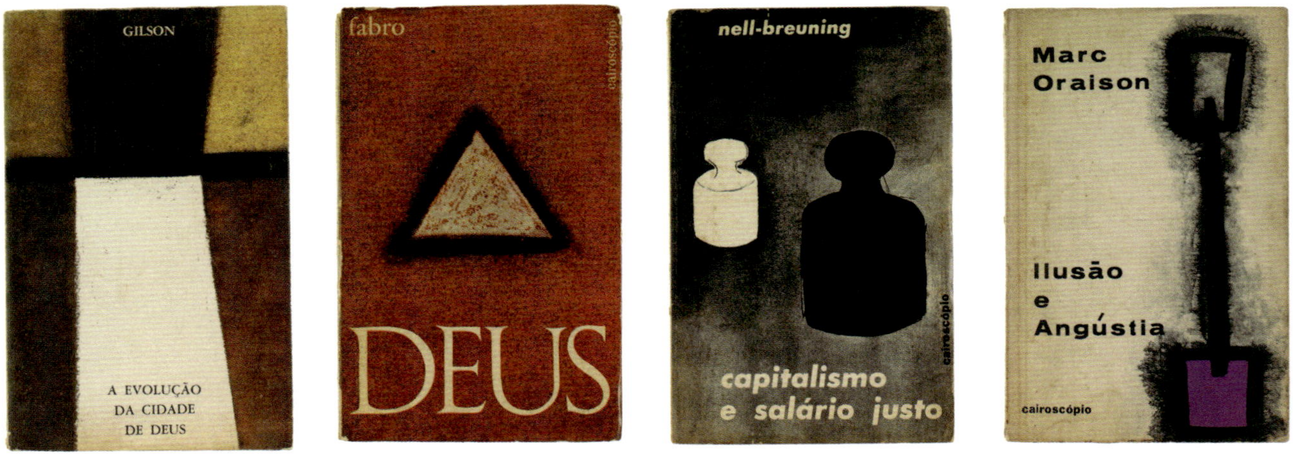

Book covers designed by Mira Schendel. mira schendel estate archive

> and background. Her rectangular forms stood out here and there, relegating the rest to a supporting role. Form ceased to be form, living plastic form, to become compositional form. Now, however, where colour once preserved itself, it no longer sets itself apart, becoming less tonal than material ... The concretism settles into density and takes on a whole other dimension, that of subjective expressiveness, with real emotional impact.[13]

On the artist's relationship with the tendency towards concrete art, the critic ends his text with the observation that Mira's abstraction 'is an inner need; it is the language of a necessarily subjective dialogue between the artist and the world'.[14]

In his introduction for an exhibition at Galeria Aremar, the art critic Theon Spanudis underscores not only the rigour of the artist's production process, but also its spiritual character:

> Everything in Mira's painting – the composition and distribution, line and colour, dialogue of forms and material – serves the sole finality of revealing the slow processes and silent rhythms of formations in formation. The earnestness, keen sensibility and religious feeling with which these processes are captured and materialised make Mira's painting a rare and singular case that, given its richness and multiple meanings, goes way beyond contrived geometrisms ... Showiness, ornamentation, an excess of colour, material or linear formation are absolutely precluded by this severe notion of composition, which works through the contained and silent fervour of religious experience to capture and reveal formative processes in their very essence.[15]

13 Mario Pedrosa, 'Mira Schendel – Pinturas' (São Paulo: Galeria de Arte São Luiz, 1963).

14 Ibid.

15 *Mira*, introduction by Theon Spanudis (Campinas: Galeria Aremar, 1964).

During this period, Mira starts to use the circular and oval shapes that will become a staple of her later work. These forms are frequently associated with an awareness of non-linear, non-homogeneous time that becomes ever-present in Mira's art, a concept that dispenses with the evolutionary temporality of Western rationality in favour of an Eastern notion of time.

In a text written for the 1964 exhibition *Mira Schendel: óleos e desenhos* (Mira Schendel: oils and drawings), at Galeria Astreia, the art critic Mario Schenberg is the first to point out the influence of Eastern philosophy on the artist's work. Schenberg, one of Brazil's leading physicists, is largely responsible for introducing Mira to this culture by presenting her with Japanese rice paper, a gift that will come to define her work throughout the 1960s. He is also the first to apply the concepts of the void, transcendence and immanence in discussing her work, notions that will become associated with it from that time on:

> Throughout 1963, Mira's work developed this sense of the void and spatiality. The romantic experience she had lived so intensely in her Lombardian youth starts to be contested by an Eastern world view, revealed to her through reproductions of the work of Chi Pai Shi, the grandmaster of contemporary [Chinese] painting. Mira gradually discovered nature. Not that grasped through ingenuity, but that which can only come from a passion for the absolute, when transcendence becomes immanence.[16]

In 1964, she produces large drawings of fruit, glasses, bottles and cups, among other objects, in ink or tempera on wet sheets of paper, though these will never be exhibited during her lifetime. She also produces collages, though these are also not exhibited. These series can be understood as a return to figuration, something she had abandoned in 1953. However, from this time on, the artist starts to work on different and sometimes completely heterogeneous series at the same time. As the curator Paulo Malta Campos observes, 'the figuration/abstraction dichotomy no longer interests her, and while she employs geometrical forms or letters as a means toward, in some way, automating her gesture through pre-established elements, she also strives for the formal solution of the still life'.[17]

In the same year, Mira produces two paintings in which she quotes *Apologia Pro Vita Sua* (1864), by John Henry Newman, in which he refers to the moment in *Iliad* when Achilles returns to battle saying, 'you shall know the difference now that I am back again'. It was the one of the earliest times she used words as visual elements in her paintings.

16 *Mira Schendel: óleos e desenhos*, introduction by Mario Schenberg (São Paulo: Galeria Astreia, 1964).

17 Paulo Malta Campos, *Percurso de Mira Schendel* (São Paulo: Faculdade de Arquitetura e Urbanismo da Universidade de São Paulo, 1991).

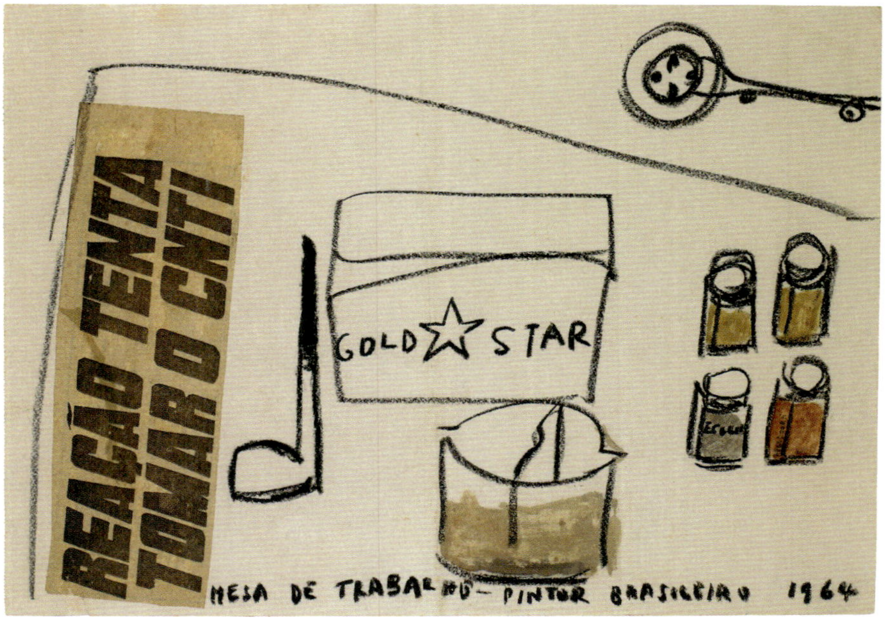

Untitled (Work Desk – Brazilian Painter)
Sem título (Mesa de trabalho – pintor brasileiro)
1964
Crayon, gouache and newspaper on paper
32 x 46 cm
mira schendel estate

1964–5 She produces her *Monotipias* (*Monotypes*), some two thousand drawings in oil on rice paper. To this day, this is one of Mira Schendel's best-known series, and it was the first to be shown abroad. On the origin of these works, the artist will declare, years later:

> I was once given stacks of ultrafine Japanese paper. I kept it, though I had no idea what to do with it. I had no plans for it. It was just given to me ... Sometime later, a year or so, I started working on that paper, but it was hopeless, as it kept tearing. It couldn't take water, it couldn't take this, it couldn't take that. It was just too thin. Then I met this girl who did monotypes, and I started to think that if I used monotype, not for the monotype effect itself, but simply with the practical goal of not tearing the paper every time I tried to use it, I could maybe draw on it. I did a number of experiments and it worked, hence the whole series of drawings on that paper which I exhibited in England...[18]

For Schendel, the *Monotipias* problematise anew such issues as the void, transparency and corporeality, and she develops a way for them to be exhibited in space, so they can be seen from both sides, in direct relation to the viewer's body.

18 Recorded interview by Mira Schendel for the Department of Art Research and Documentation at the Fundação Armando Alvares Penteado, São Paulo, 19 August 1977.

1965 Mira produces the *Bombas* (*Bombs*) series, ink drawings on wet paper, which she exhibits at Petite Galerie in Rio de Janeiro. This same year she exhibits eight from the *Monotipias* series at the 8th Bienal de São Paulo under the title *Canto dos jovens (a propósito de Stockhausen)* [*Song of the Youths (after Stockhausen)*]. In this series, Mira draws on Stockhausen's musical piece to create a universe of words written in different languages, including Italian, French, English, Croatian and German.

On Mira's relationship with language, which extends to other works, the philosopher Vilem Flusser writes:

> Mira's writings are not texts. They are not about anything, and so they cannot be read as representations. They are pre-texts. They are what texts are before they become texts. But as they are almost symbolic, as pre-texts, they cannot be 'read' as drawings either (not in the traditional sense of the term). They do not intend the thing, as drawings do; though neither do they intend, as do texts, to be about things. They should not be 'read' in a metaphorical sense, but literally.[19]

In 1965, the Brazilian artist Sérgio Camargo introduces the English critic Guy Brett to Schendel's work, and on the occasion of the 8th Bienal de São Paulo Brett and Paul Keeler, the Director of Signals, London, visit her at her home. That same year, she is invited to take part in the *Soundings Two* exhibition at Signals. The following year, Mira holds a solo exhibition at Signals in which she presents her *Droguinhas* (*Little Nothings*), among other works. The *Droguinhas* are works made of gnarled and twisted sheets of rice paper knotted together. What stands out in these works is the importance the artist places on the gesture or act. She travels to London for the exhibition and meets David Medalla, Dom Sylvestre Houedard, Li Yuan-Chia and Cyril Barrett.

1966–7 In 1966, she shows her *Droguinhas* and *Trenzinhos* at the Museu de Arte Moderna do Rio de Janeiro. By way of an accompanying text, the exhibition catalogue features a poem by the concrete poet Haroldo de Campos. During this decade, the poet was one of Mira Schendel's main interlocutors.

During her trip to Europe for the Signals exhibition, the first such visit since her emigration to Brazil, Mira visits the artist Amélia Toledo in Portugal, where she holds an exhibition of *Monotipias* at the Buchholz Gallery in Lisbon. She revisits Zurich and Milan, where, on the advice of Haroldo de Campos, she meets with Umberto Eco. In Stuttgart, Germany, she is introduced to the philosopher Max Bense and his wife, the

19 Vilem Flusser, 'Indagações sobre a origem da língua', *O Estado de S. Paulo* (São Paulo), Literary Supplement, 29 April 1967, p.1.

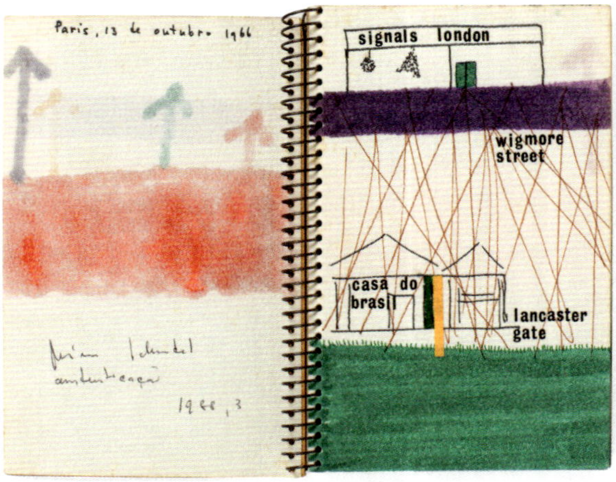
signals london
wigmore street
casa do brasil
lancaster gate

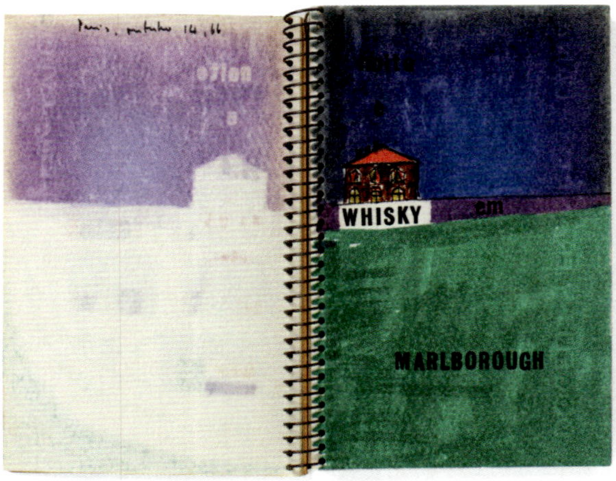
WHISKY
em
MARLBOROUGH

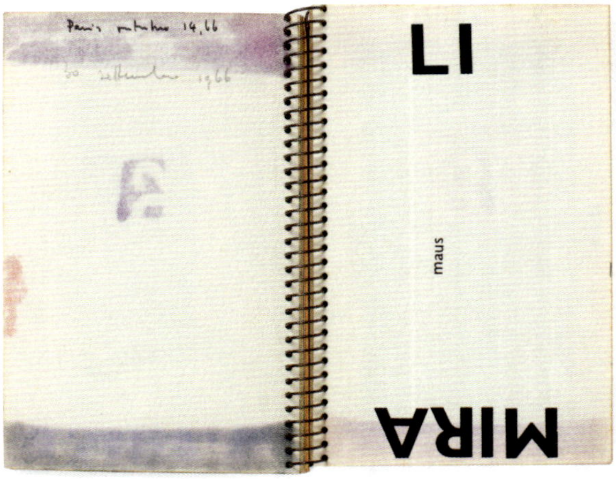
LI
maus
MIRA

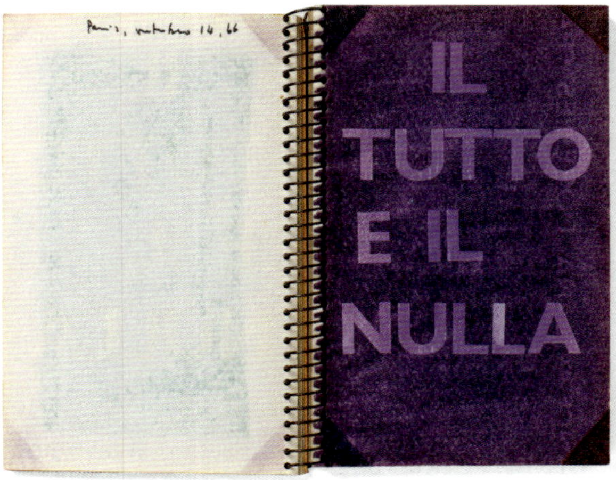
IL TUTTO E IL NULLA

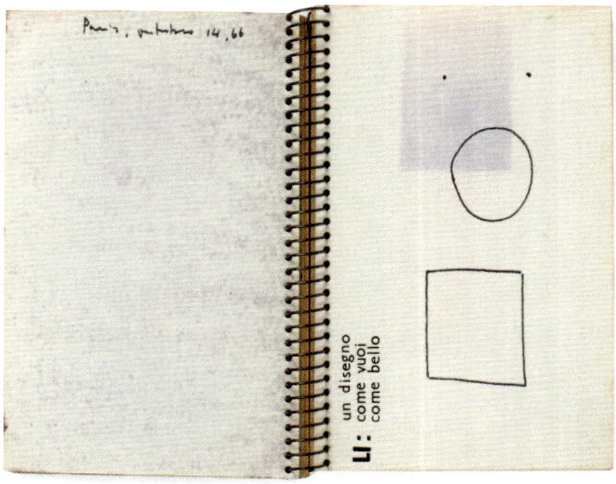
LI: un disegno come vuoi come bello

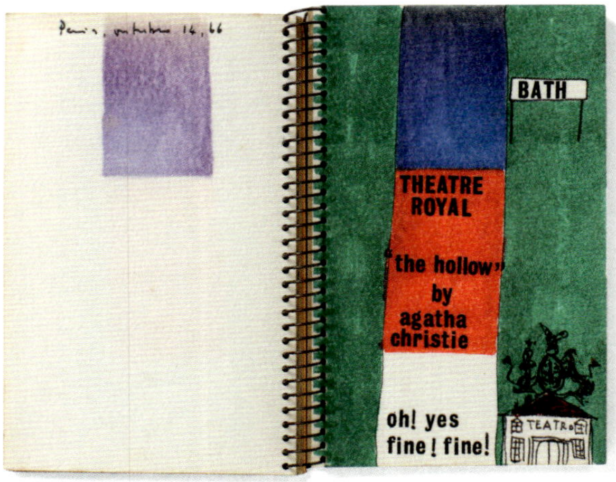
BATH
THEATRE ROYAL
"the hollow" by agatha christie
oh! yes fine! fine!

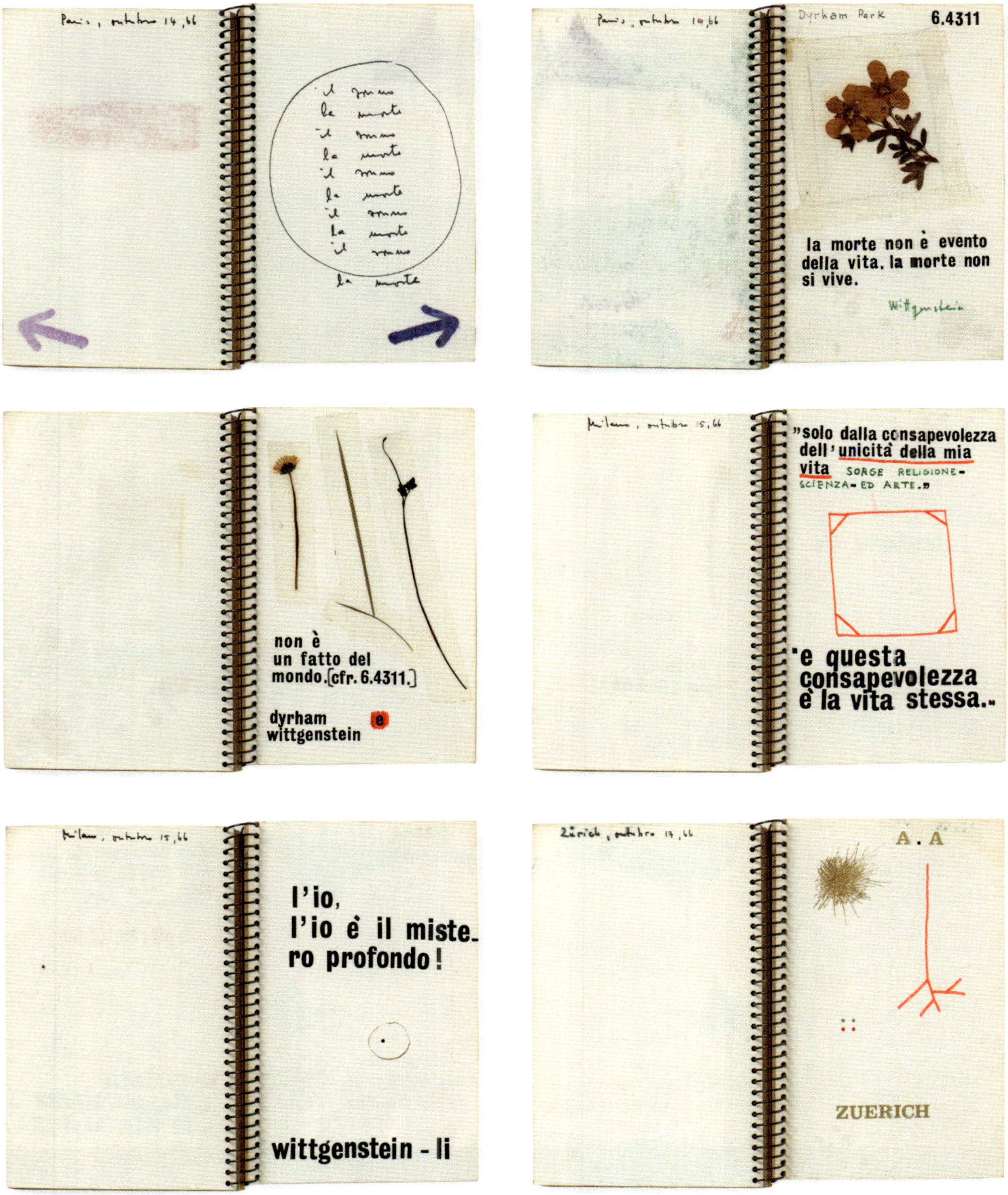

Untitled (London Journal)
Sem título (Diário de Londres)
1966
Mixed media on paper
40 x 22 cm
Melsohn Collection

semiologist Elisabeth Walther, again on the suggestion of Haroldo de Campos. She becomes a close friend of the couple, and an exhibition of her work is organised by Bense at the University of Stuttgart Gallery in 1967, for which he writes the opening text, entitled 'Graphic Reductions':

> Only what is visible is action, and action produces only visibility. Everything is quite substantial: figure outline and choice of paper, trace intensity, deferred curves; the elegant, the lazy, the subtle, the conclusive and the abrupt, the aphoristic and the arbitrary things; what one does with brush-stroke and what is like a beam. Whatever happens, comes to pass on the ultimate skin of the world's substance, right out there where the world might begin to infiltrate itself into consciousness and language.[20]

Though this long trip is her first return to Europe since leaving for Brazil, Mira does not visit her mother who still lives in Italy.

1967–8 In 1967, she presents her *Objetos gráficos* (*Graphic Objects*) at the 9th Bienal de São Paulo. In 1968, she is invited to represent Brazil at the 34th Venice Biennale, alongside Lygia Clark, Farnese de Andrade and Letycia Quadros. Mira presents twelve *Objetos gráficos* investigating the ideas of transparency, corporeality and language. She arranges them herself: the sheets of rice paper are sandwiched between acrylic and hung from nylon thread so as to be visible from both sides. In her diary, she writes that 'this is an attempt to show that the back of transparency lies in front of you, and that "the other world" is this one'.

1968–9 During another sojourn in Europe, she visits Stuttgart, Hamburg, Copenhagen and Oslo. In Oslo her work is presented at the Gromholt Galleri, and the gallery director Konrad Gromholt becomes her friend and first gallerist. She takes the opportunity to travel to the North Cape (Nordkapp) to see the midnight sun. Mira refers to this deeply impactful experience as being one of 'polarity', and she records it exhaustively in photographs and in her travel diary.

Also on this trip she visits Jean Gebser, philosopher and professor in Bern, whom Mira has been studying since 1965. Her interest in psychology, particularly the works of Carl Jung, also dates to the mid-1960s.

In 1969, she is among the Brazilian artists invited to exhibit at the 10th Bienal de São Paulo. Held during the military dictatorship (1964–85), this edition became subject to a boycott; many artists, from Brazil and elsewhere, refused to take part in protest against

20 Max Bense, *Pequena estética*, trans. Haroldo de Campos (São Paulo: Editora Perspectiva 1975), p.225.

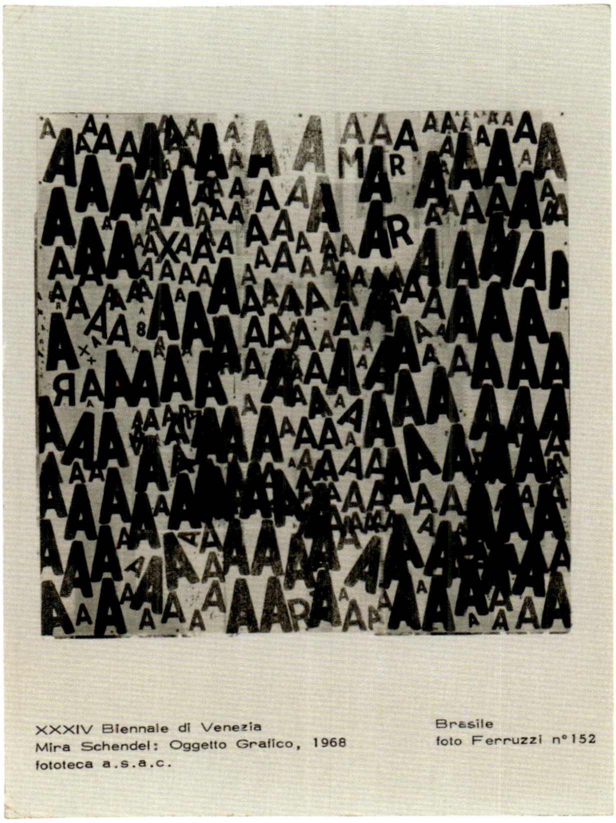

Venice Biennale Invitation, 1968
mira schendel estate archive

the draconian repression practised by the regime since the increased crackdown of 1968. Mira does not adhere to the boycott and exhibits the installation *Ondas paradas de probabilidade – Antigo Testamento, Livros dos Reis I, 19* (*Still Waves of Probability – Old Testament, Book of Kings I, 19*) [p.149].

In a letter to Gromholt, Mira speaks of this piece in the following terms: 'The theme is predominantly the visibility of the invisible, that is, of things that are in action, but without our being able to see them, such as the laws of physics or spiritual processes'.[21]

This work is a watershed in her life, as she herself noted:

> With the work for the Bienal I am perhaps beginning a more silent phase. In the drawings too. Listening (to silence also). Listening for liberation. I know (now) that it does not come in this life ... Because the ego (though its sovereignty is indispensable in this life) is limitation. All our effort in pursuit of perfection in space and time is illusory. Nonacceptance of the relative. This is a bridge we have to cross ... Say yes and no ... To be, faithfully, OF THIS world.

21 Letter to Konrad Gromholt, 25 September 1969 (mira schendel estate archive).

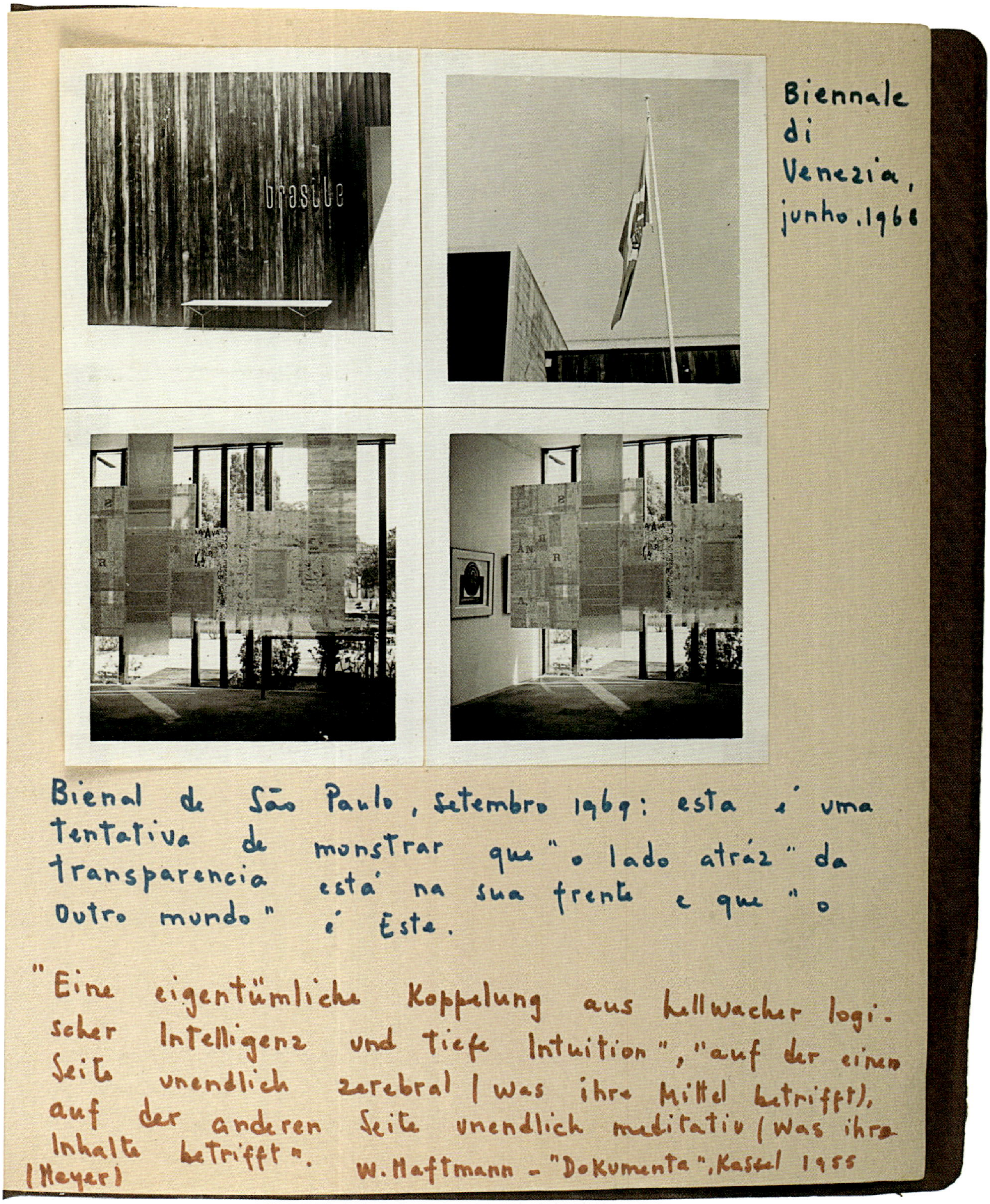

Diary of Mira Schendel, 1969
mira schendel estate archive

> And yet not be of this world. With all its love and joy and also the inevitable suffering, with devotion and without illusions.[22]

Mira Schendel's interest in discussions concerning theology and faith lead her to approach the community surrounding the Dominican order following her arrival in São Paulo. She becomes friends with Friar Chico (Áureo Pereira de Araujo), whose sermons during Sunday Mass at the Church of Saint Dominic, attended by some three thousand people, became known for associating the week's news with the gospel, generally in a manner critical of the dictatorship. Friar Chico would have a decisive role in the Movement for Peace, which emerged within the Catholic Church out of resistance to the dictatorial regime. It was he who supposedly introduced Mira to Friar Paulo de Tarso (Paulo Celso de Moura Silva) who, until he abandoned the Dominican order in the early 1970s, would remain a close friend of the artist. About her, Paulo Celso later declared:

> When I said that Mira was mystical, I meant to say that she was a person who was rooted in the real, looking for a justification of this real. For me, a mystic is one who departs from matter in order to arrive somewhere beyond matter. If he does not recognise matter, he is not a mystic, he is alienated. Mira fought with matter. She never made any concession to escape the reality of matter ... She was an interrogative volcano.[23]

1970–5 The 1970s bring transformations in Schendel's work. She shifts into new phases in her study of language and transparency, and then towards concerns with colour and painting. She does not, however, abandon her explorations of corporeality, deepened during this decade by her readings of the phenomenology of Hermann Schmitz, who Mira visits in Kiel, Germany, first in 1976 and again in subsequent years.

In the first half of the 1970s, Mira continues to produce work in which the play of graphic elements, mostly transfer lettering, still fulfils an important role. An example is her *Cadernos* (*Notebooks*) series, presented at the Museu de Arte Contemporânea da Universidade de São Paulo – MAC USP, in 1971. It is clear that in these works that Mira is exploring relations between language, time and movement. In a letter to the Gromholt in 1971, she says that she would like to make a movie 'with no story, just time, time, time, space space, space', but that there are no means for such a project in Brazil. This is perhaps why she agrees to have a film made from her notebooks for an exhibition organised by Elisabeth Walther in Stuttgart in 1975, saying at the time that she 'thought they might be good for something like that'.[24]

22 Mira Schendel (unpublished diary), quoted in Geraldo Souza Dias 2009, p.147.

23 Paulo Celso de Moura Silva's statement to Geraldo Souza Dias, in Geraldo Dias, *Do espiritual à corporeidade* (São Paulo: Cosac Naify, 2009), pp.126–7.

24 Mira Schendel, letter to Elisabeth Walther, 26 November 1973 (mira schendel estate archive).

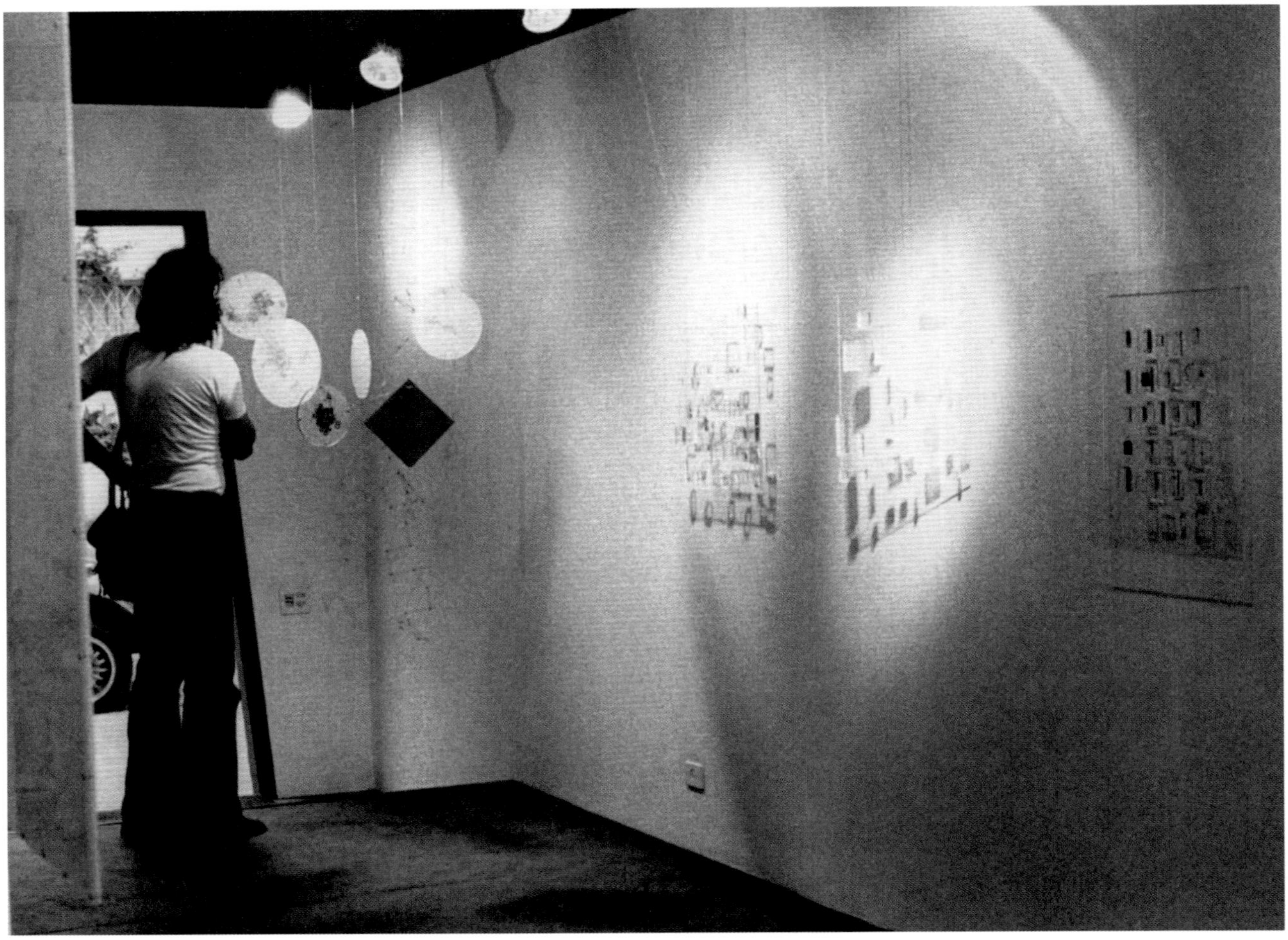

View of the exhibition at Ralph Camargo Gallery, São Paulo, 1972

In the case of the series of works on paper known as *Toquinhos* (*Little Stubs*) [p.174], begun in 1972, graphic elements in transfer lettering are associated with small coloured geometrical forms on rice paper specially dyed by the artist. With the *Datiloscritos* (*Typed Writings*) 1974 [p.166], the artist mixes typewritten lettering and handwritten signs to form compositions. In some of these works she quotes from texts that are important to her.

As for acrylic, Mira continues to use the material in the series of sculptures entitled *Transformáveis* (*Transformables*) [p.146], which she describes as a continuation of her linear drawings. In these works she explores the shadows the pieces cast across the walls:

> Max Bense was the only one who understood that it was all a three-dimensional continuation, that these things didn't function as objects, because all

> that mattered was the light and shadow, a continuation of some drawings of mine, those done on that ultrafine, transparent paper.[25]

Another series named *Toquinhos*, this time in acrylic, is developed between 1972 and 1973, the year she travels once again to Europe. Acrylic rectangles containing signs or letters are glued onto acrylic sheets, casting their shadows onto the wall in a manner similar to the *Transformáveis*. From the same time are her *Perfurados* (*Perforateds*) [p.162], in which black and white sheets of paper are punched through with holes to create patterns.

In 1974 she is invited by the São Paulo City Administration to create a work of public art. Mira designs a large Archimedes spiral in aluminium, roughly 5 metres in diameter, held aloft by a 16-metre mast. The work, intended as a counterweight to the rectangularity of the cityscape, is never made.

25 Mira Schendel, quoted in Geraldo Souza Dias 2009, p.258.

Untitled
Sem título
1974
Gold leaf and dyed paper collage on paper
37.5 x 37 cm
Collection of Pinacoteca do Estado de São Paulo. Donation of the Estate of Alfredo Mesquita, 1994

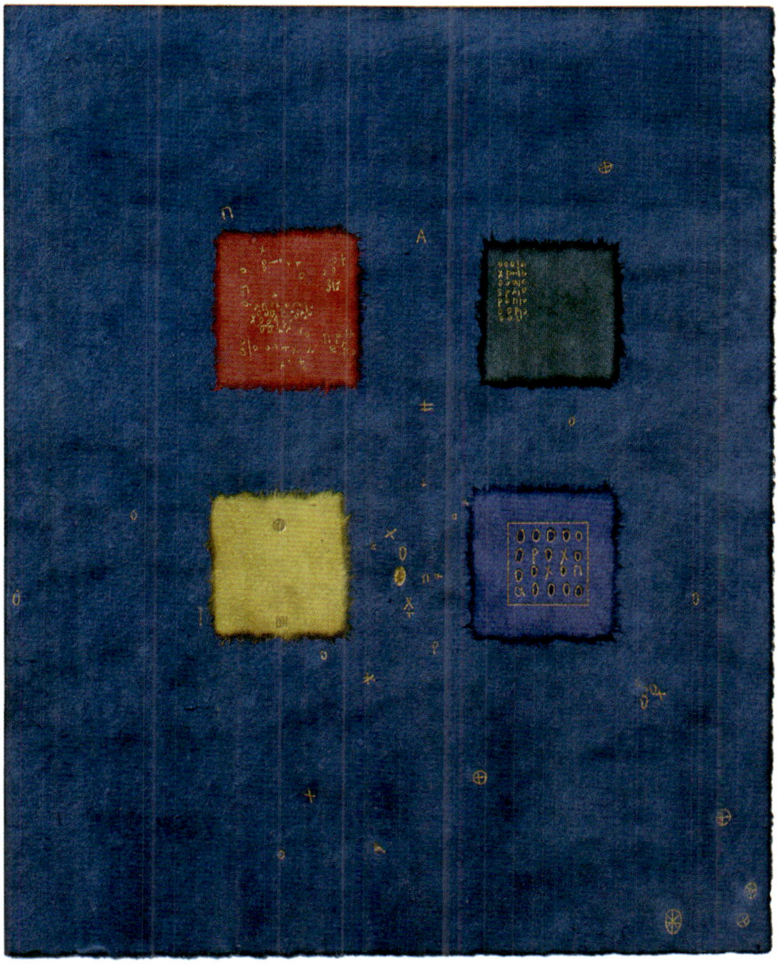

In 1975, during a debate at the 10th Contemporary Art Salon in Campinas, Mira mentions her study of Schmitz:

> From what I have learned, it was to Hermann Schmitz ... that fell the immense task of systemising data supplied by various disciplines in order to devise a phenomenology that, unlike the old school (Husserl, Scheler, Heidegger, Sartre), does not succumb to the demand for metaphysical complementation. A new phenomenology whose keystone is corporeality.[26]

1975 In 1975, Mira creates one of her most forceful series, *Homenagem ao Deus – Pai do Ocidente* (*Homage to God – Father of the West*) [p.176], which consists of sixteen spray-painted drawings with transfer lettering spelling out passages from the Old Testament, particularly drawing from the Psalms. The biblical theme harks back to her 1969 installation *Still Waves of Probability*.

Starting that same year, the artist begins a series of paintings on rice paper that antecipate the tempera and gold leaf paintings she will create in the decade to come. In this series, known as *Papéis japoneses* (*Japanese Papers*), Mira soaks the paper in watercolour to create a velvety, diffuse colour onto which she applies small and delicate inscriptions in gold (letters, numbers, arrows, etc.). In some of these works, geometrical forms are added to the composition.

The 1970s also sees her deepen her study of Jung and Eastern thought, and she creates two series in which these interests come to the fore: the *Mandalas* and the body of canvases and drawings entitled *I Ching* [p.180], presented in 1981 at the 16th Bienal de São Paulo.

1978–82 In 1978 she creates a series of landscapes, among these are the *Paisagem de Itatiaia* (*Itatiaia Landscapes*), named after a mountainous region in Rio de Janeiro state. The nocturnal landscapes are monochrome and are populated with anthropomorphic letter 'A's which Mario Schenberg likens to armies.

Her tempera paintings are shown for the first time in 1979 at the Panorama of Brazilian Art at the Museu de Arte Moderna de São Paulo. However, the first solo exhibition of this series will only occur in 1982, at Galeria Paulo Figueiredo. For the first time in her career, this series brings Mira considerable commercial success. Allying tempera with gold leaf, Mira looks to contrast the opacity of these large monochrome fields with the definition and intense shine of the geometrical forms in gold. However, Mira denies any relationship between

26 Schendel, quoted in Célia Euvaldo, in *No Vazio do Mundo* 1996, pp.94–5.

these works and religious or medieval art, which attributed a noble or divine symbolism to gold.

1986–7 Between 1986 and 1987, she produces the black-and-white tempera works that comprise her final complete series, the *Sarrafos* (*Battens*). These pieces are exhibited at simultaneous exhibitions at the Raquel Arnaud and Paulo Figueiredo galleries in São Paulo, revealing the relationship between the two groups.

The *Sarrafos* consist of large wooden panels in white tempera and gesso, onto which are attached wooden battens painted in black tempera. The effect evokes the drawn line on the page, but with none of the customary delicateness of her work on paper.

About these, Mira declares,

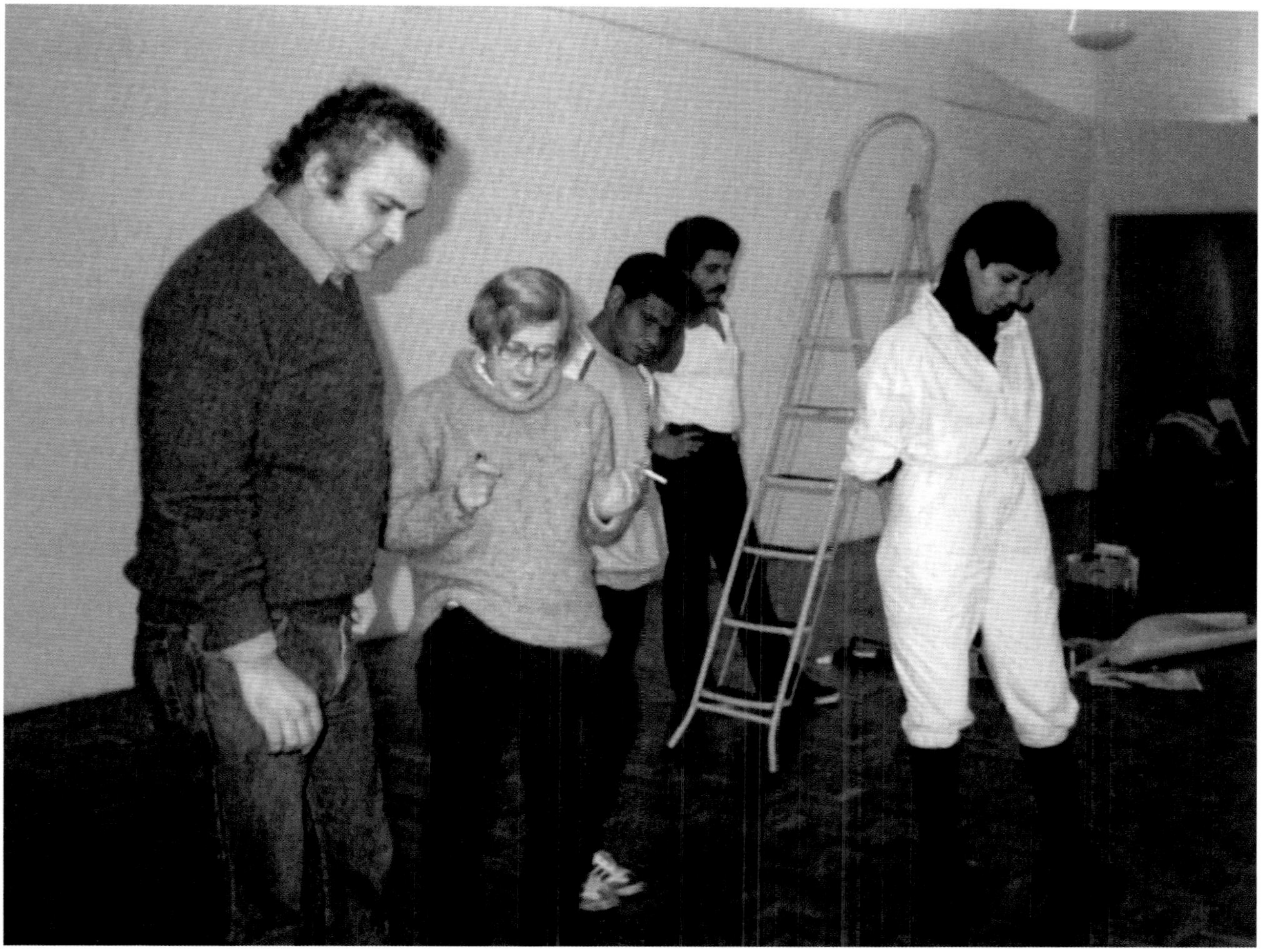

Mira Schendel with José Resende, Carmela Gross and assistants during the hanging of her exhibition at Galeria Luisa Strina, São Paulo, 1983

> This type of work started and ended with that exhibition. It was born of a moment of indecision, out of the disorder Brazil was plunged into in March of that year, when it looked like we were living in some tropical Weimar. That was the context it emerged from. I agree with Gilberto Freyre when he said that culture derives from a struggling with the problems of life. At that time, like everyone else, I was in need of direction, of some bearings. These works are a response to the marasmus of that time. I see no possibility of my continuing along that line, which was like a short story, in a way. There's no continuation.[27]

On the *Sarrafos*, the art critic Ronaldo Brito writes,

> The final series of an oeuvre made up of various, unpredictable series that encompass sundry materials, methods and procedures, Mira Schendel's *Sarrafos* reveal the full extent of the paradoxes of a poetic [practice] that seemed

27 Mira Schendel, quoted in Geraldo Souza Dias 2009, p.324.

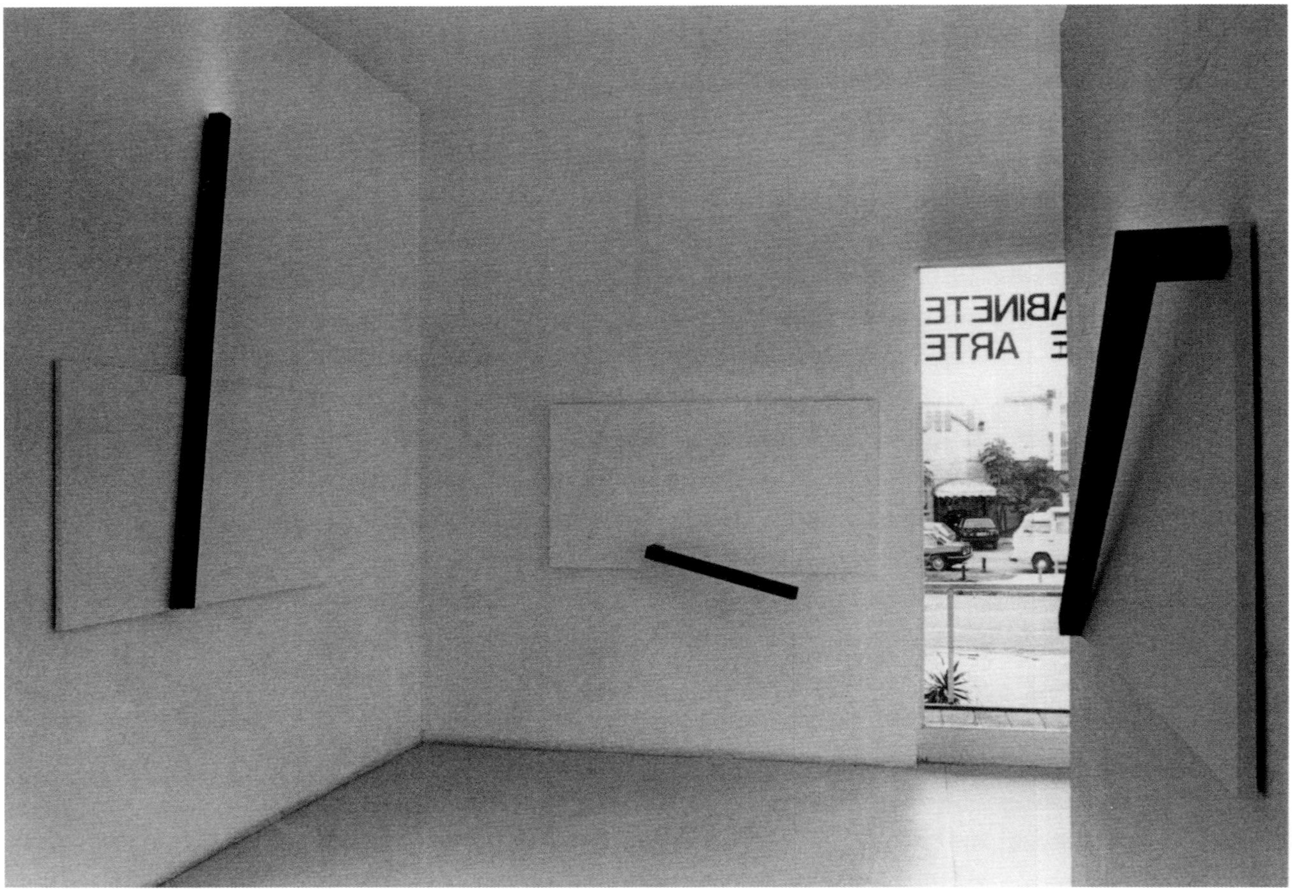

View of the exhibition *Sarrafos* (*Battens*) at Gabinete de Arte Raquel Arnaud, São Paulo, 1987

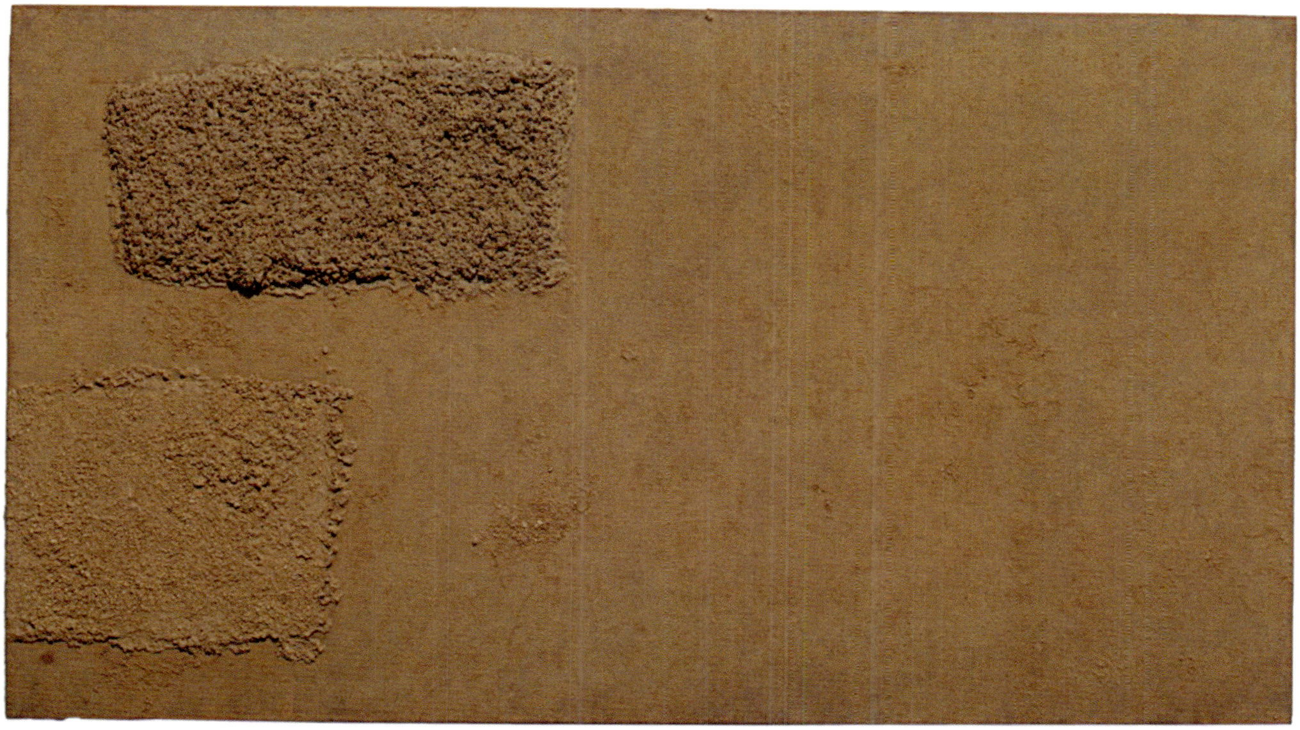

Untitled
Sem título
1988
Brick dust on wood
100 x 200 cm
Museu de Arte Contemporânea da Universidade de São Paulo, São Paulo, Brazil

> to be ruled by the coherence of random rigour: ascetic and intense, almost anonymous, and yet so singular, highly cerebral, but with exact emphasis on the sensible moment of quality.[28]

1988

In June 1988, Mira is diagnosed with lung cancer during a trip to Germany. She returns to Brazil and dies in São Paulo in July that same year. At the time of her death, the artist was developing a new process and series of works using brick dust on wood, returning to aspects of her production from the 1960s.

28 Ronaldo Brito, 'Singular no Plural', in *Mira Schendel: Sarrafos*, exh. cat., Funarte/Galeria Sergio Milliet, Rio de Janeiro, 1988.

Selected Bibliography

Books

2009
Souza Dias, Geraldo. *Mira Schendel: Do Espiritual à Corporeidade*. São Paulo: Cosac Naify, 2009.

2001
Marques, Maria Eduarda. *Mira Schendel*. São Paulo: Cosac & Naify Edições, 2001.

2000
Souza Dias, Geraldo. *Mira Schendel: Kunst Zwischen Metaphysik und Leiblichkeit*. Berlin: Galda+Wilch, 2000.

Sections of books

2011
Naves, Rodrigo. 'Mira Schendel: o mundo como generosidade', in *A forma difícil: ensaios sobre arte brasileira*. São Paulo: Companhia das Letras, 2011; pp.261–76.

2010
Pérez-Oramas, Luis. 'Abstraction, Organism, Apparatus: Notes on the Penetrable Structure in the Work of Lygia Clark, Gego, and Mira Schendel', in *Modern Women: Modern Artists at the Museum of Modern Art*. New York: The Museum of Modern Art, 2010; pp.316–33.

2009
Gonçalves Filho, Antonio. 'Mira Schendel', in *Primeira Individual: 25 anos de crítica de arte*. São Paulo: Cosac Naify, 2009; pp.184–94.

2007
Naves, Rodrigo. *O vento e o moinho: ensaio sobre arte moderna e contemporânea*. São Paulo: Companhia Das Letras, 2007; pp.89–106.

Salzstein, Sônia. 'Mira Schendel: Playing on the Surface of Language', in *Constructing a Poetic Universe: The Diane and Bruce Halle Collection of Latin American Art*. Houston: The Museum of Fine Arts, 2007; pp.192–206.

2006
Lippard, Lucy R. 'The Materials at Hand: Art, Work, and Life: Gego, Clark, Schendel, and Hesse', in *Versions and Inversions: Perspectives on Avant-Garde Art in Latin America*. Houston: Museum of Fine Arts, 2006; pp.159–94.

2005
Brett, Guy. 'Ativamente o Vazio', in *Brasil Experimental: Arte/Vida, Proposições e Paradoxos*. Rio de Janeiro: Contra Capa, 2005; pp.173–83.

2003
Brito, Ronaldo. *Experiência crítica*. São Paulo: Cosac Naify, 2003; pp.289–94.

2001
Fabris, Annateresa, 'Da palavra ao fim da palavra', in *Doação Paulo Figueiredo Museu de Arte Moderna*. São Paulo: Museu de Arte Moderna de São Paulo, 2001; pp.61–70.

Uchôa, Carlos Eduardo. 'Mira: o corpo da escritura no mundo do simulacro', in *Doação Paulo Figueiredo Museu de Arte Moderna*. São Paulo: Museu de Arte Moderna de São Paulo, 2001; pp.77–86.

2000
Salzstein, Sonia.'Mira Schendel: The Immersion of the Body in Thought', in Rina Carvajal (ed.), *The Experimental Exercise of Freedom*, vol.1. Ostfildern: Hatje Cantz, 1st ed., 2000, pp.203–33.

1998
Salzstein, Sônia. 'About the Psychic Experience of Emptiness as Form: Mira Schendel', in Luiz Carlos Junqueira Filho Uchôa (ed.), *Silences and Lights: On the Psychic Experience of Emptiness and Form*, vol.1. São Paulo: House Psychologist, 1st ed., 1998, pp.159–64.

1996
Salzstein, Sônia. 'Mira Schendel: Resisting the Present', in *Inside the Visible: An Elliptical Traverse of 20th Century Art, in, of, and from the Feminine*. Boston: Institute of Contemporary Art, 1996; pp.233–7.

Whitelegg, Isobel. 'Mira Schendel', in Gabriel Pérez-Barreiro (ed.), *Blanton Museum of Art Latin American Collection*. Austin: University of Texas at Austin, 2006; pp.371–4.

1992
Flusser, Vilem. 'Mira Schendel', in *Bodenlos: eine philosophische Autobiographie*. Düsseldorf: Bollmann, 1992.

1988
Schenberg, Mario. 'As monotipias de Mira Schendel', in *Pensando a arte*. São Paulo: Nova Stella, 1988.

1968
Brett, Guy. *Kinetic Art: The Language of Movement*. London / New York: Studio Vista, 1968..

Exhibitions

2012
Aberto fechado: caixa e livro na arte brasileira = The Enclosed Openess: Box and Book in Brazilian Art. Pinacoteca do Estado de São Paulo, São Paulo, 20 Oct. 2012 – 13 Jan. 2013. Texts by Guy Brett, Frederico Morais, Mira Schendel et al.

2011
Mira Schendel: Avesso do Avesso. Instituto de Arte Contemporânea. São Paulo, 3–27 Feb. 2011. Text by Cauê Alves.

Mira Schendel: Pintora. São Paulo Instituto Moreira Salles, Rio de Janeiro, Sept.–Nov. 2011. Text by Maria Eduarda Marques, Marco Giannotti, Paulo Pasta et al.

2009
León Ferrari & Mira Schendel: Tangled Alphabets. The Museum of Modern Art, New York, 5 April – 15 June 2009; Museo Nacional Centro de Arte Reina Sofia, Madrid, 24 Nov. 2009 – 1 March 2010; Fundação Iberê Camargo, Porto Alegreill. Text by Luis Pérez-Oramas and Rodrigo Naves.

Mira Schendel: Monotypes. Galeria Milan, São Paulo, 18 March – 25 April 2009.

2007
Campo Ampliado. São Paulo Instituto de Arte Contemporânea, São Paulo, 28 Nov. 2007 – 30 March 2008. Text by Paulo Sergio Duarte.

Documenta 12, Kassel, 16 June – 23 Sept. 2007.

2005
Amilcar de Castro, Mira Schendel, Sergio Camargo, Willys de Castro. Institutio de Arte Contemporânea, São Paulo, 29 Sept. – 10 Dec. 2005. Texts by Rodrigo Naves and Tiago Mesquita.

2004
Mira Schendel: Continuum Amorfo. Museo Tamayo Arte Contemporáneo, Mexico City, 4 March – 30 May 2004. Text by Rodrigo Naves.

2001

Mira Schendel. Galerie Nationale du Jeu de Paume, Paris, 9 Oct. – 18 Nov. 2001. Text by Geraldo Souza Dias.

2000

The Experimental Exercise of Freedom: Lygia Clark, Gego, Mathias Goeritz, Hélio Oiticica, Mira Schendel. Museum of Contemporary Art, Los Angeles, 17 Oct. 1999 – 23 Jan. 2000.

Mira Schendel, Sergio Camargo, Willys de Castro. Centro Cultural Banco do Brasil, Rio de Janeiro, 21 March – 21 May 2000.Text by João Masao Kamita.

1998

XXIV Bienal de São Paulo, Núcleo Histórico. Antropofagia e Histórias de Canibalismos. Vol.1. 24th Bienal de São Paulo. 3 Oct. – 13 Dec. 1998.

Arte Constructiva no Brasil: Coleção Adolpho Leirner = Constructive Art in Brazil: Adolpho Leirner Collection. Museu de Arte Moderna de São Paulo, São Paulo, 2 Oct. – 20 Dec 1998.

1997

Mira Schendel: A Forma Volátil: Centro de Arte Hélio Oiticica. Centro de Arte Hélio Oiticica, Rio de Janeiro, 3 June – 20 July 1997. Texts by Sônia Salzstein and Paulo Venâncio Filho.

1996

No Vazio do Mundo: Mira Schendel. Galeria de Arte do SESI, São Paulo, 30 Sept. 1996 – 26 Jan. 1997. Texts by Sônia Salzstein, Guy Brett, Rodrigo Naves et al.

1995

Mira Schendel: Art from Brazil in New York, The Drawing Center, New York, 7 Jan. – 4 Feb. 1995. Text by Paulo Herkenhoff.

1994

Mira Schendel. Galeria Camargo Vilaça, São Paulo, April 1994. Text by Rodrigo Naves.

XXII São Paulo Bienial = 22nd Bienal de São Paulo, 24 April – 29 May 1994. Texts by Paulo Malta Campos and Nelson Aguilar.

1990

Mira Schendel. Museu de Arte Contemporânea da Universidade de São Paulo, São Paulo, Nov. 1990. Text by Agnaldo Farias.

1989

Mira Schendel: Desenhos e Objectos / Cadernos, Gravuras e Xerox. Paulo Figueiredo Galeria de Arte / Espaço Fogo Paulista, São Paulo, 1989. Text by Paulo Figueiredo.

Art in Latin America: The Modern Era 1820–1980. Hayward Gallery, London, 18 May – 6 Aug. 1989; Moderna Museet, Stockholm, 16 Sept. – 19 Nov. 1989; Palacio de Velázquez, Madrid, 19 Dec. 1989 – 31 March 1990. Text by Guy Brett.

1988

Mira Schendel: Sarrafos. Funarte / Galeria Sérgio Milliet, Rio de Janeiro, Dec. 1988. Text by Ronaldo Brito.

1986

*Mira Schendel: Pinturas Recentes.*Paulo Figueiredo Galeria de Arte, São Paulo, Nov. 1986. Text by Rodrigo Naves.

1983

*Mira Schendel. 65 Desenhos, 2 Droguinhas, 1 Trenzinho, 1 quadro de 1964 e a série Deus – Pai do Ocidente.*Thomas Cohn Arte Contemporânea, Rio de Janeiro, April 1983.

1981

XVI Bienal Internacional de São Paulo. Fundação Bienal, São Paulo, Oct.1981. Text by Walter Zanini.

Arte Transcendente. Museu de Arte Moderna de São Paulo, São Paulo, 1981. Text by Theon Spanudis.

1978

O Objeto na Arte. Brasil Anos '60. Fundação Armando Alvares Penteado, São Paulo, 1978.

1975

Mira Schendel. Desenhos de 1974/75: Datiloscritos – Mandalas – Paisagens. Gabinete de Artes Gráficas, São Paulo, May 1975. Text by Haroldo de Campos.

X Salão de Arte Contemporânea de Campinas. Arte no Brasil, documento/debate. Salão de Arte Contemporânea de Campinas, Campinas, 7–30 Nov. 1975.

1974

Mira Schendel: Visuelle Konstruktionen und Transparente Texte. Schmidtbank Galerie / Institüt für Moderne Kunst, Nurnberg, 1974. Text by Max Bense and Haroldo de Campos.

1973

The Avant-garde Works by Mira Schendel. Art Gallery of the Brazilian–American Cultural Institute, Washington DC, Jan. 1973. Text by José Neistein.

1971

Museu de Arte Contemporânea de São Paulo: Amelia Amorim Toledo, Donato Ferrari, Mira Schendel. Museu de Arte Contemporanea de São Paulo, São Paulo, 21 Oct. – 7 Nov. 1971.

1968

*XXXIV Biennale di Venezia.*Brazilian Pavilion, Venice, 1968. Text by Jayme Maurício.

1966

Mira Schendel. Museu de Arte Moderna do Rio de Janeiro, Rio de Janeiro, May 1966. Text by Haroldo de Campos.

Desenhos de Mira Schendel. Galeria Bulchholz, Lisbon [n.c.]. Text by José-Augusto França.

1965

Mira Schendel. Petite Galerie, Rio de Janeiro, Oct. 1965. Text by Clarival do Prado Valladares.

1964

Mira Schendel. Óleos e desenhos. Galeria Astreia, São Paulo, Feb. 1964. Text by Mario Schenberg.

Mira. Galeria Aremar, Campinas, March 1964. Text by Theon Spanudis.

1963

Mira Schendel. Pinturas. Galeria de Arte São Luiz, São Paulo, 1963. Text by Mario Pedrosa.

1962

Mira Schendel. Galeria Selearte, São Paulo, Nov. 1962. Text by Mario Schenberg.

1954

Mira: Exposição de Pinturas. Museu de Arte Moderna, São Paulo, Oct.1954.

List of Works

Works are listed chronologically; those with precise dates are given first within each decade. Works with the same dating are in the order: painting; sculpture; works on paper. Dimensions are given as height x width x depth. Page numbers refer to illustrations.

1
Still Life
Natureza-morta
1953
Oil on canvas
64.8 x 54 cm
Colección Patricia Phelps de Cisneros

2 [p.61]
Untitled
Sem título
1953
Oil on canvas
53.3 x 64.6 cm
Museu de Arte Contemporânea da Universidade de São Paulo, São Paulo, Brazil

3
Untitled
Sem título
1953
Oil on canvas
74.6 x 74.6 cm
Museu de Arte Contemporânea da Universidade de São Paulo, São Paulo, Brazil

4
Untitled
Sem título
1954
Oil on card
30 x 25.1 cm
Museu de Arte Contemporânea da Universidade de São Paulo, São Paulo, Brazil

5 [p.67]
Untitled
Sem título
1954
Tempera and gesso on wood
51 x 66 cm
The Museum of Fine Arts, Houston, The Adolpho Leirner Collection of Brazilian Constructive Art, museum purchase with funds provided by the Caroline Wiess Law Accessions Endowment Fund

6 [p.64]
Composition
Composição
1954
Oil on wood
24.3 x 35.6 cm
Museu de Arte Contemporânea da Universidade de São Paulo, São Paulo, Brazil

7
Untitled
Sem título
c.1954
Oil on canvas
60 x 40 cm
Private collection

8 [p.62]
Untitled
Sem título
c.1954–5
Tempera on canvas
26.8 x 19 cm
Eduardo Duvivier Neto

9 [p.65]
Untitled
Sem título
1955
Tempera and sand on wood
60 x 40 cm
Private collection

10 [p.66]
Untitled
Sem título
1955
Tempera on wood
40 x 60 cm
Private collection

11 [p.63]
Untitled
Sem título
1950s
Tempera on jute
96.5 x 130 cm
Luiz Paulo Montenegro

12 [p.72]
Untitled (Painting 2)
Sem título (Pintura 2)
1960
Gouache on wood
59.5 x 39.7 cm
Colección Patricia Phelps de Cisneros

13 [p.97]
Untitled, from the series *Refrigerators*
Sem título, da série *Geladeiras*
1960
Tempera on plywood
35.5 x 26.7 cm
Colección Patricia Phelps de Cisneros

14
Untitled, from the series *Refrigerators*
Sem título, da série *Geladeiras*
1960
Tempera on plywood
43.8 x 30.8 cm
Colección Patricia Phelps de Cisneros

15 [p.71]
Untitled
Sem título
c.1960–5
Tempera on canvas
120 x 80 cm
Private collection

16 [p.78]
Untitled
Sem título
1962
Oil on canvas
74.9 x 74.7 cm
The Museum of Fine Arts, Houston, The Adolpho Leirner Collection of Brazilian Constructive Art, museum purchase

17 [p.79]
Untitled (Abstract)
Sem título (Abstração)
1962
Tempera on canvas
75 x 75 cm
Private collection

18 [p.81]
Untitled
Sem título
1963
Oil on canvas
145.9 x 114 cm
Tate. Presented by Tate Members 2006

19 [p.83]
Untitled (Landscape)
Sem título (Paisagem)
1963
Tempera on canvas
76 x 150.5 cm
Orandi Momesso Collection

20 [p.84]
Untitled (Egg)
Sem título (Ovo)
1963
Tempera and plaster on wood
132 x 90 cm
Private collection

21 [p.85]
Untitled
Sem título
1963
Tempera and plaster on canvas
100 x 100 cm
Hecilda and Sergio Fadel

22
Untitled
Sem título
1963
Mixed media on canvas
100 x 81 cm
Augusto Livio Malzoni

23 [p.75]
Untitled
Sem título
1963
Tempera on canvas
81 x 101 cm
Private collection, Dallas

24 [p.92]
Untitled
Sem título
c.1963–4
Ink on paper
48.3 x 66.5 cm
mira schendel estate

25 [p.92]
Untitled
Sem título
c.1963–4
Ink and collage on paper
48.4 x 66.3 cm
mira schendel estate

26 [p.105]
Untitled
Sem título
c.1963–5
Tempera on jute
50.5 x 50.5 cm
Private collection, São Paulo, Brazil

27 [p.77]
Untitled
Sem título
1964
Tempera on canvas
100 x 50 cm
Marcos Ribeiro Simon Collection

28
Untitled
Sem título
1964
Tempera on agglomerate
50 x 45 cm
Ricard Akagawa Collection

29
Untitled
Sem título
1964
Tempera on agglomerate
50 x 40 cm
Ricard Akagawa Collection

30
Untitled
Sem título
1964
Mixed media on wood
92 x 91 cm
Gerard Loeb, São Paulo

31 [p.89]
Untitled
Sem título
1964
Oil on canvas
130 x 162 cm
Orandi Momesso Collection

32 [p.90]
The Return of Achilles I
O Retorno de Aquiles I
1964
Oil on canvas
93 x 132 cm
Private collection

33 [p.91]
The Return of Achilles
O Retorno de Aquiles
1964
Oil on canvas
93.4 x 130 cm
mira schendel estate

34 [p.93]
Untitled
Sem título
1964
Ink on paper
48.5 x 66.5 cm
mira schendel estate

35 [p.94]
Untitled
Sem título
1964
Watercolour on paper
48.7 x 66.5 cm
mira schendel estate

36 [p.86]
Untitled
Sem título
1964
Ink on paper
48 x 66.3 cm
mira schendel estate

37 [p.86]
Untitled
Sem título
1964
Ink on paper
48 x 66.3 cm
mira schendel estate

38
Untitled
Sem título
1964
Ink on paper
48 x 66 cm
Private collection

39 [p.104]
Untitled
Sem título
1964
Ink, gouache and graphite on paper
58 x 77 cm
Estrellita B. and Daniel Brodsky Collection

40 [p.110]
Untitled (Universe), from the series *Monotypes*
Sem título (Universo), da série *Monotipias*
1964
Oil on rice paper
47 x 23 cm
Museu de Arte Moderna de São Paulo, donation of Paulo Figueiredo

41 [p.116]
Untitled, from the series *Monotypes*
Sem título, da série *Monotipias*
1964
Oil on rice paper
47 x 23 cm
Instituto de Arte Contemporânea (IAC), São Paulo, Brazil

42 [p.116]
Untitled, from the series *Monotypes*
Sem título, da série *Monotipias*
1964
Oil on rice paper
47 x 23 cm
Instituto de Arte Contemporânea (IAC), São Paulo, Brazil

43 [p.116]
Untitled, from the series *Monotypes*
Sem título, da série *Monotipias*
1964
Oil on rice paper
47 x 23 cm
Instituto de Arte Contemporânea (IAC), São Paulo, Brazil

44 [p.117]
Untitled, from the series *Monotypes*
Sem título, da série *Monotipias*
1964
Oil on rice paper
47 x 23 cm
Instituto de Arte Contemporânea (IAC), São Paulo, Brazil

45 [p.117]
Untitled, from the series *Monotypes*
Sem título, da série *Monotipias*
1964
Oil on rice paper
47 x 23 cm
Instituto de Arte Contemporânea (IAC), São Paulo, Brazil

46 [p.117]
Untitled, from the series *Monotypes*
Sem título, da série *Monotipias*
1964
Oil on rice paper
47 x 23 cm
Instituto de Arte Contemporânea (IAC), São Paulo, Brazil

47
Untitled, from the series *Monotypes*
Sem título, da série *Monotipias*
1964
Oil on rice paper
47 x 23 cm
Instituto de Arte Contemporânea (IAC), São Paulo, Brazil

48
Untitled, from the series *Monotypes*
Sem título, da série *Monotipias*
1964
Oil on rice paper
47 x 23 cm
Instituto de Arte Contemporânea (IAC), São Paulo, Brazil

49
Untitled, from the series *Monotypes*
Sem título, da série *Monotipias*
1964
Oil on rice paper
47 x 23 cm
Instituto de Arte Contemporânea (IAC), São Paulo, Brazil

50
Untitled, from the series *Monotypes*
Sem título, da série *Monotipias*
1964
Oil on rice paper
47 x 23 cm
Instituto de Arte Contemporânea (IAC), São Paulo, Brazil

51
Untitled, from the series *Monotypes*
Sem título, da série *Monotipias*
1964
Oil on rice paper
6 parts: each 48 x 23 cm
Maria Cristina and Pablo Henning Collection, Houston

52
Untitled, from the series *Monotypes*
Sem título, da série *Monotipias*
1964
Oil on rice paper
46 x 23 cm
Collection G. and J. Fainas

53
Untitled, from the series *Monotypes*
Sem título, da série *Monotipias*
1964
Oil on rice paper
45.5 x 23 cm
mira schendel estate

54
Untitled, from the series *Monotypes*
Sem título, da série *Monotipias*
1964
Oil on rice paper
47 x 23 cm
mira schendel estate

55 [p.87]
Untitled
Sem título
c.1964
Oil on canvas
115.8 x 94.8 cm
mira schendel estate

56 [p.88]
Untitled
Sem título
c.1964
Oil on canvas
92 x 130 cm
Marta and Marcio Lobão Collection

57 [p.97]
Untitled (All)
Sem título (Todos)
c.1964
Oil on canvas
162 x 132 cm
Jones Bergamin

58
Untitled, from the series *Monotypes*
Sem título, da série *Monotipias*
c.1964
Oil on rice paper
46 x 23 cm
Private collection

59
Untitled, from the series *Monotypes*
Sem título, da série *Monotipias*
c.1964
Oil on rice paper
46 x 23 cm
Private collection

60
Untitled
Sem título
1964–5
Oil on rice paper
45 x 23 cm
Private collection

61 [pp.114–15]
Sign of Signs
Segno dei Segni
1964–5
Oil on rice paper
5 parts: each 46 x 23 cm
The Museum of Modern Art, New York. Latin American and Caribbean Fund, 2008

62 [p.120]
Untitled, from the series *Little Nothings*
Sem título, da série *Droguinhas*
1965
Rice paper
20 cm diameter
Private collection

63 [p.100]
Untitled (Pass)
Sem título (Passe)
1965
Ink on paper
48 x 66 cm
Esther Faingold

64
Untitled, from the series *Bombs*
Sem título, da série *Bombas*
1965
Ink and crayon on paper
66 x 96 cm
Daros Latinamerica Collection, Zürich

65 [p.103]
Untitled, from the series *Bombs*
Sem título, da série *Bombas*
1965
Ink and crayon on paper
65.8 x 88.2 cm
Daros Latinamerica Collection, Zurich

66
Untitled, from the series *Bombs*
Sem título, da série *Bombas*
1965
Watercolour and ink on paper
46.5 x 67.5 cm
Private collection, Porto Alegre, Brazil

67 [p.101]
Untitled, from the series *Bombs*
Sem título, da série *Bombas*
1965
Ink on paper
48 x 66 cm
BBM

68 [p.101]
Untitled, from the series *Bombs*
Sem título, da série *Bombas*
1965
Ink on paper
48 x 66 cm
BBM

69
Untitled, from the series *Bombs*
Sem título, da série *Bombas*
1965
Ink on paper
48 x 66 cm
BBM

70 [p.102]
Untitled, from the series *Bombs*
Sem título, da série *Bombas*
1965
Ink on paper
47.9 x 65.4 cm
Colección Patricia Phelps de Cisneros

71 [pp.112–13]
Genesis
Gênesis
1965
Oil on rice paper
9 parts: each 46.5 x 22.9 cm
Tate. Presented by the Tate Americas Foundation 2012

72
Untitled, from the series *Monotypes*
Sem título, da série *Monotipias*
1965
Oil on rice paper
47 x 23 cm
Museu de Arte Moderna de São Paulo, donation of Paulo Figueiredo

73
Untitled, from the series *Monotypes*
Sem título, da série *Monotipias*
1965
Oil on rice paper
46 x 23 cm
mira schendel estate

74
Untitled, from the series *Monotypes*
Sem título, da série *Monotipias*
1965
Oil on rice paper
46 x 23 cm
mira schendel estate

75 [p.106]
Untitled, from the series *Monotypes*
Sem título, da série *Monotipias*
1965
Oil on rice paper
45 x 23 cm
Marcela and Israel Furmanovich

76 [p.106]
Untitled, from the series *Monotypes*
Sem título, da série *Monotipias*
1965
Oil on rice paper
45 x 23 cm
Marcela and Israel Furmanovich

77 [p.107]
Untitled, from the series *Monotypes*
Sem título, da série *Monotipias*
1965
Oil on rice paper
45 x 23 cm
Marcela and Israel Furmanovich

78 [p.107]
Untitled, from the series *Monotypes*
Sem título, da série *Monotipias*
1965
Oil on rice paper
45 x 23 cm
Marcela and Israel Furmanovich

79 [p.107]
Untitled, from the series *Monotypes*
Sem título, da série *Monotipias*
1965
Oil on rice paper
45 x 23 cm
Marcela and Israel Furmanovich

80 [p.111]
Untitled (Time), from the series *Monotypes*
Sem título (Zeit), da série *Monotipias*
1965
Oil on rice paper
47.4 x 23 cm
Inhotim Collection, Brazil

81
Untitled, from the series *Monotypes*
Sem título, da série *Monotipias*
1965
Oil on rice paper
47 x 23 cm
Marcela and Israel Furmanovich

82 [pp.108–9]
Untitled, from the series *Monotypes*
Sem título, da série *Monotipias*
1965
Oil on rice paper
5 parts: each 46 x 23 cm
Collection G. and J. Fainas

83 [p.122]
Little Train
Trenzinho
c.1965
114 sheets of rice paper and cotton thread
Dimensions variable
mira schendel estate

84 [p.123]
Little Train
Trenzinho
c.1965
Rice paper and cotton thread
46 x 65 x 15 cm
Collection Antonio Dias, Rio de Janeiro

85 [p.119]
Untitled, from the series *Little Nothings*
Sem título, da série *Droguinhas*
c.1965–6
Rice paper
Dimensions variable, approx. 90 x 70 cm
The Museum of Modern Art, New York.
Scott Burton Fund, 2005

86
Untitled, from the series *Little Nothings*
Sem título, da série *Droguinhas*
c.1965–6
Rice paper
Dimensions variable, approx. 35 x 10 cm
mira schendel estate

87
Untitled, from the series *Little Nothings*
Sem título, da série *Droguinhas*
c.1965–6
Rice paper
Dimensions variable, approx. 25 x 15 cm
Jones Bergamin

88 [p.121]
Untitled, from the series *Little Nothings*
Sem título, da série *Droguinhas*
c.1965–6
Rice paper
Dimensions variable
Private collection, Dallas

89 [p.121]
Untitled, from the series *Little Nothings*
Sem título, da série *Droguinhas*
1966
Rice paper
66.6 x 26 x 15.7 cm
Colección Patricia Phelps de Cisneros

90
Untitled, from the series *Little Nothings*
Sem título, da série *Droguinhas*
1966
Rice paper
Dimensions variable, approx. 35 x 5 cm
Maria Cristina and Pablo Henning
Collection, Houston

91 [p.99]
Untitled (How Beautiful)
Sem título (Que beleza)
1966
Watercolour and oil stick on paper
43 x 61.5 cm
Private collection

92 [p.22]
Untitled, from the series *Monotypes*
Sem título, da série *Monotipias*
1966
Oil on rice paper
47 x 23 cm
Private collection, London

93
Untitled, from the series *Monotypes*
Sem título, da série *Monotipias*
1966
Oil on rice paper
49.3 x 25.3 cm
mira schendel estate

94 [pp.137–9]
Graphic Object
Objeto gráfico
1967
Oil and ink on rice paper with acrylic
100 x 100 cm
mira schendel estate

95 [p.133]
Graphic Object
Objeto gráfico
1967
Graphite, transfer lettering and oil on rice paper with acrylic
99.8 x 99.8 cm
Colección Patricia Phelps de Cisneros

96 [p.130]
Graphic Object
Objeto gráfico
1967
Oil and transfer lettering on rice paper with acrylic
99.7 x 99.7 cm
The Ella Fontanals-Cisneros Collection

97 [p.132]
Graphic object
Objeto gráfico
1967–8
Oil on rice paper with acrylic
100 x 100 cm
Daros Latinamerica Collection, Zurich

98 [p.127]
Graphic Object
Objeto gráfico
1967–8
Oil on rice paper with acrylic
100 x 100 cm
Marta and Paulo Kuczynski Collection, São Paulo

99 [p.125]
Graphic Object
Objeto gráfico
1967–8
Oil on rice paper with acrylic
100 x 100 cm
Ernesto and Cecilia Poma Collection

100
Graphic Object
Objeto gráfico
1967–8
Oil on rice paper with acrylic
50 x 50 cm
Luiz Paulo Montenegro

101
Graphic Object
Objeto gráfico
1967–8
Oil and transfer lettering on rice paper with acrylic
100 x 100 cm
Jones Bergamin

102 [p.126]
Graphic Object
Objeto gráfico
1967–8
Oil on rice paper with acrylic
100 x 100 cm
Rose and Alfredo Setubal Collection

103 [p.131]
Graphic Object
Objeto gráfico
1967–8
Oil and transfer lettering on rice paper with acrylic
100 x 100 cm
Fernanda Feitosa and Heitor Martins Collection

104 [p.134]
Graphic Object
Objeto gráfico
c.1967–8
Oil and transfer lettering on rice paper with acrylic
50.3 x 50 cm
Private collection

105 [p.128]
Graphic Object
Objeto gráfico
1969
Oil and transfer lettering on rice paper with acrylic
100 x 100 cm
Private collection

106 [pp.40, 149]
Still Waves of Probability
Ondas parada de probabilidade
1969
Nylon thread with text on acrylic
Dimensions variable
mira schendel estate

107
Untitled
Sem título
early 1960s
Oil stick and gouache on paper
14 x 11.5 cm
mira schendel estate

108
Untitled
Sem título
early 1960s
Oil stick and gouache on paper
14.8 x 10.3 cm
mira schendel estate

109
Untitled
Sem título
early 1960s
Oil stick and gouache on paper
22.3 x 15.8 cm
mira schendel estate

110
Untitled
Sem título
early 1960s
Oil stick and gouache on paper
22.3 x 15.8 cm
mira schendel estate

111
Untitled
Sem título
early 1960s
Oil stick and gouache on paper
22 x 16 cm
mira schendel estate

112
Untitled
Sem título
early 1960s
Oil stick and gouache on paper
21.1 x 15.8 cm
mira schendel estate

113
Untitled
Sem título
early 1960s
Oil stick and gouache on paper
22 x 11.5 cm
mira schendel estate

114
Untitled
Sem título
early 1960s
Oil stick and gouache on paper
22.2 x 15.8 cm
mira schendel estate

115
Untitled
Sem título
early 1960s
Oil stick and gouache on paper
21 x 15.8 cm
mira schendel estate

116
Untitled
Sem título
early 1960s
Oil stick and gouache on paper
21.4 x 15.8 cm
mira schendel estate

117 [p.68]
Untitled
Sem título
early 1960s
Oil stick and gouache on paper
21 x 15.6 cm
mira schendel estate

118 [p.69]
Untitled
Sem título
early 1960s
Oil stick and gouache on paper
21.3 x 15.8
mira schendel estate

119
Untitled
Sem título
early 1960s
Oil stick and gouache on paper
21.4 x 15.8 cm
mira schendel estate

120 [p.69]
Untitled
Sem título
early 1960s
Oil stick and gouache on paper
21 x 15.6 cm
mira schendel estate

121
Untitled
Sem título
early 1960s
Oil stick and gouache on paper
19.8 x 13.5 cm
mira schendel estate

122
Untitled
Sem título
early 1960s
Oil stick and gouache on paper
21.3 x 15.8 cm
mira schendel estate

123
Untitled
Sem título
early 1960s
Oil stick and gouache on paper
21.3 x 15.8 cm
mira schendel estate

124
Untitled
Sem título
early 1960s
Oil stick and gouache on paper
21.1 x 15.8 cm
mira schendel estate

125
Untitled
Sem título
early 1960s
Oil stick and gouache on paper
21.2 x 15.8 cm
mira schendel estate

126 [p.68]
Untitled
Sem título
early 1960s
Oil stick and gouache on paper
21.4 x 15.8 cm
mira schendel estate

127
Untitled
Sem título
early 1960s
Oil stick and gouache on paper
18.4 x 12 cm
mira schendel estate

128
Untitled
Sem título
early 1960s
Oil stick and gouache on paper
18.4 x 12 cm
mira schendel estate

129
Untitled
Sem título
early 1960s
Oil stick and gouache on paper
21.4 x 15.8 cm
mira schendel estate

130
Untitled
Sem título
early 1960s
Oil stick and gouache on paper
21.3 x 15.8 cm
mira schendel estate

131
Untitled
Sem título
early 1960s
Oil stick and gouache on paper
19 x 13.8 cm
mira schendel estate

132
Untitled
Sem título
early 1960s
Oil stick and gouache on paper
18 x 14.8 cm
mira schendel estate

133
Untitled
Sem título
early 1960s
Oil stick and gouache on paper
18 x 14.6 cm
mira schendel estate

134
Untitled
Sem título
early 1960s
Oil stick and gouache on paper
17.9 x 14.7 cm
mira schendel estate

135 [p.70]
Untitled (Rectangles on a Brown Ground)
Sem título (Rectangulos sobre fundo marrom)
1960s
Oil on canvas
119.4 x 80 cm
Colección Patricia Phelps de Cisneros

136 [p.74]
Untitled (Facade)
Sem título (Fachada)
1960s
Oil on jute
91 x 91 cm
Luisa Malzoni Strina

137
Untitled (Facade)
Sem título (Fachada)
1960s
Oil on jute
50 x 37 cm
Jones Bergamin

138 [p.82]
Untitled
Sem título
1960s
Latex and sand on canvas
79.8 x 99.8 cm
Museu de Arte Contemporânea da Universidade de São Paulo, São Paulo, Brazil

139
Untitled
Sem título
1960s
Oil on jute
75 x 75 cm
Fernanda Feitosa and Heitor Martins Collection

140
Untitled
Sem título
1960s
Tempera on canvas
70 x 70.5 cm
Igor Queiroz Barroso Collection, Fortaleza, CE

141
Untitled
Sem título
1960s
Oil on canvas
50 x 25 cm
Rose and Alfredo Setubal Collection

142 [p.72]
Untitled, from the series *Embroideries*
Sem título, da série *Bordados*
1960s
Watercolour on paper
35 x 28.7 cm
Museu de Arte Moderna de São Paulo, donation of Zurich Brazil Seguros S.A.

143 [p.73]
Untitled, from the series *Embroideries*
Sem título, da serie *Bordados*
1960s
Watercolour on rice paper
15.3 x 15.3 cm
mira schendel estate

144 [p.95]
Untitled
Sem título
1960s
Collage, watercolour and ink on paper
50 x 70 cm
Private collection

145 [p.98]
Untitled (Yes)
Sem título (Sim)
1960s
Watercolour and oil stick on paper
48 x 38 cm
Private collection

146 [p.118]
A Fabric Net
A trama
1960s
Oil on rice paper
45.1 x 62.2 cm
The Museum of Modern Art, New York. Gift of Ada Schendel and the Latin American and Caribbean Fund, 2008

147
Untitled, from the series *Calculations*
Sem título, da série *Calculos*
1960s
Ink on paper
103 x 69.6 cm
Collection Ivo Vel Kos

148 [p.147]
Untitled, from the series *Transformables*
Sem título, da série *Transformáveis*
1970
Riveted acrylic
Dimensions variable
Private collection

149 [pp.180–1]
I Ching
I Ching
1970
Watercolour on paper
6 parts: each 45 x 23 cm
Private collection

150 [pp.182–3]
I Ching
I Ching
1970
Watercolour on paper
6 parts: each 46 x 24 cm
mira schendel estate

151
Untitled, from the series *Notebooks*
Sem título, da série *Cadernos*
1970
Ink on paper, 9 pages
23 x 31 cm
mira schendel estate

152
Untitled, from the series *Notebooks*
Sem título, da série *Cadernos*
1971
Ink and transfer lettering on paper
16 x 32 cm
mira schendel estate

153
Untitled, from the series *Notebooks*
Sem título, da série *Cadernos*
1971
Ink and transfer lettering on paper
23 x 31 cm
mira schendel estate

154
Untitled, from the series *Notebooks*
Sem título, da série *Cadernos*
1971
Ink and transfer lettering on paper
24 x 30.2 cm
mira schendel estate

155 [pp.154–5]
Untitled, from the series *Notebooks*
Sem título, da série *Cadernos*
1971
Transfer lettering on paper
13 x 15.3 cm
mira schendel estate

156 [pp.156–7]
Untitled, from the series *Notebooks*
Sem título, da série *Cadernos*
1971
Ink and transfer lettering on paper,
20 pages
16 x 30 cm
mira schendel estate

157 [p.159]
Untitled, from the series *Notebooks*
Sem título, da série *Cadernos*
1971
Ink and transfer lettering on paper,
42 pages
23 x 31 cm
mira schendel estate

158
Untitled, from the series *Notebooks*
Sem título, da série *Cadernos*
1971
Perforated paper
6 x 19.5 cm
mira schendel estate

159
Untitled, from the series *Notebooks*
Sem título, da série *Cadernos*
1971
Ink and transfer lettering on paper,
8 pages
32 x 32 cm
mira schendel estate

160 [pp.160–1]
Untitled, from the series *Notebooks*
Sem título, da série *Cadernos*
1971
Perforated paper
5.5 x 32 cm
mira schendel estate

161
Untitled, from the series *Notebooks*
Sem título, da série *Cadernos*
1971
Ink and transfer lettering on paper
21 x 31 cm
mira schendel estate

162
Untitled, from the series *Notebooks*
Sem título, da série *Cadernos*
1971
Ink and transfer lettering on paper
21 x 31 cm
mira schendel estate

163
Untitled, from the series *Notebooks*
Sem título, da série *Cadernos*
1971
Ink and transfer lettering on paper,
51 pages
11 x 19 cm
mira schendel estate

164
Untitled, from the series *Notebooks*
Sem título, da série *Cadernos*
1971
Ink and transfer lettering on paper,
12 pages
17.5 x 32 cm,
mira schendel estate

165
Untitled, from the series *Notebooks*
Sem título, da série *Cadernos*
1971
Ink and transfer lettering on paper,
11 pages
19 x 31 cm
mira schendel estate

166
Untitled, from the series *Notebooks*
Sem título, da série *Cadernos*
1971
Ink and transfer lettering on paper,
17 pages
24 x 32 cm
mira schendel estate

167
Untitled, from the series *Notebooks*
Sem título, da série *Cadernos*
1971
Ink on paper
19.6 x 21.8 cm
mira schendel estate

168 [pp.152–3]
Untitled, from the series *Notebooks*
Sem título, da série *Cadernos*
1971
Transfer lettering and graphite on paper
19.5 x 21.8 cm
mira schendel estate

169
Untitled, from the series *Notebooks*
Sem título, da série *Cadernos*
1971
Ink on paper
19.5 x 21.8 cm
mira schendel estate

170
Untitled, from the series *Notebooks*
Sem título, da série *Cadernos*
1971
Perforated paper
5.5 x 32 cm
mira schendel estate

171
Untitled, from the series *Notebooks*
Sem título, da série *Cadernos*
1971
Ink on paper
23 x 31 cm
mira schendel estate

172
Untitled, from the series *Notebooks*
Sem título, da série *Cadernos*
1971
Perforated paper with acrylic, 12 pages
19.5 x 19.5 cm
Private collection

173 [p.129]
Graphic Object
Objeto gráfico
1972
Graphite on rice paper with acrylic
97.8 x 97.8 cm
FEMSA Collection

174 [pp.48, 141]
Graphic Object
Objeto gráfico
1972
Transfer lettering on rice paper with acrylic
95 x 95 cm
Collection Clara Sancovsky

175 [p.143]
Untitled, from the series *Discs*
Sem título, da série *Discos*
1972
Transfer lettering and graphite with acrylic
27 cm diameter x 0.7 cm
Tate. Presented by Tate Americas
Foundation 2012

176
Untitled, from the series *Discs*
Sem título, da série *Discos*
1972
Transfer lettering with acrylic
22 diameter x 0.5 cm
Luisa Malzoni Strina

177 [p.140]
Untitled, from the series *Discs*
Sem título, da série *Discos*
1972
Transfer lettering with acrylic
18.5 diameter x 5.2 cm
Marta and Paulo Kuczynski Collection,
São Paulo

178
I Ching
I Ching
1972
Transfer lettering with acrylic
22 cm diameter x 0.6 cm
Private collection

179
Untitled, from the series *Little Stubs*
Sem título, da série *Toquinhos*
1972
Transfer lettering and acrylic
46 x 20.5 x 3 cm
Esther Faingold

180
Untitled, from the series *Little Stubs*
Sem título, da série *Toquinhos*
1972
Transfer lettering and dyed paper on rice
paper
47 x 23 cm
mira schendel estate

181
Untitled, from the series *Little Stubs*
Sem título, da série *Toquinhos*
1972
Transfer lettering and dyed paper on paper
49.3 x 25.5 cm
mira schendel estate

182 [p.175]
Untitled, from the series *Little Stubs*
Sem título, da série *Toquinhos*
1972
Transfer lettering and dyed paper on paper
49.3 x 25.3 cm
mira schendel estate

183 [p.174]
Untitled, from the series *Little Stubs*
Sem título, da série *Toquinhos*
1972
Transfer lettering and dyed paper on paper
49.3 x 25.5 cm
mira schendel estate

184 [p.175]
Untitled, from the series *Little Stubs*
Sem título, da série *Toquinhos*
1972
Transfer lettering and dyed paper on paper
49.3 x 25.3 cm
mira schendel estate

185
Untitled, from the series *Little Stubs*
Sem título, da série *Toquinhos*
1972
Transfer lettering and dyed paper on paper
49.1 x 25.2 cm
Private collection

186
Untitled, from the series *Little Stubs*
Sem título, da série *Toquinhos*
1972
Transfer lettering and dyed paper on paper
49.1 x 25.2 cm
Private collection

187
Untitled, from the series *Little Stubs*
Sem título, da série *Toquinhos*
1972
Transfer lettering and dyed paper on paper
49.1 x 25.2 cm
Private collection

188
Untitled, from the series *Little Stubs*
Sem título, da série *Toquinhos*
1972
Transfer lettering and dyed paper on paper
49.1 x 25.2 cm
Private collection

189
Untitled, from the series *Little Stubs*
Sem título, da série *Toquinhos*
1972
Transfer lettering and dyed paper on paper
49.1 x 25.2 cm
Private collection

190 [p.135]
Graphic Object
Objeto gráfico
1973
Transfer lettering on paper with acrylic
55.9 x 55.9 cm
Colección Patricia Phelps de Cisneros

191 [p.144]
Untitled, from the series *Little Stubs*
Sem título, da série *Toquinhos*
1973
Transfer lettering and acrylic
47 x 26 x 3.5 cm
Private collection

192 [p.145]
Untitled, from the series *Little Stubs*
Sem título, da série *Toquinhos*
1973
Transfer lettering and acrylic
50 x 58 cm
Luiz Paulo Montenegro

193
Untitled
Sem título
1973
Perforated paper with acrylic
31.2 x 31.2 cm
Museu de Arte Contemporânea da Universidade de São Paulo, São Paulo, Brazil

194
Untitled
Sem título
1973
Perforated paper with acrylic
31 x 31 cm
Paulo Kuczynski Escritorio de Arte

195
Hallelujah
Alleluia
1973
Oil on rice paper
8 parts: each 47 x 23.5 cm
Private collection

196 [p.174]
Untitled, from the series *Little Stubs*
Sem título, da série *Toquinhos*
1973
Transfer lettering and dyed paper on paper
49.3 x 25.5 cm
mira schendel estate

197
Untitled, from the series *Little Stubs*
Sem título, da série *Toquinhos*
1973
Transfer lettering and dyed paper on paper
49.3 x 25.5 cm
mira schendel estate

198
Untitled, from the series *Discs*
Sem título, da série *Discos*
1974
Transfer lettering with acrylic
24.5 diameter x 3 cm
Luisa Malzoni Strina

199
Untitled, from the series *Mandalas*
Sem título, da série *Mandalas*
1974
Ink and watercolour on paper
18 x 18 cm
Jones Bergamin

200
Untitled, from the series *Mandalas*
Sem título, da série *Mandalas*
1974
Ink and watercolour on paper
18 x 18 cm
Jones Bergamin

201 [p.171]
Untitled, from the series *Calculations*
Sem título, da série *Calculos*
1974
Ink on paper
50 x 36 cm
Museu de Arte Moderna de São Paulo, donation of Paulo Figueiredo

202
Untitled
Sem título
1974
Ink on paper
49.9 x 35.8 cm
Museu de Arte Moderna de São Paulo, donation of Paulo Figueiredo

203 [p.166]
Untitled, from the series *Typed Writings*
Sem título, da serie *Datiloscritos*
1974
Ink and transfer lettering on paper
50 x 36 cm
Estrellita B. and Daniel Brodsky Collection

204 [p.167]
Untitled, from the series *Typed Writings*
Sem título, da serie *Datiloscritos*
1974
Ink on paper
50.2 x 36.2 cm
The Museum of Modern Art, New York. Committee on Drawings Funds, 2008

205
Untitled, from the series *Typed Writings*
Sem título, da serie *Datiloscritos*
1974
Ink, transfer lettering and felt-tip pen on paper
47.1 x 32.8 cm
Museu de Arte Moderna de São Paulo, donation of Paulo Figueiredo

206 [p.169]
Untitled, from the series *Typed Writings*
Sem título, da serie *Datiloscritos*
1974
Ink on paper
50.8 x 36 cm
Private collection

207
Untitled, from the series *Typed Writings*
Sem título, da serie *Datiloscritos*
1974
Ink and transfer lettering on paper
51 x 27 cm
Private collection

208
Untitled, from the series *Typed Writings*
Sem título, da série *Datiloscritos*
1974
Ink on paper
50 x 37 cm
Jones Bergamin

209
Untitled, from the series *Typed Writings*
Sem título, da serie *Datiloscritos*
1974
Ink on paper
50 x 36 cm
Ricard Akagawa Collection

210
Untitled, from the series *Typed Writings*
Sem título, da serie *Datiloscritos*
1974
Ink and transfer lettering on paper
50.8 x 36 cm
Private collection

211 [p.167]
Untitled, from the series *Typed Writings*
Sem título, da serie *Datiloscritos*
1974
Ink and transfer lettering on paper
50 x 37 cm
Private collection

212 [p.172]
Untitled, from the series *Mandalas*
Untitled, da série *Mandalas*
1975
Ink and watercolour on paper
17.9 x 17.8 cm
Museu de Arte Moderna de São Paulo, donation of Paulo Figueiredo

213 [p.173]
Untitled, from the series *Mandalas*
Sem título, da série *Mandalas*
1975
Ink and watercolour on paper
17.7 x 17.7 cm
Private collection

214 [pp.177–9]
Homage to God – Father of the West
Homenagem a Deus – Pai do Ocidente
1975
Transfer lettering and ink on paper
16 parts: each 50.2 x 26 cm
Private collection, São Paulo

215 [p.151]
Variants
Variantes
1977
Oil on rice paper with acrylic
93 parts, dimensions variable
The Museum of Fine Arts, Houston, Museum purchase with funds provided by the Caroline Wiess Law Accessions Endowment Fund

216
Untitled, from the series *Itatiaia Landscape*
Sem título, da série *Paisagem de Itatiaia*
1978
Tempera on paper
46.4 x 23.4 cm
mira schendel estate

217
Untitled, from the series *Itatiaia Landscape*
Sem título, da série *Paisagem de Itatiaia*
1978
Tempera on paper
46.4 x 24 cm
mira schendel estate

218
Untitled, from the series *Itatiaia Landscape*
Sem título, da série *Paisagem de Itatiaia*
1978
Tempera on paper
46 x 23 cm
mira schendel estate

219
Untitled, from the series *Itatiaia Landscape*
Sem título, da série *Paisagem de Itatiaia*
1978
Tempera on paper
46.2 x 23.6 cm
mira schendel estate

220
Untitled, from the series *Itatiaia Landscape*
Sem título, da série *Paisagem de Itatiaia*
1978
Tempera on paper
46 x 23.4 cm
mira schendel estate

221 [p.189]
Untitled, from the series *Itatiaia Landscape*
Sem título, da série *Paisagem de Itatiaia*
1978
Tempera on paper
46 x 23.3 cm
mira schendel estate

222
Untitled, from the series *Itatiaia Landscape*
Sem título, da série *Paisagem de Itatiaia*
1978
Tempera on paper
46 x 23.3 cm
mira schendel estate

223 [p.188]
Untitled, from the series *Itatiaia Landscape*
Sem título, da série *Paisagem de Itatiaia*
1978
Tempera on paper
47 x 23.4 cm
mira schendel estate

224
Untitled, from the series *Itatiaia Landscape*
Sem título, da série *Paisagem de Itatiaia*
1978
Tempera on paper
46.4 x 23.2 cm
mira schendel estate

225 [p.189]
Untitled, from the series *Itatiaia Landscape*
Sem título, da série *Paisagem de Itatiaia*
1978
Tempera on paper
46 x 23.6 cm
mira schendel estate

226
Untitled, from the series *Itatiaia Landscape*
Sem título, da série *Paisagem de Itatiaia*
1978
Tempera on paper
46.3 x 23.8 cm
mira schendel estate

227
Untitled, from the series *Itatiaia Landscape*
Sem título, da série *Paisagem de Itatiaia*
1978
Tempera on paper
46 x 23.8 cm
mira schendel estate

228
Untitled, from the series *Itatiaia Landscape*
Sem título, da série *Paisagem de Itatiaia*
1978
Tempera on paper
46 x 23.7 cm
mira schendel estate

229
Untitled, from the series *Itatiaia Landscape*
Sem título, da série *Paisagem de Itatiaia*
1978
Tempera on paper
46 x 23.2 cm
mira schendel estate

230 [p.189]
Untitled, from the series *Itatiaia Landscape*
Sem título, da série *Paisagem de Itatiaia*
1978
Tempera on paper
46 x 23.8 cm
mira schendel estate

231 [p.188]
Untitled, from the series *Itatiaia Landscape*
Sem título, da série *Paisagem de Itatiaia*
1978
Tempera on paper
46 x 23.6 cm
mira schendel estate

232 [p.188]
Untitled, from the series *Itatiaia Landscape*
Sem título, da série *Paisagem de Itatiaia*
1978
Tempera on paper
46.4 x 23.2 cm
mira schendel estate

233
Untitled, from the series *Transformables*
Sem título, da série *Transformáveis*
early 1970s
Riveted acrylic
Dimensions variable
The Ella Fontanals-Cisneros Collection

234 [p.146]
Untitled, from the series *Transformables*
Sem título, da série *Transformáveis*
early 1970s
Riveted acrylic
Dimensions variable
Luisa Malzoni Strina

235 [p.146]
Untitled, from the series *Transformables*
Sem título, da série *Transformáveis*
early 1970s
Riveted acrylic
Dimensions variable
Marcela and Israel Furmanovich

236
Untitled, from the series *Notebooks*
Sem título, da série *Cadernos*
1970s
Ink and transfer lettering on paper, 40 pages
5.5 x 33 cm
mira schendel estate

237
Untitled, from the series *Notebooks*
Sem título, da série *Cadernos*
1970s
Ink on paper, 42 pages
24 x 30 cm
mira schendel estate

238
Untitled, from the series *Notebooks*
Sem título, da série *Cadernos*
1970s
Ink and transfer lettering on paper, 24 pages
19.5 x 21.7 cm
mira schendel estate

239
Untitled, from the series *Notebooks*
Sem título, da série *Cadernos*
1970s
Ink on paper, 38 pages
55 x 32 cm
mira schendel estate

240
Untitled, from the series *Calculations*
Sem título, da série *Calculos*
1970s
Ink on paper
46 x 24 cm
Private collection

241 [p.170]
Untitled, from the series *Calculations*
Sem título, da série *Calculos*
1970s
Ink on paper
50.2 x 36.2 cm
mira schendel estate

242 [p.170]
Untitled, from the series *Calculations*
Sem título, da série *Calculos*
1970s
Ink on paper
49.8 x 34.7 cm
mira schendel estate

243
Untitled, from the series *Calculations*
Sem título, da série *Calculos*
1970s
Ink on paper
49.8 x 34.7 cm
mira schendel estate

244 [p.162]
Perforated I
Perfurados I
1970s
Perforated paper
31.8 x 31.8 cm
Colección Patricia Phelps de Cisneros

245 [p.163]
Perforated II
Perfurados II
1970s
Perforated paper
32 x 32 cm
The Museum of Modern Art, New York. Purchase, 2005

246 [p.164]
Perforated III
Perfurados III
1970s
Perforated paper
32 x 32 cm
The Museum of Modern Art, New York. Purchase, 2005

247
Perforated IV
Perfurados IV
1970s
Perforated paper
32 x 32 cm
The Museum of Modern Art, New York. Purchase, 2005

248 [p.165]
Perforated V
Perfurados V
1970s
Perforated paper
32 x 32 cm
The Museum of Modern Art, New York. Purchase, 2005

249 [p.166]
Untitled, from the series *Typed Writings*
Sem título, da série *Datiloscritos*
1970s
Ink on paper
50.2 x 36.2 cm
The Museum of Modern Art, New York. Committee on Drawings Funds, 2008

250
Untitled, from the series *Typed Writings*
Sem título, da série *Datiloscritos*
1970s
Ink on paper
50.2 x 36.2 cm
The Museum of Modern Art, New York. Latin American and Carribean Fund, 2008

251
Untitled, from the series *Typed Writings*
Sem título, da série *Datiloscritos*
1970s
Ink on paper
50 x 36 cm
Private collection

252
Untitled
Sem título
1985
Tempera, gesso and oil on wood
90 x 180 cm
Private collection

253 [p.187]
Untitled
Sem título
1985
Tempera, gesso and gold leaf on wood
89 x 159 cm
Andrea and José Olympio Pereira Collection

254
Untitled from the *Black and White* series
Sem título da série *Brancos e Pretos*
1985
Tempera, gesso and oil on wood
90.2 x 180 x 3 cm
mira schendel estate

255 [p.185]
Untitled
Sem título
c.1985
Tempera and gold leaf on wood
140.6 x 90.5 cm
Collection of Paulo Joppert (in Memoriam)

256
Untitled, from the series *Little Nothings*
Sem título, da série *Droguinhas*
1986
Rice paper
Dimensions variable,
approx. 38 x 15.2 x 10.2 cm
Rodrigo Naves Collection

257 [p.186]
Untitled
Sem título
1987
Tempera, gesso and graphite on wood
90 x 180 cm
Collection Raquel Arnaud

258 [p.193]
Batten
Sarrafo
1987
Tempera and gesso on wood
96 x 180 x 47.5 cm
Jones Bergamin

259 [p.194]
Batten
Sarrafo
1987
Tempera and gesso on wood
90 x 180 x 54 cm
mira schendel estate

260 [p.195]
Batten
Sarrafo
1987
Tempera and gesso on wood
97 x 180 x 52 cm
mira schendel estate
Gift of José Resende and Sofia Telles

261
Batten
Sarrafo
1987
Tempera, acrylic paint and gesso on wood
90 x 238 x 9 cm
Andrea and José Olympio Pereira
Collection

262 [p.192]
Batten
Sarrafo
1987
Tempera, acrylic paint and gesso on wood
198 x 180 x 9.2 cm
Colección Patricia Phelps de Cisneros

263 [pp.190–1]
Untitled, from the series *Chinese Landscape*
Sem título, da série *Paisagem Chinesa*
1980s
Ink on paper
25 x 34.5 cm
Max Perlingeiro Collection, Rio de Janeiro, Brazil

264 [pp.190–1]
Untitled, from the series *Chinese Landscape*
Sem título, da série *Paisagem Chinesa*
1980s
Ink on paper
25 x 35 cm
Collection Ivo Vel Kos

265 [pp.190–1]
Untitled, from the series *Chinese Landscape*
Sem título, da série *Paisagem Chinesa*
1980s
Ink on paper
25 x 35 cm
Collection Ivo Vel Kos

266 [pp.190–1]
Untitled, from the series *Chinese Landscape*
Sem título, da série *Paisagem Chinesa*
1980s
Ink on paper
25 x 35 cm
Collection Ivo Vel Kos

267 [pp.190–1]
Untitled, from the series *Chinese Landscape*
Sem título, da série *Paisagem Chinesa*
1980s
Ink on paper
25 x 35 cm
Collection Ivo Vel Kos

268 [pp.190–1]
Untitled, from the series *Chinese Landscape*
Sem título, da série *Paisagem Chinesa*
1980s
Ink on paper
25 x 35 cm
Collection Ivo Vel Kos

269 [pp.190–1]
Untitled, from the series *Chinese Landscape*
Sem título, da série *Paisagem Chinesa*
1980s
Ink on paper
25 x 35 cm
Collection Ivo Vel Kos

270 [pp.190–1]
Untitled, from the series *Chinese Landscape*
Sem título, da série *Paisagem Chinesa*
1980s
Ink on paper
25 x 35 cm
Collection Ivo Vel Kos

271
Untitled, from the series *Chinese Landscape*
Sem título, da série *Paisagem Chinesa*
1980s
Ink on paper
25 x 35 cm
Collection Ivo Vel Kos

272
Untitled, from the series *Chinese Landscape*
Sem título, da série *Paisagem Chinesa*
1980s
Ink on paper
25 x 35 cm
Collection Ivo Vel Kos

273
Untitled, from the series *Chinese Landscape*
Sem título, da série *Paisagem Chinesa*
1980s
Ink on paper
25 x 35 cm
Collection Ivo Vel Kos

274
Untitled, from the series *Chinese Landscape*
Sem título, da série *Paisagem Chinesa*
1980s
Ink on paper
25 x 35 cm
Collection Ivo Vel Kos

275
Untitled, from the series *Chinese Landscape*
Sem título, da série *Paisagem Chinesa*
1980s
Ink on paper
25 x 35 cm
Collection Ivo Vel Kos

276
Untitled, from the series *Chinese Landscape*
Sem título, da série *Paisagem Chinesa*
1980s
Ink on paper
25 x 35 cm
Collection Ivo Vel Kos

277
Untitled, from the series *Chinese Landscape*
Sem título, da série *Paisagem Chinesa*
1980s
Ink on paper
25 x 35 cm
Collection Ivo Vel Kos

278
Untitled, from the series *Chinese Landscape*
Sem título, da série *Paisagem Chinesa*
1980s
Ink on paper
25 x 35 cm
Collection Ivo Vel Kos

279
Untitled, from the series *Chinese Landscape*
Sem título, da série *Paisagem Chinesa*
1980s
Ink on paper
25 x 35 cm
Collection Ivo Vel Kos

280
Untitled, from the series *Chinese Landscape*
Sem título, da série *Paisagem Chinesa*
1980s
Ink on paper
25 x 35 cm
Collection Ivo Vel Kos

SUPPORTING MATERIAL

281 [pp.21, 228–9]
Untitled (London Journal)
Sem título (Diario de Londres)
1966
Mixed media on paper
40 x 22 cm
Melsohn Collection

282
Collaboration with Robert Darroll
2 Visual Books: Transformation and Composition of Figures and Letters
2 Visuelle Hefte: Verwandlung und Komposition über Figuren und Lettern 1973
Film, Super 8, black and white, shown as DVD
Dimensions variable
mira schendel estate

Supporting Tate

Tate relies on a large number of supporters – individuals, foundations, companies and public sector sources – to enable it to deliver its programme of activities, both on and off its gallery sites. This support is essential in order for Tate to acquire works of art for the Collection, run education, outreach and exhibition programmes, care for the Collection in storage and enable art to be displayed, both digitally and physically, inside and outside Tate. Your donation will make a real difference and enable others to enjoy Tate and its Collection both now and in the future. There are a variety of ways in which you can help support Tate and also benefit as a UK or US taxpayer. Please contact us at:

Development Office
Tate
Millbank
London SWIP 4RG

Tel: 020 7887 4900
Fax: 020 7887 8098

Tate Americas Foundation
520 West 27 Street Unit 404
New York, NY 10001
USA

Tel: 001 212 643 2818
Fax: 001 212 643 1001

Donations, no matter the size, are gratefully received, either to support particular areas of interest, or to contribute to general activity costs.

Gifts of Shares

We can accept gifts of quoted share and securities. All gifts of shares to Tate are exempt from capital gains tax, and higher rate taxpayers enjoy additional tax efficiencies. For further information please contact the Development Office.

Gift Aid

Through Gift Aid you can increase the value of your donation to Tate as we are able to reclaim the tax on your gift. Gift Aid applies to gifts of any size, whether regular or a one-off gift. Higher rate taxpayers are also able to claim additional personal tax relief. Contact us for further information and to make a Gift Aid Declaration.

Legacies

A legacy to Tate may take the form of a residual share of an estate, a specific cash sum or item of property such as a work of art. Legacies to Tate are free of inheritance tax, and help to secure a strong future for the Collection and galleries. For further information please contact the Development Office.

Offers in lieu of tax

Inheritance Tax can be satisfied by transferring to the Government a work of art of outstanding importance. In this case the amount of tax is reduced, and it can be made a condition of the offer that the work of art is allocated to Tate. Please contact us for details.

Tate Members

Tate Members enjoy unlimited free admission throughout the year to all exhibitions at Tate, as well as a number of other benefits such as exclusive use of our Members' Rooms and a free annual subscription to *Tate Etc*. Whilst enjoying the exclusive privileges of membership, you are also helping secure Tate's position at the very heart of British and modern art. Your support actively contributes to new purchases of important art, ensuring that Tate's collection continues to be relevant and comprehensive, as well as funding projects in London, Liverpool and St Ives that increase access and understanding for everyone.

Tate Patrons

Tate Patrons share a passion for art and are committed to supporting Tate on an annual basis. The Patrons help enable the acquisition of works across Tate's broad collecting remit and also give their support to vital conservation, learning and research projects. The scheme provides a forum for Patrons to share their interest in art and meet curators, artists and one another in an enjoyable environment through a regular programme of events. These events take place both at Tate and beyond and encompass curator-led exhibition tours, visits to artists' studios and private collections, art trips both in the UK and abroad, and access to art fairs. The scheme welcomes supporters from outside the UK, giving the programme a truly international scope. For more information, please contact the Patrons Office on +44(0)20 7887 8740 or at patrons.office@tate.org.uk.

Corporate Membership

Corporate Membership at Tate Modern, Tate Britain and Tate Liverpool offers companies opportunities for corporate entertaining and the chance for a wide variety of employee benefits. These include special private views, special access to paying exhibitions, out-of-hours visits and tours, invitations to VIP events and talks at members' offices.

Corporate Investment

Tate has developed a range of imaginative partnerships with the corporate sector, ranging from international interpretation and exhibition programmes to local outreach and staff development programmes. We are particularly known for high-profile business to business marketing initiatives and employee benefit packages. Please contact the Corporate Fundraising team for further details.

Charity Details

The Tate Gallery is an exempt charity; the Museums & Galleries Act 1992 added the Tate Gallery to the list of exempt charities defined in the 1960 Charities Act. Tate Members is a registered charity (number 313021). Tate Foundation is a registered charity (number 1085314).

Tate Americas Foundation

Tate Americas Foundation is an independent charity based in New York that supports the work of Tate in the United Kingdom. It receives full tax exempt status from the IRS under section 501(c)(3) allowing United States taxpayers to receive tax deductions on gifts towards annual membership programmes, exhibitions, scholarship and capital projects. For more information contact the Tate Americas Foundation office.

Tate Modern Donors to the Founding Capital Campaign

29th May 1961 Charitable Trust
AMP
The Annenberg Foundation
Arts Council England
The Asprey Family Charitable Foundation
Lord and Lady Attenborough
The Baring Foundation
Ron Beller and Jennifer Moses
Alex and Angela Bernstein
David and Janice Blackburn
Mr and Mrs Anthony Bloom
BNP Paribas
Mr and Mrs Pontus Bonnier
Lauren and Mark Booth
Mr and Mrs John Botts
Frances and John Bowes
Ivor Braka
Mr and Mrs James Brice
The British Land Company plc
Donald L Bryant Jr Family
Melva Bucksbaum
Cazenove & Co
The Clore Duffield Foundation
CGU plc
Clifford Chance
Edwin C Cohen
The John S. Cohen Foundation
Ronald and Sharon Cohen
Sadie Coles
Carole and Neville Conrad
Giles and Sonia Coode-Adams
Douglas Cramer
Alan Cristea Gallery
Thomas Dane
Michel and Hélène David-Weill
Julia W Dayton
Gilbert de Botton
Pauline Denyer-Smith and Paul Smith
Sir Harry and Lady Djanogly
The Drapers' Company

Energis Communications
English Heritage
English Partnerships
The Eranda Foundation
Esmée Fairbairn Charitable Trust
Donald and Doris Fisher
Richard B. and Jeanne Donovan Fisher
The Fishmongers' Company
Freshfields Bruckhaus Deringer
Friends of the Tate Gallery
Bob and Kate Gavron
Giancarlo Giammetti
Alan Gibbs
Mr and Mrs Edward Gilhuly
GKR
GLG Partners
Helyn and Ralph Goldenberg
Goldman Sachs
The Horace W Goldsmith Foundation
The Worshipful Company of Goldsmiths
Lydia and Manfred Gorvy
Noam and Geraldine Gottesman
Pehr and Christina Gyllenhammar
Mimi and Peter Haas
The Worshipful Company of Haberdashers
Hanover Acceptances Limited
The Headley Trust
Mr and Mrs André Hoffmann
Anthony and Evelyn Jacobs
Jay Jopling
Mr and Mrs Karpidas
Howard and Lynda Karshan
Peter and Maria Kellner
Madeleine Kleinwort
Brian and Lesley Knox
Pamela and C Richard Kramlich
Mr and Mrs Henry R Kravis
Irene and Hyman Kreitman
The Kresge Foundation
Catherine and Pierre Lagrange
The Lauder Foundation – Leonard and Evelyn Lauder Fund
Lazard Brothers & Co., Limited
Leathersellers' Company Charitable Fund
Edward and Agnès Lee
Lex Service Plc
Lehman Brothers
Ruth and Stuart Lipton
Anders and Ulla Ljungh
The Frank Lloyd Family Trusts
London & Cambridge Properties Limited
London Electricity plc, EDF Group
Mr and Mrs George Loudon
Mayer, Brown, Rowe & Maw
Viviane and James Mayor
Ronald and Rita McAulay
The Mercers' Company
The Meyer Foundation
The Millennium Commission
Anthony and Deirdre Montagu
The Monument Trust
Mori Building, Ltd
Mr and Mrs M D Moross
Guy and Marion Naggar
Peter and Eileen Norton, The Peter Norton Family Foundation
Maja Oeri and Hans Bodenmann
Sir Peter and Lady Osborne
William A Palmer
Mr Frederik Paulsen
Pearson plc
The Pet Shop Boys
The Nyda and Oliver Prenn Foundation
Prudential plc
Railtrack plc
The Rayne Foundation
Reuters
Sir John and Lady Ritblat
Rolls-Royce plc
Barrie and Emmanuel Roman
Lord and Lady Rothschild
The Dr Mortimer and Theresa Sackler Foundation
J. Sainsbury plc
Ruth and Stephan Schmidheiny
Schroders
Mr and Mrs Charles Schwab
David and Sophie Shalit
Belle Shenkman Estate
William Sieghart
Peter Simon
Mr and Mrs Sven Skarendahl
London Borough of Southwark
The Foundation for Sports and the Arts
Mr and Mrs Nicholas Stanley
The Starr Foundation
The Jack Steinberg Charitable Trust
Charlotte Stevenson
Hugh and Catherine Stevenson
John Studzinski
David and Linda Supino
The Government of Switzerland
Carter and Mary Thacher
Insinger Townsley
UBS
UBS Warburg
David and Emma Verey
Dinah Verey
The Vintners' Company
Clodagh and Leslie Waddington
Robert and Felicity Waley-Cohen
Wasserstein, Perella & Co., Inc.
Gordon D Watson
The Weston Family
Mr and Mrs Stephen Wilberding
Michael S Wilson
Poju and Anita Zabludowicz
and those who wish to remain anonymous

Donors to The Tate Modern Project

The Blavatnik Family Foundation
Lauren and Mark Booth
The Deborah Loeb Brice Foundation
The Lord Browne of Madingley, FRS, FREng
John and Christina Chandris
James Chanos
Paul Cooke
Ago Demirdjian and Tiqui Atencio Demirdjian
Department for Culture, Media and Sport
George Economou
English Partnerships
Mala Gaonkar
Thomas Gibson in memory of Anthea Gibson
Lydia and Manfred Gorvy
Noam Gottesman
Maja Hoffmann/LUMA Foundation
Peter and Maria Kellner
Madeleine Kleinwort
Catherine Lagrange
Pierre Lagrange
London Development Agency
Allison and Howard W. Lutnick
Donald B. Marron
Anthony and Deirdre Montagu
Elisabeth Murdoch
Eyal Ofer Family Foundation
Maureen Paley
Midge and Simon Palley
Daniel and Elizabeth Peltz
Catherine and Franck Petitgas
Barrie and Emmanuel Roman
The Dr Mortimer and Theresa Sackler Foundation
John J Studzinski, CBE
Tate Americas Foundation
Tate Members
Nina and Graham Williams
The Wolfson Foundation
and those who wish to remain anonymous

Tate Modern Benefactors and Major Donors

We would like to acknowledge and thank the following benefactors who have supported Tate Modern prior to 31 March 2013.

29th May 1961 Charitable Trust
Carolyn Alexander
Basil Alkazzi
The Ampersand Foundation
Klaus Anschel
The Fagus Anstruther Memorial Trust
The Kenneth Armitage Foundation
The Art Fund
Art Mentor Foundation Lucerne
Art Monthly
Arts Council England
The Arts & Humanities Research Council
Charles Asprey
Marwan T Assaf
David and Liane Aukin
averda
Gillian Ayres
Miroslaw Balka
Fay Ballard
Lionel Barber
The Estate of Peter and Caroline Barker-Mill
The Barns-Graham Charitable Trust
Trevor Bell
Barbara Bertozzi Castelli
Anne Best
Big Lottery Fund
Billstone Foundation Sutapa Biswas
Dorothy Bohm
The Charlotte Bonham-Carter Charitable Trust
Pontus Bonnier
Charles Booth-Clibborn
John C Botts, CBE
Louise Bourgeois
Frances Bowes
Sir Alan and Sarah Bowness, and Sophie Bowness
Dr Luther Brady
Pierre Brahm
The Estate of Dr Marcella Louis Brenner
British Council
The Broad Art Foundation
The Estate of Joseph and Ruth Bromberg
The Estate of Mrs Kathleen Bush
Lucy Carter
Henry Christensen III
Patricia Phelps de Cisneros
Toby Clarke
The Clothworkers' Foundation
Ian Collins
Contemporary Art Society
Isabelle and John Corbani
Paul Coulon
Douglas S Cramer
Martin Creed
The Estate of William Crozier
Bilge Ogut-Cumbusyan and Haro Cumbusyan
Daiwa Anglo-Japanese Foundation
Thomas Dane Ltd
Dimitris Daskalopoulos
Julia W Dayton
Richard Deacon
Department for Education
Department for Culture, Media and Sport
Department for Business, Innovation and Skills
Peter Doig
Jytte Dresing, The Merla Art Foundation, Dresing Collection
The Duerckheim Collection
EDP - Energias de Portugal, S.A.
Maryam and Edward Eisler
The John Ellerman Foundation
Carla Emil and Rich Silverstein
European Union
Christopher Eykyn and Nicholas Maclean
Esmée Fairbairn Foundation
Fares and Tania Fares
The Estate of Maurice Farquharson
Dan Fauci
Fernanda Feitosa and Heitor Martins
The Finnis Scott Foundation
HRH Princess Firyal of Jordan
Jeanne Donovan Fisher
The Fisher Family
Wendy Fisher
David Fitzsimons
Representation of the Government of Flanders in the UK
Lady Lynn Forester de Rothschild
Eric and Louise Franck
Froehlich Foundation, Stuttgart
Glenn and Amanda Fuhrman
William Furlong
Gagosian Gallery
The Getty Foundation
Milly and Arne Glimcher
Goethe-Institut
Nicholas and Judith Goodison
Goodman Gallery, Johannesburg and Cape Town
The Estate of Alan Green
Margot and George Greig
Konstantin Grigorishin
Guaranty Trust Bank
Calouste Gulbenkian Foundation
Chloë and Paul Gunn
The Haberdashers' Company
Paul Hamlyn Foundation
Viscount and Viscountess Hampden and Family
Mr Toshio Hara

Hauser & Wirth
The Hayden Family Foundation
Desiree Hayter
Heritage Lottery Fund
Friends of Heritage Preservation
David Herman and the Herman family
The Hintze Family Charitable Foundation
Damien Hirst
Robert Hiscox
David Hockney
The Estate of Mrs Mimi Hodgkin
Maja Hoffmann/LUMA Foundation
Jenny Holzer
The Estate of Sir Robert Horton
The Idlewild Trust
Cristina Iglesias
Institut Ramon Llull
Joachim Jacobs
Marc Jacobs
The Japan Foundation
Milena Kalinovska
J. Patrick Kennedy and Patricia A. Kennedy
Bharti Kher
Kirby Laing Foundation
Jack Kirkland
Leon Kossoff
Jannis Kounellis
The Kreitman Foundation
Samuel H. Kress Foundation, administered by the Foundation of the American Institute for Conservation
Catherine Lagrange
Pierre Lagrange
David and Amanda Leathers
The Leathersellers' Company Charitable Fund
The Leche Trust
Simon and Carine Lee
Legacy Trust UK
The Leverhulme Trust
Gemma Levine
The Estate of Barbara Lloyd
London Organising Committee of the Olympic Games and Paralympic Games
Mark and Liza Loveday
The Henry Luce Foundation
John Lyon's Charity
Peter and Susan MacGill
The Estate of Sir Edwin Manton
Robert Mapplethorpe Foundation
Lord McAlpine of West Green
Mark McCain
The Andrew W Mellon Foundation
Mikati Foundation
Sir Geoffroy Millais
Jean-Yves Mock
Mondriaan Fund, Amsterdam
The Henry Moore Foundation
Peter Moores Foundation
Mr Minoru Mori, Hon KBE and Mrs Yoshiko Mori
NADFAS
National Heritage Memorial Fund
The Netherlands Organisation for Scientific Research (NWO)
The Embassy of the Kingdom of the Netherlands
New Art Trust
Royal Norwegian Embassy
Mr Sean O'Connor
Tony Oursler and Artangel
Outset Contemporary Art Fund
Maureen Paley
The Paolozzi Foundation
The Estate of Mr Brian and Mrs Nancy Pattenden
Stephen and Yana Peel
Andrea and José Olympio Pereira
Slavica Perkovic
Catherine Petitgas
Stanley Picker Trust
The Pilgrim Trust
PINTA Museum Acquisition Programme
Powell Charitable Trust
Gilberto Pozzi
Isabella Prata
Glenstone Foundation, Emily and Mitchell Rales
The Reed Foundation
The family of Sir Norman Reid
Frances Reynolds
Sir John Richardson
Yvonne Robinson
Barrie and Emmanuel Roman
Helen and Ken Rowe
Edward Ruscha
The Estate of Simon Sainsbury
Ibrahim El-Salahi
The Sandra Charitable Trust
Fondation Saradar
The Great Britain Sasakawa Foundation
James Scott
Robert Scott
Candida and Rebecca Smith
The Stanley Foundation
Susana and Ricardo Steinbruch
Charlotte Stevenson
Mercedes and Ian Stoutzker
Luisa Strina
Ambassador Louis and Marjorie Susman
Swiss Arts Council Pro Helvetia
The Estate of Jiro Takamatsu
Tate Africa Acquisitions Committee
Tate Americas Foundation
Tate Asia-Pacific Acquisitions Committee
Tate International Council
Tate Latin American Acquisitions Committee
Tate Members
Tate Middle East and North Africa Acquisitions Committee
Tate North American Acquisitions Committee
Tate Patrons
Tate Photography Acquisitions Committee
Tate Russia and Eastern Europe Acquisitions Committee
Tate South Asia Acquisitions Committee
Melissa Tecklenberg
Terra Foundation for American Art
The Estate of Mr Nicholas Themans
Robert Therrien
Tishman Speyer
The Tretyakov Family Collection
US Embassy, London
Petri and Jolana Vainio
The Vandervell Foundation
The Wellcome Trust
Welton Foundation
The Estate of Fred Williams
Jane and Michael Wilson
Samuel and Nina Wisnia
Poju and Anita Zabludowicz
and those who wish to remain anonymous

Platinum Patrons
Mr Alireza Abrishamchi
Ghazwa Mayassi Abu-Suud
Mr Shane Akeroyd
Basil Alkazzi
Ryan Allen and Caleb Kramer
Mr and Mrs Edward Atkin, CBE
Beecroft Charitable Trust
Mrs Abeer ben Halim
Mr Harry Blain
Broeksmit Family Foundation
Rory and Elizabeth Brooks (Chair)
The Lord Browne of Madingley, FRS, FREng
Mr Stephane Custot
Miel de Botton
Fares and Tania Fares
Mr David Fitzsimons
The Flow Foundation
Mr Michael Foster
Edwin Fox Foundation
Hugh Gibson
The Goss-Michael Foundation
Mandy Gray and Randall Work
Mrs Nathalie and Mr Luc Guiot-Saucier
Mr and Mrs Yan Huo
Mr Phillip Hylander
Anne-Marie and Geoffrey Isaac
Mrs Gabrielle Jungels-Winkler
Maria and Peter Kellner
Esperanza Koren
Mrs Ella Krasner
Mr and Mrs Eskandar Maleki
Scott and Suling Mead
Gabriela Mendoza and Rodrigo Marquez
Pierre Tollis and Alexandra Mollof
Mr Donald Moore
Mary Moore
Mr and Mrs Paul Phillips
Mariela Pissioti
Maya and Ramzy Rasamny
Frances Reynolds
Simon and Virginia Robertson
Mr and Mrs Richard Rose
Claudia Ruimy
Vipin Sareen and Rebecca Mitchell
Hakon Runer and Ulrike Schwarz-Runer
Mr and Mrs J Shafran
Mrs Andrée Shore
Maria and Malek Sukkar
Mr Vladimir Tsarenkov and Ms Irina Kargina
Mr and Mrs Petri Vainio
Michael and Jane Wilson
Poju and Anita Zabludowicz
and those who wish to remain anonymous

Gold Patrons
Eric Abraham
Jacqueline Appel and Alexander Malmaeus
Katrina Barter
Jenny and Robert Borgerhoff Mulder
Elena Bowes
Ben and Louisa Brown
Nicolò Cardi
Melanie Clore
Beth and Michele Colocci
Bilge Ogut-Cumbusyan and Haro Cumbusyan
Mr Dónall Curtin
Mrs Robin D'Alessandro
Harry G. David
Mr Frank Destribats
Mrs Maryam Eisler
Mala Gaonkar
Kate Groes
Mrs Helene Guerin-Llamas
Mr and Mrs Charles M Hale
Mrs Petra Horvat
Ms Natascha Jakobs
Tiina Lee
Fiona Mactaggart
Paul and Alison Myners
Reem Nassar
Mr Francis Outred
Midge and Simon Palley
Mathew Prichard
Valerie Rademacher
Mr Charles Roxburgh
Carol Sellars
Mrs Dana Sheves
Britt Tidelius
Mr and Mrs Stanley S. Tollman
Emily Tsingou and Henry Bond
Mrs Celia Forner Venturi
Rebecca Wang
Manuela and Iwan Wirth
Barbara Yerolemou
and those who wish to remain anonymous

Silver Patrons
Agnew's
Mrs Malgosia Alterman
Toby and Kate Anstruther
Mr and Mrs Zeev Aram
Mrs Charlotte Artus
Tim Attias
Miss Silvia Badiali
Mrs Jane Barker
Mr Edward Barlow
Victoria Barnsley, OBE
Christopher Bartlett
Jim Bartos
Mr Harold Berg
Lady Angela Bernstein
Ms Anne Berthoud
Madeleine Bessborough
Ms Karen Bizon
Janice Blackburn
Shoshana Bloch
David Blood and Beth Bisso
Mrs Sofia Bogolyubov
Nathalie and Daniel Boulakia
Mr Brian Boylan
Ivor Braka
Akex Branczik
Viscountess Bridgeman
The Broere Charitable Foundation
Mr Dan Brooke
Michael Burrell
Mrs Marlene Burston
Mrs Aisha Caan
Timothy and Elizabeth Capon
Mr Francis Carnwath and Ms Caroline Wiseman
Lord and Lady Charles Cecil
Dr Peter Chocian

Frank Cohen
Nicola Collard
Mrs Jane Collins
Dr Judith Collins
Terrence Collis
Mr and Mrs Oliver Colman
Carole and Neville Conrad
Giles and Sonia Coode-Adams
Alastair Cookson
Cynthia Corbett
Mark and Cathy Corbett
Mrs Ursula Cornely
Tommaso Corvi-Mora
Mr and Mrs Bertrand Coste
Kathleen Crook and James Penturn
James Curtis
Sir Howard Davies
Mr and Mrs Roger de Haan
Giles de la Mare
Maria de Madariaga
Anne Chantal Defay Sheridan
Marco di Cesaria
Simon C Dickinson Ltd
Ms Sophie Diedrichs-Cox
James Diner
Liz and Simon Dingemans
Ms Charlotte Ransom and Mr Tim Dye
Rafe Eddington
Joan Edlis
Lord and Lady Egremont
Jeffrey and Jennifer Eldredge
John Erle-Drax
Dr Nigel Evans
Stuart and Margaret Evans
Gerard Faggionato
Ms Rose Fajardo
Richard Farleigh
Mrs Heather Farrar
David Fawkes
Mrs Margy Fenwick
Mr Bryan Ferry, CBE
The Sylvie Fleming Collection
Lt Commander Paul Fletcher
Mrs Jean Fletcher
Steve Fletcher
Katherine Francey Stables
Elizabeth Freeman
Stephen Friedman
Carol Galley
Daniela and Victor Gareh
Mrs Lisa Garrison
Ljubica Georgievska
Mr Mark Glatman
Ms Emily Goldner and Mr Michael Humphries
Ms Josefa Gonzalez-Blanco
Mr Jonathan Goodman
Mr and Mrs Paul Goswell
Penelope Govett
Martyn Gregory
Sir Ronald Grierson
Mrs Kate Grimond
Richard and Odile Grogan
Louise Hallett
Richard Hazlewood
Michael and Morven Heller
Richard and Sophia Herman
Miss Judith Hess
Mrs Patsy Hickman
Robert Holden
James Holland-Hibbert
Lady Hollick, OBE
Marianne Holtermann
Vicky Hughes
John Huntingford
Mr Alex Ionides
Maxine Isaacs
Helen Janecek
Sarah Jennings
Mr Haydn John
Mr Michael Johnson
Jay Jopling
Mrs Marcelle Joseph and Mr Paolo Cicchiné
Mrs Brenda Josephs
Tracey Josephs
Mr Joseph Kaempfer
Andrew Kalman
Jag-Preet Kaur
Dr Martin Kenig
Simon and Jeannette Kenny
Mr David Ker
Nicola Kerr
Mr and Mrs Simon Keswick
Richard and Helen Keys
Mrs Mae Khouri
David Killick
Mr and Mrs James Kirkman
Brian and Lesley Knox
David and Sarah Kowitz
Mr and Mrs Herbert Kretzmer
Linda Lakhdhir
Ms Jacqueline Lane
Mrs Julie Lee
Simon Lee
Mr Gerald Levin
Leonard Lewis
Mrs Cynthia Lewis Beck
Sophia and Mark Lewisohn
Mr Gilbert Lloyd
George Loudon
Mrs Elizabeth Louis
Mark and Liza Loveday
Catherine Lovell
Daniella Luxembourg Art
Anthony Mackintosh
Eykyn Maclean LLC
The Mactaggart Third Fund
Mrs Jane Maitland Hudson
Mr M J Margulies
Lord and Lady Marks
Marsh Christian Trust
Mrs Anne-Sophie McGrath
Ms Fiona Mellish
Mr Martin Mellish
Mrs R W P Mellish
Professor Rob Melville
Mr Alfred Mignano
Victoria Miro
Ms Milica Mitrovich
Jan Mol
Lulette Monbiot
Mrs Bona Montagu
Mr Ricardo Mora
Mrs William Morrison
Richard Nagy
Julian Opie
Pilar Ordovás
Sir Richard Osborn
Joseph and Chloe O'Sullivan
Desmond Page
Maureen Paley
Dominic Palfreyman
Michael Palin
Mrs Adelaida Palm
Stephen and Clare Pardy
Mrs Véronique Parke
Mr Sanjay Parthasarathy
Frans Pettinga
Miss Nathalie Philippe
Trevor Pickett
Mr Oliver Prenn
Susan Prevezer, QC
Mr Adam Prideaux
Mr and Mrs Ryan Prince
James Pyner
Ivetta Rabinovich
Mrs Phyllis Rapp
Ms Victoria Reanney
Dr Laurence Reed
Mr and Mrs Philip Renaud
The Reuben Foundation
Sir Tim Rice
Lady Ritblat
Ms Chao Roberts
David Rocklin
Frankie Rossi
Mr David V Rouch
Mr James Roundell
Naomi Russell
Mr Alex Sainsbury and Ms Elinor Jansz
Mr Richard Saltoun
Mrs Amanda Sater
Mrs Cecilia Scarpa
Cherrill and Ian Scheer
Sylvia Scheuer
The Schneer Foundation
Mrs Cara Schulze
Andrew and Belinda Scott
The Hon Richard Sharp
Mr Stuart Shave
Neville Shulman, CBE
Ms Julia Simmonds
Jennifer Smith
Paul and Marcia Soldatos
Mr George Soros
Louise Spence
Mr and Mrs Nicholas Stanley
Mr Nicos Steratzias
Stacie Styles
Mrs Patricia Swannell
Mr James Swartz
The Lady Juliet Tadgell
Tot Taylor
Christopher and Sally Tennant
Mr Henry Tinsley
Karen Townshend
Melissa Ulfane
Mr Marc Vandecandelaere
Mrs Cecilia Versteegh
Mr Jorge Villon
Gisela von Sanden
Audrey Wallrock
Stephen and Linda Waterhouse
Offer Waterman
Terry Watkins
Lisa West
Miss Cheyenne Westphal
Walter H. White, Jr.
Sue Whiteley
Mr David Wood
Mr Douglas Woolf
Anthony Zboralski
and those who wish to remain anonymous

Young Patrons
Vinita Agarwal
Aziz Ahsan
Stephanie Alameida
HH Princess Nauf AlBendar Al-Saud
Ms Maria Allen
Miss Noor Al-Rahim
HRH Princess Alia Al-Senussi (Chair, Young Patrons Ambassador Group)
Miss Sharifa Alsudair
Sigurdur Arngrimsson
Miss Katharine Arnold
Maria and Errikos Arones
Miss Joy Asfar
Ms Mila Askarova
Miss Olivia Aubry
Flavie Audi
Sarah Bejerano
Josh Bell and Jsen Winte
Miss Marisa Bellani
Ms Shruti Belliappa
Mr Erik Belz
Mr Edouard Benveniste-Schuler
Miss Margherita Berloni
Raimund Berthold
Dr Brenda Blott
Mrs Sofia Bocca
Ms Lara Bohinc
Miss Camilla Bullus
Miss Verena Butt
Miss May Calil
Miss Sarah Calodney
Matt Carey-Williams and Donnie Roark
Georgina Casals
Alexandra and Kabir Chhatwani
Miss Katya Chitova
Mrs Mona Collins
Mrs Laura Comfort
Thamara Corm
Miss Amanda C Cronin
Mr Theo Danjuma
Mr Joshua Davis
Ms Lora de Felice
Countess Charlotte de la Rochefoucauld
Emilie De Pauw
Agnes de Royere
Federico Debernard
Mira Dimitrova
Ms Michelle D'Souza
Miss Roxanna Farboud
Jane and Richard Found
Mr Andreas Gegner
Mrs Benedetta Ghione-Webb
Miss Dori Gilinski
Jessica Grosman
Olga Grotova and Oleksiy Osnach
Mr Nick Hackworth
Alex Haidas
Sara Harrison
Kira Allegra Heller
Christoph Hett
Mrs Samantha Heyworth
Andrew Honan

Roelof Petrus Van Wyk
Mr Varnavas A. Varnava
Mercedes Vilardell
Tony Wainaina
Alexa Waley-Cohen
Edwin Wulfsohn
and those who wish to remain anonymous

Asia-Pacific Acquisitions Committee
Bonnie and R Derek Bandeen
Andrew Cameron
Mr and Mrs John Carrafiell
Mrs Christina Chandris
Richard Chang
Pierre TM Chen, Yageo Foundation, Taiwan
Katie de Tilly
Mr Hyung-Teh Do
Ms Mareva Grabowski
Reade and Elizabeth Griffith
Louisa Guinness
Ms Kyoko Hattori
Cees Hendrikse
Mr Yongsoo Huh
Tessa Keswick
Shareen Khattar Harrison
Mr Chang-Il Kim
Ms Yung Hee Kim
Alan Lau
Woong Yeul Lee
Mr William Lim
Ms Dina Liu
Ms Kai-Yin Lo
Anne Louis-Dreyfus
Mrs Geraldine Elaine Marden
The Red Mansion Foundation
Mr Jackson See
Mr Paul Serfaty
Dr Gene Sherman AM
Leo Shih
Mr Robert Shum
Sir David Tang (Chair)
Mr Budi Tek, The Yuz Foundation
Rudy Tseng (Taiwan)
and those who wish to remain anonymous

Latin American Acquisitions Committee
Monica and Robert Aguirre
Karen and Leon Amitai
Luis Benshimol
Billy Bickford, Jr. and Oscar Cuellar
Estrellita and Daniel Brodsky
Trudy and Paul Cejas
Patricia Phelps de Cisneros
Gerard Cohen
David Cohen Sitton
HSH the Prince Pierre d'Arenberg
Tiqui Atencio Demirdjian (Chair)
Patricia Druck
Lily Gabriella Elia
Angelica Fuentes de Vergara
Mauro Herlitzka
Rocio and Boris Hirmas Said
Anne Marie and Geoffrey Isaac
Nicole Junkermann
Jack Kirkland
Fatima and Eskander Maleki
Becky and Jimmy Mayer
Solita and Steven Mishaan
Catherine and Michel Pastor
Catherine Petitgas
Isabella Prata and Idel Arcuschin
Frances Reynolds
Erica Roberts
Judko Rosenstock and Oscar Hernandez
Guillermo Rozenblum
Alin Ryan Lobo
Lilly Scarpetta and Roberto Pumarejo
Catherine Shriro
Norma Smith
Juan Carlos Verme
Tania and Arnoldo Wald
Juan Yarur Torres
and those who wish to remain anonymous

Middle East and North Africa Acquisitions Committee
HRH Princess Alia Al-Senussi
Abdullah Al Turki
Mehves Ariburnu
Sule Arinc
Marwan T Assaf
Perihan Bassatne
Boghossian Foundation
Ms Isabelle de la Bruyère
Füsun Eczacibasi
Maryam Eisler (Co-Chair)
Shirley Elghanian
Delfina Entrecanales, CBE
Noor Fares
Maha and Kasim Kutay
Sherine Magar-Sawiris
Nina Mahdavi
Mrs Fatima Maleki
Fayeeza Naqvi
Dina Nasser-Khadivi
Ebru Özdemir
Mrs Edwina Özyegin
Ramzy and Maya Rasamny (Co-Chair)
Mrs Karen Ruimy
Dania Debs-Sakka
Miss Yassi Sohrabi
Maria and Malek Sukkar
Ana Luiza and Luiz Augusto Teixeira de Freitas
Berna Tuglular
and those who wish to remain anonymous

North American Acquisitions Committee
Carol and David Appel
Jackie Appel
Dorothy Berwin and Dominique Levy
Paul Britton
Matt Cohler
Beth Rudin De Woody
James Diner
Glenn Fuhrman
Victoria Gelfand-Magalhaes
Marc Glimcher
Pamela Joyner
Elisabeth and Panos Karpidas
Anne Simone Kleinman and Thomas Wong
Monica Kalpakian
Christian K Keese
Celine and Jacques Lamarre
Marjorie and Michael Levine
James Lindon
Massimo Marcucci
Lillian and Billy Mauer
Liza Mauer and Andrew Sheiner
Nancy McCain
Della and Stuart McLaughlin
Marjorie and Marc McMorris
Stavros Merjos
Gregory R. Miller
Shabin and Nadir Mohamed
Elisa Nuyten and David Dime
Amy and John Phelan
Melinda B and Paul Pressler
Liz Gerring Radke and Kirk Radke
Laura Rapp and Jay Smith
Robert Rennie (Chair) and Carey Fouks
Kimberly Richter
Amie Rocket and Anthony Munk
Donald R Sobey
Robert Sobey
Beth Swofford
Dr Diane Vachon
Christen and Derek Wilson
and those who wish to remain anonymous

Photography Acquisitions Committee
Ryan Allen
Louise Baring Franck
Mr Nicholas Barker
Marisa Bellani
Veronica and Jeffrey Berman
Pierre Brahm (Chair)
William and Alla Broeksmit
Elizabeth and Rory Brooks
Marcel and Gabrielle Cassard
Nicolas and Celia Cattelain
Beth and Michele Colocci
Fares and Tania Fares
David Fitzsimons
Margot and George Greig
Alexandra Hess
Michael Hoppen
Bernard Huppert
Tim Jefferies, Hamiltons Gallery
Dede Johnston
Jack Kirkland
David Knaus
Mark McCain
Mr Scott Mead
Mr Donald Moore
Mr Axel Nordin
Ellen and Dan Shapiro
Saadi Soudavar
Maria and Malek Sukkar
Mrs Caroline Trausch
Michael and Jane Wilson
and those who wish to remain anonymous

Russia and Eastern Europe Acquisitions Committee
Dilyara Allakhverdova
Maria Baibakova
Maria Bukhtoyarova
Mr Pavel Erochkine
Dr Kira Flanzraich (Chair)
Konstantin Grigorishin
Carl Kostyál
Mrs Grażyna Kulczyk
Peter Kulloi
Ms Nonna Materkova
Victoria Mikhelson
Neil K. Rector
Ovidiu Şandor
Zsolt Somlói
Tretyakov Family Collection
Igor Tsukanov
and those who wish to remain anonymous

South Asia Acquisitions Committee
Dr Amin Jaffer
Professor Nirmalya Kumar
Darashaw K Mehta
Yamini Mehta
Shalini Misra
Amna and Ali Naqvi
Fayeeza Naqvi
Mrs Chandrika Pathak
Puja and Uday Patnaik
Lekha Poddar (Chair)
Rajeeb Samdani
Mrs Faiza Seth
Azad Shivdasani
Iwan Wirth
and those who wish to remain anonymous

Tate Modern Corporate Supporters
Bank of America Merrill Lynch
Bloomberg
BMW
BP
Christie's
EY
Hildon Limited
J.P. Morgan
Le Méridien
Qatar Museums Authority
Sotheby's
Statkraft
Unilever
Vodafone Group
and those who wish to remain anonymous

Tate Modern Corporate Members
AIG
Bank of America Merrill Lynch
Christie's
Citi
Clifford Chance LLP
Deloitte LLP
Deutsche Bank
Diageo Great Britain Limited
EY
GAM (UK) Limited
HSBC
JCA Group
The John Lewis Partnership
Kingfisher plc
Linklaters
MasterCard Worldwide
Mazars
Morgan Stanley
Native Land and Grosvenor
Pearson
The Brooklyn Brothers
Tishman Speyer
Wolff Olins
and those who wish to remain anonymous

Photographic Credits

pp.127, 140, 177–9 Alexandre Santo Silva. Courtesy Marta and Paulo Kuczynski
p.133 Carlos Germán Rojas. Courtesy Patricia Phelps de Cisneros
back cover, pp.18, 24, 26 Clay Perry. © Clay Perry, England & Co. Gallery, London. Courtesy Clay Perry
p.105 Courtesy Dan Galeria
p.169 right Dawn Black. Courtesy Anton Apostolatos
p.111 Eduardo Eckenfels. Courtesy Instituto Inhotim
pp.128, 134 Eduardo Ortega. Courtesy Eduardo Ortega
p.149 Courtesy Galeria Millan
pp.70, 135, 192 Greg Stanger. Courtesy Patricia Phelps de Cisneros
p.28 Courtesy Guy Brett, London
pp.108–9 Harald Gottschalk
pp.11 bottom, 21, 48, 65–6, 71–2, 74, 77, 79, 83–4, 88–90, 95, 97, 99–101, 106–7, 110, 121 right, 126, 131, 141, 144, 146, 171–3, 180–1, 186–7, 190–1, 193, 221, 228, 229, 235 Isabella Matheus
p.85 Jaime Acioli. Courtesy Fadel Collection
pp.104, 166 left John Berens
pp.75, 147 Kevin Todora
p.220 Marco Rezende. Courtesy Marco Rezende
p.40 Marcelo Rogozinski.Courtesy Marcelo Rogozinski
p.125 Mariano Costa Peuser. Courtesy Ernesto Poma
pp. 81, 112–13 Marcus Leith and Andrew Dunkley, Tate Photography © Tate 2013
pp.121 left, 163 Mark Morosse. Courtesy Patricia Phelps de Cisneros
pp.8, 10, 12, 68–9, 73, 86–7, 91–4, 137–9, 152–7, 159–161, 170, 174–5, 182–3, 188–9, 194–5, 224, 226, 231–2 Max Schendel
p.130 Oriol Tarridas. Courtesy The Ella Fontanals-Cisneros Collection
pp.62–3, 89, 123, 145, 185 Pat Kilgore
pp.116–17 Paula Azevedo e Bruno Cals. Courtesy Instituto de Arte Contemporânea
pp.103, 132 Peter Schälchli, Zurich. Courtesy Daros Latinamerica Collection
p.129 Roberto Ortiz G. Courtesy FEMSA Collection
p.102 Rodrigo Benavides. Courtesy Patricia Phelps de Cisneros
p.98 Romulo Fialdini. Courtesy Romulo Fialdini
pp.61, 64, 82, 239 Romulo Fialdini. Courtesy Museu de Arte Contemporânea da Universidade de São Paulo
p.120 Renato Donzelli
pp.23, 167 Sam Drake, Tate Photography © Tate 2013
Cover, p.143 Tate Photography © Tate 2013
p.67 Photo © The Museum of Fine Arts, Houston. Tom Jenkins, photographer
pp.78, 151 Photo © The Museum of Fine Arts, Houston. Thomas R. DuBrock, photographer
pp.114, 115 Acc. n.: 1884. 2008. a–e. © 2013. Digital image, The Museum of Modern Art, New York/Scala, Florence
p.118 Acc. n.: 1883.2008.© 2013. Digital image, The Museum of Modern Art, New York/Scala, Florence
p.119 Inv. n.: 68. 2005. © 2013. Digital image, The Museum of Modern Art, New York/Scala, Florence
p.163 Acc. n.:117.2005. © 2013. Digital image, The Museum of Modern Art, New York/Scala, Florence
p.164 Acc. n.:118.2005. © 2013. Digital image, The Museum of Modern Art, New York/Scala, Florence
p.165 Acc. n.:114.2005.© 2013. Digital image, The Museum of Modern Art, New York/Scala, Florence
p.166 right Acc. n.: 1887.2008.© 2013. Digital image, The Museum of Modern Art, New York/Scala, Florence
p. 167 left Acc. n.: 1885. 2008. © 2013. Digital image, The Museum of Modern Art, New York/Scala, Florence